The Psychology
of Human Behavior

Second Edition

The Psychology of Human Behavior

Second Edition

Richard A. Kalish

School of Public Health
University of California at Los Angeles

Brooks/Cole Publishing Company
Belmont, California

A Division of Wadsworth Publishing Company, Inc.

L.C. Cat. Card No.: 78–97113
Printed in the United States of America

4 5 6 7 8 9 10—74 73 72 71 70

Preface

The rapid movement of events and the knowledge explosion are all too likely to outdate textbooks as soon as they are written. In an effort to keep up to date with new research, new concepts, and new events, I have written the second edition of *The Psychology of Human Behavior.*

Like the first edition, this book has been written for students who come from a wide variety of backgrounds and who may never take another course in psychology. They want to learn about the discipline of psychology, but they also want to learn about human behavior as it applies to them and their world and to their future roles in family and career. I have again attempted to provide a book with a minimum of jargon, one that emphasizes concepts and that uses only the more important psychological terminology. In writing this book, I have aimed at integrating research and theory with concepts and ideas, rather than offering a review of the latest literature; and I have sought to provide a theoretical frame of reference, rather than a totally eclectic approach.

New to this edition are discussions of contemporary issues and recent concepts, supported by more than 100 new references, almost all of them published since 1965. A considerable amount of new material has been added on memory and higher-level cognitive functioning. The recent emphasis on operant learning has influenced me and, consequently, the book. Also reflected in this edition are new knowledge about the effects of environment on intellectual functioning, innovations in community mental health care, and new understanding about the biochemistry of learning and memory, about crisis intervention in psychotherapy, and about the role of work.

Recent events on the political and social scenes are too important to ignore. Thus, this edition contains new material on alienation, student activism, drug use, status of black and brown Americans, student demands for participation in decision making on campus, and the underlying values and dynamics.

The advisory board of junior college faculty has changed a little, but its importance has not diminished. The present Board of Consultants for the revision of the *Study Guide* that accompanies this edition consists of Frank R. Blume, Department of Psychology, San Bernardino Valley College; Marion P. Cheney, Department of Psychology, Brevard Junior College, Cocoa, Florida; Dr. Preston Graham, Dean of Students, Dallas Baptist College, Dallas, Texas; Victor Halling, Department of Psychology,

Bakersfield College; John E. Hoffman, Department of Psychology, East Los Angeles College, Los Angeles, California; Donald M. Johnson, Department of Psychology, West Valley College; John E. Peters, Editor, Department of Psychology, San Diego Mesa College; and Robert Tallmon, Department of Psychology, American River Junior College.

And, of course, there is the usual legion of people who have contributed in one way or another. Prime among these was Ann I. Johnson, who participated extensively in the revision of materials dealing with sensation, perception, learning, and emotion; Miss Johnson also took responsibility for seeing that the manuscript was typed quickly and accurately. Others who deserve thanks include the reviewers, whose cogent and often irritating comments forced me to see the manuscript through less self-centered eyes: John E. Peters, San Diego Mesa College; Leslie A. King, University of Minnesota; Donald M. Johnson, West Valley College; Frances Dressler, American River Junior College; Velma A. Duvall, East Los Angeles College; Hugh Petersen, Pasadena City College; Robert L. Anderson, Eastern Michigan University; and P. James Geiwitz, Stanford University. Also deserving thanks are those who helped so much through providing illustrations: Ed Fisher, whose cartoons I have always enjoyed; Albert Kallis, Jose Lucero, John G. Warford, and the files of Antioch College News Bureau, California State College at Los Angeles Public Information Office, and the Health Sciences Public Information Office at UCLA; Columbia Broadcasting System, National Broadcasting Company, and Stan Kallis, who served as go-between for these and other television photographs. And my final thanks go to my wife, Barbara, and my children, Leah, Daniel, and Rachel, who gave me the privacy and the encouragement that this effort required.

Richard A. Kalish

Contents

Contents

The Psychology
of Human Behavior

Part One

Introduction to the Basic Principles of Psychology

Chapter One

Psychology and Psychologists

Each person begins his first course in psychology with a different set of preconceived notions about what psychology is. Some assume they will learn to "psych out" all their friends; some are afraid of what they might learn about themselves; some are positive that psychology is merely common sense. None of these anticipations is likely to be found accurate. Perhaps the wisest course for a student to follow is to be actively curious and to have as few preconceived notions as possible.

Few things excite people more than learning about themselves. Today, man has opened the vastness of space and the minuteness of the atom for exploration; yet the excitement of the universe is no greater than the excitement of our own thinking and feeling and behaving, nor is the solar system more complex than a single human being.

People readily accept the idea that it takes a great deal of study to learn about space. After all, space is unimaginably vast, and the problems of its study are obviously highly technical. The idea that learning about **behavior*** also requires study is more difficult to accept. "I've lived with myself for 18 (or 30 or 60) years. I should know myself by now, and I should know other people too."

However, the realization eventually comes that understanding the behavior of others, or of ourselves, is not so simple as it may seem. "Why do I sit watching television, when I know I have an exam the day after tomorrow?" "Why is it often easier to ask out a girl I don't particularly like than one I do like?" "Why do I just smile when that girl makes nasty comments about my friend, instead of telling her what I really think?" Such examples of everyday behavior are seldom easy to understand; consider how much more difficult it is to explain phenomena such as love and fear, marital success and vocational failure, mental illness and social adjustment.

---

* Words or phrases in bold type appear in the Glossary.

Basic Principles of Psychology

Some claim to have found the key to understanding human behavior in statements such as "Do unto others as you would have them do unto you," or "Man does not live by bread alone." Are these statements true? For the most part they express principles accepted by modern psychologists, but they hardly provide a comprehensive explanation of human behavior.

The purpose of this book is to introduce the world of human behavior as explored by psychologists. You will read about things you already know and things you may not have considered. You will find some of your questions about human behavior answered, and—if you are a perceptive and inquisitive student—you will find many new questions to ask. You may gain a better understanding of yourself and of those around you, and, hopefully, you will find the study of human behavior both exciting and enjoyable.

Psychology: What Is It?

Psychology is the science that attempts to understand, describe, predict, and influence behavior—particularly human behavior. The **psychologist** may study behavior scientifically, or he may apply the theories and research findings of other psychologists to practical problems—or he may do both.

Psychology as a Science

Psychology is defined as a science because psychologists make extensive use of the scientific method and attempt to build scientific theories of human behavior. The research psychologist begins by having curiosity, which some writers feel to be the single most important characteristic of a scientist (McCain & Segal, 1969). He is curious about a topic, and he studies all kinds of knowledge concerning this topic. From this knowledge, and occasionally from an accidental occurrence or casual observation, the scientist develops a hunch. After trying to see whether there is evidence already available to support his hunch, the psychologist may decide to state the hunch formally as a research **hypothesis**. He must then determine the proper scientific method and procedures for testing the adequacy of his hypothesis.

Once the method and procedures are established, he has to translate his ideas into action and collect data. When he has the data, he analyzes them to determine whether they bear out the initial hypothesis. Whether they do or not, they are likely to lead to new hunches and more research.

Since the purpose of a science is not just to collect facts, but to develop understanding of events, psychologists usually try to fit their findings into theories or systems of behavior. These theories or systems generate new ideas and explanations, testable through additional re-

Figure 1-1.

The girl, the automobile, and the driver are all real, but the scene in front of the driver is on film. The equipment being monitored by the girl is measuring physiological changes that occur in the driver as he actually drives the car (except that it does not move) along an actual roadway (except that it is all on film). The driver's comments and reactions will also be recorded. This is another example of how psychological methods can be applied to improve living conditions—in this instance, automobile safety. Courtesy Driving Simulation Laboratory, Institute of Transportation and Traffic Engineering, UCLA.

search. Most professional psychologists feel obligated to report their findings in a professional journal so that other researchers can use them as a stepping-stone for their own research and theory-building. Slowly, psychological scientists build, alter, and improve their theories and their understanding.

Psychologists direct a large part of their research efforts at determining relationships between **variables**, or things that vary or change. They also wish to know the conditions under which the change will occur. The **motivation** to succeed in college is one example of a variable.

The motivation of any one person will vary or change in time, and the motivations of two or more people are very likely to differ. The psychologist wants to learn what conditions will cause the *motivation to succeed* to change, and to learn what produces the differences in the *motivation to succeed* among individuals. Is the variable *attitude toward teacher* related to the variable *motivation to succeed?* Does the variable *parental reaction to education* lead to differences among students on the variable *motivation to succeed?*

To select another example: psychologists are interested in learning whether the variable *spanking* has an effect upon the variable *obedience.* If the two variables are related, as they appear to be, psychologists will probe further into the problem. How will spanking affect obedience? Is it true that the more spanking a child receives, the more obedient he will become? Is there a point beyond which increased spanking no longer leads to increased obedience and may actually produce an increase in disobedience? Do some children respond favorably to spanking, while others indicate little behavior change? What predictions regarding obedience can be made from knowing about spanking? As answers to these questions become established, new variables are added. Under what conditions will spanking lead to obedience? Will it lead to behavior changes other than obedience? Will it produce anger toward the parents? Will it lead to running away from home or pinching baby sister when no one is looking? Piece by piece the puzzle is fitted together, as the psychologist's ability to predict and describe improves.

In conducting research, the psychologist needs to be aware of three important requirements. First, he should control all the conditions of the study. If he learns that children who are frequently spanked get lower-than-average grades in school, it does not necessarily mean that the spankings or the fear of spanking produced the low grades. Perhaps parents who often spank their children are less intelligent than parents who don't; perhaps parents who spank are more concerned with obedience at home than with success in school. What other reasons can you think of?

Second, the psychologist must take precautions to remain objective, or else he risks permitting his own biases and wishes to influence the investigation. The psychologist who feels that children should never be spanked might not believe the parent of the school's top pupil who reported giving his child frequent spankings. Therefore, the psychologist must conduct his research in such a way as to keep his own feelings from interfering. He can help keep his study objective by collecting data that do not permit his personal judgments to enter.

Third, he must conduct and report the study in such a way that another investigator could repeat the project to see if he would obtain similar results (after Telford & Sawrey, 1968).

Even the reporting of the study requires a scientific attitude. Obviously all children who get spanked do not get low grades. Psychologists speak in terms of either tendencies or **probabilities**—how probable is it or "what are the odds" that a particular event will occur? If you toss a coin, the odds are 50–50 that it will turn up heads. If a child is spanked often, what are the odds that he will get low grades?

Scientists do not expect to find final answers. New information, new understanding, new hypotheses are always forthcoming. Science progresses through many small steps and few large breakthroughs. A science may be compared to an immense brick house. Each piece of research is one brick that helps the house grow. Some bricks are large, some are small, and some are not made of very good material and demand rapid replacement. Each time one part of the house nears completion, the owners decide they need an additional wing. The work never ends.

Psychology Applied

Although professional psychologists usually consider their primary concern to be research, some are more interested in applying the research findings and their own informed understanding of human behavior to practical problems. They are usually interested in the art of influencing behavior.

The psychologist who counsels a student regarding a suitable college is using the research of others to deal with an immediate problem. From previous research, he knows whether the grades and test scores of his counselee predict success in the college under discussion. He has also learned from research and experience those attitudes that seem to predict college success. His study of persuasion has probably convinced him that it would be poor judgment to argue with the student if the latter appears to make a poor choice. By studying other cases and through much experience, the counselor has become sensitive to the feelings of students and has learned, along with the *science* of psychology, the *art* of helping counselees achieve their own goals, instead of trying to impose his goals on them.

Other psychologists are hired by businesses or governmental agencies to deal with such practical problems as testing the effectiveness of a **propaganda** program to persuade the Brazilian people that Americans are their friends or determining whether a new package for breakfast cereal is more likely to entice the buyer than the old one. By building upon the research of others and adding research of their own, these psychologists try to come up with the best answers to immediate practical problems.

Psychology, then, is the science that studies behavior in order to understand, describe, predict, and influence this behavior. Psychologists use research for building theories of behavior and for applying research data to the solving of immediate problems. They also use the *art* of psychology to aid in understanding and influencing behavior.

Psychology and Other Fields

Human knowledge is not contained in a series of boxes, each set apart from the others and each representing one field of study. Human knowledge incorporates many fields of inquiry and their relationships to one another. Psychologists are very much aware of the debt they owe others as well as the use these others may make of psychology.

The next time you look at a painting or statue, ask yourself how it affects you. Does it make you laugh or feel sad? Does it move you to anger, or does it leave you feeling pleased? Art not only expresses the mood of the artist, but it may also reflect ways in which people perceive the world. One philosopher has suggested that today's artists depict people as strange and distorted because man no longer has a true sense of who he is or how he relates to the world around him (Barrett, 1958).

The artist wants to understand human behavior, and he may wish to influence behavior. The psychologist and the artist may learn from each other about the influence of color upon mood, the effects of space upon the focus of attention, the degree to which feelings and attitudes are influenced by seeing works of art, or the significance of communicating through art. Consider, also, the relevance of these comments for the advertising layout artist, the theater technician, the beautician, the hotel manager, or the printer.

Literature also "holds the mirror up to man." A good novelist can communicate the feelings of his fictional characters and make them seem more lifelike than the real people whose behavior the psychologist attempts to describe. Plays and films can produce the same result. Writers can use the understanding provided by psychologists to enrich their stories, and psychologists can gain in their understanding of human behavior by drawing from the deep sensitivity of good authors.

The relationship of other social sciences to psychology is readily apparent. Sociology, anthropology, political science, history, and economics all deal with human behavior, although not in the same way that psychology does. Sociology contributes knowledge about the behavior of crowds, the structure of the family, and the functions of institutions such as the church and the school. Anthropology investigates the ways in which people live in various cultures and subcultures, including those of the United States. Political science is concerned with politics and government, but since governments are made up of people, political scientists and psychologists can learn from each other.

While the political scientist and the political candidate are both interested in predicting the effects of political issues on the behavior of the voter, the historian desires a better understanding of the behavior of people in past generations. Both the historian and the psychologist could profit from discovering what factors enabled Lincoln to rise to such greatness; schoolteachers and parents would certainly appreciate understanding why Lincoln found reading books so exciting. Knowledge of the history of our country and of other countries helps explain the behavior of people today. To learn, for example, that the German army invaded France three times in one century may help explain the attitudes of the French toward Germans; to learn about the history of unions in the United States may help explain why your parents feel as they do about them.

From biology and chemistry, psychologists gain knowledge of the physiology of the sensory and motor apparatus, of the brain, and of the nervous system in order to understand better their effects upon behavior. At the same time, the medical doctor can use some of the findings of psychologists in treating his patients. Mathematics provides the psychologist with the statistical tools to conduct research, and the study of grammar and linguistics suggests that language may affect the thinking process. Processing data on large computers enables the psychologist to enlarge the scope of his research.

Parents, teachers, businessmen, office managers, skilled technicians, policemen, secretaries, government workers, military officers, and innumerable other groups draw upon the data of psychologists. They may wish to influence the behavior of children, potential buyers, employees, soldiers, or supervisors; they may want to predict the behavior of the competitor, the enemy, the criminal, or the boss; they may hope to understand the feelings of the spouse, the girl at the next desk, or the commanding officer; and they give to and receive from psychologists a deeper understanding of the world.

No field of study or work can exist in a vacuum. Each adds to its own store of understanding and knowledge the results of the efforts of others. What do you feel you can learn from psychology? What do you feel psychologists might learn from those in your chosen vocational field?

Psychologists: Who Are They?

Everyone uses the principles of psychology in his work and personal life, just as everyone uses the principles of mathematics and economics. However, the ability to use psychological principles does not make a person a psychologist, any more than computing a batting average or maintaining a family budget makes a person a mathematician or an economist. People considered to be professional psychologists have usually received a graduate degree, frequently the doctorate, which demands an average of six to eight years of academic training plus the ability to pass lengthy comprehensive examinations and to complete satisfactorily a work of original research.

Most professional psychologists belong to the American Psychological Association, an organization of approximately 27,000 members. Thus, there is one psychologist for every 7,500 Americans, certainly a very small proportion of the population.

Specialties Within Psychology

Although all psychologists share the understanding of a common body of knowledge, the scientific field of psychology, like other fields, is divided into a number of specialties.

The specialty chosen by most psychologists is clinical psychology. The **clinical psychologist** is primarily concerned with helping others deal with personal and emotional problems. He participates in the face-to-face relationship known as **psychotherapy**, a form of counseling that involves helping people with personal and emotional adjustment problems. In addition to performing psychotherapy, the clinical psychologist administers and interprets all types of psychological tests. He also does research, often involving various tests and various approaches to psychotherapy. He may have a private practice, or he may work with a government agency, a hospital, or an educational institution.

The **social psychologist** focuses his attention on the behavior of people and of groups in a social environment. He studies the formation and change of attitudes and beliefs, the effects of society upon behavior, and the actions of people in small groups. He is also likely to be interested in how people communicate with each other, since communication is part of a social relationship.

Quite different from the social psychologist is the **physiological psychologist**, who studies the physiology, anatomy, and **biochemistry** of the body as they affect behavior. What changes occur in the human body when the person claims to feel anger or fear? How do tranquilizer pills alter behavior? Why are some people color-blind? How is memory stored in the brain?

The **developmental psychologist** is primarily concerned with behavior and behavior changes at various stages of development. He tries to discover why some infants learn to walk later than others, how adolescent interests change between ages 12 and 18, why some people seem old at 60 while others are still vigorous at 80.

Industrial psychologists study a variety of topics, including how to design efficient machines, how to evaluate worker morale and to improve it if necessary, how to devise training programs for workers, and how to improve marketing and advertising.

These five specialties were chosen to show what a wide range of human activity is covered by the term *psychology*. Other specialties are cited in Figure 1–2. Overlap, of course, exists between the areas. A clinical psychologist may become interested in emotional problems of industrial executives, while a social psychologist may find himself studying the effects of friendship on the physical health of the aged.

The Job of the Psychologist

The largest percentage of psychologists (41%) is associated with colleges, universities, and medical schools, where they teach, conduct research, counsel, and serve as administrators. Various agencies of federal, state, and local governments also employ many psychologists (19%). Others work for public schools (10%), industry (7%), hospitals (5%), and social agencies (4%). Only a very few (6%) are self-employed (Boneau, 1968).

Psychologists use both the science and the art of psychology in their work, just as medical doctors use the science and the art of medicine in theirs. Some psychologists are involved almost completely with research, but most clinical and counseling psychologists must develop the art of being sensitive to the feelings of those they are trying to help. The industrial psychologist who is responsible for training foremen and managers must develop a high degree of sensitivity to how others feel. Also, the psychologists who teach in colleges and universities should develop the art of effectively communicating the content and the methods of psychology to their students.

Some Common Sources of Confusion

Can psychologists control behavior?   The only possible answer is "No!" When a friend tells you his troubles, he feels better afterward. The psychologist has learned much more than you may know about this phenomenon. You find that you can influence your friend's behavior by listening to him. The psychologist has more sophistication and may have learned how to have more influence than you in the same situation, but neither one of you comes near to controlling the behavior of the person with troubles. Advertisers, ministers, politicians, and doctors all influence behavior, but they do not control it. Psychologists have learned enough about people to increase the effectiveness of advertising slogans and political speeches, but increased effectiveness is far from control.

The greatest experiment in behavior control was undoubtedly the Chinese Communist **brainwashing** program, which was conducted both on the Chinese themselves and on non-Chinese in prison camps and elsewhere (Schein, 1958). These programs appear to have influenced behavior and attitudes, but they certainly did not constitute total control. Although brainwashing is often believed to have caused American pris-

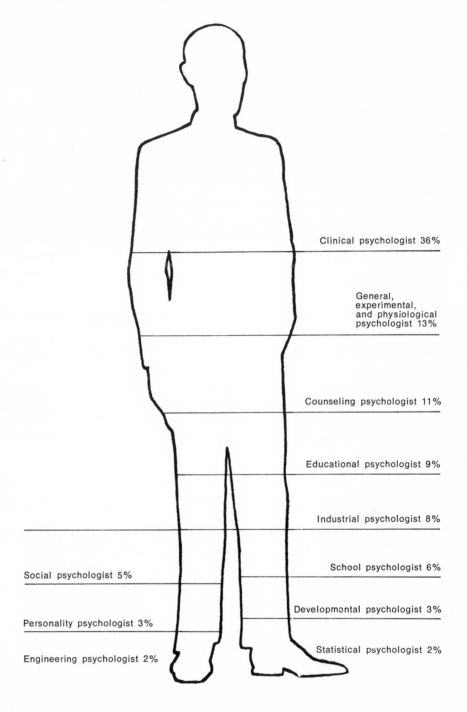

Clinical psychologist 36%

General, experimental, and physiological psychologist 13%

Counseling psychologist 11%

Educational psychologist 9%

Industrial psychologist 8%

School psychologist 6%

Social psychologist 5%

Developmental psychologist 3%

Personality psychologist 3%

Statistical psychologist 2%

Figure 1–2.

Engineering psychologist 2%

The major areas of specialization in psychology and the percentage of American Psychological Association members identifying with each area (Boneau, 1968).

oners to be ineffectual in Chinese prison camps, it rarely had long-range effects upon their behavior (Biderman, 1962).

Can a psychologist read people's thoughts?   Not at all. A psychologist, because of his training and experience, may notice a gesture that most people would ignore, or he may see in a few words meanings that others do not see. However, a good automobile salesman can size up a customer very quickly, and a competent policeman can rapidly determine what happened at the scene of a crime. The psychologist has similarly developed a sensitivity to what people are thinking and feeling. Some psychologists, through their background, training, and experience, have developed the art of *understanding* people to a high degree.

How do clinical psychologists, psychiatrists, and psychoanalysts differ?   Since clinical psychologists, **psychiatrists**, and **psychoanalysts** all perform psychotherapy, much confusion exists regarding the differences among them.

The clinical psychologist usually has received the Ph.D. degree with major emphasis in psychology. In addition to his lengthy education, he has spent a year giving psychological tests and administering psychotherapy under supervision.

The psychiatrist must be, according to law, a medical doctor. His education includes a regular college degree, a medical degree (M.D.), a year of internship, and usually three to five years of medical residency, often in a psychiatric hospital. Until his residency begins, his education is almost completely in medicine, rather than in psychology.

The psychoanalyst is almost always a medical doctor, and is frequently a psychiatrist before he undertakes the additional study, examinations, and supervised experience needed for him to be a psychoanalyst. Many psychoanalysts have practiced medicine or psychiatry for years before embarking upon the intensive training required for practicing psychoanalysis. Only a very few have had no medical training. Psychoanalysis is based directly upon the writings, lectures, psychotherapeutic practice, and personality theory of Sigmund Freud.

Methods for Learning About People

Although every scientist uses the scientific method, each scientific field studies different types of phenomena and thus needs to apply the scientific method in somewhat different ways. The psychologist, when he investigates the relationship between spanking and obedience, must use a much different approach from that of the physicist investigating the effects of temperature change on spacecraft. The major approaches used by the psychologist to obtain information include observations, case histories, tests, and experiments.

The Observational Method

Everyone observes the behavior of others and makes certain assumptions from these observations. For example, have you ever observed

Figure 1–3.

In testing intelligence, not only verbal ability and intelligence are considered, but also various kinds of motor and perceptual tasks. Courtesy Reiss-Davis Child Study Center.

what seem to be differences in behavior between commercial art majors and office management majors? Have you ever observed that left-handed baseball pitchers seem to exhibit different off-the-field behavior from that of right-handed pitchers? If so, you have used observations, but probably not in a scientific way. Such casual, uncontrolled observations may add to your understanding, but they are also very likely to be wrong. Whenever you notice an office management major or a left-handed pitcher behaving as you hypothesize, you feel your beliefs have been confirmed. When you see behavior that contradicts your hypothesis, you may tell yourself that it was only an exception, or you may find some other excuse for the behavior.

You can, however, apply the scientific method to your observations by imposing careful controls. Commercial art majors, you hypothesize, are more likely to enter into class discussions than are office management majors. By making a careful count of how often each person comments in your class, you can obtain an average class-discussion score for commercial art students and for office management students. You should make certain that you collect your observations in several different classes, since commercial art students may talk more in certain classes and less in others. The final step is to analyze your data to see whether your hypothesis is borne out. (There are many possible pitfalls in the study outlined above. Perhaps you can figure out what they are and suggest ways of dealing with them.) Of course, art or management majors in another college may differ from those you have studied, so you need to be cautious in extending the results of your research beyond the group you studied. If you take such precautions in carefully controlling your study, *controlled observations* can be a fruitful method of investigation.

The Case History Method

The use of case histories refers to an intensive study of a single individual, utilizing a great variety of information sources, such as school records, vocational evaluations, psychological tests, and interviews with the individual himself and with those who know him. All this material is integrated to provide as complete a picture of the person as possible. Not only does the case history method give an understanding of one individual, but comparison of several case histories devoted to a specific topic may also generate hypotheses to be tested on a larger scale.

Tests

A vast assortment of tests is available to the psychologist. These tests claim to measure everything from potential ability in art to moodiness, reading ability, mechanical aptitude, tendencies toward mental illness, and clerical skills. Tests have been constructed to measure achievement, aptitudes, interests, personality characteristics, memory, and numerous other aspects of human behavior. Tests serve the psychologist-as-artist by giving him a better understanding of the individuals he is trying to influence, and they aid the psychologist-as-scientist by giving him an effective way to measure many human attributes. (See Chapter 6

for further discussion of tests, including their limitations and their interpretation.)

Surveys and Questionnaires

Surveys and **questionnaires** are special forms of tests. Today's newspapers and magazines are filled with the results of public opinion surveys, attitude and personality questionnaires, and interviews. Statistics
show how the Republican voters of California feel about who should be
the next governor, how residents of Houston look upon a possible tax
increase, or how college students view their future.

However, the surveys you read in the newspapers are only a small
portion of those conducted. Business and governmental organizations
sponsor thousands of surveys annually. Our Department of State may

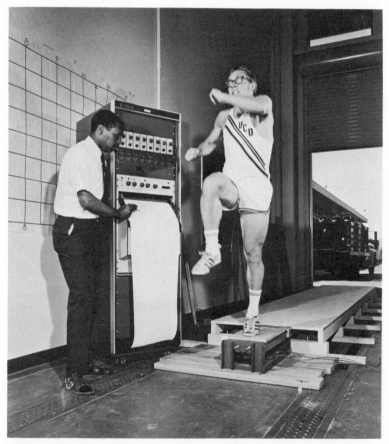

**Figure
1–4.**

Many kinds of tests are used to measure many kinds of human performance. Here
a machine measures the thrust of a long jumper. The device may aid in the selection
and training of track stars. Courtesy Public Affairs Office, University of California,
Davis.

wish to learn the attitudes of the Spanish people toward American soldiers stationed in Spain; a candidate for city council may want to know how the voters feel about local issues; a nursing supervisor may want to learn how student nurses feel about their future work.

Questionnaires are used for purposes other than the solution of immediate, practical problems. A psychologist may, for example, hypothesize that attitudes toward education are related to college grades. He could construct a brief attitude questionnaire, administer it to his students, and then check their over-all grade-point ratios at the end of the

"He's telling about how we believe in the Sacred Hippopotamus who created Man out of oyster shells—don't ask me how he keeps a straight face!"

Figure 1–5.

Obtaining accurate information in surveys is not always possible. Courtesy Ed Fisher.

academic year. Or he might believe that a relationship exists between having emotional problems and being divorced. He could then administer a personality questionnaire for measuring emotional problems to a group of divorced people and to a *comparable* group of married people. His final analysis would show which group had more emotional problems. (Once again, the studies described have possible sources of error. Can you decide what they are and suggest ways to eliminate them?)

The Experimental Method

Psychologists like to use the **experimental method** in their research, since they feel that through this method they can best control all the factors involved. In a typical psychological experiment, one group of subjects (the experimental group) is given special treatment, while a comparable group (the **control group**) is left alone or given normal treatment. The psychologist then compares the two groups to see what changes, if any, occurred in the experimental group, presumably the outcome of the conditions he arranged.

In one example of the experimental method, college students were given a long word and asked to write as many short words as possible by using the letters contained in the long word. One-third of the subjects (group *A*) were told that the average number of words made by English professors was 31; one-third (group *B*) were told that college freshmen averaged 31 words; and the final third (group *C*) were informed that prison inmates averaged 31 words. Interestingly enough, group *C* made the most short words from the long word, and group *A* averaged the lowest number. The same procedure was repeated many times, always with the same results.* Apparently the standards people set for themselves are affected by the nature of the group with which they are compared, and these standards influence the level of performance. Consider the implications for success in school or on the job.

In another experiment, subjects were told to write down words that were to be flashed very briefly on a screen. One-third of the subjects received a paper telling them that the words would deal with travel; one-third were informed that the words would relate to birds and animals; the remaining third, the control group, were not given specific instructions. Among the "words" flashed on the screen were "s a e l" and "d a c k" (Siipola, 1935). What do you think each group wrote down when it saw the above "words"? The results of the experiment indicated that a person's expectations will affect what he "sees." What relevance does this result have to human behavior outside the experimental situation?

These examples are only two out of thousands of experiments that have been conducted to learn more about behavior. Some psychologists prefer to use experiments to investigate behavior, while others use observations, case histories, tests, or combinations of all these methods.

Summary of Important Ideas

1. Psychology is the science that attempts to understand, describe, predict, and influence behavior. Psychologists make extensive use of the scientific method and of the relationships among variables.

* Based on studies in introductory psychology laboratories at the University of Hawaii, 1955–1959.

Psychology and Psychologists

2. Some psychologists concentrate on applying the psychological understanding of human behavior to practical problems, and others focus on accomplishing research.

3. The thinking and the research findings of psychologists influence and are influenced by the thinking and research findings of scholars in other fields.

4. Everyone uses psychological understanding in his daily life, but to become a professional psychologist requires extensive study.

5. Psychology is divided into numerous, interrelated specialties.

6. Psychologists cannot control behavior nor read minds.

7. The interests of the clinical psychologist, the psychiatrist, and the psychoanalyst overlap.

8. The research methods used by psychologists include controlled observations, case histories, tests, and experiments. Surveys and questionnaires are types of tests.

9. Psychological experiments make careful use of a control group, whose behavior is compared to the behavior of the group under investigation in order to determine whether the experimental condition produced a difference between the experimental and control groups.

Chapter Two

Human Needs

Among the innumerable things that psychologists study are human wants or needs and how people try to satisfy these wants or needs. A person must satisfy many needs to continue to exist. For instance, he must satisfy hunger and thirst. At birth, the human being is unable to satisfy these needs without help. Other needs, such as the need for companionship, the need for self-esteem, or the need for safety, are not part of the behavior patterns of infants but develop over the years as the result of experience.

A Book of Verses underneath the Bough,
A Jug of Wine, a Loaf of Bread—and Thou
Beside me singing in the Wilderness—
Oh, Wilderness were Paradise enow!

Perhaps Omar Khayyám, the famous poet who wrote these lines, felt that poetry, drink, food, music, and companionship (apparently female) added up to all the satisfactions he might wish for, but most people are motivated by many other **needs**. What needs would you want satisfied to turn a wilderness into a paradise?

Motivation and Its Measurement

Motivated behavior is behavior set into motion by a need felt by the individual. A need indicates that some type of satisfaction is lacking and implies that the organism is activated to reduce the dissatisfaction. Thus, a need for food signifies that a person feels the lack of food, and it sets into motion hunger-motivated behavior. The need for money means that a person feels he lacks money, and it sets into motion money-seeking behavior. Needs for affection, for prestige, or for self-respect operate in the same fashion.

> In the middle of studying for an accounting exam, Ned Rose began to feel uncomfortable. At first he was not certain why he was on edge, but he just could not concentrate. Suddenly he snapped his fingers, jumped up, and dashed to the telephone to call his steady girl friend. After he completed the call, he returned to his studying and was then able to concentrate without difficulty.

Ned was motivated to telephone his girl, even though he was temporarily unaware of his need. Nonetheless, the motivation was strong enough to activate goal-seeking behavior, which began with agitated feelings and ended with behavior that satisfied his need.

Sometimes people cannot satisfy their needs. A woman on a diet, though she is perhaps satisfying needs for popularity and self-esteem, may be perpetually hungry; a mediocre songwriter may never satisfy his need for achievement; an irritating and aggressive student may be unable to satisfy his need for companionship. A high proportion of needs can be satisfied, however, and the behavior that leads to need satisfaction is thus rewarded and is more likely to occur on subsequent occasions when the same need arises.

Individuals vary considerably in the degree to which they are motivated by any particular need. John may be highly motivated to attract attention or to express his aggressive feelings, but Jim's greatest social needs are to be neat and orderly and to form friendships with others. Jane, a student nurse, is eager to become a supervisor some day, but her classmate Jean is motivated only enough to slide through to get her certificate.

Motivation and needs are concepts, not things. They cannot be seen or heard or touched; they must be inferred or assumed from observing behavior. In the above example, by observing Ned's actions we inferred that he was motivated. The assumption that Ned had needs that motivated his behavior helps explain what he did. Many psychologists believe that motivation exists for *all* human behavior, even though the person is not necessarily aware of his motives at the time of the behavior.

If psychologists study motivation, they must have a method of measuring it. Since it cannot be measured directly in the way we measure water pressure or speed, indirect measures have been developed. One of the most common of these measures assumes that the more motivated a person is, the harder he will work to satisfy his need. Therefore, the individual who expends great effort in his college study is believed to be motivated to achieve academically; the person who spends considerable time solving people's problems is assumed to be motivated to help others.

Psychologists can measure the strength of an individual's motivation through controlled observations, through ratings by friends or teachers or others who know the person being studied, or through self-rating questionnaires. In some instances, the psychologist who wants to use the experimental method to learn the effects of motivation will try to control the degree of need. For example, studies on the effects of the hunger motive have been conducted by depriving subjects of food for a given period of time, then measuring the impact of the deprivation upon whatever variable is being considered, for example, work output, ability to concentrate, or irritability.

In making these indirect measurements of motivation and need strength, psychologists realize that their methods are subject to more error than the methods of the engineer or the chemist. At this point in the development of the science of psychology, highly precise measures are often not available. All psychologists are aware of this and attempt to be careful in their methods and cautious in their interpretations.

Self-actualization and a Hierarchy of Needs

The same qualities that distinguish the human personality from the personality of other animals also enable people to develop the need to grow, to improve, and to make use of their potential capacities. When a lower animal has had enough to eat, it rarely searches for food, and when warm enough, it rarely seeks new ways of getting warm. The animal's needs seem satisfied when it has, for the moment, all the things necessary to remain alive and to avoid discomfort and pain. Human beings, however, seem to have a need for more than this basic level of functioning.

The young child is eager to learn, to explore, and to have experiences. His parents may have encouraged his learning, but many children enjoy learning and exploration even when they receive no parental encouragement—there appears to be something in learning and in having new experiences that, in itself, excites them.

Nine-month-old Mike crawled slowly to the couch, reached up, grabbed the cloth, and painfully pulled himself to a standing position. In

Human Needs

a moment, he had fallen and bruised his chin, but five seconds later he was again pulling himself up so that he could stand. His only reward seemed to be the satisfaction, perhaps the excitement, of standing.

A beautician in Santa Barbara, California, drove into Los Angeles every Monday for ten weeks to take a series of seminars in some recent techniques. Although her shop was so busy that she was turning away customers, she felt that the 200-mile round trip was worth the effort, because what she learned enabled her to do a better job.

In both of these instances, the people seemed rewarded by the feeling that they had done something that made the most of their abilities. They had responded to their need for **self-actualization.**

What is self-actualization? According to one highly respected psychologist, Professor Abraham Maslow (1943), it is the tendency to "become more and more what one is, to become everything that one is capable of becoming." Also, to self-actualize is to accept one's own real nature for what it is (adapted from Maslow, 1955). This concept implies that people have a desire, or a need, to make something of themselves, to do as much as their potential allows.

One person may self-actualize by doing a good job of framing pictures; another, by maintaining a happy home and bringing up healthy children; a third, by leading the debating squad; a fourth, by taking shorthand rapidly and accurately; a fifth, by writing poetry to express his own feelings.

Self -

Actualization

Esteem | Self-Esteem

Love | Belonging | Closeness

Safety | Security | Protection

Sex | Activity | Exploration | Manipulation | Novelty

Food | Air | Water | Temperature | Elimination | Rest | Pain Avoidance

Figure 2–1.

Hierarchy of needs.

Before you can do an effective job of self-actualizing, however, other needs must be reasonably well satisfied. These needs, as described by Maslow (1943), form a **hierarchy of needs**, including **physiological needs**, **safety needs**, **love needs**, and **esteem needs** in addition to the self-actualizing needs.

Physiological Needs

The physiological needs can be divided into two categories: survival needs, which must be satisfied or the body processes stop and life ceases; and stimulation needs, whose functions, although not well understood, appear more closely related to the appreciation of life than to the maintaining of life.

Survival Needs

Survival needs include those produced by hunger, thirst, air hunger, elimination pressures, fatigue, temperature regulation demands, and pain avoidance. Relatively few Americans have suffered acutely from being unable to satisfy these needs (except, perhaps, for pain avoidance), but all of us have experienced these needs in milder form.

1. *Hunger.* For most people in the United States, being hungry means missing lunch and "starving" before dinner. Elsewhere in the world, and even in some American families, hunger is a major motivation, perhaps *the* major motivation, for the behavior of many people. Much of the world's population rarely receives the amount of food that an overweight American woman is allowed by a strict diet. The hungry have poor health, their life-span is short, and their infant death rate is high. Consider the overwhelming importance of food as a motivating factor for these people. Consider the motivation caused by hearing your children cry constantly because they do not have enough to eat.

During World War II, a group of Americans volunteered to undergo a starvation diet so that the effects of hunger might be studied. After several weeks of intense dieting, they displayed several types of behavior change: their dreams, thoughts, and conversations continually dealt with food; they became irritable; their activity level was reduced; and they became apathetic (Keys, Brožek, Henschel, Michelsen, & Taylor, 1950). Thus, the stronger the need, the more its impact is felt on all aspects of living.

Human Needs

2. *Thirst.* Most Americans have experienced the dry throat and mouth that accompany thirst, but very few have known the extreme discomfort of intense thirst. Those who have will acknowledge that the motivating qualities of acute thirst are overwhelming.

3. *Air hunger.* The need to breathe is so obvious and breathing is so automatic that people often forget how essential oxygen is to the body. A very brief period without oxygen will produce permanent brain damage, and a few minutes without it will lead to death.

4. *Elimination pressures.* The body must rid itself of its waste products in order to survive. Young children relieve the pressure in their bowels and bladder without hesitating (just ask any parent who is forced to change diapers), but learning reduces this freedom. Teaching children the proper conditions for satisfying the need for elimination consumes much parental energy in the early years of child rearing.

5. *Fatigue.* The human organism must have rest and sleep in order to renew its vitality. Occasionally this need becomes so strong that a person will fall asleep in class, on the job, or at the wheel of his automobile.

One group of investigators deprived four volunteers of sleep for five full days. After the first day, the subjects felt tired and irritable; after three days, they had difficulty concentrating, occasionally lost consciousness, had memory lapses, and even had **hallucinations**; by the end of the fifth day, they were, in addition, very apathetic, depressed, unfriendly, and tense. However, in spite of all these behavior changes, they were still able to perform many tasks, and none of the four volunteers displayed serious personality disturbance (Kollar, Slater, Palmer, Docter, & Mandell, 1966). However, in an earlier investigation, a person deprived of sleep for nine days did display deteriorated thinking and emotionally disturbed behavior (Luby, Frohman, Grisell, Lenzo, & Gottlieb, 1960).

6. *Temperature regulation demands.* People can adjust to variations in heat and cold up to certain limits. However, the need to be in a comfortable temperature can be extremely motivating. As a result, man has gone to great pains to provide himself with clothing, with heating and cooling devices, and with protecting shelters. The popularity of Southern California, Hawaii, Florida, and Arizona both for residents and for tourists is partly based on their comfortable climates.

7. *Pain avoidance.* People often do not realize the role that pain plays in preserving life. If you felt no pain, you would not know when a part of the body was diseased or infected, and the disease or infection could spread and cause severe damage before you realized what was happening. Thus, pain avoidance is a survival need, not because pain is discomforting, but because pain is a signal that some-

Figure 2–2.

The satisfaction of hunger and thirst needs is probably taken for granted by readers of this book, but there are millions of people in the world, including some in the United States, for whom hunger and thirst are day-to-day problems. *Top:* A Hong Kong child carrying the family's supply of water, perhaps to last several days (Photograph by Mark Davidson). *Top right:* This American child has often gone to bed hungry (Courtesy Columbia Broadcasting System). *Bottom right:* Children in India lining up for their ration of wheat during a period of famine (Courtesy Columbia Broadcasting System).

thing has gone wrong with the organism. However, it is the extreme discomfort of pain that makes pain avoidance such a strong motive.

The survival needs are the most compelling needs people have. When experiencing hunger, pain, or extreme fatigue, we can concentrate on little else except satisfying the need. To obtain food, a starving soldier is likely to surrender to a hostile enemy even with the knowledge that he will possibly be executed. Under extreme pain, or the threat of extreme pain, people have been known to violate many closely held personal convictions.

Stimulation Needs

The satisfaction of **stimulation needs**, including the need for sex, activity, exploration, manipulation, and novelty, does not appear necessary for survival. Nonetheless, complete lack of environmental stimulation is very distressing, as students in an investigation attested after they

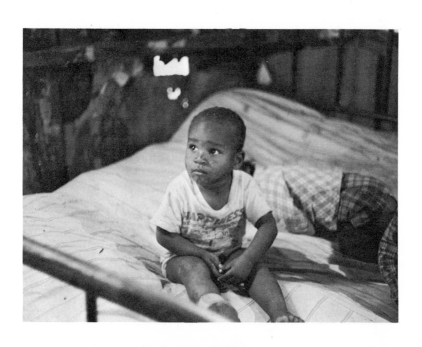

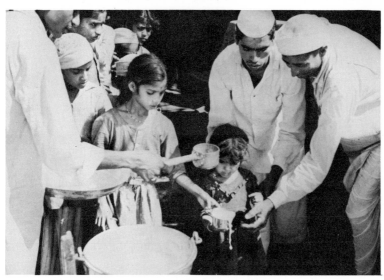

were totally shut off from their surroundings (Lilly, 1956). Children deprived of activity and stimulating human relationships seem to suffer both physically and emotionally (see Chapter 8). Also, sex is obviously necessary for the life of the species, although not for the life of any given living individual. This evidence, however, is not a sufficient basis for assuming that stimulation needs must be satisfied for the organism to survive.

At one time, stimulation needs were thought to develop through learning. Recent observations, however, have shown that animals and young infants respond to **exploratory needs** and manipulation needs without any opportunity for learning them (Festinger, 1954; Harlow, Harlow, & Meyer, 1950). Perhaps scientists will find a biochemical basis for all stimulation needs, as they have for the sex need.

1. *Sex.*   Most Americans can satisfy survival and stimulation needs with relatively little difficulty—except for the sex need. Professional writings in psychology, movie advertisements, and college bull sessions all indicate that the sex need is far from satisfied.

The desire for sex in humans results from biochemical changes within the body, but these changes are set off by information sent through the sense organs to the brain, or by thinking which began in the brain. Thinking of something with sexual meanings can lead to stirring up the sex need; seeing, touching, or hearing something with sexual meanings will also lead to sexual arousal.

How to satisfy the hunger, thirst, activity, and other physiological motives is very easy to learn. The satisfying of some needs, as the need for air or for sleep, requires no learning—we breathe and sleep without any help or learning at all. Sex is quite different. Human beings must learn how to satisfy their sexual needs.

2. *Activity, exploration, manipulation, novelty.*   It seems clear that people do not desire a state of complete rest, but seek activity and stimulation. Total lack of activity produces boredom, fatigue, and apathy. Complete isolation from stimulation, brought about by placing a person in an apparatus that completely cuts off all contact with the outside world, has led to such symptoms of mental confusion as fantasies and hallucinations (Heron, 1957).

Given the opportunity, children appear to wish to explore their environment. They wish to handle objects with their hands and—often to the amusement of older children and adults—to manipulate the objects with their tongues. Observers frequently report that children will bypass a familiar object in order to explore and manipulate a new object, implying that the need for novelty may be a factor in their behavior. Even monkeys will spend much time and effort manipulating mechanical equipment without receiving any apparent reward (Harlow et al., 1950), indicating that the act of manipulation is rewarding in itself. However, both infants and monkeys will eventually tire of any given object and will prefer to go on to something else.

You may have observed similar behavior in adults and older children, as when a man receives so much enjoyment from fixing his car that he seems saddened when it is finally in good running order. How-

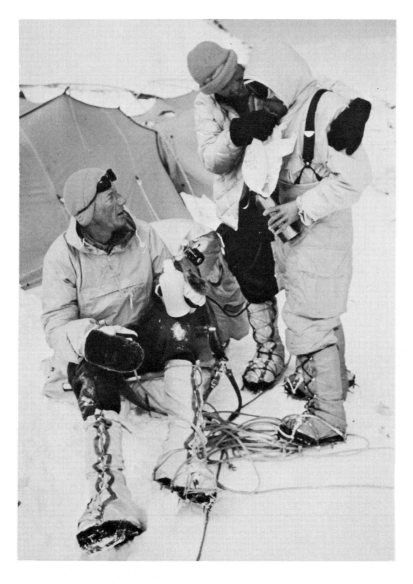

Figure 2–3.

Stimulation needs, such as the need to explore the environment, can lead to situations in which safety needs are threatened. These climbers are breathing in oxygen after their descent. Courtesy Columbia Broadcasting System.

ever, these individuals have had the opportunity to learn by having been rewarded for performing such actions. Infants have not had the same opportunities for learning, and their responses to stimulation needs probably result from inborn characteristics. The degree to which stimulation needs might be inherited is still under debate.

Adults would rarely wish to restrict a child's efforts to satisfy his survival needs; yet many adults appear unaware that the satisfaction of stimulation needs is similarly very important. Limiting the opportunity for a child to explore his environment or to be physically active may actually harm the child's normal process of development. The hunger need cannot be ignored without risking the death of the child; however, punishing the child for expressing his needs for activity and exploration may also turn out to be harmful. How do adults encourage or discourage the satisfaction of stimulation needs?

Stimulation motives appear to be related to each other and to man's general desire to receive more from the environment. For this reason, they support the contention that people have the need to make the most of their talents and capacities. In other words, one way that people desire to make the most of their environment is by manipulating and exploring it and by being active and having new experiences.

Psychosocial Aspects of Physiological Needs

The satisfaction of survival and stimulation needs involves more than biological responses. Unless their needs are acutely disturbing because they are not being adequately met, people respond to them in keeping with certain customs, traditions, personal tastes, and habits. People also attempt to increase their pleasure in the process of satisfying physiological needs: eating fish eyes would help reduce your hunger need, but you might refuse to eat them, although residents of other countries consider fish eyes a delicacy; sleeping in the flower bed by the entrance to the college library would satisfy your need for sleep, but you would not likely behave this way. You would undoubtedly prefer eating a medium-rare steak to eating fish eyes, and sleeping in a comfortable bed with clean sheets to sleeping in a flower bed. Can you see the relationship between the way you satisfy your physiological needs and the possibility of self-actualization?

Rituals, restrictions, traditions, and laws affect the methods used to satisfy all survival and stimulation needs. People eat certain foods and refuse others because of early learning experiences, not because of their food value. Eating in a clean environment, preferably with pleasant companions, seems to foster the enjoyment of food. A person who enters a smelly restaurant and notices lipstick smudges on his water glass and dried bits of food caked on his fork is very likely to lose his appetite.

31

Human Needs

"Man Does Not Live by Bread Alone."

The history of the world is filled with examples of people who gave up the satisfaction of a physiological motive in order to satisfy a motive higher on Maslow's hierarchy of needs.

> In wartime Europe, starving parents gave their only food to their children. Their love and sense of duty and responsibility were stronger than their hunger.
>
> A music student lived in near poverty, without adequate food or warmth, to save money to pay for lessons.
>
> A student, his nose completely cut from his face, helped pull his friends from a wrecked automobile before seeking personal relief (*Los Angeles Times*, July 1, 1964).
>
> Early in World War II three military chaplains drowned because they had given their life jackets to others.
>
> Hundreds of people risked abuse, beatings, and even death to help blacks win voting rights in certain communities in the United States.

Food also has great symbolic meaning. Some societies place restrictions upon doing violence to a person with whom you have recently eaten. To "break bread" with someone is an indication of friendship. Food symbolism is also apparent in religious practice. Wine, or grape juice, and wafers are vital to the Christian celebration of Communion; Orthodox Jews adhere to kosher laws that forbid them to eat any meat from pigs, goats, or shellfish; Moslems refuse to eat pig meat; and devout Hindus will not eat any part of or product of the cow.

Food preferences vary greatly. In Japan, raw fish (*sashimi*) is very popular, but oysters are eaten cooked; in the United States, oysters are eaten raw, but never fish. Many people enjoy rabbit meat, but others become sick at the thought of eating such a lovable furry creature—although they may not hesitate to eat a young chicken.

The intensity with which a physiological need is felt may also vary as a result of the social or external situation. Research into the effects of fatigue has been complicated by the close relationship between fatigue and boredom. You have undoubtedly had the experience of finding yourself wide awake, in spite of having been up all night, because you were so involved in what you were doing. The experience of feeling very tired, even after a fair amount of sleep, is a common result of boredom.

The intensity of a physiological need can similarly be influenced by social relationships. Intensely felt hunger needs and subsequent overeating have been known to result from feelings of social rejection. These observations have been confirmed by laboratory experiments in which circumstances were contrived so that the subjects who felt they had been personally rejected from a social relationship had increased feelings of hunger (Spence, Gordon, & Rabkin, 1966).

The list of social influences upon physiological needs could be continued indefinitely. What examples can you think of?

Safety and Security Needs

If you are deeply involved with satisfying your hunger need or your need to avoid pain, you will have little time or energy for anything else.

Figure 2-4.

Private ownership of guns (confiscated by police in this picture) can be used to satisfy safety needs. Do you feel that guns are an appropriate solution? Courtesy Columbia Broadcasting System.

However, once you are able to satisfy these needs, at least at a minimally adequate level, and can feel reasonably confident that the need will not return to disturb you for a period of time, you can turn your attention to satisfying safety and security needs.

Everyone needs to feel safe from such harm as meeting with physical violence, having things he values taken away, or losing the care of parents or other protectors. People who fear that the Secret Police might suddenly burst in and arrest them certainly will find it difficult to concentrate on satisfying any except the basic physiological needs. The child whose parents are constantly arguing and threatening divorce will also have unfulfilled safety needs, and his behavior may be strongly influenced by attempts to assure himself that his parents or some substitute will continue to protect him. What is the effect of the threat of nuclear war upon your own safety needs?

However, people with normal physiological and safety needs sometimes will satisfy needs higher on the hierarchy of needs in preference to those lower. Determining the reasons for this kind of preference involves the study of values, which are discussed in Chapter 17. Does anything motivate you so much that you would risk survival or safety to achieve it?

Love and Belonging Needs

Although the claim that "love makes the world go around" is at least slightly exaggerated, no doubt exists about the motivating power of the need for love and for a sense of belonging. Some evidence exists that, at least for infants, love may be necessary for maintenance of good health. Infants who lack the love of a mother or mother-substitute have been observed to become depressed (Spitz, 1949), apathetic, and physically and emotionally retarded (Ribble, 1943). Since such infants are usually also deprived of normal satisfaction of stimulation needs, we cannot be certain whether the ill-effects resulted from the lack of love or the lack of opportunity for stimulation. (See Chapter 7 for further discussion.)

In any event, the need for love and for belonging is important. People with an unsatisfied need for love or for the feeling of belonging to a group may go to great lengths to satisfy this need, even at the cost of losing self-esteem.

In his childhood, Steve Rogell had lived in a series of foster homes. At age 16, he ran away from a particularly unpleasant situation and, lying about his age, joined the Navy. Steve had no memory of his parents, both of whom died before he was three. Perhaps equally important, he had no memory of ever being loved in any of the homes where he stayed.

Shortly after leaving the Navy, Steve met and married an 18-year-old girl who greatly admired his knowledge and sophistication. Steve felt that she loved him, and he was very happy with the relationship. However, over the next few years, his wife matured and developed her capacities in many ways, while Steve remained very much the person he always was. He became tense and uncomfortable with his wife, and he began to resent her. On the one hand, she represented the love that he badly needed; on the other hand, her growing competence reminded him of how little he had matured.

His wife became increasingly irritated with Steve and, in time, she began to express this irritation. Steve, frightened of losing the one person who had loved him and whom he had been able to love, was unable to show any anger. He became submissive and constantly found ways to seek approval from his wife. Now more sophisticated than he, his wife was disgusted by the meek behavior of the man she had once looked up to, and her reactions to Steve became more and more overtly rejecting. No matter how much she attacked him, however, Steve reminded her of how much they loved each other and how much he wanted to do for her.

Love needs are not restricted to romantic love and parent-child love. They include the feeling of closeness between two good friends, the feeling of neighborliness that exists in some communities, or the feeling of good fellowship that occurs in social clubs or other social groups. Those who feel friendless and unloved exert great efforts to satisfy love needs.

Although love needs and belonging needs are related, they are far from identical. In recent years, awareness of the importance of belonging needs has increased. People who do not feel they belong to their community or who feel that they cannot relate to a group have been described as *alienated.* That is, they are strangers or unrelated persons. Since they feel unrelated to both individuals and groups, they may lack the kinds of motivation that normal social relationships lead to. Often they feel goalless and uncertain of themselves. Not being able to turn to others, they may turn increasingly inward.

Inevitably, some alienated persons will come together and satisfy their belonging needs with each other. A group of this kind may be alienated from others in the larger community, but its members may feel very much related to each other. The expatriates of the 1920s, the bohemians of the 1930s, the beatniks of the 1950s, and the hippies of the 1960s are examples of alienated groups.

Esteem and Self-esteem Needs

Once physiological, safety, and love needs have been satisfied, attention can turn toward gaining the respect of others and having respect for yourself. Steve Rogell sacrificed this opportunity when his

Figure 2–5.

Matthew's love needs are effectively satisfied, and he is also able to give love to others. Photographs by Albert Kallis.

unsatisfied love needs became so demanding that he had to beg his wife for her love.

As human beings, we all feel we have the right to be treated as people of worth. The strongest word one 3-year-old can call another is "baby," because this label implies a lesser level of competence and worth (at least in the eyes of a 3-year-old). The person who feels inadequate may channel his energy into proving his adequacy to *himself*. He may also wish to establish his adequacy in the eyes of others, but he needs most to convince himself.

Esteem needs may be satisfied through healthy or unhealthy behavior. For example, a young man wins an athletic scholarship at his college, and his parents send a notice to the local newspaper. Although they may seek this publicity partly for their son's enjoyment, they may also see their son's success as reflecting upon their own esteem. Not only the esteem accorded by others, but also our own self-esteem is affected by the accomplishments or failures of our children. Seeking esteem through one's children can become unhealthy, as in the case of the major-league outfielder of the 1950s whose father had made such demands for excellence that no human being could attain them; the esteem needs of the father produced a fairly successful ballplayer, but a very unsuccessful human who became mentally ill. The individual who lacks esteem and self-esteem may be too busy trying to convince himself and others of his worth to be able to make effective use of his abilities and potential talents.

Self-actualization Needs

Only when more basic needs have been at least minimally met can the individual turn to satisfying his needs for self-actualization. Self-actualization, as explained earlier, refers to the process of making maximum use of your abilities, of developing your talents, and of being the sort of person you really are, rather than the sort of person you believe others wish you to be.

Just as the young infant seems to need to explore his environment, just as the monkey seems to need to manipulate puzzles for the challenge, so mature human beings also wish to develop their capacities. No one is constantly self-actualizing, just as no one is constantly in the process of satisfying any one other need, but each individual has the potential within him to feel the need to self-actualize and to satisfy this need. A few examples may help clarify this complex concept.

Human Needs

John Ferguson had gone to dental school only because his mother had insisted that he follow in his late father's footsteps. One month before he would have finished the three-year graduate program, his mother died, and John dropped out of school immediately and entered another college where he earned a degree in political science. Eventually he obtained a position with the State Department. When his friends told him he was foolish to sacrifice so many years of training, he merely answered, "Dentistry is not me." He felt he could be himself and make use of his real abilities as a political scientist.

An English professor told the following story: "At the small town college where I teach, older people rarely take daytime courses, so I was surprised to notice a shiny, bald head among the more youthful ones, and I was doubly surprised when I realized this head belonged to the owner of the nearest thing to a department store our town had. He later explained that, by the time he was 45, he had made all the money he needed and had proved to himself he could run a business. But all his life he felt he could be an excellent furniture designer, and now he was returning to college to learn both the techniques and the artistic background, so that he could develop this capacity. The truth is that he didn't have much talent, but he certainly had fun."

Mary Welch was brought up in a family which believed women were not capable of being educated, and—at 17—she married a man who believed the same. Suddenly, after five years of marriage, an automobile accident left her a widow with two small children and no source of income. She took a job as waitress at a Howard Johnson restaurant and enrolled in a course to learn IBM keypunching at night, while her mother cared for her children. Slowly she realized she had ability and that she actually enjoyed the excitement of a busy restaurant, as well as the challenge of trying to improve her keypunching ability. She felt that her hectic schedule enabled her to use her talents and become more the sort of person she really was, whereas the years of living in homes that treated women as inferior and unintelligent had only held her back.

At the age of 10, Mark's parents were told by his teachers that their son spent all his time sketching and doodling. When he was 15, his father begged him to forget his drawing and study accounting so that he could eventually support himself. At 19, Mark finished business college and went to work for an accounting firm but was soon fired because he drew some uncomplimentary pictures of his boss. Mark got another job but went to art school at night. The job pays poorly, but Mark explains, "I don't really care much about pay, as long as I can concentrate on art. I just have to paint. It's just as important for me to paint as it is for you to eat."

All of these people were motivated by the need to develop their capacities and to be "themselves." Each one was fulfilling his need for self-actualizing, regardless of what the rest of the world thought.

How can you tell whether or not you are self-actualizing? First, it is necessary to realize that self-actualizing is not so sharply defined as many other psychological concepts, and you may have a difficult time deciding whether you are applying the concept properly. Four situations occur when a person self-actualizes:

1. The self-actualizing individual raises his standards and demands more of himself. By so doing, he also demands more of life and expects greater rewards from the things he does.

2. Self-improvement becomes continuous. This improvement may occur through a course in Chinese cooking, through reading books and magazines, or through a summer camping trip to the national parks. If the end result of a person's activity is that he gains in his understanding of the world or of himself, or if he becomes better able to do something, then he has been self-actualizing.

3. The individual increases his self-understanding and becomes more the kind of person he wants to be. It may seem strange to say that many people do not really like themselves, but it is true. People are ashamed of certain things they have done or wish to do or have not done or are afraid to do. The self-actualizing person behaves so that he can respect himself.

4. The self-actualizing person makes the fullest use of the abilities he has and also tries to develop new abilities. Most people will attempt only a small proportion of the many things they have the potential to do. People self-actualize when they develop present competencies and investigate new and untried areas (adapted from Coleman, 1960).

The need to self-actualize motivates people to grow and to develop their talents. However, some needs produce behavior that can only compensate for deficiencies, rather than lead to growth.

Deficiency-motivation and Growth-motivation

Behavior motivated by hunger or by fear of physical punishment results from deficiency-motivation; that is, it is motivated by things the organism lacks. You sense an uncomfortable inner tension, you wish to reduce this tension, and so you seek food or escape.

A starving man does not worry about how his food is seasoned. A child, frightened because his parents have left him alone at night without warning, would probably welcome a spanking, if that were the price of his parents' return. These people are deficiency-motivated. When they satisfy their hunger or safety needs, they have not attained any degree of personal growth; they have merely reduced a deficit.

On the other hand, when you are motivated by the possibility of truly enjoying a meal or by the pleasure of warmth and security in being with those you love, your behavior is based on **growth-motivation**. The opportunity for personal growth and pleasure, not tension-reduction, provides the motivation. You may even create mild tension on purpose, such as eating a very light lunch when anticipating an excellent dinner, to heighten its enjoyment.

Thus, behavior occurring in response to any need may, on the one hand, lead to the reduction of a deficit or, on the other hand, lead to some form of personal growth. Satisfying the hunger need can merely reduce hunger, or it can be an enjoyable process taking place in good company and pleasant surroundings. Satisfying the esteem need may merely compensate for lack of self-esteem, or it can be a wonderful experience that leaves you with a warm glow of pleasure, as when your employer commends you for having done an excellent job with a task on which you worked particularly hard.

Here, then, is the hierarchy of needs: physiological needs, safety and security needs, love and belonging needs, esteem and self-esteem needs, and self-actualizing needs. In order to focus upon the higher needs, you must first reasonably well satisfy the more basic ones. In satisfying each need, you may be motivated by deficiency- and tension-reduction, or by growth and enhancement. The hierarchy is not a rigid one, but must be considered in light of the specific background and values of each individual.

We shall return to the concept of self-actualization at many points in this book. At present, consider a few of the implications of this idea:

1. Everyone has potential capacities and talents.

2. These capacities and talents are often never developed.

3. Before developing them effectively, you usually must first satisfy physiological, safety, love, and esteem needs.

4. You are wasting a part of yourself if you leave your potential capacities and talents undeveloped.

5. Developing these capacities and talents is enjoyable and natural, not dull or strained.

6. If you try to influence others to be what *you* want them to be, you may be limiting their possibilities of developing themselves as *they* want.

Each individual has a unique personality. When he is able to satisfy his physiological, safety, love, and esteem needs adequately, he can attempt to develop his unique personality to the limits that his capacities allow.

Level of Aspiration

The strength of an individual's needs, interacting with other personal characteristics, determines his **level of aspiration** for many areas of his life. Your level of aspiration refers to the goal you anticipate achieving. The person who intends to be a straight-B student has a higher level of aspiration for grades than someone who anticipates a straight-C average.

A person's sense of happiness and satisfaction is closely related to the gap between his actual accomplishments and his aspiration level. Thus, the farther a person falls below his level of aspiration, the less happy he is, *even if his achievement level is objectively high* (Block & Thomas, 1955; Rosenberg, 1962).

When a person's achievement level begins to approach his aspiration level, he will usually raise his sights. If he finds that he is unable to succeed in fulfilling his level of aspiration, his goals may become less ambitious.

Ralph Gardner had a good intelligence and knew it. He decided to become a medical doctor, and began college with that in mind. However, because of his need to have a lot of money to spend, he devoted his energies to an outside job, and his grades remained low. After his first year of college, he lowered his level of aspiration from physician to social worker, which required graduate work but not nearly so long a training period as medicine. By the end of the first quarter of his sophomore year, he was dropped from college because of low grades. He returned in the spring quarter, now aspiring to a degree in social science, but he continued to hold his outside job, and his final grades were so low that he decided to give up college.

Ralph then got a job selling encyclopedias and was quite successful. His success reminded him that he had a good brain, and his work schedule left him free between noon and four in the afternoon; so he enrolled in a junior college to earn an Associate of Arts degree in sales management. Although his level of aspiration for education had dropped, his level of aspiration for financial success began to rise. He was soon selling an average of four sets of books a week, earning more than an average social worker makes. He aspired to earn more. After ten months, the area supervisor asked Ralph to open a new territory and recruit and train other salesmen. He persuaded some of his college friends to sell during the summer, and he made a commission on every set of books they sold, plus the normal commission on what he sold. Within two years, Ralph had received his junior college degree, had opened up two additional territories, and was next in line for assistant regional supervisor. He was now aspiring to earn the average income of a medical doctor, which he achieved at about the same age he would have completed his long medical training and begun to practice.

When Ralph first entered college, he had high levels of aspiration in both income and education. Eighteen months later, he was deeply depressed and felt he would achieve neither aspiration. He was only partially successful in achieving the educational aspiration, but he was completely successful in his financial goals.

Ralph's aspirations changed because he was able to judge himself fairly accurately. Others are less fortunate. Some set a level of aspiration beyond their abilities to achieve and then refuse to change it. Others set their level so low that it is easily achieved, but they never fully develop their talents, since they need to use only a small portion of their abilities to reach their goals.

Levels of aspiration are learned as all social motives are learned. Among the factors that influence the level of aspiration are: one's maximum potential ability; the degree to which parents and others in the environment encourage success; personality factors such as feelings of security or anxiety, which may work for or against success; early childhood experiences; and, as in Ralph's case, the person's unique history of attempts to realize a particular aspiration.

An individual's level of aspiration is also influenced by his reference group, that is, those people with whom he compares himself. If you attended a high school where 80% of the graduates went to college, your reference group would most likely have been a college-preparatory group, and you would probably aspire to higher educational achievement than your friend who went to a high school that sent very few graduates to college. One of the reasons that Ralph did not feel highly successful was that he retained his old college friends as a reference group, and he knew that they would have admired academic success more than financial success.

Unconscious Motivation

People often behave without knowing why, that is, without knowing what their motives are. When a person is unaware of his motives, his behavior results from unconscious motivation. He may become aware of the motives in the future, but—for the moment at least—he is behaving without being conscious of the underlying causes.

Many people like to believe that they always understand their own motives and that they never do anything without knowing why. Psychologists do not agree with this conclusion. They feel that much human behavior occurs without the behaver understanding all of his motives.

Consider some situations involving unconscious motivation:

Clayton Black sits in English class biting his nails. Whenever he realizes what he is doing, he quits. As soon as he becomes absorbed in the lecture again, he returns to his biting.

Jan Sturm spilled salt during lunch. He immediately threw some over his shoulder and then laughed about "silly old superstitions." Yet every time Jan spills salt, he repeats this action, although he swears he is not at all superstitious.

From the first moment you walk into class, you know you will not like the instructor, even though your friend has recommended him to you. Everything the professor does irritates you, from the tie he wears to the examination questions he asks. However, none of your friends share your dislike.

Harry's regular girl was Cynthia, but she was away at another college, and Harry had been dating Jeannie during Cynthia's absence. Although Harry spoke of Cynthia as making a "fine wife," Jeannie was more submissive and flattered Harry more. During Christmas vacation, when Harry took Cynthia home after the first date they had had in several months, he kissed her goodnight, looked into her eyes, and said, " 'Til tomorrow night, Jeannie."

Craig Kelly has a great fear of being immersed in water, especially of getting his face wet. He even hates to have shower spray on his face. Yet he admits his fear is foolish, and he cannot explain it.

The motivation for all these behavioral acts was unconscious; that is, the participants were not aware of it. How would you, as an outside observer, interpret the motivation underlying the various actions? Is there anything that is accomplished when a motive is unconscious that cannot be accomplished when motives are conscious? Will unconscious motives help a person avoid feeling guilty? Avoid taking responsibility for his own actions? Express wishes he wants to avoid thinking about? Avoid feelings of inadequacy?

Repression

When behavior results from unconscious motivation, it is often said that the basis for the behavior is repressed. **Repression**, like forgetting, is the inability to recall something. Unlike forgetting, however, repression occurs not because of passing time or disuse, but because a person is motivated to be unable to recall. You may quite easily *forget* your dentist's telephone number, but you are not likely to *forget* an appointment made two days earlier. You may have repressed the memory of the appointment, but you have not forgotten it.

Repression does not occur because you consciously want it to occur. A person does not purposely decide to repress something. It happens without his awareness. Why do people repress certain feelings and events? They repress because they have a need to do so—because the incident or feeling is so upsetting or so threatening or so disturbing to their self-esteem that they are strongly motivated to be unable to recall what happened. People repress experiences, feelings, wishes, and even thoughts. In our culture, sexual and aggressive feelings are especially likely to be repressed, because we are so reluctant to accept ourselves as the "sort of person with *that* kind of feeling."

Repressed motives may influence behavior in ways that are not always understood, although people try to make their behavior appear rational.

> When I was still in the primary grades, my parents had a strict rule that I could never hit my younger brother unless he hit me first; so I would goad him into hitting me, so that I could hit him back. Being bigger and stronger, of course, my blows were more painful than his, and, to make things even better, I always felt justified in my actions. It wasn't until I was in college that I realized what I had actually been doing.

The unconscious motivation was, of course, the desire to hit his brother. Even a third-grader realizes that hitting a child five years younger is unacceptable, and his self-esteem would suffer if he felt he had picked the fight himself. So, without being aware of why he was doing it, the older boy irritated his brother into attacking. He could thus act out his need to hit the younger boy without losing self-esteem and without bringing his parents' wrath down upon him. However, he repressed the basis for the motivation until a psychology class discussion provoked his memory. At that time, he had much less need to repress his motivation, since the hostility he felt toward his brother had long since disappeared.

Consider the person who tells his friend, "I'm only saying this for your own good," and then proceeds to criticize him with considerable vehemence. Is he really motivated by the desire to help the other person? What motives might be repressed? What might be his need to have them repressed?

Summary of Important Ideas

1. Motivated behavior is behavior set into motion by a need felt by the individual. A need indicates that some satisfaction is lacking and implies that the organism is activated to obtain the satisfaction.

2. Motivation and needs are concepts, not things. In order to measure them, indirect measures have been developed. Psychologists measure motivation through controlled observations, ratings by others, self-ratings, and laboratory experiments.

3. A hierarchy of needs implies that the individual has to find adequate satisfaction for the more basic needs before he can turn his attention to needs higher on the scale.

4. The most basic needs are the physiological needs, which include the survival needs (such as hunger, thirst, and fatigue) and the stimulation needs (such as exploration and manipulation). When the former are not adequately satisfied, the organism dies. The stimulation needs develop at least in part as the result of learning, but may well have a biochemical base.

5. People usually satisfy the physiological needs in keeping with certain customs, traditions, personal tastes, and habits.

6. The second most basic needs are the safety and security needs. Next in the hierarchy of needs are the love and belonging needs, the esteem and self-esteem needs, and—after all the previous needs are reasonably well satisfied—the self-actualizing needs.

7. A self-actualizing person makes maximum use of his abilities, develops his talents and potentialities, and becomes the sort of person he really is.

8. Some behavior is motivated by deficiencies or things the organism lacks; some behavior is motivated by growth or the desire to be better or do things in a better way.

9. Each person develops, in many spheres of his life, a level of aspiration or goals he anticipates achieving.

10. Much behavior occurs because of unconscious motivation or motivation that the person himself is not aware of.

11. When behavior results from unconscious motivation, the basis for the behavior may be repressed. Repression occurs when a person does not recall something because he is motivated to be unable to recall, not because the matter was too trivial to recall (as in forgetting).

Chapter Three

Perceiving the Environment

Psychologists have always been deeply interested in how man determines what is going on in his environment. The interest was carried over from philosophy and can be traced far back into history. Much of the early research in psychology, dating back more than 90 years, involved the relationship between what is actually, objectively, in the environment and how man interprets and analyzes it. Psychologists, in conjunction with physiologists and physicists, have studied this question in many ways, and they are still interested in it, although at a much higher level of sophistication than in the nineteenth century. The awareness that man could develop research methods to evaluate his own behavior came partly through the study of sensation and perception.

*T*he human organism is highly sensitive to its environment. It becomes aware of colors, shapes, sounds, tastes, pressures, odors, temperature change, and other environmental **stimuli** * through the senses, which might be compared to windows in a house. Without these windows, the residents of the house would not know what was going on outside. Everything that enters through these windows is transmitted to the brain, where the information is interpreted, largely in light of previous experiences. As the individual matures and has more experiences, he is better able to understand the information communicated through the senses.

Each sense is represented by **receptor** organs that receive the "message" from whatever in the environment is presenting a stimulus. **Visual** receptors are in the eye; **auditory** receptors are inside the ear; taste receptors are on the tongue. After being received by the receptor, the "message" is transmitted through the nerves to the brain, where it is interpreted and its significance communicated to the appropriate part of the body so that the organism can take some form of action.

* Stimuli is the plural of the word **stimulus,** which refers to any object or event that stirs up or stimulates behavior.

Sensation is the term applied to what occurs each time a receptor organ is stimulated. **Perception** is the process through which the various sensations are interpreted and organized into meaningful patterns.

Sensation

Traditional thought states that man has five senses: sight, hearing, taste, touch, and smell. Psychologists have changed the list of senses somewhat, adding the **kinesthetic sense** (sense of body movement, posture, and weight), the **vestibular sense** (sense of balance), and the **internal** (or interoceptor) **senses** (sense of hunger, thirst, and so forth). In addition, touch has been broken down into four different senses (pressure, pain, warmth, and cold), which are usually referred to as the skin senses.

Thus, sensory stimulation takes many forms. You are constantly being barraged with stimuli. However, your receptors are selective; that is, they respond only to certain kinds of stimulation. For example, your ear contains receptors for sound only and is not sensitive to odors or light. The receptors at the surface of the body that react when stimulated by the skin sensations are similarly highly specialized. The receptors for pressure respond only to the sensation of pressure, and the receptors for cold respond only to the sensation of cold. When you rub your eyes, you not only feel pressure, but you also see shapes and colors because the visual receptors have been stimulated, and the corresponding nerves conduct only those impulses that communicate visual stimuli.

In addition to being selective to stimuli, receptors require a certain intensity of stimulation before they will respond. Some sounds, sights, and smells, for example, are too weak to cause the receptor to respond. Thus, the sound of an ant walking has been recorded by a highly sensitive instrument, but without magnification it remains below man's sensory **threshold**. Bloodhounds can sniff their way along a trail; hawks are very sensitive to movement (Sanford, 1965); dogs can hear specially constructed whistles that are inaudible to the human ear. However, the odor, the movement, and the sound are stimuli too weak for humans to perceive. Also, many stimuli, for example, X rays, atoms, or extremely high-pitched sounds, are recognized by neither man nor animal. Man responds to only a small portion of all possible environmental stimuli.

Figure 3–1 will help illustrate what takes place during perception. When the light waves (stimuli) from the traffic light strike the eye

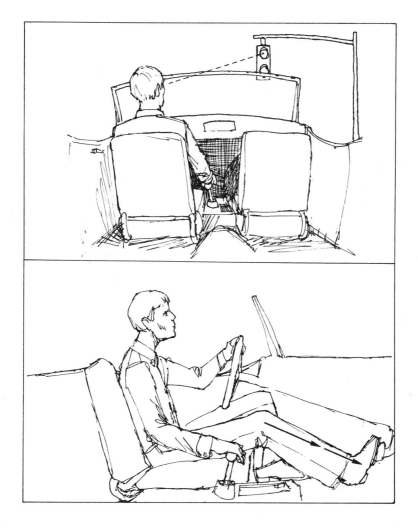

Figure
3–1.

Receiving, interpreting, and responding to stimuli.

(receptor for vision), impulses representing the colors and shapes of the light are established (response), and these impulses travel through pathways in the nervous system to the visual center of the brain, where the meaning of the stimuli is interpreted. The entire process takes only a fraction of a second. The action response—in this case, pressing the brake—may take a little longer.

Sometimes, when the same stimulus occurs repeatedly, **adaptation** takes place. Adaptation means that you are no longer aware of the sensation. For example, your first bite from a chocolate ice-cream cone is likely to seem tastier than your last; odors, after you have been around them for a while, may seem to diminish or disappear altogether; you do not feel the pressure of your clothing and ring except when you first put them on; and you may eventually adapt to living in a noisy dormitory.

Loss of Sensitivity

Humans, if they wish, can develop their sensitivity to sensory stimuli for their own enjoyment and satisfaction, but other animals cannot. A forest ranger develops his ability to see movement; a wine connoisseur develops his ability to distinguish wine bottled in 1957 from wine bottled in 1958; an opera lover can recognize when the tenor is the slightest bit flat. What sensitivities are developed by a safe cracker? A perfume tester? An art historian?

Thus, humans can develop their senses to aid self-actualization. At the same time, because we are completely dependent upon the senses for contact with the world, any reduction in sensory accuracy will reduce knowledge of what is happening in the environment. When one sense is not able to function at all, the individual is deprived of one aspect of knowledge about the world. Consider the added barriers to need satisfaction when someone is unable to see or hear. Ironically, even the sensation of pain is necessary. Without pain, you would not know that your tooth was infected or that your toe was sprained, and the ailment could become much more serious, perhaps causing grave illness or death.

Fortunately, people have learned ways to overcome the disadvantages produced by sensory handicaps. Eyeglasses and special braille books have been developed for those with visual handicaps; hearing aids and sign language enable those with auditory defects to communicate. Nonetheless, personal determination, rather than mechanical devices, often seems the major factor in compensating for sensory handicaps. Many handicapped individuals can fulfill their needs for self-actualizing as well as, or better than, people who are not handicapped.

However, even blind or deaf people retain several "windows on the world." What happens when an individual is completely isolated from his environment? Investigations have been conducted to observe people placed in an apparatus that deprives them of any contact with their environment and any stimulation of their senses. Such isolation means that they could not participate in *any* sort of activity. After a period of time, the subjects became upset and temporarily displayed symptoms commonly associated with the mentally ill (Heron, 1957).

The American community, through some of its customs, acknowledges the importance of stimulation and the difficulties of sensory deprivation. Isolation is one of the most severe punishments dealt out, whether in placing a prisoner in solitary confinement, in isolating a child in his room, or in ordering a pupil to stand in the corner of the classroom or out in the hall.

Just as lack of stimulation can become a problem, so also can overstimulation become one. The receptors, when confronted with too much stimulation, will reject the overload. In some instances, when the stimuli are too strong and too rapid, the receiving mechanism may reject all stimuli and rest for a while. Perhaps you have had the experience of being surrounded by so much stimulation all at once that you felt you wanted to get rid of all of it for a while; for example, while driving an automobile filled with shouting, jostling children.

Sensation plays a vital part in your life. When stimuli are absent, serious emotional problems may occur; when stimuli are restricted, the individual needs to adjust to his condition and find ways to compensate; but an adequate amount of sensory stimulation provides pleasure, satisfaction, and help in self-actualizing.

Perception

Perception is the process of organizing and interpreting sensory stimuli into meaningful patterns. It includes "becoming aware of objects, qualities, or relations by way of the sense organs" (Hilgard & Atkinson, 1967). The visual stimuli received by your visual receptors (eyes) when you look at the cover of this book do not tell you that you are looking at a book. They merely communicate a pattern of colors and shapes; and the brain, as the result of previous learning, interprets this pattern as a book. The auditory receptors receive spoken words as sounds, and the brain interprets these sounds as words with meanings. People who suddenly gain their sight after having been blind all their lives report that the patterns of color and shape are meaningless until they learn to distinguish what the patterns represent.

To some extent, certain types of perception seem to occur inevitably, as the result of **maturation**. Some infants as young as 6 or 7 months will crawl to the edge of a bed, but will not venture beyond or even put their hand out to see if they can continue, although they may have had no opportunity to learn through experience that the end of the bed indicates a sudden drop (Gibson & Walk, 1960). By and large, however, perception entails some learning.

In early infancy, it is hypothesized, the infant perceives his environment as a mass of shapes, colors, and sounds, along with miscellaneous pressures, temperature sensations, pains, smells, and tastes. Order slowly develops out of this chaos. One set of colors and shapes becomes identified with food or warmth; another set, which appears less frequently, may add an uncomfortable scratchy sensation to the sensation of warmth and wetness (that is, when "daddy" kisses him). The infant explores his world by touching, biting, and moving through it, and he is continuously testing to learn what it all means. Gradually he learns to identify people and objects, to locate sounds, to anticipate tastes and pressures, and to recognize relationships among the various stimuli.

Not only does the infant learn to identify people and objects, but he also learns to think of them in ways that have little to do with their physical stimulus value. After an initial meeting with someone, you would probably describe him to a friend in terms of physical appearance. After you get to know the person, however, you would focus upon nonphysical aspects. The physical appearance has undergone no significant change, but your perceptions have changed with learning. The very homely girl seems to have average or even above-average good looks when you get to know her and like her; if you love her, she may appear beautiful.

Perception, then, suggests an emotional component. Perception refers not only to the organizing and interpreting of sensory stimuli, but also to social and emotional responses. When a stimulus becomes familiar, you are increasingly likely to perceive it in terms of its meaning to you, rather than in terms of the objective stimulus that strikes the receptors.

Consider the importance of this meaning of perception for understanding human relationships, including those with persons of a different ethnic or racial group. Reactions to such persons are based upon the previous meaning these individuals had for you—often a reflection of the group to which they belong—rather than upon the objective characteristics they display. Thus, upon first meeting a person of a different group (the group might be distinguished by race, religion, sex, school, vocation, or other feature), you tend to interpret his behavior in light of your notions regarding his group.

Perceptions are influenced both by the objective characteristics of the stimuli and by the perceiver's characteristics, such as needs, experiences, set, and personal rigidity. Because of these characteristics, all people do not notice the same stimuli; neither do they perceive and interpret the same objective stimuli in identical ways.

Stimulus Characteristics

Stimulus characteristics, such as size, color, shape, movement, contrast, uniqueness, and repetition, obviously have a dominant effect upon perception. They are the essence of the sensory materials that

Figure
3–2.

What clues inform you that the pillar on the right is closer to the camera than the last one down the line? Photograph by John G. Warford.

stimulate the receptors. These qualities not only help determine the sensory stimuli, but they also influence **attention**, a familiar term that is used here in a more technical fashion to refer to the process of responding to only a portion of the stimuli in the immediate environment.

People do not attend (that is, give their attention) equally to every environmental stimulus, but select certain things for increased attention. Look at the advertisement shown in Figure 3–3. Notice that the words "Think Small" and the small automobile are the only things that appear in the very large space of the advertisement. In this instance, the uniqueness and the contrast affect your perception and attention. Uniqueness

Think small.

Figure 3–3.

Attention-getting advertisement. © 1962 Volkswagen of America, Inc. Used by permission.

results from the unusual nature of the advertisement; contrast results from the large blank area and the small picture. Even a person who had never seen an advertisement before (and who, therefore, would not realize that this advertisement is different from others) would find his attention caught by the contrast of the small object against a large blank area.

Consider some of the stimulus characteristics that influence perception and attention:

1. Size.   Large pictures and loud noise receive more attention than small pictures and soft sounds (although the advertisement in Figure 3–3 does not utilize this principle).

2. Color.   Certain colors and color combinations attract more notice than others. Food packaging and automobile license plates are both designed with attention-getting color combinations.

3. Movement.   A moving object is more likely to be noticed than a still object. Because of their apparent movement, flashing neon signs will capture your attention more than still signs of similar color and size. When you look at a number of people standing together, your eyes will shift to the one who is moving.

4. Uniqueness and novelty.   Things that are new or unusual attract your attention. A student walking across campus dressed in an Indian sari would receive attention, even if the colors of the sari were subdued, because her appearance would be both unique and novel. After you became accustomed to seeing her or if numerous Indian women in saris attended your college, you would not notice them in the same way. Uniqueness and novelty often occur together, but they do not need to. A new person in a small class is noticed, even if he is not unusual in appearance. Similarly, an extremely obese person may always get attention, even after others become used to him.

5. *Repetition.* The fact that you are shown the same television commercial over and over again is not an accident. Repetition attracts attention, even if the one stimulus by itself has little attention-getting value.

6. *Contrast.* Two sounds or two colors that contrast with each other may attract more attention than two that are similar. A tall man with a very short date will probably receive more notice than two tall people together.

Perceiver Characteristics

Perception and attention are also related to conditions within the individual, such as physiological and other needs, personal experiences, set, and personal rigidity.

1. *Needs.* A hungry person may notice, for the first time, a restaurant he has walked past on a hundred previous occasions when he was not hungry. Research has shown that hungry subjects are more likely to "see" food in a highly blurred picture than are less hungry subjects (Levine, Chein, & Murphy, 1942). The physiological need "hunger" has an influence both on *which* stimuli are attended to and on *how* these sensory stimuli are perceived and integrated into meaningful patterns.

Love needs may function in a similar fashion. You vaguely notice a group of six people talking together, and suddenly you realize that one of them is a person for whom you have strong affection. A few moments later you are able to give a complete description of the clothes, posture, and mood of the loved person, but you are not even certain who the other five are, because you did not attend to them.

Psychological needs affect not only attention, but also perception itself. One investigation showed that the need for self-respect and for the respect of others affected the perceptions of some subjects:

> A group of students were placed in a half-circle facing a pair of posters. One of the posters contained three lines of different heights,

while the other contained one line identical to one of the three lines on the first poster. Each student called out, in turn, the line on poster *A* that was the same as the one on poster *B*. Then another pair of posters was presented, and the procedure was repeated. On the third pair of posters, all the students but one called out the *wrong* line (since all but one had been trained by the experimenter to do so). The student who was not "in" on the study sometimes called off the correct line and sometimes called off the same line as all the others, even though it was obviously incorrect to the objective observer. Then the procedure was repeated with other naïve subjects.

When later asked why they responded incorrectly, the subjects gave several reasons: (1) "I figured the group was wrong, but I thought I'd better go along"; (2) "I saw them differently than the others, but I felt something was wrong with me"; (3) "I saw them the same way the group called them" (Asch, 1951).

Thus, in the first instance, group pressure won out; in the second, the personal insecurity and uncertainty of the student caused him to answer against his better judgment; in the third, the student stated that he actually perceived the lines as being a *length they were not!* If the perception of the length of a line can be so much affected by the need to go along with the group, many other perceptions must be similarly affected. If one boxer is strongly favored by the crowd, will the referee and judges be affected in their decisions? "I know it happened because I saw it with my own two eyes." Is that always sufficient proof?

2. *Experiences.* Previous experience also affects attention and perception.

A 4-year-old American child, living in Paris while his father was assigned there by his company, was playing in a sandbox at a large park. A French child of the same age approached and, holding his shovel above his head, called out in French, "Do you want to play with me?" The American was unable to understand the words, but he responded in light of previous experience with children who held shovels over their heads—he slugged the French boy in the stomach.

People necessarily interpret the environment in terms of their own background. If your experiences are such that a raised shovel means "fight," you respond accordingly.

When you observe two Japanese men bowing and smiling to each other, you perceive them as being friendly, whereas their culture demands that people show such behavior even when they do not like each other. An American observer may have no idea which of the two bowing men is the manager and which is his assistant, while a Japanese observer

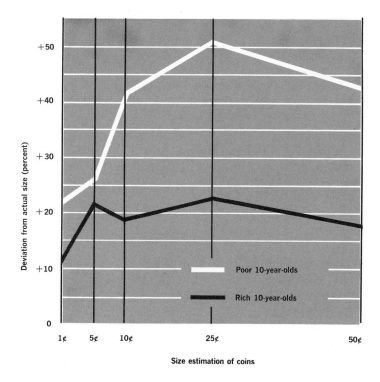

Motivational factors and perception. Reproduced by permission of the American Psychological Association. The top curve represents the size estimation of coins made by poor 10-year-old boys asked to adjust a circle of light so that it was the same size as a designated coin. The bottom curve shows the estimates of rich boys. Although all the boys tended to overestimate the size of the coins, the poor boys overestimated more than the rich boys (Bruner & Goodman, 1947).

Figure 3–4.

Size estimation of coins

could easily tell by the depth and frequency of the bowing because *his* experiences have taught him what cues to attend to for such information.

3. *Set*.   Because of previous experiences and learning, we often anticipate that certain things will occur before they actually happen. That is, we have a *set* or expectation that they will occur. The basketball referee knows that the visiting team's center has fouled out in three successive games, and he develops a set that this man is likely to foul. With this set, the referee is more apt to interpret the center's actions as a foul than to interpret as a foul the same actions by another player.

Even a simple suggestion can produce a set that will lead to inaccurate perceptions:

Professor Blanchard, a friend of the author, told of this demonstration. First he set a bottle of yellowish liquid on the table in front of him and turned to the large class. "I want to test your power of smell today. This bottle contains a very bad-smelling chemical. When I take the stopper out, the odor will slowly drift back, and it should be strong enough to reach even the back rows. Please raise your hand when you first smell the chemical." Professor Blanchard then removed the stopper. First a few hands in the front of the room went up; within a few minutes most of the students had raised their hands.

The chemical solution in the bottle was colored water, without any odor at all; yet well over half the students believed they smelled something, or at least raised their hands to indicate they did.

4. *Personal Rigidity.*   Some people display the personality characteristic of being rigid or inflexible. This quality appears to affect perception. In one well-known study, subjects were shown a series of simple drawings of a dog; in each new drawing, however, the dog looked a little more like a cat, until the dog was obviously no longer a dog but a cat. Those indicating a high degree of racial prejudice were more likely than the average subject to continue to insist that the animal was still a dog, while the more flexible subjects recognized the change more rapidly (Frenkel-Brunswik, 1949). This is an excellent example of the close relationship that exists between perceptual processes and personality.

Although everyone is susceptible to the sorts of perceptual distortions described above, frequent or extreme distortions are probably not often made by individuals successful in self-actualizing. The self-actualizing person can see the world more nearly as it really is, rather than as he wants it to be. Conversely, misinterpretation of sensory stimuli produces errors in judgment along with the errors in perception, and would thus reduce the chances a person has to make maximum use of his abilities.

Perceptual Constancy

In order to make better sense of the world, we often interpret sensations quite differently than the actual objective stimuli suggest. This misinterpretation occurs particularly with perceptual constancy. Place a coin flat in your hand and put your hand in front of you, a little below eye level: does the coin look round? Probably it does, even though the visual sensation you are receiving is not that of roundness. If you were to draw that coin to look exactly as it now appears, the drawn coin would be far from round. When you look at an automobile a couple of hundred feet away, it looks as big as the one only 20 feet away, although once again the objective visual sensations you are receiving must be reinterpreted to communicate the size equality.

The process of perceptual constancy causes us to perceive objects as appearing to be what we think of as normal, regardless of objective sensory stimuli. The two examples above illustrate shape constancy and size constancy. Perceptual constancy also occurs for color and brightness.

Distorted Perception

Perceptions can be distorted because of qualities of the stimulus and because of qualities of the perceiver. The best-known examples of the former are **illusions**. An illusion is a mistaken perception. You think you see or hear or feel something, but the circumstances have fooled you. When you look at a stick half immersed in water, the stick appears broken, even though you know it is straight. The road ahead of you reflects the sun in a way to give the illusion of a puddle of water.

One form of illusion has been popularly called "optical illusion." Several examples of this illusion are shown in Figure 3–5. Another form of illusion is the illusion of movement. The moving red neon arrow, upon closer inspection, turns out to be several different red arrows blinking on and off at the proper speed and sequence. A motion-picture film is nothing more than a rapidly changing sequence of stills giving the

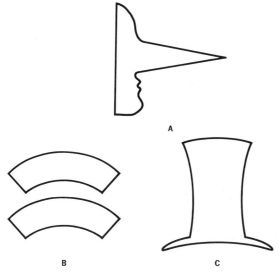

Figure 3–5.

Distances are not necessarily what they seem. In A, the nose is as long as the figure is high; in B, the two arcs are identical; and in C, the brim of the hat is as long as the hat is high.

impression of motion. Characters in films from the 1920s appeared to walk with jerky movements because they used fewer individual stills, and the film moved less rapidly through the camera.

Qualities of the perceiver may also distort perception. From time to time, someone reports hearing voices or seeing visual stimuli when no stimulus is present. These perceptions are hallucinations, or perceptions that occur without stimuli. Although hallucinations are most commonly associated with severely mentally ill or alcoholic individuals, they can occur to normal persons under extreme circumstances. Sometimes a dream or even a daydream will seem so real that it feels like a hallucination. (See Chapter 5 for a discussion of dreams.)

Hallucinations and illusions are often confused with each other and with **delusions**. The differences are vitally important. An illusion causes a person to confuse or distort existing stimuli, usually because of the qualities of the sensation. A hallucination is a perception *without* external stimuli. A delusion is a belief, and will be discussed in Chapter 15.

With so much emphasis on the factors that alter and distort perception, there is danger of underestimating the accuracy with which we perceive. In spite of inevitable subjectivity and lack of 100% accuracy, inaccurate or distorted perceptions only occasionally have a meaningful influence upon the lives of normal people.

Summary of Important Ideas

1. The human organism is aware of the world around it through the senses. These senses include vision, hearing, smell, taste, the skin senses, and others, such as the sense of body movement and the sense of balance.

2. Perception is the process of interpreting the sensory stimuli received from the environment by the receptors and communicated to the brain through impulses in the nervous system.

3. Some sensations are too weak to activate the receptors.

4. Although partial reduction of sensation, as through blindness, can be compensated for, people completely deprived of sensory stimulation may become emotionally upset.

5. The infant explores his world through his senses. Gradually he learns to identify people and objects by their stimulus patterns.

6. The term *attention,* when used technically, means the process of responding to only a portion of the stimuli in the immediate environment.

7. Attention and perception are influenced by stimulus characteristics such as

size, contrast, and movement. They are also affected by perceiver characteristics such as needs, experiences, set, and personal rigidity.

8. Perceptual constancy refers to a process by which we interpret sensations to coincide with what is normal, rather than perceiving them as objective sensations.

9. Distorted perceptions include illusions and hallucinations.

Chapter Four

Principles of Learning and Their Application

Once the psychologist becomes interested in how human beings are stimulated by objects in the environment, he wishes to know about the processes of learning and forgetting. Learning affects the interpretation of stimuli, and so perceptual processes and learning processes are closely related. Interest in learning principles descended from philosophers of centuries ago and led to the development of techniques for the study of behavior. Sensation, perception, learning, thinking, memory, motivation, and emotion (emotion will be discussed in Chapter 13) are usually considered to be the basic processes of human behavior.

Throughout history men have been curious about the processes of **learning**. How do people learn language, values, motor skills, social behavior? Very little behavior is totally uninfluenced by learning, and much behavior would be impossible without a great deal of learning. As a result, the study of learning principles has become basic to the study of the psychology of human behavior.

Learning takes place whenever a relatively permanent change in behavior results from experience or practice. Like motivation, learning cannot be measured directly, but must be assumed to occur when a change in performance is observed. When you see a 1-year-old walk, you know that he has learned this behavior because he was not able to walk three months earlier. However, you are not observing the actual learning process, but rather, you are observing the learner's performance, which is overt behavior. Similarly, your instructor in this course will probably grade you on your examination scores and other evaluations of performance, since he assumes that these performances represent learning.

The measurement of learning is further complicated by the fact that performance, although strongly influenced by learning, is also affected by such factors as fatigue, motivation, and health. Thus, the psychologist's ability to measure learning is far from perfect. Only when he can introduce accurate measuring devices into the brain will the psychologist be likely to overcome these sources of inaccuracy.

The importance of learning cannot be overestimated, since virtually all behavior involves some learning. You learn to talk, eat, be interested in politics, feel insulted, want money, thread a needle, love your parents, plan a budget, drive an automobile, respect or dislike yourself, and satisfy your physiological, safety, love, esteem, and self-actualizing needs. Without the ability to learn, people would be little more than vegetables and would need constant care to continue to exist.

Organisms, of course, are not merely a collection of assorted processes such as sensing, perceiving, learning, and thinking. A person must be looked upon as a unified whole rather than as a series of parts. Thus, although perception and learning are discussed in different chapters for the sake of convenience, try to keep in mind the continual interplay between these and all other behavior processes. Your perceptions are based upon what you have learned through previous experiences; your learning is most strongly influenced by what you perceive.

Kinds of Learning

In developing principles of learning, psychologists must account for both simple learning, such as an infant learning that he can stop crying for his bottle when he sees his mother enter the room, and complex learning, such as learning how to design the plans for a skyscraper. The present discussion will include two forms of simple learning: classical conditioning and operant learning. The latter part of the chapter will deal with more complex forms of learning, and Chapter 5 will discuss thought, including problem solving, concept formation, and language.

Classical Conditioning

Physiologist Ivan Pavlov conducted the first systematic studies of **classical conditioning** over 60 years ago. After observing dogs salivate when their food was brought to them, Pavlov demonstrated that they would learn to salivate to a previously neutral **stimulus** such as a bell, sounded a moment before the arrival of the food (Pavlov, 1927). Originally the stimulus *food* produced the **response** *salivation*. After many trials during which the buzzer was sounded prior to the presentation of food, the buzzer became the stimulus for salivation. The salivation

Figure 4–1.

Many principles of learning hold true for both humans and animals. Courtesy Columbia Broadcasting System.

response occurred involuntarily—the dog could not control its salivation. This process, in essence, is classical conditioning.

You can try out a little demonstration on yourself. Next time you are with a group of friends, yawn. A great big soulful yawn! Make it realistic! Then watch the way the others begin to yawn, or try not to yawn. When you were a very young child, the stimulus of another person yawning would not have led to your responding with a yawn, but you have been conditioned to yawn when observing others yawn. (By the way, do you feel like yawning now? If not, try reading this paragraph once again, slowly, and think about yawning.)

Classical conditioning helps explain more than such simple behavior as yawning and salivating. Let's begin with a reasonably well-accepted statement: year-old infants enjoy being cuddled by their parents. That is, the stimulus of warmth and physical contact of the parent will produce in the infant a response indicating pleasure, such as gurgling and smiling. Assume that this year-old infant has had many such experiences with both his mother and his father. He has, by now, come to associate the presence of his parents with the warm, pleasant physical contact that produces the gurgling and smiling. What happens? He now responds to the sight, perhaps even the sound of the step, of his parents with gurgling and smiling. His response occurs virtually inevitably to the approach of his mother or father. Gurgling and smiling did not originally occur in response to his parent, but through the constant association of *warmth and affection* with *parent close to me,* the infant has become conditioned to respond in this fashion.

The original stimulus *warm human contact* produced the response *gurgling and smiling;* after many experiences with the parent, the stimulus *sight of parent* produced the response. Thus, it can be said that the infant is conditioned to gurgle and smile at the sight of the mother; that is, he has learned to give this response virtually automatically.

After a while, the infant responds with gurgling and smiling to all adults. This process is called **stimulus generalization,** since the infant's response to his parents has been generalized to other adults. Then his older brother, who is jealous of the baby, enters the picture. Whenever the brother comes by, the baby is likely to get a pinch or a squeeze. The baby then learns **discrimination** between adults and older brother. If his brother's friends are pleasant to him, the baby may learn further discrimination, this time between his older brother and other boys of the same age.

Each time the stimulus-response sequence occurs, **reinforcement** of learning takes place. That is, each time the sight of the parent is followed by cuddling, reinforcement occurs. The more reinforcements, the more thoroughly the infant learns to respond to his parents with pleasure, and the longer it would take for his responses to cease if his parents ceased their cuddling.

The response, however, may not follow the stimulus forever. A process called **extinction** can occur. When, for example, Pavlov stopped feeding the dogs following the sound of the buzzer, they eventually ceased to salivate when they heard the stimulus. If the infant's parents stop giving him love and warmth, he will stop his smiling and gurgling.

Or will he? Human behavior is complex. Although classical conditioning is a very useful model, like other models for understanding human behavior, it has shortcomings. There was a time when many psychologists felt that classical conditioning could explain virtually all learning and that all human behavior could be controlled as easily as the salivation of dogs or the yawns of your friends. This belief no longer holds, and classical conditioning is usually seen as only one form of human learning.

Operant Learning

In classical conditioning, the original stimulus-response sequence is part of the person's potential behavior. That is, the infant gurgled and smiled in response to being cuddled without having to learn to smile. Much learning, however, is of a different nature; it involves rewarding the learner for the proper response and either not rewarding or punishing him for improper responses. Eventually, the individual learns the correct response.

Four conditions are necessary for **operant learning** to take place: (1) the learner must have the motivation to do something, to behave in some fashion; (2) he must have the potential for producing the correct response; (3) when he gives the correct response, he must receive some kind of **reward** or **reinforcement**; and (4) if he does not give the correct response, he must be motivated to continue to respond until he does.

Each time the correct response occurs and is followed by reinforcement, learning has taken place. On each successive occasion, the correct response should occur sooner and the number of incorrect responses should diminish until, finally, the correct response will regularly follow the stimulus.

Sometimes the person does not produce the correct behavior but does respond in the proper general direction. He is reinforced for that approximate response until he gives it regularly; then the reinforcement is stopped until he again behaves a little more in the correct general direction. Consider a young child learning to catch a ball; you do not reinforce his behavior only when he makes a perfect catch, but also every time he comes a little closer to making a perfect catch. You continue this process until he has learned how to catch a ball correctly.

A young girl wants to thread a needle. She knows generally what to do, but cannot do it properly. Each time she fails to get the thread through the hole, her response is not reinforced. Finally she responds correctly and is successful. The next time she tries to thread a needle, she succeeds more quickly.

A clumsy student wants to learn to make lay-ups on the basketball court. He makes attempt after attempt, most of them failures. However, his occasional success is reinforcing, and he begins to repeat those responses that lead to baskets. Slowly he learns, through success and failure, to sink a high percentage of his shots.

Principles of Learning and Their Application

A man receives a brand-new, expensive camera. He reads the directions, then goes out to take pictures. He tries to adjust the camera to account for light, glare, distance, and so forth, but his early photographs are either too blurry or too dark. Eventually he learns to judge the conditions properly, by remembering what he did when his pictures turned out well. The correct responses—that is, camera adjustments—are reinforced; they tend to be repeated, and, as a result, his pictures improve greatly.

In classical conditioning, the initial response is made involuntarily —the dogs salivated and you yawned, not because of decisions but because the conditions led almost inevitably to the responses. Eventually the response—again almost inevitably—occurs following a previously neutral stimulus, such as the buzzer. In operant learning, the individual does something to the environment—he makes many voluntary responses until one is reinforced. As B. F. Skinner, a major pioneer in this field, has said, "the behavior operates upon the environment to generate consequences" (1963). When the consequences are rewarding, the behavior is reinforced and is more likely to occur again when the circumstances are repeated.

Each attempt by the individual to respond correctly to a stimulus is termed a **trial**; each rewarding of a correct response is termed a **reinforcement**. The more rapidly and the more frequently a person's trials are reinforced, the faster he will learn.

Extinction also occurs with operant learning. When a previously successful response is no longer rewarded or reinforced, the person will eventually stop making that response under the given circumstances. When the photographer decides that his pictures are not good enough or the basketball player finds that his shooting success has reached a standstill, he alters his previous behavior and emits new responses.

Extinction is not the only way of eliminating a response. Negative reinforcement may also be used. This process refers to finding some way to leave a particular response unreinforced or to punish the responder until he stops the response. The child who sucks his thumb is punished for his action in a variety of ways, until he eventually stops. Using punishment for negative reinforcement is not always successful, as anyone who has tried to stop a thumbsucker has found out. Sometimes the attention that punishment provides is more rewarding than the penalty of the punishment itself. On other occasions, the punishment marks that behavior as something special, so that the person recalls—and perhaps repeats —his response on subsequent occasions. Negative reinforcement can also take the form of not offering an expected reward, such as when your best jokes get only a deadpan reaction.

Two applications of operant learning. Operant-learning methods have been widely applied in working with schoolchildren. One 4-year-old child cried after the slightest frustration. His teachers tried to help him, but achieved little success. Finally, when they began to ignore him, so that his crying was not rewarded, his tears came no more often than any other child's (Harris, Wolf, & Baer, 1964).

Another example was that of a nursery school child who always played by himself. To alter this behavior, his teacher would give him extra attention every time he approached another child, regardless of the reason, but would ignore him as long as he played by himself. Initially the teacher provided the reinforcement whenever the child merely *stood next* to another child; later she rewarded the child only when he *played next* to another child; finally she rewarded him only when he *played with* another child (Harris et al., 1964). This careful use of operant-learning methods in encouraging social relationships has been repeated in a variety of settings.

Another familiar application of operant-learning principles is the teaching machine. A question appears in the machine, and the learner writes down the answer or says it to himself. Then, through some action by the learner, such as turning a handle or pressing a button, the correct answer to the question appears in the machine. If the learner's response is correct, he is rewarded by a sort of psychological pat on the back—reinforcement occurs on that trial. The learner thus receives immediate positive reinforcement if his response is correct and negative reinforcement (that is, no reward) if incorrect.

Teaching machines have potential use (1) at all levels of general education; (2) in special education, particularly for the mentally handicapped and slow learner; (3) in industrial training; and (4) in the military (Leib, Cusack, Hughes, Pilette, Werther, & Kintz, 1967). Their success, however, varies with the situation, the machine program, the student, and the purposes of the educational program (Leib et al., 1967).

Students both in high school and in college have stated their approval of teaching machines for a variety of types of learning. Over 75% of one group of college students believed that machines enabled them to get more out of their introductory psychology course than they otherwise would have gotten (Holland, 1960). Teaching machines offer many advantages to the student, such as enabling him to work at his own speed and to check immediately whether his response was correct or incorrect. Teaching machines are undoubtedly very useful as a supplement to the instructor's teaching and the text. They provide an effective way to study for examinations; and under some limited circumstances, they may actually replace an instructor or a textbook, but—at least at present—they cannot substitute for a competent teacher or a well-written book.

Figure 4–2.

Teaching machines serve many purposes. *Top:* A young child with emotional difficulties is helped to overcome them through reinforcements for appropriate responses on a teaching machine. *Bottom:* A college student is examining another kind of teaching machine. Courtesy of School of Education, UCLA. Photographs by Jose Lucero.

Remembering and Forgetting

Learning is very closely related to remembering. If no learning occurs, there is nothing to remember. Conversely, if no remembering occurs, learning is without value. Learning refers primarily to acquiring the capacity for behavior change, whereas remembering implies the continued capacity to act upon the learning. When you say that you have learned to ride a bicycle, you mean that you have acquired the skill to ride; if, ten years later, you claim that you still remember how to ride a bicycle, you mean that you are still capable of acting upon the earlier learning. Stating this another way, the ability to ride a bicycle is stored in your memory and is available to recall.

Figure 4–3.

Music is very meaningful to the Cuna Indians of the San Blas Islands, off Panama. Learning to play their native instruments is part of their cultural education. Courtesy Braniff International.

Principles of Learning and Their Application

Kinds of Remembering

The three major ways in which remembering is exhibited are *recall, recognition,* and *relearning.* Recall refers to the act of bringing to your thoughts an image or representation of what has occurred earlier. Recall is tested by asking the person a question or asking him to perform a task. What does your best friend look like? What foot do you use to press on the brake? Show exactly how you set up accounting books for your company. When did you last have an ice-cream cone? These responses all require recall. Your instructor measures your recall of the course content when he gives you an essay exam.

Recognition refers to your awareness that something is familiar, that you have experienced or perceived it previously. You recognize people from their photographs, or you recognize the new Chevrolet from its familiar trademark. A multiple-choice exam is a measure of recognition, since the alternatives are presented to you and you select the one that you recognize as correct. You do not need to recall, that is, bring the answer to mind, because the answer is in front of you.

Relearning is a less frequent indication of remembering. Relearning merely means that a second attempt at learning something, usually much later than the first, will take less time and effort than the initial attempt, because something of the original learning stayed with you. If you were brought up until the age of 4 in a home in which Spanish was spoken, at 18 you might no longer be able to speak the language. However, it would take you less time to learn that language than it would take someone who had never had the early contacts. The increased rapidity of learning in a relearning situation implies the existence of some memory.

The Nature of Forgetting

You may have heard that everything you have ever perceived or experienced in any fashion is stored somewhere in your brain, and that, given the proper circumstances, it could be remembered. If such were the case, nothing would ever be truly forgotten. We could only say that some perceptions and events were extremely difficult to recall.

Psychologists have not been able to prove or disprove this hypothesis, but much contemporary evidence points to a two-factor theory of memory. The first factor is *short-term memory* and refers to sensations and other experiences that are remembered only very briefly, such as the name of a person you meet at a party. It is forgotten ten seconds later; the memory is not, to use computer jargon, stored. The second factor is *long-term memory;* it takes place when something about the experience causes it to be stored. In this instance, a biochemical change occurs in the brain and the memory remains there. In some recent experiments with lower animals, psychologists have been able to alter long-term and short-term memory independently of each other by altering the body chemistry. In related research, investigators have found that rats who were brought up in a stimulating and varied environment and given many experiences developed brains that could be distinguished by chemical analysis from the brains of rats that were reared in isolation (Krech, 1968).

Thus, the nature of remembering and its opposite, **forgetting**, may be two-fold. For some experiences, the memory time span is very brief or even nonexistent, the result of inadequate impact of the event. For other experiences, the long-term variety of memory makes forgetting more complicated. It might occur because of *disuse, interference,* or *motivated forgetting*.

To state that forgetting takes place because of disuse implies that the chemical base in the brain deteriorates. Since our own experience suggests that we have greater difficulty recalling events of the distant past or events that we are not reminded of, the disuse approach has appeal. However, you may also have had the opposite experience—you suddenly recalled the name and face of a person you have not even thought of in 15 years. People often report dreaming of events that had not crossed their thoughts for 30 or 40 years. Other evidence has been supplied through recall under hypnosis.

Interference implies that something has gotten in the way of remembering. The interference may be retroactive; that is, later learning interferes with the ability to recall earlier events. Retroactive interference means that you recall recent events better than earlier events because, in a sense, the recent events squeeze the earlier events from your memory. Another form of interference is proactive interference, used to describe the process by which early learning makes it more difficult to recall what you have learned afterward. If both proactive and retroactive interferences operate, you should be able to memorize the first part and the last part of a poem or a list of terms more easily than the middle part. Indeed, that result is just what both personal experiences and numerous research studies have shown.

In Chapter 2, the term *repression* was introduced to describe what happens when a person is unable to remember something because he is motivated to be unable to remember. The concepts of repression and unconscious motivation will be used several times in this book. Obviously repression provides an additional explanation of why we are unable to remember.

It is not necessary to debate the three factors that adversely affect recall of long-term memories, since all three may operate simultaneously. As with many problems, the evidence on forgetting is far from complete, and the immediate future is likely to bring some exciting developments.

Another unknown in the psychology of remembering is the point at which forgetting takes place. For memory to occur, three things must happen: (1) you must be aware that the event has taken place; (2) you must be able to store that material; and (3) you must be able to bring that information into focus when you need it. In the two-factor theory of memory, short-term memory implies that the original awareness was minimal and the memory was never stored; long-term memory implies both storage and retrieval from storage. But at what stage in that sequence does forgetting usually occur? When psychologists can determine that point, they will have made a major step in understanding the dynamics of memory.

One of the most exciting—and at the same time disturbing—developments is the possibility that man will be able to improve his memory through chemical means. There is some evidence that both normal and mentally retarded persons *slightly* improve their ability to remember after taking glutamic acid (Vogel, Broverman, Draguns, & Klaiber, 1966). Psychologists have been able to affect the performance of animals by altering their brain chemistry, and they have been able to affect animal brain chemistry by altering their experiences. The question, then, is: What happens when we begin to apply these methods to human beings? Can you think of both good and bad consequences?

Application of Learning Principles to Effective Study

Many principles of learning and memory, developed through research, can be applied to the problems of effective study. These principles are not magic formulas for success, and they cannot be substituted for self-discipline or individual competence, but—combined with proper motivation and effort—they can help students make maximum use of their abilities.

Warm-up

It takes a few minutes or more for an athlete to get warmed up. The same principle holds for students. Each time you begin to study, you need a little time to warm up. A typist does not work at top speed in the first ten seconds of typing; a mechanic called to the telephone in the middle of a complicated task may take several minutes figuring out what he was doing before the interruption. Since warm-ups do consume time, study should be planned to minimize them by avoiding frequent shifts from one kind of task to another.

Frequency and Spacing of Repetitions

Football players do not merely learn their plays until they go through them correctly one time; they drill and drill until a mistake is almost impossible. Such drill is repetition to the point of **overlearning**. Overlearning will both improve learning and reduce the rapidity with which forgetting takes place.

However, boredom and fatigue may decrease learning and the effective use of intelligence. Therefore, going over the same material in the same way repeatedly, until boredom occurs, is not efficient. Both retroactive and proactive interference increase when you study the same material for a long period of time. Such learning is termed **massed practice** and is exemplified in cramming for an exam.

Distributed practice, or spaced practice, is more effective than massed practice, both for recalling the material a few hours later and for recalling it many months in the future (Anderson, 1967). Spaced practice is particularly effective for meaningful materials, but it loses much of its force when the distributed-practice sessions are too brief or separated by too long a period of time. The more frequently adequate practice sessions are held, the less forgetting that occurs. Thus, periodic reviews are recommended.

Whole Versus Part Learning

Whole learning is the learning of material by going over it in its entirety on each study occasion; part learning involves taking a small segment, learning it well, and then going on to the next segment. It is very difficult to say which is better for any given individual under given circumstances. The best advice seems to be to study the largest units that are meaningful to you (Hovland, 1951).

Knowledge of Results

Knowledge of previous results, or **feedback**, is helpful in studying, especially because you can correct previous errors and know your weaknesses (Anderson, 1967). Imagine shooting a rifle at a target but never knowing whether you hit it or not! How much learning would take place? Would your performance improve? The same difficulty exists when you do not make good use of previous learning and performance by studying your mistakes on an examination. Teaching machines make good use of this principle.

Meaningfulness of Subject Matter

Psychologists have shown that people learn facts, ideas, and relationships faster and remember them longer when they have meaning (McGeoch & Irion, 1952). For this reason, you can improve your ability to recall by trying to understand the relationships between what you are studying and other aspects of your academic or personal life. You may find it difficult to memorize the battles of the Civil War, but by plotting them on a map and trying to understand their consequences in the politics of the Civil War, the battles are no longer isolated incidents, but part of a meaningful pattern. To make the study of the Civil War meaningful to you, you might contemplate how its outcome changed our country and how different the United States might be today if the South had won.

Think about the courses you find the least interesting: How can you relate the material to your own life? How can you find a meaningful pattern that ties the material together? How does it fit in with other courses you are taking?

Transfer of Training

Positive transfer of training occurs when learning one type of task facilitates learning another task. In negative transfer, the learning of one task interferes with learning a second. An example of the former would be learning to use an electric typewriter after first learning how to use a manual one. The latter would be exemplified in your attempts to get used to calling your girl friend by her new married name.

Sometimes people learn work habits or study habits that harm their chances of learning better ways of working and studying. Early approaches are difficult to overcome. Because of negative transfer, a factory worker who has worked on one machine for ten years might find it very difficult to use a new machine. However, learning the principles, rather than the specifics, of a task can lead to positive transfer.

Active Set

How often have you had to reread the same paragraph four or five times because none of the ideas seemed to "stick"? You were not actually attending to your reading; you did not have an active set to learn. A method for studying textbooks has been developed that helps establish an active set and, simultaneously, enables you to follow other principles of effective learning such as being familiar with what you will read in advance, making reading meaningful, or responding immediately.

This method of textbook study is called **SQ3R** and consists of five steps:

1. Survey. In order to gain an active learning set, it is useful to have an idea of what is ahead. Before taking a long automobile trip, you usually look at a map of the entire route; similarly, you can survey the book you are going to read by skimming the material and reading the summary carefully.

2. Question. To encourage an active set, it is useful to be searching for something. If you look for the answer to a particular question in a book, you are more likely to have an active set than if you are only trying "to cover the pages assigned." Make up your own questions by turning each major heading into a question and writing this question down. If you were applying SQ3R to this text, you would jot down, "How can principles of learning help study?"

3. Read. You obviously need to read the material. With your question in the back of your mind, read actively to answer the question.

4. Recite. To complete the process, you need to answer the question. It is suggested that you first answer the question aloud, and then jot the answer down under your question in your notes. Once again, you are forced into activity so that you can better check your own reading adequacy.

5. Review. The previous three steps are repeated for each major heading, probably between four and eight per chapter. The final step, which is primarily repetition rather than active set, is to reread the summary and review your notes. Such repetition is useful in helping you see the entire chapter as a meaningful pattern, rather than as isolated segments (Robinson, 1961).

Proper use of SQ3R will not only produce an active set for learning, but will also supply you with a brief chapter outline, enable you to recall the material longer, and reduce daydreaming. (See the Appendix for examples and some additional suggestions in using SQ3R.)

Studying with a group can also improve your active set to learn. When other people ask you questions from the text or your professor's lectures, you must answer them aloud. You are forced to learn the material well enough to explain it to the satisfaction of others in the group.

One important purpose of teaching machines is providing an active set for learning. Both the *Question* and *Recite* steps are usually incorporated in programmed instruction procedures.

Summary of Important Ideas

1. Learning is the process that takes place whenever a relatively permanent change in behavior results from experience or practice.

2. Learning cannot be measured directly, but must be inferred from observing performance.

3. In classical conditioning, a stimulus is presented a moment before a second stimulus. If the second stimulus elicits a response, the first stimulus will eventually elicit the same response, assuming the procedure is repeated often enough.

4. Additional learning takes place through generalization and discrimination. Extinction weakens the bond between stimulus and response; reinforcement strengthens the bond.

5. Operant learning requires motivation to respond, the possibility of producing the correct response, and a reward for producing the correct response. When the correct response is not emitted spontaneously, operant learning can be guided by eliciting the correct response through a series of approximations.

6. Operant learning has been applied to personal and academic problems in such ways as encouraging better social relationships among children and providing the basis for programmed teaching machines.

7. Learning and memory are closely related. If no learning occurs, there is nothing to remember; without memory, learning is valueless.

8. Evidence for memory occurs through recall, recognition, and relearning.

9. A two-factor theory of remembering has been proposed. The factors are long-term memory and short-term memory.

10. Memory has a biochemical base. When the relevant body chemistry is altered, memory is affected.

11. Forgetting may occur through disuse, interference, and motivation to forget.

12. Principles of learning and memory may be applied to study. Application of these principles includes making proper use of warm-up, using the optimum number of study sessions spaced in optimum fashion, making proper use of whole and part learning, obtaining knowledge of results, making material meaningful, using transfer of training principles, and applying SQ3R.

Chapter Five

Thought and Language

Learning and remembering provide the base from which more complex aspects of intellectual capacities can be considered. Humans must learn not only simple responses to simple stimuli, but also complex responses to complex stimuli. They must learn to solve problems, gain insights, and form concepts. In brief, they must learn to think. Since language is such a basic part of the thought processes of humans, thought and language will be discussed here in the same context. The nature of intelligence emerges from considering thought and language, and Chapter 6 will examine intelligence and its measurement. Thus Chapters 4, 5, and 6 take us from the simplest all the way to the most sophisticated forms of learning.

The complex nature of humans becomes immediately apparent when we contemplate their thought processes. Although lower forms of animals do think, make decisions, and act intelligently, a wide gap exists between the capacities of the most intelligent of lower animals and the average man. Writers of science fiction sometimes create characters whose intelligence is as far beyond that of humans as ours is beyond lower animals; yet the science, technology, and social institutions of these wonder-creatures are often not beyond the potential achievement of man. Hopefully man will use his thinking ability to save the future of the human race from the effects of the destructive potential this same ability to think has permitted him to evolve.

The Beginnings of the Use of Symbols

You have undoubtedly observed that people not only learn to do things for immediate satisfaction, but they also learn when the reward is

Figure
5–1.

Man's ability to use thought and language has permitted him to develop amazing scientific achievements, such as the Mercury space capsule shown here. This ability has enabled him to create and, unfortunately, also to destroy. Courtesy Columbia Broadcasting System.

a symbolic reinforcement, such as money, which has no value in and of itself, but receives value in terms of what it can purchase. Chimpanzees can learn to work for poker chips that can be exchanged for food a day later (Wolfe, 1936), indicating that they can learn a relatively sophisticated symbolic relationship. People also work for money to buy things, but—for some people at least—money eventually becomes important in its own right, perhaps because of its association with previous satisfaction of needs. When the chimps found that their poker chips would no longer get them food, the response that they emitted to obtain the chips (that is, work) met with extinction, and they stopped working. People, on the other hand, will work hard to obtain far more money than is needed to purchase the goods and services they desire. The accumulation of wealth for its own sake seems to become autonomous, or independent, of other need satisfactions.

Both humans and some lower animals learn to respond to symbols with as much fervor as they respond to what the symbol stands for. A smile, a word of encouragement, a raised fist are all symbols that we learn to associate with other stimuli, until the symbol becomes as meaningful and as motivating as the initial stimulus.

Problem Solving

Much human learning involves seeing relationships and working out new solutions. Sometimes problems are solved largely by *trial and error*. Thomas Edison is said to have made several thousand attempts, each time trying a different method or material, before he produced the electric light. His efforts were, of course, far from random, for there had been considerable previous thought, but there was also much trial and error. A personal experience of the author's also illustrates problem solving by trial and error, which, in this instance, turned out to be more successful than careful thought and planning:

> Our newly purchased French automobile seemed to intrigue and baffle all American mechanics who were entrusted to repair it. As long as we remained in Los Angeles, we had little difficulty, but one summer we decided to take a cross-country camping trip, and the car's water pump fell off 20 miles from Kansas City. The local dealer was reassuring, but his mechanics were less so. They put on three successive water pumps, none of which lasted more than a few miles. A total of five man-hours went unsuccessfully into what should have been a one-hour task. Finally, just before closing time, the head mechanic came back over for the umpteenth time, leaned over to face the water pump, touched and twisted and yanked and pushed every conceivable contrivance. Then I noticed that he began turning a bolt that had been partly hidden and completely unnoticed. As he turned it, he began to grin, then he got up, said "Try 'er," and walked away. The water pump lasted the remaining two years we owned the car.

The *step-by-step* method is usually used in solving algebra problems or in figuring out what is causing your faucet to leak. Although the step-by-step process in problem solving is often obvious, at other times the solution of a problem may seem to happen all at once. Such experiences may result from some step-by-step process that has gone on without our knowing it, but we end up with the feeling that the solution came suddenly.

In these instances, the solution is often referred to as resulting from *insight*. Insight has been differentiated from other kinds of problem solving in several ways: (1) it comes suddenly; (2) it occurs smoothly and without hesitation; (3) it may come before the person actually tackles the task of solving the problem; and (4) it may reveal a novel solution (Osgood, 1953), or at least a solution that is original for that person. In terms of these characteristics, the auto mechanic (above) or the student solving an algebra problem has not used insight. Three-year-old Danny, however, did use insight:

> After a hard morning of playing on the monkey bars at his school, Danny arrived home to demand a cookie "Right now!" His mother reminded him that lunch would be ready in ten minutes and he could have a cookie for dessert. Mother's logic was not persuasive, but the fact that the cookies were on the kitchen counter about two feet out of his reach was persuasive—or at least it had been on previous occasions. This time, with his climbing of monkey bars fresh in his mind, Danny pulled out two of the kitchen drawers to form steps and quickly clambered up to the counter and the cookies.
>
> Danny saw the relationship between two previously unconnected acts, climbing on monkey bars and getting a cookie, whereupon a sudden insight occurred.

Not all persons go about solving a problem in the same way. For a given problem, one person may apply trial-and-error techniques, another may try to solve it logically step by step, and a third may experience a sudden insight.

Concept Formation

The question of how humans develop their understanding of concepts is today undergoing extensive investigation by psychologists. How do you learn what is meant by the terms *democracy, manly, three, total, blue* (the color), *opposite,* or *Swedish?*

One way in which concepts develop is through abstracting from experiences with the concept in a number of different settings. The young child hears the word *blue* applied to a blue coat, the blue sky, his sister's blue eyes, and his blue blanket; slowly he recognizes that blue refers to the color. If he has previously formed an understanding of the concept *color,* he could merely be told that blue was the color of the coat, sky, and so on. Once the child has learned what common quality of the coat, the sky, his sister's eyes, and his blanket is encompassed by *blue,* he can generalize blueness to other objects. Through the responses of others, he will gain an understanding of the outer limits of blueness: when does blue become black or white or purple or green? And, if he hears his father ask his mother why she is so blue, he may become confused all over again.

Very young children tend to develop concepts through concrete features shared by various items: for example, automobiles and trains are

**Figure
5–2.**

Concept formation consists of learning that one response describes a number of related things. Courtesy Fillmore H. Sanford.

similar because they are both hard, fast, and have horns. A later step in **concept formation** is to respond to the function of the items; for example, automobiles and trains are similar because you ride in them. The most mature phase of concept formation is to recognize the similarity between trains and automobiles because both belong to the abstract concept *vehicle* (Reichard & Rapaport, 1943).

Some concepts are very difficult to grasp, not only for young children but also for mature people, particularly when the concept is abstract and there is nothing physical to point to. Sometimes abstract concepts mean something quite different to different people. Thus concepts such as *democracy, religion, love,* and *independence* are only understood through varied experiences with situations in which the words are applied.

Thinking

Where does the topic of learning stop and the topic of **thinking** begin? The answer is an arbitrary one of definition. Concept formation and problem solving form a borderland between learning and thinking.

Human beings are able to combine the many symbols, concepts, and other results of learning into thinking. Imagining the future or trying to make sense of the past is thinking. Creating a comic strip, designing the body of a new sportscar, or solving a problem in algebra all involve thinking. Criticizing a movie or deciding to break a date are forms of thinking. Whether the thinking will lead to good or poor results is not the point; the point is that thinking takes place. Animals show a form of behavior that can be called thinking, but the difference between thinking by men and "thinking" by animals is very great.

Thinking has been described as "any process or activity not predominantly perceptual. . . . Judging, abstracting, conceiving, reasoning, and . . . imagining, remembering, and anticipating are forms of thinking" (English & English, 1958).

Thinking may work under our control, or it may be partly or completely outside our awareness. In working out an accounting problem or in trying to figure out the identity of the criminal in a murder mystery, we use controlled thinking—we try to guide our thought processes to gain a particular goal. Thinking for school or for work is frequently controlled thinking.

Rigid Thinking

Many people are rigid in their thinking. They seem to say, "Don't bother me with facts or new ideas—I know what's right." They are referred to as people with closed minds, because they are not willing to consider new information. People who have racial **prejudice** tend to be more rigid in their thinking than people who do not. They have more difficulty in discarding old ways of thinking and trying new ways (Frenkel-Brunswik, 1949).

A person's prejudices against (or for) other people may make his thinking less effective. A man who is prejudiced against a particular newspaper may not believe something it publishes, even though it is obviously true; a person prejudiced against Italians may not recognize the important contributions made by Italians. To be prejudiced means to prejudge or judge in advance. If a judgment is made in advance of adequate information or understanding, its accuracy may be reduced.

Prejudices may be based on **stereotypes**. A stereotype is a "rigid and oversimplified or biased perception" (English & English, 1958) that leads to rigid and oversimplified thinking. Even the origins of the word emphasize this meaning: the term comes from printing and refers to something that is difficult to change once it is set in type.

Think of the stereotype "All sailors like to drink heavily." This particular stereotype, often held in communities located near Navy installations, may make it more difficult for sailors to get dates or make

Basic Principles of Psychology

friends off base. Therefore, they tend to drink more, and the stereotype is made to appear true. When a person believing in the stereotype meets a sailor who claims he does not drink, he may not believe the sailor; he has a set for the sailor to be a heavy drinker, and this set reduces the logic and perceptiveness of his thinking.

The above situation is also an example of the **self-fulfilling prophecy.** The stereotype that sailors will drink increases the chances that they

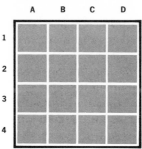

1. Buzzing insects
2. Organs of vision
3. What older brothers do to younger sisters
4. Without difficulty; with _____
A. Lions do it
B. Mosquitoes do it
C. Dogs do it
D. Snakes do it

Figure 5–3.

Complete this crossword puzzle. The answer is at the end of the chapter. Be careful of rigid thinking.

will drink, thus making the original prophecy appear valid. If adults prophesy that teen-agers are bound to be troublemakers, they will treat teen-agers accordingly, and the teen-agers are more likely to respond by becoming troublemakers. Stereotypes can easily lead to self-fulfilling prophecies. What other examples occur to you?

Rigid, stereotyped, and prejudiced thinking may distort the accuracy of perceptions, hinder the effectiveness of learning, and provide an untrue picture of the world. Since, under these circumstances, a person "knows" certain things to be true when they actually are not, the effectiveness of efforts for achievement and self-actualization may be negated. When people insist on doing things the same old way and when they allow their biases to interfere with the accuracy of their thinking, they reduce their competence to run a business, enjoy leisure, or help their children to mature.

Thinking Without Conscious Control

More often than you may realize, thinking occurs without conscious control. While you are driving alone in an automobile, thoughts come and go quickly, moving from one idea or image to another with relatively little control.

Sitting in psychology class, you hear the instructor remark, "The birth of a new infant into the family often produces a problem for the older children." Your thinking begins to wander back to when your sister was born, the way your parents sent you to stay with your aunt and uncle for a month, how nice your aunt is and how bald your uncle is, whether you will be bald when you are as old as he, how old he looks today, why he looks older than your father, how your father reacted to your little sister when she was born, how you did not really begin to like her until she was about 14 years old. Then you find yourself listening to the lecture again. Your daydreams might have taken a minute or two, but the thoughts, although set off by the professor's statement, were carried on by your own associations.

Sometimes uncontrolled thinking can be used to solve problems.

"My short story's hero was about to be killed, and I couldn't figure out a decent way to get him out of the spot. Nothing seemed right. I sat and looked at my typewriter for 30 minutes, but nothing came to me, so I decided to hit the sack. Suddenly, just as I was squeezing the toothpaste tube, the idea hit me: Let him get killed and rework the ending. I used the idea and it worked beautifully."

The writer had a *set* that his character had to remain alive, and he had "written himself into a corner," but kept persevering along one line: how to get the character out. Later, while dwelling on some trivial matter, his thinking was no longer controlled or channeled—in a sense he had been freed from the rigidity that had controlled his thinking—and he was able to arrive at a new type of solution not previously considered.

Creative people often make use of uncontrolled thinking, since thinking that is overly controlled will run along the same old paths (see the discussion on creativity in Chapter 6).

Fantasies and Dreams

Fantasies, or daydreams, and dreams are examples of thought processes that occur with little or no conscious control. Although the external environment may provide the trigger that sets a fantasy or dream off, the images that form usually have little relationship to what is going on outside the person. Dreams and fantasies are related to hallucinations only to the extent that all three refer to apparent perceptions taking place without any external sensation (see Chapter 3).

Fantasies

Humans have the ability to recall a situation in "their mind's eye," or to create a situation that has never occurred. Such creations are called daydreams or **fantasies**. Before calling a girl for a date, a college freshman rehearses the event through fantasy; a student in police science "pictures" what he will say when he catches one of his professors speeding—especially if that professor had flunked him; an unpopular girl fantasizes dating the most popular boys at the college.

Fantasies and daydreams can be helpful in achieving self-actualization. You rehearse the future to see "how it fits"; you anticipate, through fantasy, things that may happen, and you are better able to cope with them when they do occur; you blow off steam harmlessly by yelling at your professor, arguing with the boss who fired you, and making your girl friend's ex-steady look foolish—all through fantasy. Fantasy can also help in other ways: Have you ever created, through fantasy, a short story plot, a new office procedure, or an improvement on the dress pattern you recently purchased?

However, fantasy can be carried too far. When you begin to find daydreams easier than making an effort, when your fantasies become so interesting that real life seems dull, then fantasies can become harmful. People with severe mental illness confuse fantasy with reality, so that their fantasies seem true to them.

Dreams

Everyone dreams every night. Strong evidence has accumulated to indicate that people dream four or five times each night, for an average of 20 minutes per dream (Dement, 1960). You may not remember your dreams—you may even insist you do not dream—but the weight of scientific research has reasonably well established that dreaming is a normal, usual, and probably necessary process. Recent studies show that not being allowed to dream is very upsetting. If dreams are interrupted one night, the number of dreams will increase the following night; if dreams are interrupted several nights in a row, anxiety and irritation result (Dement, 1960).

During the day, everyone has feelings, desires, and fears that he cannot admit, even to himself. One explanation of dreams is that these feelings cannot make themselves known during the day, when you can control your thoughts; but at night when, in a sense, your guard is down, they appear in disguised form. What you actually "see" in your dreams, according to this theory, is called **manifest dream content**. The real significance of the dream, which is often disguised because the dreamer finds it impossible to admit to himself that he has such thoughts and feelings, is termed **latent dream content**. The manifest content is often bizarre, making no apparent sense, but the latent content, if interpreted correctly, makes very good sense. Psychologists and psychiatrists often interpret dreams in an effort to help people understand certain feelings they may not be able to admit, even to themselves.

The following incident is a good example of how dreams and their interpretation can affect normal human relationships. Notice that it was the student, not the psychologist, who finally recognized the full significance of her dream.

Penny Joseph, a lively and attractive graduating senior, entered my office close to tears. She had been having the same dream, off and on, for about four weeks, and she always awoke from it in a state of panic. The dream setting was at the family dinner table, where Penny, her parents, her two brothers, and her fiancé were eating Sunday brunch. But, Penny insisted, someone else was at the table, although no one could see him and only Penny seemed aware of his presence. This "presence" came closer and closer to Penny, until she woke up drenched with perspiration, her heart pounding.

I suggested that the "presence" might represent certain hesitancies Penny had concerning her coming wedding, and that she had some common fears about getting married. She agreed that this was part of the solution, but not all of it. After about 30 minutes of discussion, I asked whether anyone in her family disapproved of the wedding. She shook her head, then her hands began to clench. "Now I know," she said.

It turned out that Penny had been married when she was 18, but the marriage was annulled the following year. Since the marriage had occurred in a distant state and few people knew about it, she and her family had agreed never to tell anyone (her ex-husband had subsequently been imprisoned on several counts of robbery, and the entire incident was a very painful one). When she fell in love with Robert, her fiancé, she had intended to tell him, but "the moment was never right." Robert's family was known to be "stuffy" in their concern about reputation, and Penny feared that they would not approve the marriage if they learned of her past. By the time wedding plans were begun, Penny totally lacked the courage to talk to Robert about her past.

The "presence," of course, was her ex-husband. When I asked if anyone in the family disapproved of the marriage, she suddenly realized that he was, in a way, a member of the family and that he would certainly have disapproved. He had often hit Penny during their marriage, and he had beaten up an old high school boy friend who he felt was "just too friendly." He also threatened to kill anyone who "lays a hand on my woman." Penny was afraid to tell Robert, yet felt guilty about not telling him and fearful that her first husband would find her. His "presence" certainly overshadowed the entire family and the happiness of the future marriage.

Consider Lorrie's dream, which occurred during her freshman year at college:

"I dreamed I was running after a little pig. I chased the pig through the town, in and out of houses, across streets, to the edge of town, and back to our house. I finally caught the ugly little thing, picked her up and started to carry her to the butcher, when she suddenly turned into my baby sister."

When Lorrie was 16 and deeply involved in dating, cheerleading, and high school dramatics, her mother gave birth to a baby girl. Lorrie's brothers were both in college at the time. You can interpret this dream yourself.

Very few dreams, however, lend themselves to interpretation as easily as these. Each dream must be considered in light of the unique personality and life circumstances of the dreamer. Penny's dream, for example, could never have been understood without a full knowledge of her background. For this and other reasons, psychologists consider most dream-interpretation books to be without merit.

Language

The capacity of a child to develop an understanding of concepts is closely bound up with his ability to comprehend language. Language, in

Thought and Language

its broadest sense, is any communication between two or more individuals. Concepts are communicated largely through verbal symbols, but gestures, facial expressions, body movements, diagrams, and mathematical formulas also communicate and are a type of language.

Every known human society has a spoken language with a grammar and rules of grammar; every spoken language is organized around these rules. In addition, every spoken language has (1) pronouns; (2) ways of communicating concepts of time, space, and number; and (3) words meaning true and false (Miller, 1964). Although animals can communicate, only man has a true language.

Sometimes it seems that people use a language without rules. Thus you may have heard the claim that residents of some ghetto areas do not use rules of grammar or of vocabulary. However, evidence indicates that such persons, although they may not use generally accepted rules, do indeed follow an accepted grammar and accepted definitions that are well understood within their own community. When there is need to communicate with people outside the community, the lack of similar grammatical rules and word definitions can be confusing, particularly when people from both groups believe that they are speaking the same language.

Language is used to communicate many phenomena, including descriptions of physical things and of events, expressions of feelings and attitudes, and abstract concepts. Thus, people can learn to use language properly only to the extent that they have also learned about the world and have understood concepts. Words are learned through abstracting and generalizing, just as concepts are learned. Can you explain how the principles of operant learning might be applied to the process through which a young child learns the meanings of new words?

Languages differ not only in vocabulary and grammar, but also in how they classify phenomena. In English, the word *aunt* refers to your father's sister, your mother's sister, your father's brother's wife, and your mother's brother's wife. However, other societies use four different terms to describe these four different people (Murdock, 1949). The author was told that residents of Yap, a small mid-Pacific island which is part of Micronesia, use over 30 distinctly different words to describe kinds of water, for example, ocean water, bay water, stream water, fresh water. Being on a small island, the Yapese find water a very important element in their lives.

Words not only describe physical realities, but they also attach implied values to the physical reality. "I am slim; you are thin; he is skinny." Each may be the same height and weight in reality, but the greater the distance between the speaker and the person spoken about, the more unpleasant is the meaning of the term. *Nigger, Negro,* and *black* all refer to the same physical reality, but their meanings are very different. The

Basic Principles of Psychology

same is true of *broad, woman,* and *lady; pachuco, chicano,* and *American of Mexican ancestry; fuzz, cop,* and *police officer.* The meanings and implications of words are studied by the science of semantics.

Nonverbal Communication

Words are not the only means of communication. Communication occurs through a raised eyebrow, a cough, blushing, spitting, taking a girl's hand, crying, sending a gift, or kicking someone in the shins. All these events, and many more, communicate feelings, ideas, beliefs, and intentions.

Folklore has it that a hearty handshake and a firm glance mean that a man is honest. The truth is that the salesman who is trying to persuade you to buy an encyclopedia or a new car you do not need is also aware of this folk belief. **Nonverbal communication** can easily be as complex as verbal communication.

A college freshman on a blind date to the movies tries to hold hands. What does this mean? Is he showing honest affection? Is this the lead-up to "making out"? Does he just enjoy holding hands? Then his date slips her hand away from his. What is she communicating? Is she trying to get rid of him? Does she want him to think she is a "nice girl"? Do her hands perspire and embarrass her?

Nonverbal communication can also produce misunderstandings between people of different cultures who have established differing patterns of expected behavior.

A very sociable American doing business in Manila came to like one of the Filipino businessmen with whom he was dealing. They met for dinner that evening, and the American, who was feeling the effects of two martinis, slapped the Asian across the back. The Asian looked at him in amazement, then realized that the American had meant it to be a friendly gesture. However, the business deal fell through, and the two companies did no further business.

Among the most important forms of nonverbal communication are facial expression, touching, gestures, self-manipulation (such as scratching), changes in body position, and head movements (Mehrabian, 1968). During conversations—or even during periods of silence—these occurrences signify as much as words. Research has shown, for example, that you are more likely to relax during a conversation with someone to whom you feel superior than with someone who you feel is superior to

Thought and Language

you; for example, you are more at ease with your younger brother's friends than with your professor, and this fact is communicated to the other person (Mehrabian, 1968). Frequently the actual words of a conversation contradict the other forms of communication. Thus, you may continue to say, "Yes, that's very interesting," but your eyes move around the room and you slump back in your chair—both actions communicating that you hardly find the speaker's statements interesting.

Even in the verbal part of communication, the words themselves

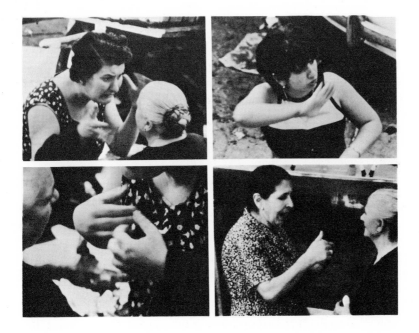

Figure 5–4.

Facial expressions and hand movements communicate a great deal. Courtesy Columbia Broadcasting System.

carry only part of the meaning. Your tone of voice may communicate something quite different from the words. Sometimes the speaker will produce this disparity on purpose, but often he does not realize that what he is saying contradicts what he is communicating. Your words say, "I had a very nice time this evening"; your voice says, "It was really rather dull"; and your movements say, "I'm very eager to get out of here."

Whether we communicate through words, through actions, through tone of voice, or through physiological change, communication is vitally important. In order to make the most of your abilities, you need to be able to communicate effectively to others and to receive the real meanings of what others are communicating to you.

Summary of Important Ideas

1. People respond to symbolic reinforcements.

2. Much human learning involves problem solving. Problem solving may occur through trial and error, through step-by-step logical consideration, or through a sudden insight.

3. The understanding of concepts develops at least in part through abstracting from experiences with the concept in several different settings. More abstract concepts are more difficult to grasp.

4. Thinking may remain under conscious control or may occur outside a person's awareness. Fantasies and dreams are examples of the latter.

5. Fantasies, when not carried too far, have an important and useful function in problem solving and creativity.

6. Everyone dreams frequently. Without the opportunity to dream, emotional upsets may occur more often.

7. When thinking becomes rigid, stereotypes may form. Stereotypes often lead to prejudices, and both reactions limit an individual's ability to think logically and accurately.

8. Language is any communication between two or more individuals. All societies have a spoken language with a recognized grammar and recognized word definitions.

9. Semantics is the science of word meanings and word use.

10. Nonverbal methods of communication are as important as verbal methods. To receive communication accurately, one must be sensitive to nonverbal communication.

	A	B	C	D
1	B	B	B	B
2	I	I	I	I
3	T	T	T	T
4	E	E	E	E

Here is the answer to the crossword puzzle shown in Figure 5–3. Did you figure it out?

Chapter Six

Human Abilities

This chapter, which closes the first section, "Introduction to Basic Principles of Psychology," discusses intelligence and creativity as examples of human abilities. The measurement of human abilities by means of psychological tests is also examined here.

The 1968 science fiction film *Planet of the Apes* proposed that man, through his destructiveness, would reverse the present flow of evolution and revert to being a less intelligent being, whereas apes would develop into higher beings and eventually take over the planet. The prospect, although far-fetched, is not completely impossible. For the foreseeable future, however, no animal—not even the relatively intelligent monkey or porpoise—is likely to approach the intelligence of a normal human.

Without his superior intelligence, the human would lack the self-awareness to study himself, to attempt to self-actualize, or to transmit his values, ideas, and material goods across time and space. He would be unable to build upon the knowledge and products of past generations and to plan for future generations. He would not be able to prolong life through science and medicine or to destroy life through wars and other forms of destruction. Man's intelligence even enables him to search for ways to improve his intelligence.

What Is Intelligence?

Intelligence refers to the ability to grasp abstract concepts and symbols (such as language), the ability to learn, and the ability to cope with new situations (English & English, 1958). It also includes the ability to profit from experience and the ability to solve problems. This explanation is necessarily broad, since a great variety of specific acts may be termed intelligent.

It is intelligent behavior to ride a bicycle, recognize a person you met last week, and know the difference between a bush and a tree; it is intelligent behavior to count, to read a blueprint, and to spell; it is intelligent behavior to learn the meaning of concepts such as afternoon, love, round, and democracy; it is intelligent behavior to know what to do when your best friend is in trouble, when you see an automobile accident, and when you have a fight with your brother. In the following argument, Pete and Mike are in a hopeless deadlock because each is referring to a different type of intelligent behavior.

Pete: My kid brother is really bright. He can take his bike apart and put it back together all by himself, and he gets along great with the other kids—he's a real leader.

Mike: Yeah? Pretty good, but my sister is a real whiz. She cracks top grades in her class, and she won an award in Sunday School.

Pete: She may be bright, but she isn't *that* bright. She doesn't have more than one or two friends. Besides, she still thinks Santa Claus is a real person.

Mike: Well, your brother isn't so smart either. He forgot his lines in the school Christmas play, and he was a semester behind in his reading for a long time.

Numerous difficulties can occur when we talk about an "intelligent person." An individual might exhibit a high degree of intelligence in his verbal behavior, yet display very limited intelligence in any acts that demand an understanding of mechanics. Because of such occurrences, psychologists have become interested in "factors of intelligence." Some of the factors more commonly described include the following:

—the ability to use words effectively (verbal ability)
—the ability to reason effectively
—the ability to memorize easily
—the ability to know how to behave effectively in social situations
—the ability to work well with numbers (numerical ability)
—the ability to act quickly when necessary
—the ability to perceive spatial relationships
—the ability to work effectively with the hands (motor ability)
—the ability to understand principles of mechanics

A person above average in one factor of intelligence is likely to be above average in others. A child with a good memory is also likely to be above average in handling numerical concepts, in reasoning, and in adjusting to new social relationships. Exceptions do exist, and psychologists are constantly conducting research to determine more accurately the nature of the factors of intelligence and the relationships among them.

One investigator has divided intellectual abilities into two basic categories: *crystallized general ability* and *fluid general ability*. The former depends upon social and cultural experiences and includes capacities directly related to learning, such as vocabulary, mathematical knowledge, mechanical ability, and memory. The latter refers to abilities less related to formal education or the surrounding community, for example, many forms of judgment and reasoning (Cattell, 1968).

Environmental Influences on Intelligence

Most psychologists and educators believe that intelligence is influenced by both heredity and environment, by both what we are born with and what happens to us after birth. Psychologists are not certain, however, *how* important heredity is and *how* important environment is. They know, for example, that the measured intelligence of a child is noticeably related to the measured intelligence of both his mother and his father (Conrad & Jones, 1940). Does this mean that the child inherited the intelligence through genetic means? Or does it mean that intelligent parents help their child learn more than do less intelligent parents? Both elements probably enter into the situation. (See Chapter 7.)

Some families do much to encourage their children to develop intellectual abilities; others do nothing. Families who take time to talk intelligently to their children, even when the children are very young, aid in the children's use and development of intelligence. The attitudes of parents toward learning, books, and school are also important: children whose parents ignore or make fun of education and books are less likely to be successful in intellectual tasks related to school progress.

Parents not only influence their children's intellectual competence by their attitudes, but also by their use of language. A person whose language ability is poor will not do well on intelligence tests or in school. When children are reared in an environment where parents seldom talk to them, the children do not learn much language in the home. They are, then, inadequately prepared for schoolwork and quickly fall behind. As a result, they come to dislike school and pay even less attention to language, which further reduces their test scores. A vicious circle is set up. This is particularly likely to occur to children from socially and economically poor homes.

Some children are faced with another problem: the language spoken in their home is different from that spoken in the community. Living in a home in which English is either not spoken or is poorly spoken, the child uses English less frequently and may have some difficulty thinking in English. He will probably not speak English as well as others of his age (Soffietti, 1955), which may lead to lower performance on intelligence tests and in classroom work.

Not only can parents affect the development of verbal ability, but the parent-child relationship also can have an effect on intelligence that extends beyond language and verbal symbols. The willingness of parents to encourage, rather than stifle, the child's needs to explore and manipulate his environment may affect many of the factors of intelligence. Can you suggest ways in which parents might influence a child's mechanical ability or social ability?

The home also influences measured intelligence indirectly by affecting the physical health of the individual. For example, where diet is poor, intelligence seems to suffer (Harrell, 1947), and persons suffering from certain serious medical problems may be less able to develop their intellectual capacities.

Environmental Influences on School Performance

Good health care, nutrition, educational opportunity, and family relationships are not provided equally to every American child. The more fortunate are amply taken care of, and most Americans probably have at least an adequate amount of each, but some children seem to be lacking all four. These children are most frequently from very low-income families. They are frequently of Negro, Mexican, Puerto Rican, or American Indian descent, although substantial numbers are "white Anglos."

Many problems arise because these children have difficulty succeeding in school. Middle-class children succeed in school partly because the values internalized at home are similar to those that guide the school. They also find that their family life has very probably prepared them for school. Just the opposite is often the case with disadvantaged children.

Human Abilities

> The lower-class child . . . tends to have a poor attention span and
> to have great difficulty following the teacher's orders . . . he generally
> comes from a nonverbal household: adults speak in short sentences, if
> indeed they speak at all. . . . The child has never been obliged to listen
> to several lengthy sentences spoken consecutively.
>
> In school, the middle-class teacher who rambles on for several
> sentences might just as well be talking another language . . . lower-
> class children have a limited perception of the world about them: they
> do not know that objects have names . . . , or that the same object may
> have several names. . . . They also have very little concept of size or
> time.
>
> The lower-class youngsters are poorly motivated, because they
> have had little experience in receiving approval for success in a task or
> disapproval for failure; but school is organized on the assumption that
> children expect approval for success. And since the parents . . . do not
> ask the youngsters about school, the children have no way of knowing
> that the parents *do* very much want and expect success (Silberman,
> 1964).

The parents of these children usually wish to help their youngsters,
but they may lack the necessary financial resources or the awareness of
what to do and how to do it. Since many belong to ethnic minority
groups, their attempts at helping themselves are often rebuffed by the
rest of society because of racial prejudice. As the children grow up and
have families, they pass their disadvantages on to their own children, in
much the same way as the educated person will pass on his understanding of the world to his children.

Many children from disadvantaged homes do break the circle and
escape from the problems they grew up with (this breaking away is not
the same as leaving their ethnic community, which is an entirely different matter). Perhaps they were influenced by a parent or other relative, a
teacher, a social worker or policeman, or by some inner resource not fully
understood. Here is a word picture of the obstacles faced by one such
hypothetical student from a disadvantaged home; it is by no means an
extreme example.

> He comes from a home that is physically crowded, permitting him
> little privacy and no space of his own. His father has not been around
> the home for many years, and he has to take care of his younger
> brothers and sisters—not a serious matter except that it drains consider-
> able time and energy and requires taking on adult worries. His mother
> works, so he has to prepare many of the meals; most of them end up
> being cereal or sandwiches. He knows nothing of nutrition and has no
> way of getting enough food, even if he did know. Because of his
> inadequate diet, he functions at a low energy level and with limited
> alertness. Economic uncertainty is constant.

Because the use of language in the home is often restricted to one-syllable words or nods and grunts, he is behind his age group in language development. Also, since his early environment lacked stimulation, his memory and learning skills have rarely been challenged. He has not learned middle-class concepts of time or middle-class notions of reward and punishment, so he finds the demands of his middle-class teachers strange and unrealistic. Since he knows many people who have failed, failure in school is neither unanticipated nor terrifying. And once he begins to fall behind, the chances are he will fall farther and farther behind (based on Powledge, 1967).

A very thorough study of the achievement of 600,000 American students in 4,000 schools, grades 1 through 12, was completed in 1966. Results indicated that differences in achievement were due largely to home background, type of age-peer associations, and teacher characteristics, rather than to the school itself. This finding suggests that the disadvantaged child who is surrounded by other disadvantaged children is in a worse situation than he would be if he were part of a school population of more varied backgrounds (Coleman, Mood, & Campbell, 1966).

The behavior of teachers toward their students should not be underestimated as a factor in the intellectual growth of children from low-income homes. Like everyone else, teachers respond to others in terms of their prior expectations, often based on stereotypes. In one study, teachers were told that certain of their pupils were considerably more intelligent than their classmates. Although the teachers did not realize it, these pupils had been selected at random and were neither more nor less intelligent than their classmates. Nonetheless, by the end of the school year, these children, previously known to be comparable to the other pupils in intelligence, had improved considerably more than average, as reflected by various measures of ability. The investigators concluded that the teachers treated these children as superior and expected greater achievement from them, and the children responded to this treatment by actually improving (Rosenthal & Jacobson, 1968).

Today a combination of federal and local programs has been established to help the children who are most likely to face the difficulties that arise in disadvantaged homes. The emphasis in these programs is on very young children, particularly preschoolers. By giving them a variety of educational and social experiences, including encouragement to express ideas through talking, it is hoped that they will have fewer barriers to surmount in achieving success in school.

As more experience with these programs is reported, the need for follow-up becomes increasingly apparent. The children who as 3-year-olds received help through a program such as Operation Head Start will in later years continue to need extra help from the type of person who helped them originally. Although the programs are still in their early stages of development and although racial antagonisms and political squabbles have slowed their success, they indicate that a beginning, at least, has been made in attacking the difficulties besetting many children.

The question may arise: "Why succeed in school? After all, look at all the problems those middle-class, academically successful people have. And look at the way they chase the buck, rather than pay attention to those things that would help humanity." Do you feel this point has merit? How would you respond?

Psychological and Educational Tests

Testing has become part of our way of life. For better *and* for worse, psychological and educational tests have found their way into schools, colleges, businesses, industries, government agencies, welfare agencies, medical centers—everywhere you look.

Because of the importance of testing in psychology, a great deal of effort is expended in determining how good each test is. This determination is made by evaluating the **validity** and the **reliability** of a test. A test is valid to the degree that it really measures what it was designed to measure. It is reliable to the degree that it measures consistently.

Consider your final exam in English last semester: What was it designed to measure? Knowledge of grammar? Ability to write? Understanding of literature? Did it measure what it was designed to measure? If so, it was valid. Now, how consistently did it measure? If you had taken a very similar examination one week later, would you have gotten roughly the same score? If you had received a high score on one test and then a low score a week later on a similar test, your scores would not have been dependable; that is, they would not have been reliable.

An Air Force psychologist was approached by a young recruit who was unhappy about being assigned to the motor pool rather than receiving mechanical training to work on an engine crew. The psychologist pointed out that his test scores showed low mechanical ability, but the recruit objected. He had taken those tests, he explained, at seven in the morning after riding most of the night on a crowded train and arriving in time to get only three hours of sleep and a hurried breakfast. Most of the others taking the tests had gotten to the base in plenty of time for a good sleep and leisurely breakfast. The psychologist agreed to retest the young man, and his scores were considerably higher the second time.

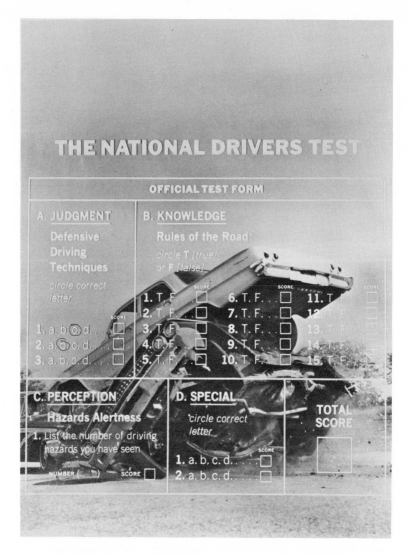

THE NATIONAL DRIVERS TEST

OFFICIAL TEST FORM

A. JUDGMENT	B. KNOWLEDGE
Defensive Driving Techniques	Rules of the Road
circle correct letter	circle T (true) or F (false)

	SCORE		SCORE		SCORE
		1. T F...☐	6. T. F... ☐	11. T	☐
	SCORE	2. T F...☐	7. T. F... ☐	12.	
1. a. b ⓒ d...☐	3. T F...☐	8. T. F... ☐	13. T	
2. a ⓑ c. d...☐	4. T F...☐	9. T F... ☐	14. T F	
3. a. b. c. d...☐	5. T F...☐	10. T. F... ☐	15. T F	

C. PERCEPTION	D. SPECIAL	TOTAL SCORE
Hazards Alertness	circle correct letter	
1. List the number of driving hazards you have seen		
NUMBER ( ) SCORE ☐	1. a. b. c. d.....☐ SCORE	
	2. a. b. c. d.....☐	

Figure 6–1.

A test used on television to enable home viewers to check their driving knowledge. Courtesy Columbia Broadcasting System.

Sometimes a test can be valid in general, but not under a specific set of circumstances. How valid would a typing test be for a person with a fever and a terrible headache? Can you think of other instances when a normally valid test is not valid under specific circumstances?

Since grades are based partly or completely on tests, whatever factors affect the validity of tests also affect the validity of grades. Occasionally a student will believe his grade was not valid. If the grade is too low, he may complain to the professor, although he virtually never complains if the grade is too high.

Some tests make use of national **norms**. In such instances, your score can be compared to the scores of hundreds of other people. You may be told that nationally you are in the thirtieth percentile (30%ile) in clerical ability, or the seventy-third percentile in scientific interest. The score means that you have as much as or more clerical ability than 30% of those who were used for comparison, or you have as much as or more interest in science than 73% of the norm group. (Remember that these percentiles do *not* mean that 30% of your answers were correct, or 73% of your statements showed scientific interest.)

Psychological tests measure many kinds of characteristics, including general intelligence and factors of intelligence, aptitudes and achievement, interests, needs, and personality characteristics. Also, many principles of testing hold true for surveys of attitudes, beliefs, values, and other kinds of psychological and educational measurements.

Measuring Intelligence

Intelligence, like motivation and learning, cannot be measured directly, but must be assumed from performance. The best-known tests of intelligence are probably the Stanford-Binet Intelligence Test, the Wechsler Intelligence Scale for Children (WISC), and the Wechsler Adult Intelligence Scale (WAIS). These three tests attempt to measure general intelligence, and they offer an overall score. They also assume that their results are only minimally influenced by culture and formal education. Other intelligence tests emphasize the measurement of factors such as those described on page 92; they provide scores for the individual factors and also an overall score.

Most test results are reported in percentile form. Some, however, use what are called standard scores, utilizing a statistical approach that will not be discussed here. Both the Stanford-Binet and the Wechsler use standard scores now (previously they had used another method); thus, both tests arbitrarily assign the score of 100 to a person who has been shown to have average intelligence for his age group, with higher scores implying higher intelligence (for that age group) and vice versa.

Many factors influence the degree to which an individual can make maximum use of his potential abilities, including his potential intellectual competence. The IQ (intelligence quotient) test, a normally valid measure when we become aware of its limitations, can nonetheless be influenced by environmental and personality factors.

Intelligence is one aspect of the total personality, and it inevitably interacts in dynamic fashion with other personality attributes. Self-esteem, for example, affects performance on IQ tests, and performance on IQ tests affects self-esteem. The case of Eddie illustrates many of the principles discussed in this chapter.

Eddie: A Case History

At the time of testing, Eddie was finishing second grade. He was reported to the principal because he was totally unable to read, he could not draw even the simplest house or person, he constantly day-dreamed, he paid little attention to the teacher, and he did not get along well with the other children. His teacher believed he was well below normal in intelligence and might need special treatment.

The psychologist who tested Eddie had been his counselor at summer camp, and he and the boy liked each other. In addition, being tested gave Eddie an excuse for leaving class and an opportunity for getting individual attention. While he was with the psychologist, he was talkative and happy, unlike his apathetic, classroom self.

The first test Eddie took consisted of drawing a person (described in Goodenough, 1926). The maturity level of his drawing, compared to others of his age, showed Eddie to be in the upper 5%, an amazing performance for a child whose teacher stated he could not draw a man that even remotely resembled a man. He then took the Stanford-Binet Intelligence Test and scored in the upper 10%. Eddie scored in the top 10% on every test, except one that demanded reading, which he could not do.

Eddie was obviously a child of high ability. Why was he doing so poorly? The answer was found mainly in his family relationships. His father, frustrated in his work, constantly criticized the teachers and the school system and sometimes even made fun of the entire process of education, claiming it was a waste of time; at the same time, he demanded that Eddie study hard and get good grades. His mother, a weak person who worried more about her imaginary illnesses than she did about her children, both feared and resented her husband and gave Eddie neither affection nor discipline. Eddie admired his father, but did not know how to please him, so he withdrew by becoming apathetic.

Eddie's case is a good example of the value of intelligence testing as an aid in understanding the problems of the individual. It also points up the importance of thinking in terms of different kinds of intelligence, since Eddie had good verbal and reasoning abilities, but was not able to learn how to behave socially. The effects of his home environment upon his personality and his school performance were very dramatic.

The IQ test has three major limitations. First, it is only an *estimate* of intelligence. Even though it is shown to be a good estimate in most instances, a variety of situations may interfere with its accuracy. The child may react negatively to the person giving the test and, therefore, become unwilling to respond; he may have been brought up in a home where a foreign language was always spoken; he may have a bad cold that interferes with his test performance; or he may have been upset by an argument between his parents that morning, which keeps him from concentrating effectively. In addition, he may just not care whether he does well or not.

Second, the IQ test can measure only the kinds of intelligent behavior related to items on the test. Most tests given in schools measure the aspects of intelligence that are related to school success, such as memory, knowledge of vocabulary, ability to follow directions, verbal reasoning ability, or arithmetical skill. They say much less about the kinds of intelligence that enable a person to be popular, to repair a transmission, or to make a wise choice in a presidential election.

Third, although psychologists have tried to construct an IQ test that is not influenced by previous learning experiences, such a test is clearly an impossibility. Therefore, to some extent, IQ scores reflect the opportunity the person has had to learn, although in theory a measure of intelligence should not be affected by learning opportunity.

In spite of its shortcomings, the IQ test can predict success in academic work from elementary school through college, in vocational achievement, and even in leadership (Anastasi, 1958; Mann, 1959). However, the IQ test is merely a measuring device, and, as with any measure, it is subject to error and to misinterpretation.

Measuring Aptitude and Achievement

Intelligence tests are used primarily for educational purposes. When the focus is on employment, tests of aptitude and achievement are used most commonly. An **aptitude** is the capacity to become competent, assuming adequate training; **achievement** refers to a person's present level of competence. Although aptitude and achievement are related, they are not identical.

Innumerable aptitude tests are available, and some are widely used in employee selection. Many firms use selection tests to measure verbal, mechanical, numerical, clerical, and sales aptitudes. Achievement tests measure some of the same qualities, but are likely to include more factual material than aptitude tests. Thus, a test of mechanical aptitude would present problems that could be answered correctly by a person before he had taken courses in mechanics, and an achievement test of mechanical ability would ask questions that would require previous study or experience.

The final exam for this course will undoubtedly be an achievement test, since your instructor will wish to know your level of understanding of the materials studied.

Evaluating Interests

Many people confuse aptitude tests and interest tests. Students will frequently claim to have taken a test showing they have a high aptitude for medicine or engineering, but further checking will show that the test actually measured interests.

Two tests of interests are widely used. One, the Kuder Preference Record, is familiar to many students; it requires that you indicate which of three activities you like most and which you like least. The second major interest test, the Strong Vocational Interest Blank, gives students letter grades according to how closely their interests compare with successful men or women in different career fields.

Since a person's interests are highly predictive of what he will enjoy doing vocationally, they also predict vocational success. However, interests can be evaluated through means other than tests. You can examine your activities: What do you enjoy doing? How do you spend your time? What do you stick to? What do you do well? High school and college courses and activities can be evaluated in the same way. If your self-evaluation matches your test scores, you can usually assume you are on the right track. If the test scores disagree with your perceptions of yourself, a careful consideration of what might be causing the differences is in order.

Evaluating Needs and Personality Characteristics

Students probably find personality tests the most interesting and the most irritating of all psychological tests. Part of the difficulty undoubtedly arises from not understanding why the questions are worded as they are. Sometimes students want to know whether "never" in a questionnaire means "absolutely never, not even once," or whether it implies less restrictiveness. Also, students commonly complain about being forced to answer by checking one of five alternatives, even though the real answer may lie somewhere between the alternatives or not even be offered. Scores on personality tests are often given in terms of percentiles.

Figure 6–2 shows the categories used in constructing one of the best-known tests of personality and needs. Although the categories are stated in terms of needs, for example, need for achievement and need for dominance, you will readily see that needs are one aspect of personality.

Counselors use a combination of tests and interviews to help a student evaluate his personality and needs. The validity of personality tests is lower than the validity of aptitude or interest tests, and not enough is known about why or how certain personality attributes fit a person for specific vocational fields. However, objective self-evaluation is very difficult—although many people pride themselves on their self-understanding—and one's personal insights often need to be supplemented by tests and interviews.

---

1. Achievement—the need to accomplish things well and quickly, to be successful in what is done, to overcome obstacles.

2. Deference—the need to follow someone else, to have a leader.

3. Order—the need to be neat and orderly.

4. Exhibition—the need to attract attention, to be noticed.

5. Autonomy—the need to be independent, to gain freedom, to defy authority.

6. Affiliation—the need to form friendships, to love others, to join groups, to please people.

7. Introception—the need to be imaginative, subjective, to participate in romantic action.

8. Succorance—the need to get help or sympathy, to be dependent.

9. Dominance—the need to influence or control others, to lead, to organize.

10. Abasement—the need to apologize, to accept punishment.

11. Nurturance—the need to help others, to express sympathy.

12. Change—the need to avoid routine, to be involved with change.

13. Endurance—the need to work hard, to avoid distractions.

14. Heterosexual—the need for relationships with the opposite sex.

15. Aggression—the need to express aggressive feelings, to harm, to punish.

Figure 6–2.

Personality needs measured by the Edwards Personal Preference Schedule (Edwards, 1954; based on the list of needs developed by Henry A. Murray, 1938).

Projective Tests

The previously discussed tests all are based upon checking the best of several alternatives. Another entirely different kind of test is the **projective test**. Rather than providing a checklist, these tests are open-ended. In the Thematic Apperception Test (TAT), the subject is shown a series of pictures and asked to tell a complete, spontaneous story to match each picture. In the House-Tree-Person Test, the subject is asked to draw a house, a tree, and a person all in the same picture, and then he discusses what he has drawn. The examiner later evaluates the stories or the discussion, usually written down verbatim, and looks for themes suggesting relationships with others, attitudes toward self, hopes for the

Figure 6–3.

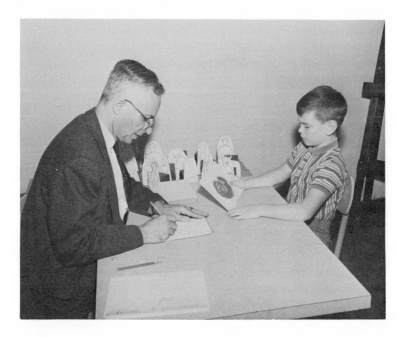

This child is telling a story about the picture in front of him; in the background are drawings of human figures that he has just finished using to act out a story. Both these approaches are types of projective techniques. Courtesy Reiss-Davis Child Study Center.

future, emotional reactions, or typical modes of behavior. The assumption underlying projective testing techniques is that the individual will reveal his own feelings in his stories and drawings.

There are many types of projective tests available, in addition to the two mentioned above. One is the Rorschach Inkblot Test, a very complex test that is difficult to evaluate; it involves a set of ten cards, each containing one inkblot to be interpreted by the subject. Another test is the Sentence Completion Test, which contains the beginnings of sentences, to be completed by the respondent as he wishes. Another example is the Word Association Test, which presents a series of words to which the respondent replies with the first word that comes to mind.

The justification for projective tests and their scoring is highly complex, and need not be further considered here. Research evidence indicates that projective tests have lower validity and reliability than the more objective tests. Nonetheless, clinical psychologists and psychiatrists often claim that the tests are extremely useful for understanding an individual. Because they are not limited to a series of alternatives for checking, projective tests can get at more subtle and more complex aspects of the personality, which may compensate for the hazards of depending on the subjective interpretations of the examiner.

Tests are subject to numerous kinds of error and have many short-comings. Some tests, such as those appearing in newspapers and magazines, are fun to take, but may have little or no validity and should not be taken seriously. However, not even the most carefully constructed tests are valid in every instance. Validity of tests of personality and interest is related to the ability and willingness of the individual to respond honestly and without self-deception. When the person taking the test is motivated to distort the results, either to fool someone else or to maintain his own inaccurate self-concept, many tests cease to be valid.

Tests can also be used improperly; for example, they can be employed to make decisions without allowing for exceptions, or they can be administered to persons who are unfamiliar with tests and whose scores therefore will not accurately reflect their actual abilities. Nonetheless, *in combination with other methods of evaluation,* tests are very useful in making decisions and in understanding individuals.

Creativity

In recent years, the nature of creativity and its measurement have been the focus of much concern by psychologists. Being creative is not the same thing as being intelligent. People with extremely high IQ scores may show little creativity, and those with average or even below average intelligence may exhibit highly creative behavior at times. On the whole, though, various measures of creativity do show relationships to various measures of intelligence; that is, those people who do well on tests of creativity tend to do well on tests of intelligence. It is difficult to say whether the people who score well on these tests are also more productive, since there are so many types of productivity that using this criterion in comparing creative with noncreative people is questionable. We cannot evaluate a person's output and decide that the more he produces, the more creative he is.

Figure 6–4.

In the heart of the Watts section of Los Angeles stand these towers—the work of one man—created from pipes, bottles, stones, and odds and ends. Do you feel that the Watts Towers are an example of healthy creativity? Photograph by Steve Renick.

Human Abilities

Creativity is defined as the "ability to find new solutions to a problem or new modes of artistic expression" (English & English, 1958). Novelty and originality are also implied by creativity, and the creative person is frequently assumed to be making some form of contribution to the community (Piers, 1968). In some ways, creativity is the opposite of rigidity. The creative person can see new and unusual relationships or find new and unusual uses for things.

A businessman may be creative in finding a way to enter a previously untouched market; an artist who turns out one basic type of painting with many slight variations is not creative, although he may be a competent craftsman. A housewife who creates her own recipes for homemade soup and bread is more creative than an author who writes only "formula stuff."

There is real danger in discussing who is or what is creative, since psychologists are far from agreeing among themselves how to judge creativity. However, one investigator found that 15 characteristics are most often cited by psychologists in describing creative people: (1) strong motivation, (2) involvement in what happens, (3) curiosity, (4) persistence, (5) dissatisfaction with things as they are, (6) self-sufficiency, (7) autonomy, (8) independence of judgment, (9) self-confidence, (10) self-acceptance, (11) sense of humor, (12) intuition, (13) tolerance for ambiguity, (14) desire to deal with complex ideas, and (15) flexibility (Piers, 1968). The similarity between these characteristics and Abraham Maslow's description of the self-actualizing personality is striking (see Chapter 7).

Recent research has compared highly creative students with highly intelligent (but not especially creative) students. The former were less well liked by their teachers, placed more importance on a sense of humor, and were more likely to choose unusual vocations. Perhaps of more importance, the highly creative students were much less interested in working toward what most of us consider to be success; they preferred to wander off in their own directions, doing what they wished (Getzels & Jackson, 1962).

Every society has many pressures against creativity and in favor of conformity. Creative people do things differently, and people who do things differently are often a bit frightening to the others. Sometimes creative people have ideas that seem to oppose the accepted way of thinking and living. Sigmund Freud and James Joyce are examples of men who have been attacked for their creative ideas. Modern art has also been widely attacked by people who make no attempt to understand it.

To differentiate the truly creative from the merely clever or the crackpot is not always easy. However, some people are so fearful of new ideas and new ways of doing things that they accuse all change of being dangerous or peculiar.

Figure 6–5.

Artistic expression is one way in which creativity can be demonstrated. Courtesy Columbia Broadcasting System.

As an example of how disturbing new and different ideas can be, an incident involving a student nurse and her supervisor is appropriate:

> The student had been dating an intern known for being critical of the methods used by the nursing supervisor, who had been very slow to take advantage of new ideas. When the student asked her supervisor why she did not try some of the newer approaches, the older woman sputtered, "Is that what that young doctor told you? Why don't you stand on your own two feet and do as *I* tell you?"

Developing Creativity

Is there anything that parents, teachers, or other members of the community can do to encourage the development of creativity? A recent

"I don't know what there is about it. I just get this feeling that if it works things'll never be the same around here!"

Figure 6–6.

Creativity can also be applied to improving productive output. Courtesy Ed Fisher.

study of parents whose children displayed unusual scientific creativity showed that the degree of parental control appeared to be the major factor in influencing their creativity. Creative students felt that their parents respected their integrity and permitted them to take responsibility, rather than exerted strict controls (Datta & Parloff, 1967).

Other studies suggest that creativity would be stimulated through (1) not requiring that children respond rigidly and not demanding "everything in its place and a place for everything"; (2) stimulating the enjoyment of new experiences and discouraging rigid routine; (3) rewarding flexible thinking; (4) not trying to make children be like everyone else, but rewarding them for being different; and (5) permitting children to accept their own "irrational impulses" (based on Berelson & Steiner, 1964).

Educating people to be creative is not an impossibility. A few attempts toward such education have shown some hope for the future. Even public schools might do a better job of encouraging creativity if they could gear their programs to permit students to discover principles and ideas on their own, rather than emphasize the kind of presentation in which the teacher does the work (Piers, 1968).

The following individuals fit the author's criteria for being creative. Though you may not approve of what each of these individuals has done with his creative abilities, consider the creative nature of their accomplishments. Whom would you add to the list? Whom would you eliminate? Why?

Some Representative Creative People

Joan Baez (singer and songwriter)
Martin Buber (philosopher)
George Washington Carver (scientist)
Charlie Chaplin (actor)
Charles Darwin (scientist)
Walt Disney (artist-businessman)
Thomas Edison (inventor)
Albert Einstein (scientist)
Henry Ford (businessman)
Benjamin Franklin (inventor, writer, political figure)
Sigmund Freud (psychiatrist)
Mahatma Gandhi (political figure)
Helen Hayes (actress)
James Joyce (author)
Gustav Mahler (composer)
Horace Mann (educator)
Karl Marx (political theorist)
Rod McKuen (poet)
Pablo Picasso (artist)
Knute Rockne (football coach)
Carl Rogers (psychologist)
Charles Schulz (cartoonist)
Frank Lloyd Wright (architect)

Summary of Important Ideas

1. Intelligence refers to the ability to grasp abstract concepts and symbols, including language; the ability to learn; the ability to solve problems; and the ability to cope with new situations.

2. There are many factors of intelligence. A person who is above average in one factor is likely to be above average in another, but many exceptions exist.

3. Heredity and environment both influence intellectual functioning. Considerable evidence and much theorizing support the idea that the home and community environment can restrict or foster a person's ability to function intelligently.

4. Children from disadvantaged homes may perform at a lower level in school than their actual potential allows.

5. Psychological and educational tests have become virtually a way of life. As a result, considerable effort has been put into developing good tests.

6. A good test must be valid and reliable.

7. Most test results are reported in *percentiles.* Some, including the best-known intelligence tests, the Stanford-Binet and the two Wechsler tests, use *standard scores;* they assign a score of 100 to a person of average intelligence for his age group, with higher scores implying higher intelligence and lower scores implying lower intelligence.

8. The validity of IQ tests is limited in several ways, but the tests are still valuable when used properly.

9. Aptitude refers to a potential ability; achievement denotes a competence already attained.

10. Interests, needs, and personality characteristics are also measured by tests. Although objective tests are used most commonly, projective tests are also administered.

11. Creativity implies novelty and innovation. Although related to general intelligence and to productivity, creativity can occur when both these characteristics are not pronounced.

12. Creativity can be fostered by parents and teachers through the right kind of attitudes.

Part Two

Development of Human Behavior

Chapter Seven

An Introduction to Personality Development

From the preceding chapters, you might assume that the human is a combination of separate elements rather than a single, unified organism. The divisions were made only for convenience, and the present chapter will discuss the individual as a whole, rather than as a series of parts. The discussion will consider various ways of looking at the human personality and will lead into the next chapters, which deal with human development. You may find it helpful to relate the ideas of the previous chapters, particularly the hierarchy of needs as expressed by Abraham Maslow, to the material in the first half of this chapter, especially to the section entitled "An Introduction to Personality."

When psychologists look at people, what do they see? Do they see living beings whose behavior is beyond their own control, who are helpless in the face of the pressures of their environment? Or organisms that will harm others unless kept in careful check? Or animals that differ from other animals only because they can walk upright and talk?

Different psychologists look at people differently. This book presents the view that people will try to make use of their capacities, if given the opportunity, and that people can become successful in using these capacities in spite of great environmental pressures. Further, the author assumes that most, perhaps almost all, behavior called "good" and "evil" is learned. Finally, the book takes the position that the factors distinguishing humans from lower forms of animal life are numerous and vital.

Human Behavior: Some Apparent Contradictions

Nothing illustrates the complexity of humans better than some apparent contradictions in their behavior. People are adaptable and creative, yet strangely rigid. Their behavior varies according to their culture, yet shows consistency from culture to culture. The behavior of any one individual changes from situation to situation, yet remains consistent through time. People can communicate across space and time, yet are often unable to understand those they love the most. Their behavior results from the most subtle and intricate factors, yet this complex behavior is to some extent predictable. To consider these apparent contradictions is to become aware of man's fantastic range of abilities, feelings, and achievements.

Adaptable, Yet Rigid

More than any other creature, the human can change his environment to please himself. Over the centuries he has learned to build structures and manufacture clothing to protect himself against extreme cold, and to create air-conditioning devices to protect himself against extreme heat. He has devised medicines to prolong life and bombs to destroy life.

He can live on the earth, under the earth, in the air, in outer space, on the water, and under the water. He has obtained power from lower forms of animal life, from water, from heat, and from splitting the atom. He can create clothing out of chemicals, build computers that play chess, and send words and pictures over thousands of miles in a matter of seconds. He can establish laws and customs to control his own behavior, so that millions of people can live within a short distance of each other without constant conflict.

In spite of his amazing ability to alter his environment to suit himself, man displays disturbing signs of rigidity. Once he takes a stand on an issue, he is extremely reluctant to admit he is wrong. He gives up his superstitions very slowly, if at all, and hesitates a long time before altering any of his more important values, even when the world around him is changing rapidly. He likes new gadgets and appliances, but has a difficult time accommodating himself to new architectural styles or new teaching methods. He is much more adept at finding ways to win wars than at finding ways to stop wars.

An Introduction to Personality Development

Thus, although man has made immense strides in creating and adapting his physical world, he has been less successful with his personal and social world.

Changeable Across Cultures, Yet Consistent

"There are only two indisputable truths in psychology," one professor remarked in his first psychology lecture. "The first is that people are similar, and the second is that people are different."

For example, every society has a family system of some sort, but the systems differ. In the United States, the family usually consists of mother, father, and children, but the Tibetan woman may marry two brothers simultaneously (Peissel, 1965), and a married couple in Japan is likely to reside with the husband's parents and take care of them as long as they live.

Such emotions as love, anger, joy, and jealousy are known throughout the world; yet each society permits different ways of showing emotions, and the members of any given society may express emotions differently from each other. In France and Italy, anger is often shown directly. In Japan, anger toward a child or a servant may be expressed directly, but not anger toward an equal. Yet *some* Japanese express anger toward equals, and *some* Frenchmen and Italians are inhibited in showing anger.

Changeable Through Time, Yet Consistent

Behavior varies not only as the result of societal influences, but also because of the immediate situation. A normally placid person may erupt with anger if his steak is overdone; the child who is talkative and socially aggressive at home hides behind his mother's chair when the family is visiting friends; the teacher who is normally patient with children becomes highly irritable after a sleepless night. Although the behavior of any one person is consistent (that is, reliable—see Chapter 6) to a substantial degree, it is also subject to change as the result of the specific situation. A balanced perspective between situational influences upon behavior and enduring characteristics must be maintained.

Effective in Communicating, Yet Ineffective in Communicating

Man is the only creature that can communicate effectively across time and space. A telephone call can connect a travel agent in Kansas City with a hotel manager in Calcutta; a radio enables people to commu-

**Figure
7–1.**

People are the same, and people are different. People receive satisfaction from dance,
but they choose different forms. Courtesy Columbia Broadcasting System.

nicate with an astronaut hundreds of miles in outer space; a television set allows a track fan in Vermont to watch an Olympic track meet in Mexico City.

Not only do men send and receive communications across space, but they can also send and receive communications across time. A technique has been developed that will determine the age of a rock; ancient scrolls have been found recently that report what life was like 2,000 years ago; records of our present civilization have been buried, and civilizations in the future may uncover them and understand the present era better. Only man has the ability to send messages into the years ahead or to understand the messages left by people years and even centuries ago.

Despite man's achievements in communication, people often cannot communicate with those closest to them. Parents give their children great love and care, yet the children often find themselves unable to explain their deepest feelings to their parents. A wife wants desperately to tell her husband that she needs more of his attention, and a high school student wants to ask his parents to respect his privacy; but fear and inhibition prevent the expression of these feelings. Man has learned more about the scientific techniques of communicating across time and space than about communicating deep feelings to those he loves.

Complex, Yet Predictable

No two individuals look or behave exactly alike—even identical twins are slightly different. Each person combines physical appearance, personality, abilities, and attitudes in a unique fashion. Nonetheless, psychologists have found that, within limits, human behavior may be predicted. In spite of its complexity, behavior is not a complete mystery. A psychologist can administer a brief test to 100 entering freshmen and judge which ones are likely to graduate. His judgment will be far from perfect, but it will be much better than guesswork or making the decision from an interview.

Predictions of many kinds of behavior are possible. If you are more stubborn than average, you are also likely to be neater than average (Sears, 1936); the correspondence does not always hold, but the relationship has been shown to exist. If you are forced to express your views in public, your views will be less likely to change later (Hovland, Campbell, & Brock, 1957). If you are under stress, you may run faster than you normally could, but if the stress is too great, you may "freeze." Thousands of such predictions can be made with varying degrees of accuracy, although the uniqueness of people has prevented psychologists from making their predictions with complete accuracy.

The Behavior of Humans and of Lower Animals

The human is considered the highest form of animal life. Although, *by definition,* he is an animal and shares many characteristics with other animal species, the human differs from lower animals in distinct ways. Both humans and other animals seek food and shelter, care for their· young, exhibit aggression and fear, and enter into relationships with other individuals and with groups. However, humans have vastly higher intelligence, the ability to walk upright, and the ability to use tools. You can easily add many other examples.

For the purpose of studying human behavior, six main differentiations between people and lower animals are pertinent:

1. People develop more slowly.   Therefore, the effects of the environment have more time to operate. Since infancy and childhood are longer for the human than for other forms of animal life, his experiences during these periods may have more lasting effects.

2. People study themselves.   No other creatures study themselves. As a matter of fact, no other creatures seem aware that they exist and thus can be studied.

3. People develop interests that have nothing to do with keeping alive.   Many animals enjoy play, new experiences, and companionship, but only at a relatively primitive level. People can become interested in such activities as reading, travel, television, sports, talking, collecting matchbooks, studying ancient civilizations, and playing poker.

4. People use symbols in thinking and communicating.   The symbolic language of animals is very limited, but people have developed a great variety of symbols, including words, gestures, and numbers, which open entire new worlds for them.

5. People can govern their behavior by occurrences far away in time or in space.   A man may act in a certain way because he wishes future generations to think well of him. A student can learn what happened in 1492 or in 1933, or he can anticipate what might happen in 1984 or 1999. People can alter their behavior by learning what is happening in Bogor, Indonesia, or Indianapolis, Indiana (the above were adapted from Diamond, 1957).

6. People change the environment of each generation.   You are living in a world much different from the one your grandparents knew when they were your age. Most of the changes are the result of human accomplishments. A dog or a horse, on the other hand, lives in the same sort of world in which his grandparents lived, except for the changes produced by humans. Humans can acquire, accumulate, alter, and transmit values, ideas, and material goods (adapted from Sanford, 1965).

These differences between human and animal behavior allow the human wonderful opportunities for personal growth, for controlling his environment, for using his abilities, and for enjoying his life. They also offer him great destructive potential. How well do you think the human has used the abilities and opportunities he has? You can see immediately the importance of knowing history in order to answer this question.

An Introduction to Personality

The theme of this book is human behavior and, therefore, the human **personality**: its nature and development, the way it adjusts to the world, its feelings, its values, its problems, and the ways in which it deals with these problems. Although you all have an idea what the term *personality* implies, the psychologist's definition may differ from yours in several ways.

Personality can be defined as the **dynamic** organization of characteristic attributes leading to behavior, and distinguishing one individual from other individuals. It refers to the total individual and includes (but is not limited to) needs, motives, methods of adjusting, temperament qualities, self-concepts, role behaviors, attitudes, values, and abilities. The term covers behavior the individual himself is aware of, behavior of which he is not aware, behavior evident to others, and behavior evident only to himself.

This definition is extremely broad and requires some additional explanation of the terms used:

Dynamic. A dynamic person is forceful, always moving, filled with energy. In psychology, to refer to personality as dynamic is to say that the human is constantly changing and that each change affects the entire personality in such a way that the original change is itself affected, thus setting off another series of changes. No element of personality is isolated from any other element—nothing operates independently, in a vacuum. Consider the impact of a seemingly insignificant behavior change in a hypothetical case:

Ever since he was a child, Jack Swarthout had felt a strong need to be with other people. When he took introductory psychology, he read about needs and motives, and he gained insight into his own feelings. It bothered him that he was so dependent on others, so he mentioned it casually to his girl friend, who agreed that he should worry less about having a large group of friends. Jack began to look differently at the people he spent time with, and he realized that many of them were shallow and boring, so he began to do more things on his own or with only one or two friends. He liked his new activities, and he felt pleased with himself for being able to be alone. Soon he found that he was able to have close relationships with a few people, and he recognized that he had never had really close friendships before, not even with his girl friend. His altered reaction to his friends affected their responses to him, which in turn further altered his reactions. Each event and experience also had an influence on Jack's need to be with other people.

Personality is dynamic, interacting, changing.

Organization. Personality is neither a single entity nor a combination of entities, but an *organization* or a "whole." An automobile is not a shell; neither is it merely an assortment of separate parts. In order to work, an automobile must be an organization of individual parts into a whole automobile. Personality also is organized into a whole.

Characteristic. An example of behavior fairly typical of an individual is said to be *characteristic* of him. If a man is consistently kind and gentle, but will strike anyone who threatens to strike him first, we would still call him kind and gentle, because such behavior is more typical of him.

Behavior. Any observable action is behavior. Eating a ham sandwich is behavior; so is each separate step in eating a ham sandwich, such as making the sandwich, raising it to the lips, biting it, chewing it, and swallowing it. Two people may both eat ham sandwiches frequently enough to consider this act to be characteristic or typical, but each will make, bite, and chew the sandwich in different ways.

Thinking is also behaving, since thinking involves brain-cell activity, which is indirectly observable through a device such as the electroencephalograph. Any expression of an attitude or a need, even if only in thought, is thus a behavior. Other examples of behavior include figuring out whether you received the correct change at a store, wondering whom to vote for in the next campus election, becoming angry when you hear someone tell a lie about your friend, and trying to listen to the professor who speaks so quietly that you can barely hear him.

To repeat the initial definition of personality in other terms: Personality is *the changing and interacting organization of typical qualities into a whole that leads a man to behave as he does and that makes him different from other people.*

An Introduction to Personality Development

The Self-concept

A very useful way to understand the human personality is through consideration of the **self-concept**. The definition of self-concept is deceivingly simple: Self-concept is your picture or image of yourself. Like personality, self-concept is a dynamic organization of characteristic qualities, but—unlike personality—self-concept is a picture of those qualities *as seen by the individual himself.* Your self-concept includes *your* picture of your abilities, of your effect upon others, of your temperament and other elements of personality, and of your physical qualities, such as health and appearance.

Self refers to what you really are. Self-concept refers to what you think of yourself, your picture or image of yourself, or what you really *feel* you are.

Ron Vance had two older brothers, both brilliant and outstanding college students. Ron was constantly expected to live up to the standards set by his brothers, which he could not do although he was well above average in intelligence. Over the years he developed a self-concept of being "not too bright," and he increasingly avoided situations that called for intelligence or schoolwork.

Your self-concept reflects how you feel about yourself. Like any feeling, it may be partially unconscious or based on unconscious needs. You are likely to have some elements in your self-concept that you are not fully able to recognize.

Patricia Tratner was more than 30 pounds overweight, even though her friends had been telling her for years that she would be very attractive if she would reduce. Consciously, her self-concept became "I would be attractive if I could only reduce." However, until she sought help from a psychologist, she was unable to realize why she had never lost weight. Pat's unconscious self-concept was that of a hopelessly unattractive person. She was unconsciously motivated to remain overweight because if she did lose weight and was still unattractive, she could no longer make excuses. Once she gained insight into her unconscious self-concept, she was able to lose weight and, more important, to worry much less about whether she was physically attractive or not.

Many forms of behavior that appear inconsistent or irrational on the surface begin to make sense if you can learn about the self-concept of the people involved. For example, a 14-year-old girl became furious during Christmas dinner because she was seated, as she had been for years, with the children. Her self-concept, however, was that she had attained sufficient age and status to eat with the adults, and being seated with the younger children disturbed her self-concept.

The self-concept has been extensively investigated. The results of one study (summarized in Figure 8–4, page 152) suggest that an individual's self-concept, in combination with his attitudes toward others, can tell a lot about his behavior. Research has shown that people whose self-concepts are unpleasant are more likely than average to be poorly adjusted (Calvin & Holtzman, 1953).

The Body-image

The physical changes that occur throughout your lifetime are accompanied by changes in your self-concept and in your **body-image**, which is the picture you have of your physical being, including appearance and health. To express it in different words, your body-image is your body self-concept.

During the early years of life, the body-image must change quite rapidly to remain accurate in light of the actual physical changes that occur. Like all facets of the self-concept, your body-image is largely a reflection of how you feel others perceive you. If you are considered physically attractive, you are likely to have a corresponding body-image. Your body-image inevitably affects other aspects of your self-concept, as well as your behavior and your responses to others—and thus, the subsequent responses of others to you. As a result, a dynamic interaction takes place, involving body-image, self-concept, and behavior of the self and of others.

If the way others respond to you satisfies your needs, you may try to do something with your appearance to encourage more such responses; if the reactions of others are displeasing, you may try to alter your appearance. A girl who is complimented on her hair may take better care of her hair as a result; a boy who is teased because he is so skinny may try hard to gain weight.

A person with a healthy self-concept will not be overly disturbed by not being considered physically attractive, since he accepts himself as a worthy individual. However, the individual whose self-concept causes him to feel insecure may place too much emphasis upon the need to be thought physically attractive. You can make some interesting guesses about a person's self-concept and body-image by observing what he does to his physical appearance: notice clothing, hair style, cleanliness, use of makeup and jewelry, style of eyeglasses, posture, walk, smile, and so forth.

The body-image extends beyond the outward physical appearance, and includes physical health and handicaps that cannot be seen. Being

An Introduction to Personality Development

color-blind, having a rheumatic heart, or needing a filling for a cavity all affect the body-image.

Body-image and the physically different. Just like the racially different Negro and the religiously different Jew, the physically different person suffers job discrimination, social discrimination, and ridicule.

> Mary Frost had been severely burned as a child, and her face was badly scarred. After becoming a skilled stenographer, she found jobs difficult to obtain. One executive commented to his assistant after Mary left his office, "The rest of the staff would have nightmares after looking at that face all day."

Physical problems, even relatively minor ones, can have a negative effect upon a person's body-image. One's ability to adjust to problems involving physical appearance is only partly the result of the appearance itself; it is also related to the individual's general self-concept and his feelings of adequacy.

Figure 7–2.

How would you evaluate the body-image and self-concept of this boy? Courtesy Crippled Children's Society of Los Angeles.

Dave Korngold lost a leg when he was 4 years old, and was fitted with a wooden leg almost immediately. His parents, wisely, did not overprotect him, but treated him like a normal child who needed love and care and freedom to explore his environment. During World War II, when Dave was still in junior high school, the director of social work at a nearby veterans hospital asked Dave to show the returning amputees how well he could get around.

A popular person with both boys and girls, Dave never lost his sense of humor. His favorite story concerned a junior high school touch football game when he became angry with several members of the opposing team. After a particularly long run by the opposition, Dave casually leaned up against a tree and suddenly pulled off his wooden leg and waved it like a club at his opponents. They were so startled that their playing completely disintegrated, and Dave's team won.

Dave had a normal, healthy childhood and adolescence, and is now successful in the entertainment field.

Dave did not find his body-image unpleasant—it was merely one of the facts of life. If his parents had been less understanding or too protective, Dave might have considered himself a cripple. As it was, he considered himself a normal person who happened to have one leg.

Another physical difference affecting body-image is being overweight or underweight (although today the former is a more serious matter). Being too heavy, which is primarily the result of too much eating and too little activity, often produces an unpleasant body-image. Overweight people, contrary to their stereotype, are not jolly. They are often unhappy. They dislike their body and often have difficulty finding certain types of social relationships, such as dates. Obese people are also the butt of humor on television and in movies, which further worsens their body-image and their overall self-concept.

The Ideal Self

The self-concept reflects the image an individual has of himself. The **ideal self** is his image of himself as he would like to be. The ideal self of a young child is usually a parent; older children tend to idealize glamorous or historical figures; adolescents and adults select a combination of several people or an imaginary or hypothetical person for their ideal self (Havighurst, Robinson, & Dorr, 1946). Thus, as we mature, the ideal self becomes more complex.

People try to live up to their ideal self, but they usually fall short. When a person's self-concept falls far short of his ideal self, he is likely to show maladjustment (Rosenberg, 1962) and confusion (Block & Thomas, 1955). He is dissatisfied with himself and feels that he has failed to become the sort of person he wishes to become.

At the same time, people who claim that their self-concept and ideal self are almost identical may also be unstable. Research has shown that these individuals have an unusually great need to be liked and accepted by others and that they dislike expressing their emotions (Block & Thomas, 1955). All in all, the self-concept of the healthy personality is close, but not too close, to the ideal self.

Traits and Roles

In addition to the self-concept, two other descriptions of personality stand out as being particularly useful: **traits** and **roles**. Each of these has its place in the study of human behavior.

Traits

A personality trait is a behavior characteristic that differentiates people from each other. Psychologists talk about such traits as thriftiness, boastfulness, friendliness, foolishness, or honesty. To describe an individual in terms of a trait implies that the trait is fairly typical of his behavior.

People talk in terms of traits all the time. "John seems to be a happy guy." "Jeanne just isn't as thoughtful as she used to be." "Greg is too shy to be a good salesman." However, it is important to remain aware that describing a person by traits is oversimplifying, since his actual personality is both unique and dynamic. John is not always happy; Jeanne is still thoughtful in many ways; Greg might make an excellent salesman after he learns the routine.

Roles

Any given society has many *positions,* such as male and female, leader and follower, minister and doctor, or teacher and student. In each society, a certain pattern of behavior is expected of the individual who occupies a given position. This anticipated behavior pattern forms the *role* associated with that position. Thus, the role of the minister is to be concerned with spiritual matters, and many people become upset when a minister seems to be trying hard to make a lot of money for himself, since that appears inconsistent with his role. The role of the adolescent male in the United State is much different from the adolescent male role in many other countries. In what ways do you suppose these roles differ?

Personality develops and changes very slowly but constantly throughout one's life-span. These changes interact dynamically with the demands of the society to form age roles. Certain types of behavior are expected of people as a function of their age. For example, consider the different types of study habits you anticipate from a 10-year-old and from a college freshman, or the different sex behavior thought appropriate for a high school junior, a 30-year-old, and a 70-year-old.

Age roles must often be considered in interaction with other roles. Dress styles of teen-agers are usually brighter, less traditional, and probably skimpier than dress styles of 50-year-olds—differences that are determined by age roles, at least during this part of the twentieth century. However, dress styles also differ according to sex roles, social-class roles, and work roles. When roles are combined, new and more precise images emerge; for example, consider the dress styles of a young, upper-class college girl and of an elderly working-class retired man.

When a person ignores role expectations, he risks various punishments from the community. These punishments often involve social avoidance, personal criticism, and mockery. When a young man marries an elderly woman, both are seen as stepping out of their proper age roles and both receive criticism; if the marriage is between a young woman and an elderly man, the criticisms are milder.

On certain occasions, the violation of age roles is rewarded. A teen-ager who behaves like people ten years older than himself is often complimented by being called "mature," and an active and productive 80-year-old is similarly seen in a positive light. Certain kinds of behavior are considered appropriate substitutes for expected role behavior, but others are not. Problems of sex role behavior are discussed in Chapters 12 and 15.

The Self-actualizing Person

To say that an individual has a normal personality suggests that he does not suffer from a major personality inadequacy or severe emotional disturbance. However, normality merely implies "all right." As the previous discussion (in Chapter 2) of self-actualizing indicated, being normal is only part-way to getting as much from life as possible. Once basic needs are reasonably well satisfied, the individual can turn his attention to making the most of his capabilities and to being completely himself.

Self-actualizing should be seen as a process and not as a condition or state. A person cannot say, "I am in a state of self-actualization," as he might say, "I am in a state of good physical health." He would need to say, "I am in the process of self-actualizing." The difference is important, since self-actualizing needs to be seen as something that you are experiencing, not as something that *is* and that you either have or do not have.

Abraham Maslow, in studying psychologically healthy, self-actualizing persons, decided that they differed from other people in 13 basic ways (cited in Maslow, 1962).* (You may wish to review the earlier material on self-actualization in Chapter 2.)

Characteristics of the Self-actualizing Person

1. Superior perception of reality.   The self-actualizing person does not have such strong prejudices or fears or rigidities that he must reinterpret the world to suit himself. People who constantly blame communists or capitalists for all the troubles in the world are not accurately perceiving reality.

2. Increased acceptance of self, of others, and of nature.   Some people do not like themselves. They are overly critical and unforgiving regarding themselves. They do not think that they are worthwhile people. In addition, they are unduly critical and unforgiving of others, and may also feel that people in general are just no good. The self-actualizing person recognizes that he and all other people have limitations, but that he can nevertheless accept himself and others as worthwhile. Such acceptance does not rule out self-criticism, but means that the person enjoys a basic self-confidence, employing self-criticism to produce changes, rather than to induce a deadening depression.

3. Increased spontaneity.   Psychologically healthy persons can be relaxed and spontaneous. They need not worry unnecessarily about what others think, and thus they can behave more naturally. "Spontaneity" does not mean that they violate the rights of others or that they enjoy shocking others, but that they *can* act impulsively and emotionally.

4. Increase in problem centering.   Since self-actualizing persons are not overly concerned with personal problems and with satisfying status needs, they have the energy and the desire to deal with the particular problems or activities that strike them as challenging.

5. Increase in detachment and desire for privacy.   These days, there is so much emphasis on getting along with others that we often neglect the importance of privacy. The self-actualizing person enjoys privacy and the opportunity to concentrate on his own thoughts and ideas.

---

* The headings are taken verbatim from Abraham Maslow, but the explanations are the responsibility of the author of this book, as he interprets Maslow.

A Buddhist Legend Clarifies the Healthy Personality °

Once the Enlightened One came upon a couple of young boys having a fist fight. One of them was on the ground, with the other sitting on him. When they saw Lord Buddha approaching, they both jumped up and stood apologetically before him. Lord Buddha asked the winner what caused him to knock his friend down. "He called me a liar," the boy said.

"Are you a liar?" asked Lord Buddha.

"No, sir," was the reply.

"Then why did you fight?" asked the Enlightened One. "You know, you are the best one to decide whether you really lied or not. If you did lie, you should thank your friend for bringing it to your attention. If you had not lied, you know that your friend was mistaken. In either case, there seems to be no cause for such temper. You certainly do not knock a person down when he greets you by calling you a handsome and wonderful fellow, do you? You either thank him, or tell him he is mistaken, but you do not hit him."

In this legend, Buddha shows that the healthy personality has enough self-acceptance not to be bothered when an accusation is untrue, and has enough acceptance of others not to become angry when a friend makes an error.

° From Chatterjee, M. N., *Society in the making.* Ann Arbor, Mich.: Edwards Brothers, 1942. P. 30.

6. Increased autonomy *and resistance to being dominated by the* **culture.** Self-actualizing persons can remain independent of the pressures around them. They can evaluate the world they live in, without being blinded by the fact that they are living in it. They remain faithful to their own values and are not susceptible to the pressures of propaganda.

7. Greater freshness of appreciation and richness of emotional reaction. Self-actualizing people are not bored with life and do not need to run after new thrills. They can enjoy new experiences and see new elements in doing "the same old thing." They can find stimulation and pleasure in a conversation, a baby, or an old piece of driftwood.

8. Higher frequency of all-absorbing experiences. From time to time, some of us have an experience that is so enthralling, so exciting, and so absorbing that we virtually lose track of time and place. We are "taken out of ourselves." Self-actualizing people report this experience more often.

9. Increased feelings of brotherhood to man. The phrase "brotherhood of man" is often used without real meaning. The emotionally healthy person truly understands this concept. It is not just that he has friends, but that he feels he is a part of all mankind. Whatever happens to any man happens to all men, and thus happens to him.

10. Good relationships with others.   People with healthy personalities are able to have a few very close, meaningful relationships, although they may not necessarily be popular with a large group.

11. More democratic beliefs.   Self-actualizing individuals accept people for what they are, not for the labels (such as race, religion, or vocation) attached to them. They believe every human is entitled to dignity and esteem.

12. Greatly increased creativity.   Several of the previously described characteristics indicate the creative abilities of the psychologically healthy person. He is not overly involved with his own problems; he can respond spontaneously; he is relatively free from domination by his surroundings. Therefore, he can see new relationships and consider new ideas without being hampered by prejudices and rigidity.

13. More subtle sense of humor, which lacks hostility.   Self-actualizers find more humor in the world, but the humor is not at the expense of someone else. They do not find it funny when someone else is embarrassed or criticized. They enjoy laughing with people, but not at people, and they do not look upon personal misfortune as a cause for laughter. (This final factor is not listed with the others, but appears elsewhere in Maslow's writing.)

Additional Characteristics of the Self-actualizing Person

Abraham Maslow described the characteristics of the self-actualizing person that he had observed through his research. They by no means exhaust the list of possible characteristics of self-actualizing individuals. The author will suggest a few more.

14. The ability to make decisions, to accept responsibility for decisions, and to face the consequences of decisions.   Too often people do not wish to make decisions, because decisions involve responsibility. Inevitably, some decisions will be wrong, but the psychologically healthy person can make decisions when called upon. Since he is problem centered, his decisions are—on the whole—based on objective evaluation, rather than on his own personal needs or anxieties.

15. Increased goal-directedness.   The self-actualizer is working toward goals, rather than just "living" without any idea of what he wishes to do or why. His goals may not please others—they may even be considered foolish—and he may not achieve all his goals, but his behavior is not random or aimless.

16. High integrity.   Integrity means being honest, not merely to the letter of the law of honesty and decency, but also to the spirit. A

**Figure
7–3.**

Overcoming the forces of a hostile nature is self-actualizing for some people. For one person, this challenge is met by climbing Mount Everest; for another, by taking photographs in the depths of the ocean. Courtesy Columbia Broadcasting System.

healthy personality has integrity himself and can accept others as having integrity.

17. *Appropriate flexibility.* At times, people must be able to change their attitudes and ways of thinking. Flexibility, or lack of rigidity, does not mean bowing to the slightest pressures; it does mean being willing to consider change when the circumstances have changed or the information available has changed.

18. *High social consciousness.* Although the self-actualizing person is often detached and values privacy, he does not shut himself off from the world. He is willing to take a position on an issue, even though his position may be unpopular.

19. *High social awareness.* Emotionally healthy people are aware of the effects they have upon others. They respond to others as "complete and whole individuals" (Maslow, 1962). To them, other people are not objects or tools, but humans.

20. *High ability to give and to receive.* We all need to be able to give to others, both materially and in terms of our time, our energies, and our interest and concern. Since the self-actualizer recognizes the importance of giving, he realizes the importance of being a gracious receiver. To give without being able to receive is as degrading to others as receiving without being able to give.

21. *Increased insight.* People are limited in the degree to which they can understand themselves, but the psychologically healthy person finds that because he feels secure and accepted, not much interferes with his self-understanding. He observes how others react to him, when he succeeds and when he fails, when he seems motivated and when he is unmoved. Through such observation, he can increase his self-understanding.

The healthy, self-actualizing person is certainly not perfect. The above characteristics are not what every self-actualizing person lives up to, but they are more descriptive of the self-actualizer than of others. You may think of qualities that have been omitted, or you may feel that some of the characteristics listed have been overestimated in importance.

Influences on Human Development

The very first moment of being occurs in the mother's womb, when the sperm from the father unites with the ovum from the mother. The cell that emerges from this joining and eventually matures into the human fetus is called a **zygote**. At the time the zygote is formed, the future individual inherits certain characteristics from each of his parents, through microscopic bits of life called genes and chromosomes. These inherited characteristics are referred to as **genetic** or **hereditary** in origin.

The Nature-nurture Controversy

Behavior genetics is the area of study that concerns itself with hereditary (or genetic) and environmental aspects of behavior. A question that has long plagued psychologists is the degree to which heredity and environment contribute to various human characteristics. Debate over this question has traditionally been known as the *nature-nurture controversy.*

When the infant is born, he is different in appearance from all other infants—unless he has an identical twin. There is little doubt that such characteristics as eye color, hair color, bone structure, and facial features are inherited, which accounts for children resembling their parents.

Other characteristics are believed to be heavily influenced by genetic factors, but are also affected by the environment. Your height and weight, for example, depend both upon your gene structure at conception and upon health, nutrition, and eating habits in later life. Your *potential* intellectual capacity may well be inherited, but your ability to make use of this intelligence is influenced by the environment.

The newborn infant differs from other infants in ways that go beyond physical appearance. He displays patterns of activity, irritability, and mood that seem to be inherited; at least the possibility that they have been learned is definitely limited. These patterns are expressed through differing amounts of movement, of crying, of sucking behavior, and of sleep. Some psychologists claim that these behavior and temperament differences developed during the nine months in the womb; others contend that heredity is by far the major influence.

People often make statements such as, "He has his father's temper," or "He cries easily, like his mother." The implication is that temper and readiness to cry are genetically inherited. Geneticists and psychologists are not at all certain how important heredity is in determining these kinds of behavior. Both heredity and environment interact dynamically in causing a person to develop a hot temper or a tendency to cry; but it is not necessary to assume that heredity and environment contribute in the same proportion to the temperamental or crying behavior of every individual.

Some characteristics are only minimally and indirectly affected by heredity. Political attitudes, religious values, enjoyment of television shows, or interest in watching or playing baseball are virtually completely the result of previous learning; yet, heredity may play an indirect part. People who are, for genetic reasons, very intelligent, irritable, or emotional may, because of their inherited characteristics, find a particular political viewpoint or type of entertainment more appealing or less appealing.

In essence, heredity influences certain personal characteristics substantially or almost totally, but has a very limited and indirect effect on others. Thus, assuming proper motivation, an individual is capable of producing considerable change in certain personal characteristics, but will remain very much restricted in changing other personal qualities. Genetic structure may be seen as setting the outer limits on behavior and other characteristics. Just as inherited limitations prevent humans from flapping their arms and taking off into the air, inherited limitations restrict the range of innumerable other kinds of behavior. Later learning and experiences can modify behavior, but they cannot change the basic inherited framework within which each individual must work. However, learning and experience are the primary influences upon attitudes, values, and most of those behaviors that we consider "good" or "bad."

Parents often make the mistake of treating all their children alike, even though the needs and desires of the children may differ considerably. The job of a parent is made much more difficult by the unequal needs and differing personality patterns of children.

Some Relevant Research

Careful observations of patients suffering from certain medical problems have led scientists to talk about **inherited predispositions.** Two people who lead the same sort of life and are equally healthy both become ill with a strep throat. Person A contracts rheumatic fever, but person B is not affected. Person A, therefore, may have genetically inherited a predisposition or weakness toward rheumatic fever. He did not inherit rheumatic fever, but he inherited a susceptibility to contract the disease, whereas person B inherited a strong resistance to the illness. Considerable evidence is available that one person may have a greater inherited predisposition to become mentally ill than another, although they both lead equivalent lives and face equally stressful situations (Kallmann, 1953).

Many studies, including the one mentioned directly above, have investigated differences between **identical twins** and **fraternal twins.** Since identical twins come from the division of a single fertilized egg, they share an almost identical heredity; they are nearly identical to each other in appearance and are inevitably of the same sex. Fraternal twins are born when two separate eggs are fertilized; their heredity is no more the same than that of any two children of the same parents, and they need not look alike or be of the same sex.

Fraternal twins share with each other a highly similar environment, just as identical twins do, but they share a much less similar heredity than do identical twins. As a result, in behavior presumed to have some genetic basis, identical twins should resemble each other more than fraternal twins resemble each other. Research results bear this conclusion out. Identical twins have been found more similar than fraternal twins on measures of intelligence, interests, and personality (Nichols, 1968); on the length of time it takes to react to stimuli and on other tasks involving sensory and motor responses (Osborne & Gregory, 1966); and on the likelihood of becoming mentally ill (Kallmann, 1953).

Other studies have shown that the intelligence of foster children is more similar to that of their biological parents than to that of their foster parents (Honzik, 1957), even though a good foster home appears to increase the IQs of foster children beyond scores otherwise expected (Skodak & Skeels, 1949).

Interaction of Heredity and Environment

Much of what was once considered to be genetically inherited is now recognized as having been learned, often during the early years of life. A young girl whose mother is always arguing with her father may learn to feel that men are crude and must be argued with. When she grows older and marries, she argues with her husband, much as her mother had argued with her father. The casual observer may assume such behavior to be genetically inherited, whereas most behavioral scientists believe it is learned.

Of greatest importance to the proper understanding of human behavior is the recognition that heredity and environment interact with each other. Neither stands in isolation. Being tall or short, being Caucasian or Polynesian, being male or female, being what our society considers beautiful or what our society considers homely, these are all genetically determined characteristics. Each of these qualities affects the way others respond to us. Since the responses of others to us help determine our self-concept, the degree to which our needs are satisfied, and our opportunities for self-actualization, genetically transmitted characteristics have an important indirect influence on human behavior. Genetic qualities affect the individual's environment, which inevitably affects his behavior. Can you see how the resulting environment might act to affect the genetic inheritance of the next generation?

Think of some people you know and try to understand how their heredity interacted with their environment to make them the sort of people they are. How about Napoleon? Albert Einstein? Martin Luther King, Jr.? Elizabeth Taylor? Elgin Baylor?

Inherited characteristics probably affect personality in four basic ways: (1) people inherit certain physical characteristics such as facial features and certain medical conditions; (2) people inherit predispositions to certain mental and physical illnesses; (3) people inherit predispositions to certain types of behavior; and (4) all these qualities interact with the environment to influence personality indirectly as well as directly.

Biochemical Basis of Human Development

Within the past decade, psychologists have turned increased attention to biochemical aspects of behavior. One of the most promising areas of investigation in this field is the study of DNA (deoxyribonucleic acid) and RNA (ribonucleic acid).

DNA, an acid found within the genes, regulates the development of the cell. A mechanism within the DNA molecule maintains the continued development of the cell and guards against malformation. DNA also produces RNA, which is critical in the development of substances that regulate chemical reactions within body cells.

One of the most exciting prospects of DNA and RNA research is that these substances have been linked with learning and memory. With learning, the RNA concentration in certain parts of the brain increases. When RNA is artificially increased, learning appears to occur more rapidly. Thus it seems that another important piece of evidence for the genetic basis of certain aspects of behavior has been found.

Summary of Important Ideas

1. Humans are adaptable, yet rigid; their behavior varies according to their culture, yet shows consistency from culture to culture; individual behavior changes from situation to situation, yet retains a consistent quality; people communicate across space and time, yet are often unable to understand those they love most; their behavior results from the most subtle and intricate factors, yet is still predictable.

2. People differ from lower animals in many important ways.

Development of Human Behavior

3. Personality is the dynamic organization of characteristic attributes leading to behavior, and distinguishing one individual from other individuals.

4. The self-concept is the picture an individual has of himself. The conscious self-concept and the unconscious self-concept are usually similar, but not necessarily identical.

5. The body-image is the aspect of the self-concept that involves physical health and appearance.

6. The ideal self is the image a person has of himself as he would like to be.

7. A role is the pattern of behavior expected of a person with a given position in society. The positions include such categories as male, female, physician, student, leader, or teen-ager.

8. Self-actualizing persons have been found to differ from most other people in many ways, for example, in having better perception of reality, increased spontaneity, and greater freshness of appreciation.

9. Psychologists and geneticists have been concerned with determining the degree to which heredity and environment contribute to various human characteristics. Some characteristics seem to be primarily the result of genetic transmission, and others are developed through interaction with the environment.

10. The dynamic interaction between heredity and environment affects much human behavior.

11. Psychologists are beginning to study the biochemical bases of behavior.

Chapter Eight

The Early Years

The previous chapter formed a bridge between the basic principles of human behavior and the development of human behavior. Psychologists and others emphasize the study of the early years of life because they are strongly convinced that experiences during this time leave an unerasable mark upon responses to situations in later years, even though an accurate memory of the early experiences may be lacking.

Experiences during the earliest years of life probably have a greater effect upon later behavior patterns than do experiences at any other time in the life-span. Even though the infant and young child face a limited range of situations and lack a conscious memory of what occurs, the first two or three years of life are tremendously important. The mature personality is largely the product of early parent-child relationships, early experiences of all sorts, and the interaction between these factors and the genetic qualities the infant inherits.

Prenatal Influences on Development

A newborn infant has already had a history of roughly nine months of existence. Although his brain and senses were not well developed during that period, his condition was still influenced by the health of his mother and by what is termed the **intrauterine environment**. Thus, his later appearance, intelligence, and behavior *may* be affected by what occurs between conception and birth.

Development of Human Behavior

Women who maintain an adequate diet during pregnancy are more likely than poorly nourished women to give birth to healthy babies, and the birth itself and the recovery are much easier for them (Ebbs, Tisdall, & Scott, 1942). Although being undernourished is certainly harmful for the mother and the fetus, "eating enough for two" is not the proper alternative. Moderate amounts of food, with particular attention to a well-balanced diet, undoubtedly are most effective. In countries where pregnant women cannot receive adequate food and medical care, many infants die during the **prenatal** period.

When the mother contracts certain illnesses during her pregnancy, the future health, intelligence, and physical condition of the infant may be adversely affected. These illnesses include German measles (during the first three or four months of pregnancy), syphilis, tuberculosis, and some strains of influenza (Montagu, 1958). Physical illness of the pregnant woman is not the only condition that may affect the fetus. Such environmental factors as restricted oxygen supply or irradiation "can substantially alter the course of development" (Telford & Sawrey, 1968), particularly if they occur at the stage of development when the fetus is most susceptible. There appear to be critical stages in fetal development; if the fetus is subjected to certain influences at the proper critical period, harm may occur, but if the same influence occurs later, the harm will be diminished or nonexistent.

Women who are unhappy about being pregnant appear to have more problems during pregnancy, more medical difficulties at delivery, and less well-adjusted children in subsequent years (Engström, Geijerstam, Holmberg, & Uhrus, 1964; Wallin & Riley, 1950). Although it is not known how the unhappiness of the pregnant woman is related to future problems, it is possible that the anxiety felt by the mother might cause a physiological change that affects the future infant. Another possibility is that women who are unhappy about being pregnant are more careless in taking proper care of themselves. They might ignore good nutrition, not get adequate rest, pay no attention to an illness, or not bother with prenatal medical examinations. And, inevitably, women who do not like the idea of being pregnant may well resent the child after he arrives, and will treat him in such a way as to lead to adjustment problems later.

Other conditions of the mother that may disrupt the normal development of the fetus include heavy drinking, which usually reduces the likelihood of a healthy diet; use of certain narcotics; smoking, which seems related to low birth weight and prematurity (Lowe, 1959); exposure to X rays or to atomic fallout; lack of oxygen; a major illness or accident; and a condition that occurs when the parents have incompatible blood types.

The Neonatal Period

The infant in the first two or three weeks of life is called a **neonate**. A century ago, the neonatal period was a time of danger to the future health and life of the individual, and the proportion of infants who died before they were two weeks old was quite high. Improvements in maternal health, hospital conditions, and general medical care have been major factors in producing an amazing drop in the death rate at birth and during the neonatal period. Unfortunately these improvements have not been distributed evenly throughout this country, and infant mortality is about twice as high for nonwhites as for whites. In spite of excellent health facilities for those expectant mothers who can afford the cost or who know where to seek free help, the infant mortality rate in the United States is higher than that in 13 other countries.*

A distressing outcome of the greatly improved health care and health services has been the much-publicized **population explosion**, contended by some to be among the biggest problems facing the last third of the twentieth century. Can you explain the significance of this term and its relationship to reduced infant mortality? What other recent technological, scientific, or social changes have affected the population explosion?

Behavior Differences at Birth

"To be honest, I didn't really enjoy my son until he was about a year old—that's when he began to have a real personality." In spite of a common belief that all babies are alike, definite individual differences are evident at birth.

Even during the first two or three days of life, infants display considerable differences in responding to noise or other stimuli (Schachter, Bickman, Schachter, Jameson, Litachy, & Williams, 1966). Subsequent observations during the first few months show differences in motor behavior (movements), reactions to frustration, and readiness to smile (Diamond, 1957). Some infants are generally more responsive to their environment, more easily stimulated by what goes on around them. These personality differences occur so early and with so little opportu-

---

* Metropolitan Life Insurance Statistical Bulletin, May 1967, p. 48.

**Figure
8–1.**

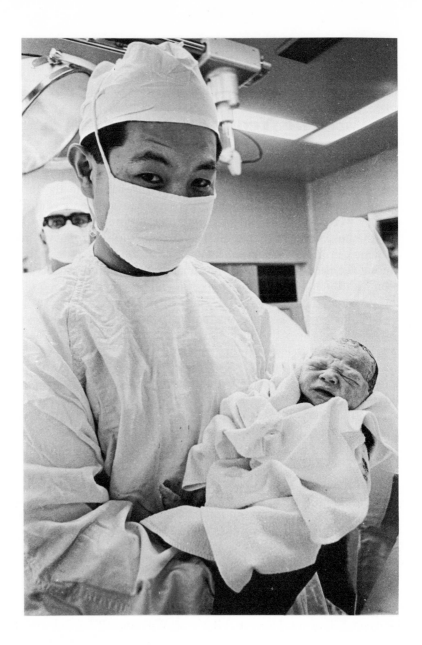

The supposedly "just-born" infants you see in the movies are actually several weeks old. Real infants look more like this one immediately after birth. Courtesy UCLA.

nity for learning that they seem to be at least partly the result of inherited factors.

Birth and Right After

Many physicians and psychologists feel that modern American women become so tense and fearful about giving birth that the birth process becomes more difficult and painful. This, in turn, may create a negative attitude toward the infant, who caused the discomfort. Medical men try to encourage mothers-to-be to look upon childbirth as a natural event, neither very dangerous nor necessarily especially painful.

A few expectant mothers follow a program of **natural childbirth**, which combines various physical exercises with encouragement to develop mentally healthy attitudes regarding childbirth (Dick-Read, 1960). In some instances, the husband will remain with his wife during labor and sometimes even during delivery, if his presence is felt to contribute to the security feelings of the mother.

Although only a small proportion of women use natural childbirth methods, medical and social attitudes toward proper behavior of mothers-to-be have changed considerably over the past 50 years. At one time, expectant mothers were encouraged to rest as much as possible, to stay off their feet, and to remain at home unless it was necessary to leave. Today they are encouraged to get mild exercise, to remain moderately active, and to follow their normal schedules to the degree they can do so without feeling discomfort.

After the infant is born, some mothers prefer to use a **lying-in** arrangement in the hospital. With lying-in, the newborn is placed in a small room adjacent to the mother's room or in the same room with the mother, so that the baby is immediately available to her, instead of being in a special ward some distance away.

Some expectant mothers have the sort of attitudes that make natural childbirth and lying-in very rich, worthwhile experiences. Other women are undoubtedly better off adhering to the more traditional methods.

Early Development

At birth, infants have only a minimal awareness of their environment. Although their senses are fairly well developed at birth and mature quickly in the following weeks, neonates have little basis for interpreting the stimuli that they do receive. Even very young infants, however, will exhibit certain responses to some noises, odors, tastes, colors, and tactual stimuli; for example, they may avoid an unpleasant odor or look for longer periods at one color or pattern than at another (Kidd & Rivoire, 1966).

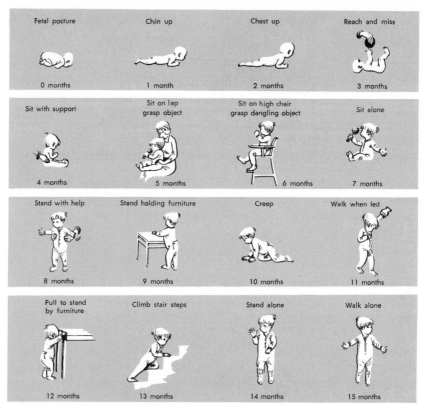

Figure 8–2.

Motor development in children. The averages pictured do not, by any means, imply that infants who develop faster are bound to be highly intelligent or that those who develop later are doomed to slow learning throughout their lives. Normal infants show a wide range in development. Adapted from Shirley (1933); by permission of the University of Minnesota Press.

An infant's early movement is largely mass activity. That is, his entire body will move in response to stimulation of one part of the body. Neonates can suck and swallow, which allows them to take food, but these actions are **reflexes** that occur automatically without learning. Motor behavior, such as grasping, crawling, and walking, develops more slowly than sensory abilities and varies considerably from child to child.

Figure 8–2 shows the average age at which certain behavior is first observed, but it is perfectly normal for children to develop much later or much earlier than these averages.

The neonate sleeps about two-thirds of the time, but—as parents learn to their dismay—will wake up every few hours, crying to be fed. Slowly, as his body grows larger, he can take more food at a time and will need to eat less frequently. Crying and other forms of agitation can be soothed not only through feeding, but also by gentle rocking, pleasant sounds, or a sweetened pacifier, even as early as the second or third day of life. Babies differ in how easily they can be soothed and also as to the stimulus that works the best (Birns, Blank, & Bridger, 1966).

During the early weeks and months of life, individual differences among infants interact dynamically with their environment. One investigation revealed that babies who were active did not seem to need much environmental stimulation, but made normal progress with the minimum amount of mother contact necessary for adequate care. Inactive infants, on the other hand, made similarly normal progress only if their mothers provided stimulation for them through personal interaction. Inactive babies with unresponsive mothers gave the impression of being comparatively immature (Escalona, 1965).

The effects of parental stimulation during these early months are frequently underestimated. One study found that even 5-month-old infants were measurably more active and attentive if their mothers spent time playing with them and providing other types of interaction (Kagan, 1968). Studies of this nature raise some fascinating practical questions. For instance, one investigation showed that infants seem to recognize strangers around 5 or 6 months, but display fear of them between 7 and 9 months (Bronson, 1968). This observation suggests that introducing a parent substitute at this age may lead to some difficulty; but would the difficulty have permanent impact? Might this early stimulation affect production of DNA or RNA and, perhaps, influence later memory?

The question of the impact of early experiences needs further study. How serious is the effect on the life situation of a 12-year-old boy of his having received little stimulation during the first year of life? Is there a particular age at which certain kinds of stimulation should occur in order to have maximum effect? If stimulation is lacking at a certain age, can it be compensated for later? One study showed that monkeys that were raised in isolation (that is, without either parents or playmates) exhibited great fear when they were placed with other monkeys for the first time. Those that were isolated for a relatively brief time eventually learned normal behavior patterns, but those that experienced longer periods of isolation were never fully able to compensate for them. In later years they displayed many forms of antisocial behavior, including violence (Harlow & Harlow, 1967).

Maturation

Some behavior results from **maturation**, which means that it develops almost inevitably—assuming a normal environment—without being taught. For example, walking is largely the result of maturation. The human must reach a certain level of maturation and readiness before he can learn to walk; at that point, he will probably learn to walk with or without aid. Effective help and encouragement might hasten the process by a few weeks, but no more.

Maturation is almost impossible to speed up. The rate of maturation is primarily the result of heredity, although inadequate physical health, nutrition, or learning opportunity can retard maturation. Parents who pressure their child to learn certain tasks, such as climbing stairs or buttoning, before he is ready will find that their efforts have little long-range effect upon the ability of the child to do the particular task. If the parents push too hard, the results may be negative, because the child is being forced to do something he cannot do successfully. He may become anxious and fearful over his inevitable failure and develop feelings of inadequacy and a lowered self-concept.

Child-rearing Methods and Personality

Psychologists believe that experiences during the first few years of life are vitally important in shaping the entire personality. As a result, they have spent much time and effort exploring the methods parents use to rear their children and the various parent-child relationships that occur. Some of the specific aspects that have been studied include early feeding experiences, early toilet-training experiences, and early sex-behavior training.

These experiences are very important for several reasons: (1) Early experiences set the stage for later expectations. (2) Since early experiences have not been contradicted by other experiences, they may have greater and more lasting impact. (3) The child's attitudes toward himself begin to develop at a very early age. (4) Early experiences may affect later unconscious motivation.

Attitudes of parents toward children may be described in many ways, but two dimensions are indicated frequently in research and in theories: (1) warmth (or acceptance) versus hostility (or rejection); and (2) control (or restrictiveness) versus permissiveness (or independence) (Maccoby, 1964). It is generally assumed that these two factors, rather than the specific techniques of child rearing, are of primary importance. Thus, in considering the topics to follow, we must consider the behavior of individual parents as to the degree of warmth they show and the degree of independence they allow their children.

Early Feeding Experiences

For the infant, hunger needs and their satisfaction are among the most compelling forces in life. If the hunger need remains unsatisfied too long, he may develop fear or anxiety regarding his ability to obtain food. Children who have suffered severe hunger during their very early years have been later observed to stuff food into their pockets, even when the supply was plentiful. If early eating experiences are tense, uncomfortable occasions, the child may develop negative attitudes not only toward eating, but also toward the individuals associated with these early events.

The most meaningful experiences infants have with eating are the initial breast or bottle feeding, weaning from the breast or bottle, and contact with solid food.

Breast feeding. For years, many physicians and psychologists have strongly advised those women who are physically capable to breast-feed their babies. Among the reasons frequently mentioned were: (1) Breast feeding leads to close physical contact between the mother and the child, providing a sense of security for the infant and pleasure for the mother. (2) As the child begins to learn, he will associate the warmth of his mother's body and the satisfaction of his hunger with his mother as a person, helping to build a strong affection between the two. (3) Breast feeding often helps a woman "feel like a mother" (Spock, 1957). (4) Mother's milk is likely to be right for the baby and free from germs, whereas bottled milk often necessitates preparation and adjusted formulas. (5) Breast-fed babies have fewer illnesses and better chances for survival (Jeans, Wright, & Blake, 1954).

Although a considerable body of research exists on the later personality of nursed versus bottle-fed infants, no final conclusions can be drawn. Many of the studies found breast-fed children healthier, happier, better adjusted, and more successful in school (for example, Hoefer & Hardy, 1929; Rogerson & Rogerson, 1939); other studies discovered no differences between the two groups (for example, Sears, Maccoby, & Levin, 1957; Sewell & Mussen, 1952). No research, however, has shown bottle-fed babies to be better off than breast-fed infants.

These results may be explained, in part, by the finding that mothers

Development of Human Behavior

who breast-feed are more likely to be happy about having children and are more likely to enjoy cuddling their babies. These maternal attitudes even seem related to the amount of breast milk the mother will have (Newton, 1968). Therefore, the later good health and adjustment of breast-fed babies may well be, at least in part, the result of maternal behavior other than breast feeding. Breast feeding is just part of a pattern of warm, positive responses toward infants, and it is this pattern, rather than any one aspect of it, that leads to better physical and mental health. Since most authorities recommend that the baby be held (rather than propped) during feeding, the main value of breast feeding could be the cuddling and affection the infant receives during feeding.

One unfortunate outcome of the emphasis upon breast feeding is that many women who are physically unable or personally unwilling to breast-feed may feel guilty and inadequate. If, as hypothesized above, the main value of breast feeding is the cuddling the infant receives, mothers who use bottle feeding can compensate by other forms of care and affection. This point is particularly important, since American mothers are less likely to nurse their infants than are mothers from most societies in the world (Whiting & Child, 1953).

Weaning.   Eventually the young child must be removed from the breast or the bottle and taught to drink without sucking. According to the famous Dr. Spock, most infants are ready to begin this step between 7 and 10 months, although they may begin taking sips from a cup as early as 5 months (1957). Anthropological investigations of small, less developed societies show that **weaning** of the child from the breast begins typically between ages 2 and 3. Of 52 groups investigated, only the Marquesans weaned their children earlier than Americans (Whiting & Child, 1953).

Weaning should occur gradually, preferably by the elimination of one feeding at a time (Spock, 1957). An infant who is shifted suddenly from the breast or bottle to the cup may find the experience upsetting. Mothers in some of the societies described by anthropologists wean their children very gradually, allowing them to continue feeding from the breast from time to time, until they are as old as 5 years (Whiting & Child, 1953), and in one society until around the age of 12 (Gorer, 1938).

Feeding Problems.   Feeding problems in childhood, especially in infancy, often plague mothers. Unfortunately for parents, the appetites of their children are rarely predictable. Sometimes children eat a great deal; at other times, very little. Without warning, a child may go on a hunger strike and eat nothing at all or refuse to eat solid food. Since the mother often becomes frantic, she communicates her anxiety to the child, who is likely to respond by becoming more anxious and unhappy himself. Unless something is medically wrong, a child will eat when he becomes hungry, and a jumpy, frightened mother is not going to increase his appetite.

Feeding problems among one group of children studied could not be traced to bottle feeding, weaning, or strictness of the feeding schedule. In this research, children with feeding problems were found to have had more severe toilet training, more physical punishment, and less warmth from their mothers than children without feeding problems (Sears et al., 1957). Here, then, is additional evidence that the degree of warmth and of parental restrictiveness, rather than the specific training techniques, is important in determining later personality adjustment.

Toilet Training

Primitive societies usually do not begin **toilet training** until the child is around 2, and the Bena of Africa may wait until he is 5 (Whiting & Child, 1953). American families, however, usually start toilet training toward the end of the first year, sometimes placing the child on the "potty" as early as 5 months and finishing toilet training at about 18 months on the average (Sears et al., 1957).

Some parents feel a glow of pride in toilet training their child before he is 9 or 10 months old, even though pediatricians and psychologists discourage attempts at toilet training too early. Being toilet-trained demands a certain degree of maturation: the child must learn to associate the physical pressure within his body with the acts of elimination; then he must be able to withhold the waste until he can get (or be taken) to the toilet. Many children will toilet-train themselves if left alone; when they are around 2 years of age, they wish to imitate their parents and their older friends or brothers and sisters. The later that training begins, the less time it takes (Sears et al., 1957).

It may seem strange that psychologists and pediatricians place so much stress upon toilet training, but there is a good explanation. Toilet training is likely to be the first attempt of parents to train their child; it often involves the first taste of real discipline and the first fear of disappointing the parents. Perhaps most serious, the child is often frustrated because he cannot please his parents by doing what they expect of him. He may thus develop a self-concept of inadequacy, which could generalize to other phases of living. Since toilet training, unlike other types of child training, continues for many weeks or even months, fear of possible failure in satisfying the parents can become extreme. The child may even come to feel that being toilet-trained is the most important thing in his life. His parents praise him when he is successful, scold him when he is unsuccessful, and discuss it constantly. Sometimes the child thinks that the valuable thing is the feces, not the act of getting to the toilet:

Development of Human Behavior

Karen Reiter's parents placed great emphasis upon toilet training, and they were very unhappy at Karen's slow learning. At 26 months, Karen made many mistakes, and the family did everything they could to get her trained. Karen was a sensitive child who wanted to please her parents but seemed unable to learn this particular trick. One evening, while her parents were entertaining three other couples for dinner, Karen called to her parents to ask whether she might bring out "something to show you." Her father, thinking she wanted to show the guests her brand-new furry slippers, called back "Yes." And Karen trooped out, her pajama pants around her knees, displaying the bowl from the "potty"—full.

Parents may also demand too much of their child during toilet training. Some children are physiologically ready to be trained much earlier than others, and even children who have been trained will have accidents from time to time, especially on occasions of stress, such as at the birth of a new brother or sister or when the parents are arguing. The severity of toilet training, rather than the age at which it begins, is more closely related to emotional upset (Sears et al., 1957).

Children may consciously or unconsciously ignore their toilet training as a form of aggression against their parents. A child who is apparently trained, then suddenly wets or soils, not only insults the training techniques of his parents, but also produces a job of cleaning up that parents usually abhor. Chronic bed-wetting, sometimes interpreted as aggression against the parents, is more frequent among children who received very severe toilet training (Sears et al., 1957).

While the author was working with young children, he developed a particularly close relationship with 3-year-old Barbara, who was living in a type of orphanage. After several months of frequent contact, he told the child that he had to leave for another job. Although he did all he could to break the news gently, and another psychologist had agreed to take up where he left off, the child was very upset. During each of their last three meetings, she soiled her pants at least once, although her most recent previous mistake had been nearly a year earlier. Was Barbara expressing aggression or responding to stress, or both?

Toilet training is closely related to cleanliness training. Parents who desire rapid toilet training often emphasize other forms of cleanliness and neatness (Sears et al., 1957). The child who fails in his toilet efforts is reminded how "dirty" he is. A few years later, the same body parts will again become the center of attention as a place where modesty must be maintained. The demands for cleanliness and the demands for modesty interact to make that part of the body a forbidden, exciting, "dirty" area.

Perhaps you feel that the importance of early feeding and toilet-training experiences has been exaggerated in this chapter. If so, discuss these topics with friends who have young children. Regardless of their specific experiences, you will quickly see what an important part this early training played in the lives of the parents, and you can imagine how important it was to their children, who had much less in the way of outside activities to distract them.

Sex Training

Young children invariably locate their genital areas during the normal process of becoming familiar with the sight and feel of their own bodies. Exploring or handling the sex areas is likely to elicit punishment from parents, although most mental health authorities would probably say, "Ignore it."

In some societies, sex play among children is accepted as natural

Figure 8–3.

Modesty is not natural; it must be learned. Photograph by John G. Warford.

(Whiting & Child, 1953). Also in the United States, children frequently explore each other's bodies, perhaps while claiming to play *Doctor*, although they usually hide their game from adults. Parents often oppose any sort of sex activity among children, and in one study over one-half of a group of mothers expressed definite opposition to sex play (Sears et al., 1957).

When punishment for sex play is severe, it may produce sexual-adjustment difficulties that work against future mental health. The early training of many American adults has created fear, anxiety, avoidance, and even impotence and frigidity in sex behavior and affection.

To convince their children to avoid any sex behavior, some parents make up stories or relate "facts" that are not accurate; for example, "If you touch yourself there, you will get sick or go crazy." Statements of this nature may create an immediate sense of panic, as well as long-range fear and avoidance of all forms of sex. The usual types of sex exploration and manipulation in which children indulge are unlikely to be harmful, unless the children feel anxious or guilty because they have been persuaded that their activity is sinful and unclean.

Nonetheless, adults are often frightened and offended by children's sex play, occasionally with justification. If the sex behavior involves two or more children, or if an older child is participating, one expert suggests that adults consider trying to convince the children to stop (Spock, 1957). Among effective approaches are distracting the children, getting them involved in other activities, or expressing mild and general censure (for example, "That game isn't really so good—why don't you ride your bikes for a while?"). Such approaches reduce the behavior without drawing attention to it.

Methods of child training are considered important by most societies, and contemporary America is certainly not an exception. If infants are fed, toilet-trained, and sex-trained as part of a pattern of basically loving and affectionate parent-child interactions, the specific training techniques probably are of secondary consequence. What is of primary consequence is how early rearing affects the development of the individual's self-concept and his relationships with the important people in his life.

Significant Others and the Self-concept

The self-concept develops through interaction with other people, beginning in infancy. A young child's judgment of himself can be only a reflection of how he feels others are judging him, and those "others" who have a particularly great impact are referred to as **significant others**. For most infants and young children, significant others are the parents, and it is through his parents' eyes that the child evaluates and pictures himself. Significant others form a sort of psychological mirror (Cooley, 1902; Sullivan, 1953). The child looks to his parents to learn who and what he is, and what he sees reflected back forms his picture of himself.

Thus, if the child feels his parents love him, he will feel he deserves this love; if he feels his parents think him stupid, he will believe it of himself. He is not able to judge himself or them, but tends to accept their viewpoint of himself (and of much else in the world) as right and proper. If his parents have treated him well or cruelly, paid attention to him or ignored him, shown him love or shown him nothing but the back of their hand, he can only feel, "If these people do this to me, I must deserve it." He has no other basis for comparison at his age.

Elaine Lander's parents were well into their forties when she was born, and her sister and brother were both in high school. She was, by any definition, an unwanted child. Her mother, a private secretary to a business executive, quickly hired a housekeeper to care for her and returned to work. Her father was irritated with having to worry about diapers and baby-sitters again, especially when he was working unusually hard to save money for the older children's college education. Whenever either parent had to feed or change or otherwise handle Elaine, they did it as quickly as possible, not really caring whether she was bounced around a little in the process. They rarely bothered to give her that extra attention and affection that babies need.

Both parents constantly referred to her as a "damned nuisance." They had no sympathy for her crying and little interest in how she developed, other than making certain she received good physical care. As Elaine grew older, she began to recognize how her parents felt about her. When she played make-believe games, she would yell at herself, "You're a bad girl, Elaine, and a nuisance and a damned and a not-hurry-up. You're an icky."

She matured into a quiet, reserved, fearful girl who was constantly apologizing for bothering others. She hated to approach people for friendship, since she viewed herself as being unworthy of friendship. Her parents had rejected her attempts at gaining their friendship, and she feared similar rejection from others. She later became a successful and popular nursery school teacher.

As a very young child, Elaine accepted her parents' view of her as valid. She was unable to say to herself, "I'm really a very good person, but my parents are too busy to notice me." All she could feel was, "If my parents (who are my world) do not notice me, then I am not worth noticing." By the time she was mature enough to evaluate herself with greater objectivity, her self-concept and her behavior patterns were well formed, and change was extremely difficult. Why do you think she was able to succeed as a nursery school teacher?

To make matters worse, children who feel unaccepted often behave in ways that irritate others. They may be so hungry for people to accept them that they are unable to disagree or to turn down a request for a favor, and they gain a reputation for being weak. Or they may react in just the opposite way: having been unable to trust the significant others in their lives, they are unable to trust or wholeheartedly like anyone else; and since others will usually respond to being disliked by disliking in return, the person's self-concept of inadequacy is made to appear true. This is another example of the self-fulfilling prophecy discussed in Chapter 5.

As the child matures, he is constantly coming into contact with other people who may influence his self-concept. They respond to his

Acceptance of self	Acceptance of others	Personality traits exhibited
Good	Good	Healthy self-confidence, accepts responsibility, has faith in mankind, optimistic.
Good	Poor	Critical of others, overestimates own acceptability.
Poor	Good	Timid, modest, popular, feels open to attack.
Poor	Poor	Dissatisfied, dependent, frightened, great need for security, impulsive.

Figure 8–4.

Relationship of acceptance of self and acceptance of others to certain personality variables (adapted from Fey, 1957).

appearance, intelligence, verbal ability, temperament, or friendliness. Being treated by others as an attractive, intelligent, capable individual will help encourage a corresponding self-concept. If this self-concept agrees with the very early self-concept developed through the parents, the child is likely to mature into a healthily adjusted adult. On the other hand, being considered by others as an unclean, unintelligent, lazy person can create a corresponding self-concept. Even if the parent-child relationship is healthy, the negative reactions of later contacts with other people can partially undo the good the parents have accomplished. If—and this is more serious—the parent-child relationship was not good, later negative experiences will reinforce and perhaps make worse the already negative self-concept.

In any case, it would appear that changing the self-concept in a direction that contradicts the early learning from significant others becomes increasingly difficult as the person becomes older. This is why

The Early Years

psychologists place such great emphasis on. the importance of early parent-child relationships: they set the stage for the child's entire life.

Self-perpetuating Aspects of the Self-concept

Although the individual's self-concept develops in response to the responses of others, the responses of others are a direct reaction to the individual's self-concept. For example, the more frequently people on welfare are condemned as "no good and lazy," the less likely they are to seek work. They seem to be saying, "Since I'm lazy, I couldn't find work or do a good job anyway. Since I'm no good, why bother trying?" When they do get jobs, they may be unnecessarily sensitive to criticism. Then the rest of the community reacts by condemning them more strongly for being lazy or for being irritable when criticized. A few people rebel against the evaluation of others and do better than they otherwise would, but most accept the evaluation as largely true.

Community responses to welfare cases are self-perpetuated through the children of people who are on welfare. The children recognize that many people stereotype their parents as lazy, unintelligent, and unclean, and that these stereotypes are extended to them as well.

> These youngsters do not know who they are, what they can be, or even what they want to be. They are afraid, but they do not know of what. They are angry, but they do not know at whom. They are rejected, and they do not know why. So they make up answers. . . . And perhaps worst of all, they accept without question the world's judgment of them as not simply unlovable, uncultured failures, but as one such failure in a vast sea of failures (Washington, 1964).

If the children are members of certain minority groups, such as the black American, the American Indian, or Americans of Puerto Rican or Mexican ancestry, these feelings of failure may be intensified.

Other Influences of Significant Others

Significant others influence the lives of their children in other ways than in the development of the self-concept. First, they serve as models for behavior. Regardless of what parents tell children, the examples set by the parents are vitally important. When parents who swear insist that their children not swear, they are not really saying that swearing is wrong; they are saying swearing is wrong if someone is around to punish you for it, or swearing is wrong if you are a child. Second, parents provide most of the rewards and punishments in the early lives of their children. It is their smile or frown, their gift or slap, their love or rejection that means the most to the child. Later in life, other people also become important, but the parents are the most influential figures in the first few years, and they usually remain so.

Development of Love

Significant others are associated with warmth, love, and affection. They are also associated with the satisfaction of the infant's hunger, thirst, and temperature-regulation needs. When the parents are not there, discomfort remains; when they are there, discomfort ceases. When the parents are not there, love and affection are missing; when they are there, love and affection are present. Thus, the absence of parents is associated with the absence of those things that are important.

Because they are associated with such important satisfactions, the parents become valued for themselves. Just as some people like money for the sake of money rather than for what it will buy, infants come to love their parents for themselves rather than just as bringers of good things. This is the beginning of true love and affection.

Psychologists and psychiatrists have emphasized in many ways the importance of love and affection for infants, but a series of studies conducted over the past several years has captured the imagination of both laymen and professionals. Although this research has been carried on with monkeys rather than people, the implications for human beings are obvious.

Two "monkey mothers" were constructed, identical to each other except that one had a wire body and the other's body was made of sponge rubber and covered with terry cloth. Baby monkeys showed a strong preference for the terrycloth mother, even when they were fed by a bottle inserted through the wire mother. When frightened, the animals would run for the soft, cuddly mother (Harlow, 1958). The soft mother offered a type of reassurance, which might be compared to the physical affection the human mother offers her child. Later, these monkeys who were raised without normal mothers were themselves unable to perform adequately as mothers (Harlow & Harlow, 1962a). This result indicates that inadequate mothering will affect not only the children but even later generations.

Perhaps the major implication of these studies is that physical contact and cuddling are important for the proper development of infants and young children. Some people feel they have discharged their obligations as parents if they fulfill the physical needs of the child, such as food, clothing, housing, and basic cleanliness. Much evidence has been gathered suggesting that this minimal care provides only minimal benefits for the children. Again we face the double-barreled question: is inadequate physical contact a major factor in development, and if so, can those children who lacked sufficient cuddling make up for it later? Since we cannot go back in time, can we do anything to make up for lost time?

Offering a child love—not only physical affection but emotional warmth—is a great help in establishing a later healthy personality. The child develops the self-concept "I am lovable," which leads to feelings of adequacy and self-worth. You may recall that the needs for love and for self-esteem must be reasonably satisfied before an individual can become concerned with self-actualization.

Separation from Significant Others

A parent often must leave his child. The absence may be permanent, such as through death or some divorces; it may be temporary, when a parent is very ill, takes a long business trip, or is in the military or in prison. If the absence occurs before the child is 4 or 5 months old, his awareness of the world is probably not well enough developed to cause him to be upset. After this very early age, however, the infant has established enough rich associations with his parents that their extended absence might be very disturbing.

When a significant other leaves, the child may suffer **separation anxiety**. He senses that the source of love and satisfactions has left him, and he becomes fearful. Parents may notice that even when they leave for an evening, their child resents their absence. A child who wakes up in the middle of the night and finds a strange baby-sitter instead of his parents will become very frightened or upset. Of course, if the child knows the baby-sitter and has expected her to be there, his fear will be negligible. Even a schoolchild who comes home after school to find his mother unexpectedly away is likely to be frightened.

When a child whose mother died before he was 5 reaches maturity, he is more likely than average to be emotionally disturbed, to show signs of mental illness, or to be delinquent, unless an adequate replacement can be found or the father can do a good job of compensating. Types of separation other than death also lead to increased chances of later emotional problems (Barry & Lindemann, 1960).

Being separated from a parent produces emotional upset in two major ways: (1) The child has lost an important person upon whom he depended for many satisfactions; and the loss, which is reflected in great excitement and confusion in the home, is very disturbing. (2) A home with only one parent is often less stable because of pressures of money, the decreased time the remaining parent has available to spend with the child, and other factors. If the separation is caused by death, the child may become confused about the meaning of death and its effect on him; children often think of death as a punishment, and they may become afraid that they, too, will die soon.

Development of Human Behavior

The topic of death is rarely discussed in our society. People get fidgety and irritable when the matter is brought up, often claiming that it is too depressing to talk about. Nonetheless, death is part of life, and children eventually learn its significance. The relationship between separation anxiety and feelings regarding death is not fully understood, but fear of death in adulthood may be a direct result of early fears of being separated from a parent.

Separation anxiety has also been observed in children who entered a hospital or other institution when they were between 15 and 30 months of age, especially when circumstances allowed little or no contact with their parents. Their reactions occurred in three stages: (1) *protest,* when they showed active distress, crying, and eager searching; (2) *despair,* when they became withdrawn and inactive; and (3) *detachment,* when

Figure 8–5.

Apathy and withdrawal are commonly observed results when adult attention is lacking. Courtesy The Library of Congress.

they seemed to have recovered from despair, but in fact attempted to avoid emotional involvements with people (Bowlby, 1960).

Since infants and young children in hospitals and institutions often receive little personal attention and no affection from the busy nursing and institutional staffs, they lose their spirit and enjoyment of life. Even when given good physical care and diet, children in institutions develop more slowly and have a higher mortality rate than children raised in private homes. They are also more likely to have later behavior problems and to show apathy (Spitz, 1949).

> Roberta lost both her parents when she was 18 months old and was placed in an institution for children. A year later she was a tense, tearful child who fought constantly with others and could not adjust well to the nursery school the institution supported. At that point, she was referred to the institution's psychological clinic. For several months she met twice a week with one of the psychologists there and did nothing but play; the psychologist gave his full attention to Roberta, sometimes playing with her, sometimes just watching as she played. At the end of ten weeks, both Roberta's housemother and her nursery school teacher commented spontaneously that her behavior had improved greatly.

The changes in Roberta's behavior illustrate the importance of feeling loved and cared for. Although replacement figures can compensate for the absence of significant others to some extent, the best life situation for children undoubtedly occurs when significant others do not change.

Summary of Important Ideas

1. The physical condition of the expectant mother influences the well-being of her future child; her emotional state *perhaps* also has an influence.
2. Ways in which infants' behavior differs at birth include motor behavior, activity level, and responsiveness to noise.
3. At birth infants have a minimal awareness of their environment, although their sensory apparatus appears adequately developed. Development is rapid in the first few months.
4. The degree of warmth and autonomy provided by the parents, rather than specific child-rearing techniques, seems to have primary influence on later behavior and adjustment of the child.
5. Breast feeding is considered, *on the whole*, superior to bottle feeding, but parental love and affection are more important than the method of feeding.

6. Child-rearing practices in the United States are more severe than in most preliterate societies.

7. Toilet-training methods are important to the development of children, largely because parents place so much emphasis upon control.

8. A young child's evaluation of himself reflects the reactions of others toward him; the most important of these others, usually the parents, are called *significant others.*

9. Young children accept the views that significant others have of them, usually without criticism or evaluation.

10. The love of a child for his parents develops from the satisfaction they provide him, which includes satisfaction of his biological needs, in combination with his receiving warmth, affection, and autonomy from the parents.

11. When a significant other leaves, the child may exhibit signs of emotional disruption and separation anxiety.

Chapter Nine

The Developing Child

Chapter 8 focused largely on the biological, psychological, and social beginnings of human behavior, with emphasis on the first two years of life. The present chapter extends the concerns both in time and in space; it continues with the chronology of child development and also shows the child beginning to recognize the world beyond his parents.

*L*ife is not a series of time categories but a continuing flow that we describe in time periods for convenience. The total human personality and all aspects of this personality develop and change continuously throughout the life-span. Personality development is most remarkable during the years of childhood and depends to an appreciable extent upon the parent-child relationship.

The Parent-child Relationship

The satisfaction that a child feels with himself, his life, and the world around him often reflects the satisfaction felt by his parents. Parents happy in their marriage, in their work, in their social relationships, and in their general approach to life seem to be better parents. Parents who are bitter, frustrated, and unfriendly often allow their unhappiness to interfere with their relationships with children.

The mother, unable to have the concert career she had desired, pushes her daughter into seeking a concert career, for which she is not capable.

The father, disliking his wife and distrusting women in general, convinces his son that women are to be avoided.

The father, a failure at work, is a tyrant in his own home, the only place where anyone listens to him.

The mother, unhappy in her marriage to a cold, aloof husband, turns all her attention to her son, whom she coddles and overprotects.

Unhappy and poorly adjusted children do not inevitably result from unhappy parents, nor do happy parents inevitably have happy children, but the chances are much more favorable for these relationships than for the opposite. Among the many factors related to healthy parent-child relationships are (1) the parents' ability to allow the children freedom and responsibility, (2) the children's opportunity to express their feelings, (3) the degree to which the children have been aided in self-actualization, and (4) parental methods of controlling or disciplining behavior.

Allowing Freedom and Responsibility

Freedom and responsibility go together. Children need to receive freedom and responsibility when they are young and to an increasing degree as they mature, so that they will be accustomed to independence when they begin college, move away from home, or take their first job. Parents who overprotect their child, for whatever reason, are not preparing him adequately for adult life. Children need to be allowed to grow up and to leave home, without feeling that they are hurting their parents. (In some societies grown children would not wish to leave their parents, but we are here concerned with the mainstream of Western culture.)

Parents face a major dilemma. On the one hand, children have definite limitations, and they will inevitably fail at certain tasks and make incorrect decisions. On the other hand, in order to mature into self-sufficient adults, children need to try difficult tasks and make difficult decisions. An adult may "know better" than the child, but the child has to find out for himself much of the time; an adult may "do it better," but the child wants to do it himself.

Danny, at 12 months, refused to take any food that he could not get to his mouth through his own efforts, and this included ice cream, which he loved. His parents had to watch him go through strenuous effort and many spills in order to eat. It was hard on the floor, on his clothes, and on his parents, but Danny showed great pleasure in his achievements.

Lee's parents were in a hurry, and her father lifted her into the family car for a quick get-away. Lee protested loudly, scrambled out of the car, glared at her father, then pulled herself into the vehicle without help.

The Developing Child

Riding a bicycle, getting dressed, drawing grandmother a birthday card, crossing the street without help, all are ways in which children establish that they are autonomous, competent individuals. Parents who are overprotective prevent their children from developing freedom and responsibility and may encourage them to become highly dependent or else may provoke aggressive rebellion.

Children mature at different rates, and not all children of the same age will be sufficiently mature to take the same responsibilities or be given the same freedoms. One 10-year-old can be trusted to go shopping for his mother, but another cannot; 12-year-old Ted can be believed when he says his homework is completed, but 12-year-old Tom must be checked.

It seems logical that children who are prevented from taking appropriate responsibility and freedom will develop a self-concept of being inadequate: "My parents don't think I'm competent, so I guess I'm not competent." On the other hand, children who are pushed into responsibilities long before they are ready may feel their parents are rejecting them; also, they are likely to fail at their tasks and as a result develop a self-concept of inadequacy. The most successful children seem to be those who are encouraged to take responsibility at appropriate age levels and whose parents can tolerate mistakes and misjudgments as part of the child's process of growing up.

Statements Children Can Get Along Without

1. You know I love you—look how much money I spend on you.
2. Your brother likes to kiss me—he must love me more than you do.
3. You're my child—you're supposed to love me and respect me.
4. When I was your age, things weren't so easy.
5. If I only had had the chances you kids get today.
6. Do you always have to do what the other kids are doing? If they all jumped off the Golden Gate (or Brooklyn or any other) Bridge, I suppose you would jump off also.
7. I used to love helping my mother around the house.
8. When you get older, you'll think back to all the time you wasted.
9. I don't know what's going to become of you when you get older.
10. It took me a long time to realize that my parents knew what they were talking about, and I always regretted not paying attention to them sooner.
11. Do you always have to spend your money on such trash?
12. Is that any way to talk to your parents?
13. I don't know why you can't do it—your sister always did it that way.

Development of Human Behavior

Communicating Feelings

Parents have feelings, and so do children. Both have the right to express their feelings. There are occasions when a mother is entitled to become angry with her child; there are times when children are entitled to express unhappiness with their parents' actions. If the basic relationship is good, and if the parents do not threaten to withdraw their love or administer violent physical punishment, an expression of anger may actually improve the situation. Children and parents can learn to respect the emotional expressions of each other if they are secure in their relationship.

Good communication consists of more than freedom to express feelings. Ideas, wishes, plans, and activities also need to be communicated from parents to children and from children to parents. Some parents are always too busy to explain things, and others are always too busy to listen. Both sets of parents are inhibiting the ease of communication that should be available between parents and children. Children do not need to be told everything that is going on or permitted complete conversational control—parents deserve privacy and a life of their own —but children are members of the family, and members of a group are entitled to be listened to and to be informed.

Helping Children Self-actualize

Most parents wish to see their children make as much of their own talents as they possibly can, whether the talents involve artistic ability, sales ability, administrative ability, technical ability, or social ability. Parents are often less aware of their role in helping their child become more himself, which is also part of the child's process of self-actualization. Adults are often intent on bringing up their child to be as much like the parents as possible, regardless of how the child feels.

Consideration of Maslow's need hierarchy may be useful in discussing how parents can help their children self-actualize. Parents would never purposely deprive their children of adequate food or sleep, and lack of fulfillment of survival needs is seldom a problem in the United States. Nonetheless, parents may, often without realizing it, deny sufficient satisfaction of stimulation needs. By doing too much for a child, an unthinking adult may inadvertently stifle the child's need to explore and manipulate his environment.

Maureen, a very pretty 3-year-old whose parents both worked, was left with a full-time maid. The maid, a gentle, elderly woman, became very much attached to Maureen and soon developed the need for Maureen to be dependent on her. She slept with Maureen when the child napped, refused to let her play at other children's homes, and even fed her, although Maureen could easily feed herself. Maureen became dependent on the maid and soon internalized the self-concept that she was helpless, a self-concept that the maid unknowingly encouraged.

Not only was Maureen overprotected, but she was also overindulged. She was always able to get what she wanted by crying or throwing a tantrum. The maid was so afraid of losing the child's affection and so devoted to her that she frequently spent her own salary on gifts for the girl. Maureen made occasional attempts to break away by playing with other children, but the maid hovered around, and the other children soon preferred to avoid this well-meaning, but irritating, supervision. When offered the alternative of a dish of ice cream with "the kids" or a walk to the store with the maid, Maureen decided to take the walk. (P.S. The maid bought her ice cream anyway.)

Overprotection is not the only way of restricting the satisfaction of children's stimulation needs. Some parents are overly punitive and frighten their children from exploring their environment. Others worry that new activities might be too time-consuming, too demanding, or too dangerous for the child, so they always do things for him.

Safety needs and love needs interact dynamically with each other. Parents who show their child much love and affection are also providing the child with a sense of security. A parental show of affection can rarely be an error, unless the love has strings attached or is so overwhelming that it smothers the child. "I'll love you if . . ." is not really giving love, but trading love. What husband would appreciate hearing his wife say, "If you buy me a new dress, I'll love you"?

Some parents, because of their own upbringing, find it difficult to show physical affection or even other forms of love. Nonetheless, children seem to sense when they are loved and, also important, respected. To say that parents should respect their children does not imply that the children be allowed to dominate their parents, but that they be treated as unique and worthwhile individuals, in spite of their immaturity. Even those adults who provide security and love for their children do not always show their children this sort of respect. They may repeatedly communicate to their children how immature they are and how dependent they are upon the parents. By emphasizing their children's inadequacies, the parents may be encouraging in them a lack of self-esteem.

What about self-actualization? How can parents take positive steps, over and above more general considerations such as love and respect, to help their children use their talents? There are innumerable answers to this question, of which the following are only a few:

1. Reading to children, even before they can understand all that is said, will expose them to the immense world of words and books.

Children whose early contacts with books are happy ones are not so likely to find books and words a problem in school. Perhaps equally important, a period set aside each day for reading will assure the child that he can share a pleasant, relaxed few minutes with his parent—even when he knows every word of his favorite book by heart.

2. Children ask many questions, often foolish ones and sometimes impossible-to-answer ones. Asking questions is their way of learning about the world, and the adult who tries to answer them truthfully is reassuring and satisfying.

3. Children need to spend time with their parents, to do things together with them. Having a picnic, going for a drive, or taking a walk are simple things families can easily do together. Fathers in particular, since they are away from the home so much, can greatly enrich the father-child relationship by having some type of activity they can share with their children. In France, it is common for a father to take his children somewhere on Thursday afternoon (school is not in session then), while mother stays home.

4. There comes a period for each child when he wants to learn to count or read or tell time—which marks an opportunity for the parents to encourage him, without pushing him. A warm, noncritical parental attitude of encouragement will probably do more good in the long run than any specific learning that might occur. If the child has been bribed or pressured into learning the alphabet, his success in school is not necessarily improved just because he knows something sooner than the other children; but if his knowledge grew out of his own motivation, such learning may be advantageous.

5. Children benefit from an appreciation not just of books, but also of art and music, of nature and science, of the behavior of machines and the behavior of people, of white-collar work and blue-collar work. The ability to appreciate a diversity of activities, interests, and people will help a child discover his own talents and respect the talents of others.

Self-actualization does not come about automatically when parents follow a rigid set of rules. Rather, it develops slowly when parents satisfy the more basic needs and provide an exciting and stimulating environment, while respecting the child's individuality and his need to succeed in his own unique way.

Placing Limits on Behavior

When children are born, they do not know how society expects them to behave. Their parents take on the responsibility of placing limits on their behavior to make it acceptable. In different families, different sorts of limits will be established. One family will allow the child to play

The Developing Child

in mud; another will not. One family will keep the child out of the living room; another will give the child freedom to play in any room.

Once the limits are set, children appear to be better adjusted if the limits are enforced consistently. To discipline a child for throwing the jelly spoon at his sister on one occasion, but to laugh about it on another occasion, is an example of inconsistent limits on behavior. The child is uncertain as to what is expected of him.

The methods used to keep behavior within limits are also important. Whereas punishment is probably the most common approach to maintaining limits, other methods are also available. Too much use of punishment merely draws attention to the forbidden act, but does not reinforce the correct response. Like the teaching machines that give no response for a wrong answer but reward the right one, parents can often find a way to ignore improper behavior and reward correct behavior.

Punishment has other dangers: it may cause the child to become angry with the parent for the punishment, instead of with himself for the improper act; it can induce frustration, which may lead to future aggressive behavior; it can become unnecessarily severe and cause undue pain or overly severe restrictions; it indicates incorrect behavior, but may ignore correct behavior.

Such arguments against punishment do not imply that discipline, controls, or even punishment are never effective. The child may endanger himself by shoving a nail into an open socket; he may endanger others by ramming his tricycle into a playmate; or he may endanger property by twirling a large stick close to a breakable lamp. In each of these instances, the adult may be able to reduce the danger in the child's behavior without resorting to punishment, but sometimes the unique demands of the situation require punishment. How would you, in each of the above situations, change the behavior without the use of punishment?

Interestingly, children may interpret parental lack of limits as an indication that the parents do not really care.

> "It was raining cats and dogs that day—I must have been about 9—and I asked my father if I should wear my rubbers. He told me to do what I thought was best. Well, I knew what was best, but I wanted him to tell me, because it seemed like he didn't really care. He wouldn't, so I went without my rubbers and caught a terrible cold. I hated my father for giving me that cold, and I hated him more because he reminded me that I made the decision."

The maturation level of children is an important factor in the type of limits set upon their behavior and the sort of enforcement used. Very young children do not understand language well enough to respond to

Figure 9–1.

Children enjoy expressing themselves through music and art. *Top:* Courtesy Antioch College News Bureau. *Bottom:* Courtesy UCLA Extension: Arts and Humanities Division.

"Don't!" Thus a mild slap on the hand may be necessary. Of course, parents who take necessary precautions in child-proofing their house will avoid many problems.

At certain ages, children do not recognize the significance of what they are doing. They may spread jam on the tablecloth, shoot big brother's dart gun at the neighbor's baby, or curl up and sleep underneath Aunt Molly's car parked in the driveway. Sometimes they will hit another child as a release for their own frustrations. Constant punishment for acts they do not understand may be highly frustrating, especially for very active children. Still worse is disciplining a child for failing at something beyond his physical or intellectual powers to achieve. A child who is not ready to be toilet-trained or who is not ready to memorize the alphabet will find punishment extremely frustrating, and it will be of little value in producing the desired behavior.

Considerable doubt exists about whether a spanking is more cruel or less cruel than having the child miss a planned-for movie or keeping him in from playing. We do know, however, that a spanking in combination with reasoning works much better than a spanking by itself, and that warm, loving mothers get better results from spanking than do cold, aloof mothers (Sears, Maccoby, & Levin, 1957). Studies of underdeveloped societies indicate that more theft occurs in groups that are very punitive than in groups that show great love toward their children, implying that stealing may be a way to make up for not feeling loved (Bacon, Child, & Barry, 1963). In these instances at least, harsh physical punishment certainly did not lead to more responsible behavior.

Each parent has to work out a system of enforcing limits that is appropriate for his own personality, his child's personality, and the specific set of circumstances involved. After an argument with her father-in-law, a mother may be harsher in punishing her son; after a fatiguing day at work, a father may not have the energy to discipline his daughter; after an especially exciting birthday party, a child may need to unwind before going to bed. Children and parents can adjust to each other's habits and to individual circumstances, as long as the children never feel that parental love may be withdrawn.

Real parental love does not depend on whether the child eats his cereal, refrains from hitting his baby sister, or gets good grades in school. Parents who threaten to withdraw their love for any reason imply that their love is neither very strong nor very dependable. Their love is not given freely, but must be earned. Such threats—like brutal physical punishment, which is used more to satisfy the parents than to discipline the child—may produce the immediate behavior desired but will also bring about long-range feelings of anxiety, resentment, and fear. Such parental behavior will probably have more harmful effects in the long run.

Giving Children "Antiparent" Weapons

Children, except those in **overindulgent** homes, cannot command their parents directly; they must find indirect methods. Infants may learn that going for long periods without eating is a good way to gain attention; spitting up food and vomiting are also effective in upsetting and controlling parents. At age 3, bed-wetting or soiling, especially if the parents have been bragging about how clean their children are, is a wonderful way to annoy adults. Even if children are punished for their behavior, they have learned how effective their misdeeds can be—the punishment may actually convince them that they "have a good thing." Constant whining may be the best way for 4-year-olds to get a rise out of Mom and Dad.

Older children may use more obvious forms of aggression. When 4-year-old Tod says, "Daddy, you're pooey," his father merely responds, "Oh?" However, the father of 4-year-old David gets angry and gives a stern lecture. David now has a weapon he can use against his father, whenever he is willing to risk punishment.

Although punishing children may be effective, it draws attention to the incorrect behavior and does nothing to emphasize the proper behavior. Parents who insist upon the correct behavior and then reward the child for doing the correct thing are usually doing a more effective job of inducing the child to behave in an acceptable fashion than are the parents who punish the wrong behavior but do nothing more. The former are applying principles of operant learning to the situation, since positive reinforcement often seems to be more effective in changing behavior than negative reinforcement in the form of punishment (see Chapter 4). Nonetheless, mild punishments, even spankings, may be useful in certain situations, and no evidence is available that mild punishment is, in itself, harmful.

Development of Internalized Attitudes

So far the chapter has emphasized the parents' role in the parent-child relationship. However, we are not concerned with the parents' behavior for its own sake, but with the effect it has upon the child. As the child matures, he moves farther from the sphere of direct parental influence. Knowing this fact, parents try to teach their children, while they are still very young, behavior patterns and attitudes that they will follow the rest of their lives.

Before a child is 3, he has begun to develop a sense of what is considered right and what is considered wrong. At first this occurs without his questioning or knowing what he is doing. As his parents punish him for this and reward him for that, the child learns what is expected of him. He also learns from observing how his parents behave.

Since the significant others in a child's life are *the world* for him, he accepts their ideas and their behavior as correct. This acceptance leads to the process of **internalization**, through which the child accepts his

Figure 9–2.

Children learn many actions by observing their parents. Photograph by John G. Warford.

parents' ideas and values as his own. When he is older, the child will also internalize the ideas of others in his society; he will learn these ideas through his friends, through school, and through what he reads and hears and sees about him. However, in the beginning years, the parents provide almost the only source of **values**.

The values that the child internalizes have a strong influence on his behavior, because his own sense of right and wrong, rather than fear of outside authority, controls his actions. This value system, through which a person approves or disapproves of his own actions, thoughts, and feelings, is the conscience.

To some extent, the development of the conscience and of other internalized values is conscious. The child observes his parents enjoying reading, so he picks up a book—even though he may hold it upside down. He internalizes the value that reading is "good" and "proper." However, the greater part of the process of acquiring conscience is **unconscious**. As the mother and daughter walk down the street, the mother spies a mangy stray dog and yanks her child away. Shortly after, the girl wants to pet another dog, but her mother tells her not to, that it is probably dirty. Slowly the child builds into her own belief system the value that dogs are to be avoided. She has internalized, or taken for herself, her mother's attitude toward dogs. Thereafter, when she wants to pet a dog, her conscience may tell her that it is wrong. These values will interact, in a dynamic fashion, with her personal experiences with dogs.

Sometimes, personal experiences contradict internalized values, but more frequently they are interpreted to support previously held beliefs: the young girl who had internalized the belief that dogs are bad may see a friendly dog run toward her but will interpret its behavior as potentially vicious. Since the sight of the dog has undoubtedly created a feeling of fear and tension, avoiding the dog will reduce the tension. Thus, the act of avoiding the dog is reinforced because of the reduction of fear, and therefore this behavior probably will be repeated on later occasions. In this way the value that dogs are bad and that avoiding them is good will be reinforced, just as the infant's pleasurable response to his mother was reinforced (see page 63). That is, the avoidance of discomforting stimuli can be just as reinforcing as receiving pleasurable stimuli.

The process of internalizing values can be seen very clearly in young children:

> Seth Regan, a bright 3-year-old, had been carefully taught not to color on the floor. One afternoon, his mother heard loud shouts and slaps from Seth's room. She raced in and saw Seth slapping his hand as hard as he could, shouting, "No! Naughty! Don' do dat!" Then she saw that he had accidentally crayoned off the drawing paper and onto the floor.

Shame and Guilt

There are three basic reasons why an individual avoids doing something he would like to do and has the capability to do: (1) he recognizes that the punishment will be too great; (2) he experiences **shame**, the feeling that his family or country or some valued group would disapprove of his actions; and (3) his conscience or internalized values will not let him—that is, he feels it is wrong, or feels **guilt**. In many situations, all three feelings occur. For example, a young man would like to avoid military service, but will not pretend he has poor hearing or vision, which would allow him to stay out. Why? Because (1) he is afraid of the punishment if the faking is uncovered; (2) he knows that friends and family would be ashamed of him; and (3) he feels such behavior is unethical and unfair to others. The last two reasons may be understood in terms of the unhappiness produced by too great a difference between self-concept and ideal self.

For most Americans and Europeans, internalized values and conscience are the major restraints against committing unethical and illegal acts. Americans will feel a sense of guilt when they do something to violate their consciences. Not only overt behavior, but even thoughts and feelings may elicit guilt so disturbing that the individual will avoid the action, the thought, or the feeling in order to avoid the disrupting sense of guilt. You often are confronted with the knowledge that you could do something unethical or illegal with little chance of being punished; yet you behave honestly. The feeling of shame may enter into your decision, but the chances are that you wish to avoid the extreme discomfort caused by a guilty conscience.

In Japan, and elsewhere in Asia, the emphasis is not on guilt but on shame, especially on bringing shame to the family (Benedict, 1946). Thus, Japanese tend to be very polite to their friends and in their own homes because they wish to avoid shame. However, they may be very rude in crowded department stores and rush-hour subways, where no one can identify them and cause shame to occur. The American, who typically is more polite in public, is more likely than the Japanese to show rude behavior to family and friends.

In both **shame societies** and **guilt societies**, the family and the home are probably the greatest influences on behavior. The American conscience and the Japanese sense of shame will not develop adequately if they are not given encouragement by significant others. If children do not have respect or affection for their parents, they will not internalize parental attitudes (if American) or worry about bringing shame to the family name (if Japanese).

Investigations have disclosed that American children who were reported to have strong consciences had been brought up in families that used praise and reasoning rather than physical punishment. These children were shown warmth and acceptance by their parents and thus were more inclined to internalize the values of their parents while maintaining a positive self-concept. Children of warm and loving mothers were more likely to develop healthy consciences than children of cold and aloof mothers (Yarrow, Campbell, & Burton, 1968). Although parents usually wish their children to be influenced by their conscience, some parents may encourage their children to develop an unnecessarily strong conscience.

> Mary Fogarty was a physically affectionate mother, but she also demanded a great deal from her children. Whenever one of her children showed the slightest sign of misbehaving, Mary threatened to withdraw her love from him, and she would give extra attention to her other children. By being so affectionate, Mary gained the devotion of her children. Once having gained their devotion, she was able to force them to meet her demands, because failure was punished by rejection and obvious favoring of the other children. As the Fogarty children grew older, even thoughts of disobeying their mother caused anxiety and feelings of guilt.
>
> Jack Fogarty, Mary's oldest child, was especially afraid of his mother's disapproval. He developed an exaggerated sense of guilt. On one occasion, his teacher stated that one of the students had broken a classroom window during the lunch hour. Although Jack was in the cafeteria with several of his friends during the entire lunch period, he felt compelled to explain to his teacher that he had not been responsible, even though no one suggested he had been. Another time, a teacher announced that she had caught a student cheating on an examination. Again, Jack, who had never been accused of the incident, needed to tell her he was not involved.

In Western nations, if no sense of guilt exists, there is little control of behavior, since, in many instances, neither fear of punishment nor avoidance of shame provides adequate motivation. However, although lack of conscience is a matter of serious concern, the opposite is equally a problem. Some people have an exaggerated conscience and feel guilty about actions, thoughts, and feelings that are not expected to elicit guilt.

Some typical behavior patterns emerge from chronic and intense guilt feelings. Examples include the person who is always apologizing for anything that might even remotely be interpreted as wrong; the person who is afraid to make a decision for fear that his decision will hurt someone's feelings; or the person who is so worried that his actions will be seen as "bad" that he is unable to concentrate upon the important, day-to-day tasks of living.

Psychologists attempt to reduce these irrational or exaggerated guilt feelings through psychotherapy. Have you ever experienced guilt that was so strong you could not concentrate on your studies?

Sex Role

The impact of internalized values is especially strong when sex roles become involved. The proper behavior for males and females is a part of the social structure of every society, and the person who behaves inconsistently with what is expected of his sex is a partial outcast in his community.

Sex-role behavior is learned from three basic sources: first, from observing the parent of the same sex as a model and by behaving as he does; second, by internalizing his values as they relate to sex role; and, third, from being rewarded by significant others (and, to a lesser extent, by other people) for appropriate behavior, while being punished—or at least unrewarded—for inappropriate behavior.

From the very earliest years, boys and girls are treated differently. Children learn what sex they are almost as soon as they learn their names, and even children of 2½ years are aware of proper sex roles (Vener & Snyder, 1966). Boys and girls are dressed differently, given different toys to play with, and rewarded for different sorts of behavior. Young girls are given dolls and encouraged to hold them like "Mother holds baby sister"; young boys are given trucks and airplanes. Boys are often allowed to get dirty or to be noisy, but girls may be punished, if only by a hard look, for exactly the same behavior.

The older the child becomes, the more important he finds it to behave in ways considered proper for his sex. He is also likely to find it more difficult, since the community often makes conflicting demands. Thus, parents communicate the importance of high academic achievement to their sons, at the same time assuming that intellectual activity may be somewhat unmanly and that school might be restrictive. Girls, on the other hand, "are expected to . . . accept the schooling process, but they are assumed not to be capable of serious intellectual achievement." In addition, school success may be seen as much less important for girls than for boys (Stone & Church, 1968).

What happens to the development of the sex role in single-parent families? Different studies suggest somewhat different patterns, but there is evidence that the absence of the parent of the same sex as the child is more critical than the absence of the parent of the opposite sex. Rates of delinquency and school dropouts increased when the parent of the same sex was absent because of death or divorce (Gregory, 1965). Boys who lost their fathers while they were still preschoolers exhibited less typically masculine behavior; for example, they were less aggressive and less interested in body-contact sports (Hetherington, 1966). Even chances for later marital satisfaction diminish somewhat if the parent of the same sex is absent (Renne, 1968).

Contact with adults of both sexes is probably helpful in learning proper sex-role behavior. The girl, for example, needs a woman whom she can imitate and whose values she can internalize. She also needs a man, so that she can observe how men treat women and how women respond to this type of treatment. If one parent is missing, the children may turn to other relatives, family friends, teachers, or other community members to learn their sex role. What would you predict to be the sex-role development of a boy brought up in a home where the parents are divorced, the father has disappeared, and the mother frequently criticizes men in the harshest terms?

When the wife completely dominates the husband, the children may not know whose behavior patterns to internalize—those of the strong mother or the weak father. The same problem occurs when one parent is very cold or hostile to the children and the other is warm and affectionate. The child of the same sex as the unpleasant parent does not want to be like that parent; yet, if he becomes like the admired or affectionate parent, he will internalize the attitudes and behaviors of the opposite sex.

Freud's explanation for the development of the sex role suggests that the male child, at around 3 years of age, develops an extremely strong attachment to his mother, even to the point of wishing to replace his father in his mother's affections. At the same time, he begins to fear his father, who, being bigger and stronger, might hurt him if he really competed for the mother. During the next few years, the boy learns that although his mother loves him, she restricts her more intimate feelings to his father. Finally, the boy realizes that he cannot win in the competition with his father, and so he attempts to become as much as possible like the man his mother loves. In this way, a boy begins to imitate his father and to internalize the father's values and behavior, and thus learns the male sex role.

There seems little doubt that the best situation for proper sex-role development occurs when both parents are warm, have a good relationship with each other, provide a good parent-child relationship for their children, and do not deviate too far from acceptable sex-role behavior. However, as is so often the case, the absence of the situations listed above does not doom a child to later sex-role problems.

Development of Aggressiveness and Dependency

Like conscience and the sex role, aggressiveness and dependency develop through interaction between the child (his inherited behavioral

The role of the American boy differs from the role of the boy in Saudi Arabia. Courtesy Standard Oil Company (N.J.).

predispositions and his previous experiences) and significant others. The influence of significant others is much more complicated than people often assume. It is naïve to accept the popular notion that all that parents need to do to avoid dependent or aggressive behavior in their children is offer them love and security (Yarrow, Campbell, & Burton, 1968). Nonetheless, love and security are undoubtedly important factors.

All people have aggressive feelings, especially after a frustrating experience; similarly, all people have the need to be dependent upon others on occasion. Both aggressive behavior and dependent behavior are frequently punished when children exhibit them openly. The child who hits a playmate over the head with a metal truck is more likely to be punished than the child who never leaves his mother's side, but neither behavior is considered appropriate for a growing child.

Aggressiveness

Most healthy, normal children express some aggressive behavior. Parents who punish aggression, expecially when the punishment is physical, seem to encourage further aggression by their children. If the children are afraid of expressing their aggression directly, they may do so indirectly, perhaps through their play or their fantasies (Sears et al., 1957).

However, parents who completely overlook aggressive behavior do not reduce aggression either. One investigation revealed that the least aggressive children have parents who showed they dislike aggressive behavior, but did not use physical punishment or extreme threats of punishment. The most aggressive children had parents who provoked aggressive behavior by using physical punishment frequently, but did not show particular disapproval when their children were aggressive (Sears et al., 1957).

Dependency

When a child is punished for aggressive behavior, he feels frustrated, and his own aggressive acts multiply. Similarly, when a child is punished for being dependent, he becomes more dependent, probably because of fears that his parents are rejecting him as an individual when they reject his attempts at being dependent. Recent research has verified that these relationships exist (McCord, McCord, & Verden, 1962; Sears et al., 1957).

Healthy dependency will cause the child to wish to please his parents, so that he will internalize their values and, eventually, the proper sex role. In Sears' study, the unhealthily dependent children had parents who were either rejecting and punitive or else **overprotective**

(Sears et al., 1957). Children who are prevented from exploring the world while they are young, either because their parents are too fearful or too restrictive, may be afraid to explore later. Such children develop a self-concept of being people who need their parents, rather than a self-concept of being independent and self-sufficient. Children who feel loved and therefore secure have a self-concept of being adequate people, and are not afraid to venture into the world at the proper time.

Relationships with Other Children

Although the parents are the most meaningful significant others, other people become increasingly important to children as they grow older. Both playmates and **siblings**, a term used to indicate both brothers and sisters, are among the most influential of these other people.

Sibling Rivalry

The first child in the family has no competition at all—until a sibling is born. The first child has the full attention of his parents—he is king. Then a competitor appears on the scene. Not only is he a competitor, but he seems a very successful competitor. All the aunts and uncles and grandparents and friends who used to tell 4-year-old Joey how cute he was, now tell Joey how cute Lisa is. To top it all off, Joey's mother was taken away to the hospital, while Joey was shipped off to live with grandmother. As soon as he returned, he was warned, "Shut up, keep out of the way, and don't bother the baby."

After this introduction, Joey is expected to show love, loyalty, devotion, and respect to the little monkey that cries at all hours, cannot even talk, and is absolutely no fun to play with. Often, the result is **sibling rivalry**, an intense competition between two children in the same family, frequently leading to hostile feelings.

To some extent, older children can be prepared for the arrival of a new sibling.

Leah, aged 2½, was well prepared for the birth of a new sibling. She felt the movement in her mother's "tummy" and even claimed, "I have a baby in my tummy, too." She took great pride in becoming a big sister, a feeling her parents encouraged, and she was made to feel that

Development of Human Behavior

the baby would be hers as much as her parents'. When the baby arrived, her parents made an extra fuss over Leah and depended upon her help in various ways, such as getting diapers out of the drawer and patting the baby's back when he needed to be burped.

Jerry was 3½ when his sister was born. His parents talked about the coming baby and told Jerry he would love her and protect her; but when the baby came, Jerry was shushed, ignored, told to play outside, and rarely allowed to see the baby. When he did see his sister, he was instructed to kiss her and fuss over her. Within a few months, Jerry had learned that the best attack was to pretend to be showing affection; while apparently kissing his sister, he would bite or pinch her. His parents punished him severely, and Jerry withdrew completely from his sister. In later years, his sister turned out to be a very popular girl, but Jerry had very little to do with her.

When the older child is not properly prepared for the new sibling and not allowed to play a part in the new infant's life, several forms of reaction can occur: (1) active or subtle aggression directed against the baby; (2) increased attempts to gain attention from the parents, including—if necessary—naughty behavior, even though it may be punished; (3) attempts to get even with the parents; (4) withdrawal from the parents, to avoid the possibility of further emotional hurt; (5) **regression**, or returning to earlier forms of behavior such as bed wetting, crying, or wanting a bottle.

Sibling rivalry can become intense and bitter, since the children are fighting for the attention of the most important people they know. Some parents make matters worse by comparing them with each other: "Robert made good grades in school—why can't you?" "Mary Jean didn't wet her panties when she was 3."

Occasionally, sibling rivalry is so intense that grown children are afraid to leave home, for fear that the remaining sibling will oust them from the good graces of the family. Most incidents of severe sibling rivalry disappear after the children go to college or establish their own homes. By then, the individuals have achieved a sense of personal adequacy without being so dependent upon their parents. However, the effects do not always disappear.

Playmates and Friends

Friendship among young children is usually limited to children in the immediate neighborhood and to children brought to visit by family friends. These peer-group friendships become more stable over the years, until—by third or fourth grade—a child may feel very uncomfortable when moving into a strange community (Hurlock, 1959).

The Developing Child

Early social relationships may be very important for later adjustment. Generalizing from laboratory studies with monkeys, social relationships among those of the same age group grow stronger with maturation, but mother-child relationships weaken (Harlow & Harlow, 1967). These healthy social relationships are enriching, and may partially compensate for inadequate parent-child relationships. Motherless monkeys who were allowed to play with each other showed normal social development, but comparable monkeys with no play opportunity were severely retarded socially (Harlow & Harlow, 1962b).

Children are not very subtle in their behavior. If they do not like a particular child, they will let him know it. The unpopular preschool child is described as one who "attacks vigorously, strikes frequently, or pushes and pulls." Other traits which lead to unpopularity include overdependence on adults, unwillingness to accept the routine of other children, and disrespect for the property of others (Hurlock, 1959).

In later childhood, playmates are usually of the same sex; and social class, race, and religion begin to influence friendships. Personality is undoubtedly as important as any other quality in leading to the avoidance of certain people. The value of being accepted by a friendship group is very important to people of all ages. Children are no exception.

Importance of Play

Children's play is very important to proper development, although adults may think of it merely as a pleasant way for children to pass time. One reason for the importance of play is that it provides initial experience in entering into social relationships with others of the same age. At first, children play by themselves. Soon, they enjoy having another child around during their play; however, each child will play with his own things, by himself. The only contact between the two may be arguments when both want the same toy at the same time. This kind of play is known as **parallel play**, since the children are not interacting. When they are about 2½ or 3, children begin to play with each other, although if one child is older, play may begin much earlier. Through such play, they learn the need for sharing and for give-and-take.

Play also allows children to use their imaginations. They can act out the behavior of their parents through playing house; they can travel to the zoo, take an airplane trip, or visit the planet Mars, all through the wonderful device of play. At the same time, they can try out new roles by being Mommy or Daddy, and thus experiment with their future behavior.

Children have many aggressive feelings that are not permitted direct expression but can be expressed through play. A young child who is angry with his parents may gain some satisfaction by punishing a doll;

a boy who has been spanked for breaking a dish can build a skyscraper of blocks and smash it to the floor.

Many other feelings besides aggression can be expressed through play. The little girl who is very attentive to her doll may be behaving as her mother has behaved with her, or she may be trying to compensate for a lack of maternal affection. (Can you suggest other interpretations?) She imagines herself as the doll, and thus can receive from mother (herself) the love she does not receive from her real mother.

Another benefit of play is that it leads to learning. This learning may take the form of new motor skills, such as hopping or skipping; increased verbal ability, which results from trying to communicate with others; and increased ability to understand and get along with others. Play gives children exercise, provides excitement, and is entertaining.

The attitude of adults can contribute to the value and pleasure of play or can detract from it. Adults limit the value of play when they demand quiet, interfere or make frequent suggestions, constantly ask questions, tease, or try to show the child "how to do it right." To encourage appropriate play, adults can treat each individual child with respect, allow him freedom to make noise and get dirty (unless there are good reasons not to), enjoy the child's enjoyment, and provide him with toys that stimulate his imagination.

Figure 9–4.

Creative play provides many excellent learning opportunities for children. Courtesy Columbia Broadcasting System.

The Developing Child

Childhood friendships and play are part of normal development, and they provide a necessary channel for the satisfaction of many important needs. However, in the case of most children, healthy parent-child relationships are undoubtedly the major factor in producing healthy adjustment and the possibility of self-actualization in later years.

Summary of Important Ideas

1. Parents who are satisfied with their own lives seem to be better parents. They are more likely to permit their children the proper balance of freedom and responsibility.

2. Many parents desire to see their children self-actualize through optimum development of their talents. Unfortunately, not all parents are able to create the best environment for such development.

3. Certain limits need to be placed on the behavior of children. These limits should be enforced with consistency, but with minimal punishment.

4. The child begins to develop a conscience when he is 3 years old. He tends to accept the values and behavior of significant others as his own and to incorporate them into his conscience. This process is called *internalization*.

5. Inappropriate behavior is prevented by shame, by guilt or conscience, or by fear of punishment. Some cultures emphasize shame, and others maintain control through guilt.

6. An appropriate amount of conscience is more likely to be developed by children brought up in warm, loving homes. In some instances, conscience and resulting guilt feelings become unnecessarily self-punishing.

7. Proper sex-role behavior is part of the social structure of every society. Interaction with people of both sexes aids in the development of acceptable sex roles.

8. All people experience aggressive feelings and dependent feelings.

9. Sibling rivalry often develops between two children in the same family.

10. Social relationships with age peers are very important, even to young children. Such relationships can, to some extent, compensate for inadequate parent-child relationships.

11. Play enables children to learn to get along with others, to use their imaginations, to express many feelings indirectly, and to learn new motor and verbal skills.

Chapter Ten

Adolescence and the Beginnings of Young Adulthood

As your reading progressed from Chapter 7 to the present chapter, you may have noticed that the orientation shifted. No more is the individual discussed solely in terms of how the world affects him; he is now seen as becoming progressively more responsible for his own behavior. The 6-month-old has little to say about how people respond to him but the 16-year-old has a great deal of control over his life situation. Chapter 8 had nothing to say about the relationship of the infant to others of his age, because—by and large—no relationships exist; Chapter 9 had a section on peer-group relationships; Chapter 10 is largely a discussion of the interaction between individuals of the same age level.

The decade between ages 12 and 21 is often considered a time of preparation for eventual maturity. Physically the individual attains full strength, maturity, and reproductive ability. Socially he accomplishes three major developmental tasks: (1) he moves from his parents' family and readies himself for becoming a parent in his own family, thus reducing his old family ties and establishing ties with a new family unit; (2) he ceases to receive *nurture* and becomes capable of giving nurture himself; (3) and he learns to work and to love (Group for the Advancement of Psychiatry, 1968). By the end of this period, the individual is expected to be ready to take his place as a self-sustaining member of the community.

The years of adolescence and the beginnings of young adulthood involve more than mere preparation and transition. The process of maturing occurs with dynamic interaction among physical changes, personal changes, social changes, and changes in the surrounding environment. During this decade the individual awakens to the world around him and to his own sense of identity.

Postponing entrance into adult society until a person is in his twenties is a recent development. In a sense, the idea of adolescence as a distinct period in the life process is relatively new, probably the result of the extensive education demanded in the modern world, and possibly because this age group is no longer needed in the labor force. In past centuries, the individual assumed adult responsibilities while still in his teens, often married before 20, and seldom lived beyond 50.

Even recently, many **preliterate** (or primitive) societies inducted the male child into official manhood around age 13, when he becomes physically and sexually mature. Known as **puberty rites**, ceremonies of induction often included painful rituals and demanded that the boy show his ability to fend for himself. At this time, the boy was taught some of the tribal secrets and was thereafter considered in many ways to be an adult. (Why do you suppose the girls were usually ignored in this procedure?) In these societies, the male moved directly from childhood to manhood, without an intervening adolescence. Our society, however, recognizes adolescence as a separate phase. During this phase the person is especially aware of changes in the physical body, in the sense of individual identity, and in the form and meaning of social relationships, including sexual relationships.

The Changing Human Body

The growth rate of children, which is very rapid during the very early years, tapers off until girls are about 10 and boys are about 12 (Tanner, 1961). At these ages, the growth rate suddenly spurts ahead for about two or three years. Since this **growth spurt** begins sooner for girls, there is a period of a year or two when girls are taller than boys, the only time during the entire life-span when this is true.

Puberty

Before the end of the growth spurt, the child begins to enter **puberty**, the period in his life when he becomes sexually mature. Most girls begin puberty, which is marked by the first menstrual period, between ages 12 and 14, although the range is from 10 to 17 (Cole & Hall, 1964). The determination of when puberty begins is less precise for boys, but it occurs about one year later than for girls.

Have you heard your parents make the comment "Kids certainly seem to be growing up faster these days than when I was young"? Their observation is not merely the result of their having forgotten what it is like to be young. Since puberty results from both genetic factors and such environmental factors as health and nutrition, those countries with higher standards of living have noted over the past several decades a steady decrease in the age when puberty begins (Garrison, 1968).

Physiological changes accompanying puberty are well known. They include the growth of body hair and—primarily for boys—the growth of facial hair; changes in the outlines of the body and the beginning of breast development for girls; the cracked voice for boys, which embarrasses them so frequently and which eventually matures into the adult male voice; and the beginning of menstrual bleeding for girls—at first irregularly, and later, every month.

Acne

Acne is the medical problem which "causes more . . . maladjustments between parents and children, more general insecurity and feelings of inferiority, and greater [emotional] suffering . . ." than any other (Sulzberger & Zaidens, 1948). No really effective cure has been found for acne, or pimples, even though it is extremely common, particularly during the late teens and early twenties (Cohen, 1945).

The specific causes of acne are not known, although dermatologists believe that the following factors contribute to the condition: poor diet, particularly eating too much oily food such as chocolate and peanut butter; constant touching and picking; inadequate cleanliness (which might include overuse of cosmetics and hair spray); poor general health; fatigue; and emotional stress (Sutton, 1941). Cleanliness, only one of many possible factors, may be overemphasized both by adolescents and by adults.

The degree to which emotional stress affects acne is not known, but research indicates that a combination of genetically inherited skin qualities and stress may interact to aggravate acne. Severe acne sufferers give off a large amount of facial oil when under stress, and those with little acne produce much less of this oil, which is believed to contribute to acne (Lorenz, Graham, & Wolf, 1953).

The major problem caused by acne is its effect upon the body-image. Many sufferers, particularly girls, become frantic at the sight of even a few red or white or black marks. They buy creams, salves, soaps, and special cosmetics; they go on special diets, use sun lamps, and take X-ray treatments. Whether these methods work or whether the acne merely disappears in time, most cases are eventually cured.

The Developing Self

Who are you? Not your name or your physical appearance or your family history, but the *real* you. What is the real you? The you no one else really knows, that perhaps you do not really know yourself. In other words, what is your *self?* Not your self-concept, but your actual self.

A confusing question? Certainly, but a question that begins to have meaning during adolescence. According to one well-known psychoanalyst, the question of **identity** is the major "psychosocial crisis" that faces people between ages 12 and 21. In order for them to continue toward self-actualization, they must—and usually do—overcome this crisis (Erikson, 1956).

How do you know when you are being yourself? As you behave, you become aware of your behavior and decide, partly consciously and partly unconsciously, whether the behavior represents "the real me" or not. When the behavior is not consistent with "the real me," you may feel "I am not myself." This feeling is upsetting and causes emotional discomfort. You may also be concerned about the effect you have on others when you are not yourself (adapted from Jourard, 1963).

People become unhappy when others treat them as though they had no identity—no "real me." We talk disparagingly of large, impersonal universities as factories, even while recognizing that their educational programs may be of high quality. You are probably pleased when someone remembers your name, because that signifies his awareness of your identity; you are an individual, apart from the thousands of other people he has met. People talk longingly of small towns, where "everyone knows everyone else," because the individual has identity in these communities. Identical home designs, the impersonality of large medical clinics, the use of numbers instead of names to identify students, the vast growth of computers, are all cited as examples of the loss of identity of the individual, regardless of their contributions to efficiency and "the better life."

In a world where many people complain about a lack of identity, it is not surprising that the adolescent is still seeking his, still wanting to know "the real me." In his search, he tries out new behavior patterns and new styles of living to see which ones are comfortable. For example, adolescents experiment with styles of handwriting, with variations in spelling their names, with an assortment of nicknames, with hairstyles and clothing styles, with speech mannerisms. The adolescent tries each of them on like a new pair of shoes, walks around a bit, then decides whether it fits comfortably or not.

During the years of adolescence, young people also try out more important styles of behaving.

> "It's some years ago, but I can still remember. One day I thought I'd be romantic and dashing, but that didn't work too well, so the next day I was the sweet-and-understanding type. That was better, but I still tried out a few others: I was the silent-and-in-emotional-pain type, the happy-go-lucky type, and the big-spender type. But each time I came back to the sweet-and-understanding type. Even though I was aware of what I was doing, I kept feeling that I was really being myself. Today I don't try to be any type any more, but I guess that I still think of myself as more like the sweet-and-understanding type than anything else. Of course, I do know I'm not always either sweet or understanding."

Adolescents are strongly motivated to find out "Who am I?" and then to behave consistently with what they feel this self to be.

In attempting to learn who they are, adolescents and young adults have the added problem of having to get a handle on a rapidly moving society. "Young people are . . . forced to make major decisions which will critically influence their lives, yet the increasing complexity of society has reduced assurances that their decisions will lead to [appropriate] goals" (Trent & Medsker, 1967). While trying to gain a sense of personal identity, teen-agers need to have an awareness of their goals, which they can formulate only in terms of what they want to do in the future. However, many in this age group feel bewildered about why their life was not so satisfactory after high school graduation as they had anticipated, and they feel frustrated because of their powerlessness to produce any change (Trent & Medsker, 1967). They do not understand what they should do to make their future satisfying in such an uncertain world.

The Adolescent Role

Strange as it may seem, those of adolescent age form a minority group that is the object of **discrimination**, **prejudice**, and **segregation**. And they respond, much as members of other minority groups, by forming their own society with its own rules and customs, a society that resembles the general society in most ways, but with some behavior distorted or exaggerated.

Adolescents in the United States are given no real place in their community. They are no longer satisfied with being children; yet adult opportunities, such as regular employment, sex and marriage, and independence and responsibility for their own behavior, are not available. They are reminded of their second-class citizenship by everything from restrictions on buying a bottle of beer to editorials in newspapers. Adults often consider them unstable, immature, and potentially violent. They are treated as being dependent and ineffective (Ausubel, 1954). Adults often feel that the only proper task for adolescents is to complete their education (Menninger, 1968), and even that accomplishment is not to help the adolescent self-actualize, but to produce more signs of achievement and productivity to help support the society run by adults (Kalish, 1968).

Three changes have taken place in the adolescent role over the past 60 years. First, teen-agers have much more personal money than before. Although they earn money to make their own purchases, their earnings are no longer necessary for the well-being of the family. Second, their schooling has been extended so that few adolescents are in the labor force. Third, and perhaps because of the first two, the dependent role of the adolescent has been extended, so that he is well advanced in physical, sexual, and intellectual maturity before he can make his own decisions and lead his own life. Perhaps this kind of dependency encourages the adolescent to prove his maturity to himself and others by turning to violence and thrill seeking (Soskin, Duhl, & Leopold, 1968). Today's adolescents are most certainly kept away from engaging in society (Menninger, 1968).

Since adolescents are essentially told they have no place in adult society, they inevitably turn to each other for support. In this way, they become extremely dependent upon what other adolescents think of them. The teen culture becomes much more important than the adult culture. After all, the adult culture says "Keep out!" and the teen culture says, "Welcome, friend and fellow sufferer!"

In years past, and in many parts of the world today, adolescents have received a great deal of responsibility, ranging from household chores to working side by side with adults in the field and the factory. These tasks were not just busy work, but work essential for keeping the family going. In our country today, we do not need adolescents to take on these responsibilities, and we have deprived them of the feeling that they are making a real contribution. The Latter-Day Saints (Mormons) encourage their young people to participate in community responsibility; perhaps their low rate of delinquency and school dropout is partly a result of their willingness to allow youths a mature role.

Of a large sample of teen-age boys, 43% thought that the responsibilities and opportunities that allowed them to take on an adult role contributed greatly to making them feel important and useful. Nothing else was nearly so highly rated (Boys' Clubs of America, 1960).

In spite of the importance of their own culture, teen-agers exhibit

Figure 10–1.

Tastes in music, hairstyle, and clothing originally established by adolescents often become acceptable to a large segment of the adult population. Courtesy Columbia Broadcasting System.

very much the same values as the general adult culture that surrounds them. True, there has been much teen-age violence, which seems to be a way for them to handle frustrations they are too immature to cope with otherwise. However, consider the violence that adults exhibit: the murder of literally millions of civilians in Nazi concentration camps, the ruthlessness of the communist regime under Josef Stalin, or the violence of the Ku Klux Klan in our own country. If teen-agers exaggerate the importance of the automobile in building their self-esteem, think about the symbols of status that their parents require.

Perhaps adults overemphasize the differences between the teen culture and their own. It has been shown, for example, that the social, political, religious, and other values of teen-agers closely resemble the values of their parents (Hyman, 1959). Also, adolescents have (1) a higher opinion of adults than their parents have of themselves, and (2) a higher opinion of adults than their parents believe they have (Hess & Goldblatt, 1957). Like many minority groups, adolescents admire the majority group and internalize their values.*

Emancipation and Primary Status

As long as teen-agers live with their parents, and are almost completely dependent on them for financial support and guidance and either

---

* Or have things changed since these studies were conducted?

unable or unwilling to be responsible for their own behavior, they are identified as their parents' children. One author has described this position as **derived status**, because teen-agers *derive* their *status* and identity directly from the status and identity of their parents, and the parents are considered largely responsible for what their children do (Ausubel, 1954).

In their own teen-age culture, adolescents have **primary status**. Here the teen-ager is not known as Mrs. Johnson's boy, but as Jack Johnson. He is responsible for his own status.

Although parents encourage their late-adolescent children to take responsibility and behave in a mature fashion, they often find it difficult to allow these children an equivalent amount of decision-making power and to accept them as mature and responsible individuals (Ausubel, 1954). The adult seems to be saying, "I'll give you freedom and decision-making power when you prove to me that you are mature." The teen-ager responds, "How can I prove I'm mature when you don't treat me as a responsible person?"

Sometimes, in an effort to emancipate himself and establish primary status, a teen-ager will leave home against his parents' wishes. Boys may enlist in the military, and girls may seek marriage; both, of course, can get work. Our society seems to perceive a married person or a working person as deserving primary status, and studies suggest that the main purpose for teen-age working is to become more independent of parents (Boys' Clubs of America, 1960). Many college students need to learn to cope with the frustrations of remaining financially dependent upon their parents, while friends are emancipating themselves through marriage and full-time jobs.

Not all adolescents seek emancipation. Freedom can be frightening, particularly for people whose physiological, security, and love needs are not adequately satisfied. To leave home and become established on your own demands giving up many of the comforts and satisfactions that you have been accustomed to. More than that, it demands that you make your own decisions and take responsibility for your own actions. Many people prefer to allow others to make decisions for them. If they leave home, they quickly find a person or an organization to tell them what to do and how to behave. Adolescents and adults who are very uncertain of themselves and have little self-respect may find freedom too difficult and may prefer others to do their thinking for them.

Slowly, however—often painfully slowly in his own eyes—the adolescent gains freedom from his parents and emerges into the community as a person in his own right. Once the general community of adults gives him primary status by accepting him for himself, he no longer needs the teen culture for support. He can now take his place in the adult community and will very quickly become responsive to its demands.

Some adolescents and college students face a more difficult task in their relationships with their parents. For them, the problem is not how to become emancipated, but how to deal with "problem" parents. All parents are, at various times, seen as problems by their children, but some present special difficulty. Thus, we read about adults who are too immature to take responsibility, who are too temperamental to hold a job, whose heavy drinking or sexual promiscuity or violent behavior gets them into constant trouble. We often forget that these people frequently have children who face experiences that other children do not face; for example, rarely having a meal set before them, finding a different man in their mother's bed every month, or being severely beaten. These children will become emancipated at an early age and with minimal conflicts (Ausubel, 1954). However, consider the other problems they may need to deal with.

Friendships

Since his peer group gives the adolescent primary status and individual identity, acceptance or rejection by this group is vital to most teen-agers. Unlike the adult who knows the limits of what he can do and still be socially acceptable, the adolescent is less sure of his identity and is not willing to risk a blunder that might cost him status in the age group that does accept him.

Because he is uncertain how far he can safely venture from the demands of the group, the adolescent is willing to accept pressures from his peers that he would vehemently reject from his parents. When he was young and his parents were the major significant others, he accepted their demands with little questioning. Now his friends are the primary source of satisfaction of his security, love, and esteem needs, and the adolescent wants to do his best to see those needs continually satisfied.

When adults criticize the adolescent friendship group, they are attacking the basis of the adolescent's status and esteem, and he becomes very defensive. He may become even more defensive if he recognizes the adult comments as largely true, since this possibility is very damaging to his self-concept. In the long run, however, and with some obvious exceptions, the qualities that make an adolescent popular with his peer group and acceptable as a date are qualities that adults approve.

All people have the potential to enter into warm and mutually rewarding friendships. The value of friendship is widely recognized, and most college students state that they would rather have a few close friends than a large circle of casual acquaintances.

The person with a healthy personality can both give to and receive from friendship—friendship is not a one-way street. You find that your friendship bolsters your self-concept by helping you recognize that others can like and respect you, and also that you are able to give another the liking and respect that bolsters *his* self-concept and helps him become a more complete person.

Deep and sincere friendships are very satisfying, but they also present the possibility of loss. When you like someone, you place trust in him and become dependent upon him in certain ways. If he disapproves of your behavior, you are more than normally upset; if he ignores you, moves away, or dies, you may feel you have been cheated, even when you recognize how unfair such a feeling is. You have invested a part of yourself in him just as you invest money in a bank, and you count on some sort of return. If you get nothing in return, or worse, if the investment is destroyed, the emotional pain can be great. In any form of friendship, and especially in love and marriage, people take a chance on being hurt. In order to gain from a relationship, you must risk something. The emotionally healthy person has sufficient feelings of self-adequacy that he can take this risk; on the other hand, some individuals may experience too much anxiety in risking a close friendship, and are unable to give, or even to receive, in a close relationship.

Some people have been so badly hurt by others that they are unable to trust people enough to enter into a friendship. Foster children, for example, who are moved from home to home, are often unable to trust others. In their experience, each time they allow themselves to like a new foster family, they are moved to another home.

Building Healthy Friendships

Good friendships are based on many factors. Friends tend to be of the same racial, religious, social, and age groups; they tend to have similar intelligence and get similar grades; they tend to live or work near each other.

In addition to having similar background characteristics, friends also have similar needs, interests, reading habits, morals, and scores on personality tests (Ausubel, 1954; Banta & Hetherington, 1963; Izard, 1963). These factors enable people to satisfy each other's needs and to communicate with each other with understanding, a condition just as important in healthy friendships as in good marriages. Thus, in friendships, as in all healthy human relationships, the parties resemble each other in certain ways, but also complement each other by satisfying each other's needs.

Healthy friendships are built on the satisfaction of healthy needs. They are also built on many other factors. Dr. Carl Rogers, a well-known and highly respected psychologist, makes the following conclusions about self-awareness and friendship:

*It does not help, in the long run, to act like someone I am not.**

To pretend to be someone or to know something or to feel in some way that is not true to yourself builds neither friendship, nor trust, nor your own self-concept.

I find I am more effective when I can listen acceptingly to myself, and can be myself.

People should try to understand how they really feel about others and not condemn themselves if these feelings are not what they "should be." If you are bored or irritated with people, you should recognize how you feel and not be self-critical.

I have found it of enormous value when I can permit myself to understand another person.

Instead of trying to judge the words or behavior of another person critically, it is more valuable to try to understand why he does what he does.

I have found it enriching to open channels through which others can communicate their feelings to me.

People are often reluctant to discuss their real feelings for fear they will be laughed at or criticized. It is rewarding to allow them to express their feelings to you, even if you disagree with them.

I have found it highly rewarding when I can accept another person.

It is not easy to accept another person for himself, without basing your acceptance on his race or his money or his beliefs or his age. Yet accepting others along with their feelings and attitudes and values— even if they disagree with yours—is rewarding.

The more I am aware of myself and others, the less I wish to rush in to "fix things."

In relationships with other people, you gain more by being yourself and trying to understand and accept others, rather than trying to change them (Rogers, 1961).

Healthy friendships are a source of satisfaction to both parties and help both parties become more complete and individual. Although friend-

* The italicized statements are either directly quoted or slightly altered from Dr. Rogers' original statements.

ships do place some restrictions on behavior, the overall result of a good friendship is that both individuals feel liked and respected and enjoy more freedom rather than less.

Dating Relationships

Between puberty and engagement, the American youth is immersed in the problems of dating. Dating means much more than a way of spending time and having fun. It influences attitudes and behavior in many ways.

1. *Dating affects the self-concept.*   A girl knows she is well liked when she receives many calls for dates and is frequently asked to go steady. Her self-concept develops accordingly. The boy will react similarly; if he finds girls are interested in dating him, his self-concept will be favorably affected.

2. *Dating is an indication of prestige and reputation.*   Students are judged not only by their own accomplishments, but also by the popularity and accomplishments of those they date. Dating a less popular girl or boy will certainly do nothing to raise prestige. Prestige is gained by dating a popular person, a member of the leading crowd, a student leader, or—particularly for high school girls—an athlete.

3. *Dating affects other aspects of social life.*   The girl tends to find herself in the social group selected by her date. Much of her nondating social activity may also become centered in this group. When the boy and girl sever the relationship, they are often embarrassed or upset by having to face the friends who had known them as a couple.

4. *Dating is an opportunity for learning.*   Often overlooked in discussions of dating is the learning it can offer. The demands of married life in the United States are great because so much is expected of marriage. Both the husband and wife *expect* the mate to understand them, to be sensitive to their needs, and to supply love, affection, and companionship. To deal with the complexities of selecting the correct spouse and living enjoyably with that person, a great deal of experience and understanding are needed. Some of this occurs through observing the relationship between the parents, but much can be learned through the give-and-take of dating.

Dating thus allows young people to get to know many potential spouses in a very personal, face-to-face situation, which in some ways is a preliminary to the marital relationship. The teen-ager can test out certain behavior, attitudes, and roles in a relatively harmless arrangement. He

10–2.

Figure 10–2.

Despite increased political activism on college campuses, getting a date is still important. Photograph by John G. Warford.

---

can gain an understanding of the type of behavior that appeals to him in the opposite sex, and what in his behavior appeals to the opposite sex. In many societies, marriages are arranged and dating opportunities are limited or nonexistent, and the expectations each married person has of his spouse are usually different from those of Americans. Talk to people from other countries, and see if you can learn how different marital roles require different sorts of experience before marriage.

Dating: Other Places and Other Times

Dating as practiced by most college students is a recent phenomenon, occurring mostly in the United States, Canada, and some European countries. The idea of a boy asking a girl to spend an unchaperoned evening with him was unknown a century ago. The couple might have gone for a Sunday afternoon walk, or they might have sneaked away from the community picnic to be together, but such activities are a far cry from the present dating behavior. Not only have styles of dating changed, but also the age at which teen-agers begin to date has been getting steadily younger.

In African, Asian, South American, and some European countries, dating "American style" is either virtually unknown or else is limited to a very small proportion of the population, usually the more wealthy and sophisticated. Even in those European countries where dating is common, group activities occur more frequently than the single date or double date, and going steady is usually avoided until the young people are in their late teens.

Chaperones are still very common in such places as the Philippines and Latin America. A young couple going to the movies is accompanied by an older relative or a trusted family friend. Sunday afternoon strolls are popular in many parts of the world, although parents may demand that even these walks be chaperoned, at least from a distance.

When a boy in Iraq wants to meet a girl he has seen, he must first ask his parents or a close friend to find about the girl. Then he will try to arrange for his parents to call upon the girl's parents and take him along, or for the mutual friend to introduce them. Eventually he will be admitted to the girl's house without his parents, but they will never be left alone until they are engaged. In the meantime, the couple may be passing exciting love notes back and forth through a mutual friend or a servant. This may be poetic and romantic, but it is very different from American dating style.

A Japanese girl expressed what many students around the world probably feel: "I would like to be more free than I am, but I would not like to be free like American girls. They do too much with boys that is wrong. American parents are not strict enough with their daughters. And I know from talking to American students that their freedom does not make them any happier than we. No nice Japanese boy would marry a girl who behaved like an American girl."

Attitudes Toward Dating

Nearly half of a large group of teen-agers stated that they began to date at 13 or 14; most of the rest began at 15 or 16 (cited in Cole & Hall, 1964). Girls begin to date earlier and often date older boys. By their senior year in high school, about 80 percent of all students claimed to be dating regularly (Gallup & Hill, 1961).

Many investigators have asked high school and college students to list the most important characteristics in a date or a future husband or wife. The lists are all a little different, but a University of Michigan study of qualities wanted in a date is fairly typical. These students selected as most important (1) being pleasant and cheerful, (2) having a sense of humor, (3) being a good sport, (4) being natural, (5) being considerate, and (6) having a neat appearance (Blood, 1956).

The same study had other significant results. For example, men seemed to feel they needed a car in order to date, but girls did not consider cars so important. Similarly, men felt their dates preferred them to be in a good fraternity, have money, dress well, go to popular places, be good dancers, and be able to drink. The girls, however, put much less emphasis on these factors than the men thought they did (Blood, 1956).

What are your motives for dating? Undoubtedly, you have many, and they differ from those of your friends to some extent. There is reason to believe that men and women do not have the same primary motives in dating. Women seem more concerned about courtship, whereas men find recreation of greater importance (Skipper & Nass, 1966). Physical attractiveness and implied sexual relations also play an important part. One research team arranged dates for college students on a chance basis. They then obtained numerous personality and ability test scores on all the students and also an evaluation by outsiders as to the physical attractiveness of each student. Later they asked each participant how much he liked his partner and whether he wanted another date. The *only* basis for approval found in this study was physical attractiveness: the more attractive the date, the more the person was liked (Walster, Aronson, Abrahams, & Rottmann, 1966). In surveys, students do not express so much concern for physical attractiveness, but apparently the concern is there. The results of this study suggest definite limitations on some kinds of survey research—and also on computerized matchmaking.

Going Steady

College students frequently go steady or have previously gone steady. About one-fourth of a large group of high school students indicated they were going steady (cited in Cole & Hall, 1964). Going steady offers the advantages of getting to know one person very well, of feeling accepted by at least one person, of giving and receiving emotional warmth, and of not having to worry where the next date is coming from.

The disadvantages of steady dating include the possibility of getting bored with each other but being unable to break the habit, of moving into an overly intense sex relationship, of having limited social contacts, and of undergoing emotional strain from fear of break-ups and suspected unfaithfulness. The biggest problem of going steady, however, is that it can lead to marriage before the individuals are ready.

Changing Perspectives on Going Steady

In 1925. "None of the popular girls will go with the same fellow more than a couple of times a month—unless she really intends to marry him. Why, I dated eight different men last month alone. I guess that's why I'm considered just about the most popular girl around."

In 1945. "I've been going steady with Chuck for six months, but I think we're going to break up soon. That's a shame, because before that I went steady with Eddie for over a year. The really popular girls are the ones who go steady with someone they really like for at least several months, because anything less than that just isn't worth it."

In 1955. "I've been going steady with Jerry for three weeks already, but it's all over now. Besides, I want to go steady with Frank—he attracted me already last month when I was going steady with Rich."

In 1965. "This going-steady business is for kids or for almost-engageds. Marty and I are going *steadily,* but not steady. None of that exchanging rings or anything. We like each other and we're what you might call a couple, but we're each free to do what we want. I get kind of a kick out of playing the field once in a while, and we don't want to get too involved."

In 1985. ? ? ? ?

Going steady does not necessarily imply future marriage, but may be simply a matter of obtaining a secure relationship. On the one hand, it can be a retreat for the insecure who do not wish to face the competition and games of dating around. On the other hand, it can be a wonderful, although often painful, emotional experience for those who are emotionally and intellectually mature enough to keep it in perspective.

Joe Porter was not very popular in high school. When he got to college, he began dating Karen Himmel, a rather plain, dull girl, and they quickly decided to go steady, both of them feeling very much alone in the large college they attended. One day, Joe was told that Karen had been rushed to the hospital after a suicide attempt. This incident occurred right after Joe had told Karen he felt they should break up. Joe felt so guilty for causing such drastic behavior that he proposed to Karen in the hospital, and she accepted. They were married at the end of the school year, and are still married, now with two children. Joe has never loved Karen, but he feels he is paying his debt for the anguish he caused her. He never learned that Karen had called the dormitory mother just after taking the sleeping tablets and had dramatically announced, "I'm going to kill myself."

Not many steady couples are married because of a faked suicide attempt, but less dramatic incidents are common. Fortunately, many young couples deal with a steady relationship in a mature way.

For those of college age and immediately after, steady relationships may be changing in their implications (see page 210).

From Apathy to Alienation to Activism

In 1961, an article in a popular American magazine claimed that "In general, the typical American youth shows few symptoms of frustration, and is most unlikely to rebel or involve himself in crusades of any kind. He likes himself the way he is, and he likes things the way they are" (Gallup & Hill, 1961). Most observers would have agreed that year.

Hippies

A very few years later, the hippie appeared on the scene. He claimed that he was dropping out of society. He no longer trusted or respected the Establishment, that is, the middle-class adults who seemed to be the decision makers in society, and he no longer wished to respond to their rewards. Instead of seeking satisfaction through achievement in school and work, he turned to his own personal inner world. To make this world more exciting, he experimented with a variety of drugs, called psychedelic or consciousness-expanding or mind-blowing drugs (see Chapter 19 for additional discussion). His concern with the inner world made the external world seem unimportant, so he ignored his health and paid little attention to his living conditions. In renouncing the values of the Establishment, he also rejected its limits on sexual behavior and on cleanliness; he rejected cigarettes and neatness; he rejected liquor and work.

Many different kinds of hippies made their appearance. Some were too young to be real hippies, so they were called teenie-boppers. Others were too "uptight" to become full-time hippies, so they became weekend hippies and would descend in droves on Greenwich Village in New York, the Haight-Ashbury in San Francisco, or the Sunset Strip in Los Angeles after school each day and on weekends. Others admired the hippies and spent much time with them, but remained with their education, jobs, and families. As more police, tourists, and part-time hippies moved in, the real hippies began to leave the familiar spots and retreat to more isolated areas.

The effect of the hippies on the rest of the community was predicta-

Adolescence and Young Adulthood

ble. Their parents were often powerless to do anything, since many hippies were of legal age to leave home and those who were not continued to run away from home anyway. The political and business communities attempted to force the hippies to leave by arresting them for loitering or for drug use, and they probably had some effect. Since the hippies displayed little violence, although begging and petty theft seemed to increase over time, their main challenge to society was in terms of values. Their physical appearance challenged the beliefs that the Establishment held in regard to neatness and acceptable dress. Their

Figure 10–3.

Whether selling underground newspapers or picking flowers, hippies have been a common sight in many American cities. Courtesy Columbia Broadcasting System.

sex behavior, use of drugs, and rejection of acceptable methods of work and consumption were particularly infuriating to the Establishment.

The Establishment firmly believed that work, achievement, learning, and productivity were good, but the hippie ethic denied the worth of all these values. Hippies and other young people began to ask their elders why, if attaining these values was so wonderful, did the members of the Establishment need to depend so much on alcohol, tobacco, aspirin, tranquilizers, and antidepressant pills. The background of the young people and that of their parents' generation were often so different that mutual understanding was difficult. Many members of the Establishment had lived through a depression and a major war, and the feelings they had developed regarding work and money were much different from the sentiments of those who had known primarily an affluent society that was not engaged in an all-out war.

The hippies were, undoubtedly, alienated. They lacked a relationship to the larger community around them (see Chapter 2), and thus lacked one of the bases for a sense of identity, although they did establish their own communities. Many of them criticized what they felt was the immorality of the Establishment in its treatment of ethnic minorities, of the poor, and of the Vietnamese during the war.

Activists

Just around the time that magazines and television networks began to do stories on the hippies, the rest of American youth became active again. Paralleling the extreme militancy and activism of youth in France, Germany, Mexico, Japan, and elsewhere, college-age Americans turned to fighting for what they wished. Although they shared with the hippies a distaste for the Establishment, the activists did not drop out, but joined in. The activist movement probably began partly as a result of the 1965 student participation in voter registration in the South, and partly through the Free Speech Movement at the University of California, Berkeley. Anger was generated primarily at the United States position in the Vietnam War and at conditions in the urban ghettos.

The activists picketed speakers, spoke out through publications and campus forums, and eventually became involved in violence, although it is difficult to determine how much of the violence was brought about by the students and how much by the authorities. Only a small portion of American college students have been activists; even where they are strongest they probably never number over 10% of the student body at any one time. However, activists have influence out of proportion to their numbers, partly because they are vocal, partly because they represent the brighter, higher-achieving students (Block, Haan, & Smith, 1968), and partly because many of their views appeal to nonactive segments of the campus populations.

The impact of the activists upon the Establishment was, if anything, greater than that of the hippies. The hippies had dropped out and presented a challenge only to those whom they happened to meet. The activists, however, were making demands everywhere, including demands for additional decision-making powers on college campuses; and they backed up their demands by displays of numbers. Many colleges and universities saw violence: property was destroyed and serious injury occurred.

Who were the activists?

First, they tended to come from families in which the father was a professional man or higher-level businessman. Second, both they and their parents tended not to have strong church affiliations or traditional religious beliefs. Third, they placed emphasis on intellectual and artistic activities, on serving others, and on self-expression, and so did their parents. Fourth, they were above-average students (Flacks, 1967). They were more flexible, more objective, more independent, more imaginative, and—perhaps because of the pressures put on them—more tense and anxious (Trent & Craise, 1967).

In what did the activists believe?

They did not seek more material goods for themselves. Many actually gave up material gain in order to help others live a better life (Keniston, 1967). Nor were they alienated from all Establishment values. In many ways, they believed in the traditional values expressed by the leaders of this country. One activist who later became a professional psychologist felt that the activists had eight major orientations:

1. They did not like to be bound by conventions; they wanted to feel free to "do their thing."

2. They opposed many forms of authority.

3. They emphasized the importance of everyone participating in government, and they were particularly upset when some people were denied that opportunity.

4. They wanted to be flexible and resented rigid philosophies.

5. They were strongly opposed to hypocrisy and phoniness.

6. They felt that people should be a part of their community and be involved in their community.

7. They distrusted religious, legal, educational, and other institutions.

8. They rejected careers in the sciences and industry for careers in fields permitting self-expression, such as painting or movie production, and in fields allowing service to others, such as social work (Flacks, 1967).

At the same time that some students were demanding that college administrations permit them new and broadened decision-making roles, other groups—sometimes consisting of the same students—were insisting that more attention be paid to ethnic minority communities. Student leaders of black, Mexican-American, and Oriental origins emerged to intensify demands that more minority group students be admitted to colleges and, simultaneously, that more services be provided for these students, since their previous schooling was often so poor that they might have difficulty in handling college-level work in competition with stu-

202

dents from white communities. Confrontations between student leaders and college administrators became common, and, in November 1968, the students at San Francisco State College succeeded in forcing the college to close down in order to avoid possible violence and to consider student demands.

The activists seemed to be so angry with what they observed that they were intent on changing society rapidly and extensively, perhaps

Figure 10–4.

In 1968, many college students participated actively in the Democratic Presidential primaries. Courtesy Columbia Broadcasting System.

violently. But what other kinds of students were around? First, there were the apathetic majority who remained primarily involved in their own concerns and who accepted enough of the existing society to refrain from noticeable objection. Second, there were the hippies and other alienated groups. Third, there were those called "individualists," those who actively supported change in society, but in a conservative direction, although they did share some basic values with the activists. Fourth, there were the constructivists, people who tried to produce change in society by their own work and example; they might have worked alongside an activist in a black ghetto, but would probably not have walked the picket line with him. And fifth, there were the people who became antisocial delinquents (Block et al., 1968).

The specific nature of alienation changes and the specific nature of protest changes, but both alienated people and protesters remain in one form of another. In our rapidly changing world, the nature of social movements will also undergo rapid change. In what ways do the hippies and activists of today differ from what you have just read? To what extent does the first paragraph in this section (page 198) describe students today?

Summary of Important Ideas

1. The decade from 12 through 21 is not only a transition from childhood to mature responsibility and opportunity, but it is also a time of increased concern about the world and about a sense of personal identity.
2. Adolescence is not a distinct developmental period in all societies.
3. The growth spurt begins shortly before puberty. During and after puberty, many sex-related physiological changes occur.
4. Many adolescents are involved with the search for identity and the desire to understand *who* they are.
5. Adolescents are a minority group that is discriminated against; they have rejected the role of children but are not accepted as adults. Eventually, they are emancipated and attain primary, rather than derived, status in the general community.
6. The importance of the peer group is that it is the only source of primary status for the adolescent.
7. The person with a healthy personality can give to and receive from friends.
8. American students are deeply concerned with dating. Dating relationships are valuable in developing mature roles, but also involve certain hazards.
9. Going steady is a common practice in the United States.
10. Hippies are alienated from most American social values and have chosen to drop out of society. Activists are alienated from a portion of generally accepted values, but have chosen to fight rather than drop out.

Chapter Eleven

Courtship and Marriage

The period between ages 18 and 21 is often a transitional time for American youth. In past centuries this transition may have come earlier, but demands for both vocational and personal competence have extended the time of dependence upon parental and school authority. During this brief period the adolescent becomes an adult in the eyes of the law. Since others' responses toward him tend to mirror the legal definition, he is labeled "of legal age" and "mature." He is forced to make decisions for himself that had always been left to others. Among the most important new decisions he must make are those involving sex behavior and those leading to marriage.

Throughout the history of the world, thoughtful parents have taken great pains that their children avoid inappropriate sexual relationships and that they enter into appropriate marriages. So concerned were they that many would never dare leave the decisions to their children; the parents themselves made these vital arrangements. Although the parents desired to find a spouse their child could like or even come to love, family finances, family reputation, social class, religion, and various forms of bride payment, or dowry, were the deciding factors in choosing mates.

Even today, in many parts of the world, marriages are arranged by parents, often without asking the prospective bride and groom for consent. Although Americans are frequently upset by this custom, our own high divorce rate has been cited by people of other nations as evidence that love marriages are not particularly successful.

Sex, marriage, and divorce are matters of immediate interest to every high school graduate. Today, more than half of the girls in this country are married before their twenty-first birthday,* and many are pregnant at the time of marriage. One-half of American men are married by the age of 23. Thus, almost every college student has seen some of his

---

* *Information Please Almanac,* 1966.

personal friends marry—and perhaps divorce. In addition, recognition of the role of sexual relationships in dating, courtship, and marriage is very much a part of the contemporary campus scene.

Sexual Relationships

A great deal is said in popular literature about sexual enjoyment both in and out of marriage, perhaps so much that many people overestimate its value. Sexual compatibility may greatly enrich a good marriage, but it cannot save a basically poor marriage. Sexual relationships before marriage, although potentially explosive and sometimes ending in disaster, may also be overestimated as to their impact upon subsequent love relationships.

When an unmarried couple decide to test their sexual compatibility before marriage, they may be fooling themselves. For many people the sexual act changes its significance so much after marriage that the premarital experience may have little relationship to later satisfaction. For example, a person who has internalized the value that premarital sexual intimacies are totally inappropriate may seem sexually cool before marriage, but very warm after the wedding, when the fear and anxiety are reduced. On the other hand, some people find great excitement in an illicit sex relationship, but do not respond physically to the long-range affection required in marriage.

Sexual enjoyment reaches its greatest moments within a marriage between two people who love each other. Yet, a good marriage can exist where sexual enjoyment is only moderate or even low. Sex is only one way of expressing affection. A look of understanding, a touch on the arm, a smile, all express affection between man and woman. In a healthy engagement or marriage, these forms of affection are more common and, perhaps, more important than strictly sexual expression.

Sex Behavior

Dr. Alfred Kinsey published his famous reports on the sex behavior of Americans two decades ago, but a continuing and highly emotional debate has been raging around these books ever since (Kinsey, Pomeroy, & Martin, 1948; Kinsey, Pomeroy, Martin, & Gebhard, 1953). Although his statistics are open to criticism, they appear to be reasonably accurate and have been found similar to those resulting from other studies.

Although some people believe college students are sexually promiscuous, Kinsey found their sex experiences more limited than those of people outside college. People from the middle class, which includes most college students, were less likely to have been sexually intimate outside of marriage than those from the lower class.

Almost all college students had kissed and necked at one time or another, and many had done so on numerous occasions. Petting (involving the breasts or genitals) is less common, but more than nine out of ten college men and women had done some petting by their twentieth birthday, about one-third reaching complete sexual release through orgasm in this fashion.

In many instances, necking and petting do not lead to intercourse, but consume enough time and allow enough excitement so that intercourse does not take place. Rather than hazard the risks of sexual intercourse, college men frequently indulge in mild love-making, then get release through masturbation at a later time. Although some people still believe masturbation leads to mental illness, no evidence exists to support this assumption, except that guilt arising from fears over masturbation can be emotionally disturbing. Middle-class parents often accept masturbation as a way of keeping their sons from engaging in intercourse, but lower-class people consider it both foolish and dirty. Almost all boys and many girls use masturbation as a form of sexual release, so that it hardly can be considered strange or unnatural, and its use is especially frequent among college students.

A form of sexual release common among adolescents is the sexual dream. In these cases, the sleeper will dream about sexual activity. The manifest content (what you "see") may or may not be sexual, but the latent content (what the dream represents) will be. (See Chapter 5.) During the dream, he (and it is usually the male) will have an orgasm, which may or may not wake him up. Such an experience may be very distressing to adolescents not aware of what is happening.

Homosexual and other deviant relationships occur more often than is usually realized, although most of those reporting homosexual experiences were involved only in isolated incidents. About 10% of the adult men had maintained homosexual behavior over an extended period of time (Kinsey et al., 1948).

Some people claim that Kinsey's data were highly exaggerated; others contend that the sexual involvement of today's college students exceeds Kinsey's figures. In either case, college provides new freedoms and responsibilities in regard to sex behavior.

New Freedoms and Responsibilities

Less parental supervision and more flexible time demands give the college student increased freedom for social life and dating—and, inevitably, for sexual relationships. His concept of the role of a college student may also encourage a freer attitude toward sex behavior. College freshmen are no longer so sexually innocent as they were (or as others liked to think they were) 50 years ago. Although they participate less in sexual intercourse than nonstudents of the same age (Kinsey et al., 1948, 1953), they are aware of what occurs in the world around them. If television shows and high school reading lists are sometimes censored, the daily newspaper, popular monthly magazines, and bull sessions are not. With the increased freedom and increased awareness, the college student needs to increase his understanding of the consequences of what he is doing and to accept responsibility for what he has done.

There are many types of sex behavior. A mature and complete sexual relationship between two people who love each other is one type; a group of eighth-graders giggling at obscene postcards exemplifies another. A world of difference stands between these two kinds of behavior. Sex behavior may satisfy growth motives, or it may satisfy only deficiency motives.

John Small entered my office rather timidly and asked if he might talk with me a few minutes. After much embarrassment and hesitation, he finally got to the point. John had begun dating only a year earlier. He was fairly popular with the girls, although very shy in his dating behavior. Many of the other fellows had talked freely of their sex experiences, and John had begun thinking something was wrong with him for never having had any.

Now, in the middle of his first college semester, he had reached the point with a girl he had been dating when he felt he could "go further" than kissing, but he did not know whether he should. He did not ask his sister or his parents, although he was close to them, because he knew they would merely say "No" and not wish to talk about it. John did not want an answer—he wanted an opportunity to discuss. For over an hour that afternoon, he discussed his feelings about sex in general and his behavior with the girl in particular. At the end of the discussion, he had not made up his mind, although he had explored most of the pros and cons. However, he no longer appeared to be in such conflict.

Not all students have the insight and maturity that John showed, but he had reached the point in his life where any such decision he made had to be his own—others could no longer make decisions for him.

Sex can be used to deepen and enrich a happy marriage, or to degrade a human relationship as one person uses sex to exploit the other. Sex can bring pleasure, satisfaction, even fun; or it can bring guilt, fear, and anxiety.

Each individual has internalized values regarding sex. Beginning with toilet training and modesty training, children learn to keep the genital area private and clean, and touched as little as possible. Later they are taught that sex without love and affection is not appropriate. Although many are fortunate in internalizing the value that sex in marriage is to be enjoyed, others have had early learning experiences and have faced parental and community attitudes that make difficult any sort of later sexual enjoyment without ensuing guilt and anxiety.

Evidence exists that once sex behavior is initiated, guilt does not inhibit continuation of that behavior. Apparently both males and females participate in sexual relationships that initially cause guilt, but they will continue the activity until the guilt diminishes, then go on to more advanced sexual behavior until the guilt associated with that also decreases (Reiss, 1968). Thus, guilt, although serving as an inhibiting force, does not eliminate sex activity.

To some extent, sex behavior results from the opportunities offered by the immediate situation. The pressures of the family normally oppose extramarital sex, but pressures of dating and courtship encourage it. Therefore, whatever circumstances reduce the influence of the family, for example, distance from home or divorce, will also reduce the inhibitions on sex (Reiss, 1968).

Other cultures differ from ours in their sexual attitudes. Some restrict sex so effectively that even sex in marriage is not enjoyed. Others teach that sex is a basic part of affection. Still others restrict nonmarital sex officially but allow it to occur unofficially: "Don't do it, but if you do it, don't get caught." And a number of cultures allow premarital sex to occur with little objection, but demand complete faithfulness in marriage (Ford & Beach, 1951; Murdock, 1957).

Behavior in other cultures does not determine appropriate behavior for our culture. There are people who contend that complete sexual freedom would improve mental health. However, many circumstances having no relationship to sex contribute to our emotional problems, for example, intense competition, need for status, uncertainty about social role, or desire for material possessions. There is not sufficient evidence that Americans would suddenly become mentally healthier if they became sexually free (Ausubel, 1954).

The major problem about sex is undoubtedly the conflict that arises between (1) the values we have internalized and religious and legal pressures, all of which demand that we avoid sex outside of marriage, and (2) the constant barrage of stimuli from movies, publications, conversation, and just plain knowledge of what is going on, all of which suggest, "Have fun—do it now." This conflict is part of the world we live in, and each person must work out the most effective way that he, as an individual, can adjust to the dilemma.

Those who cannot cope with their sex conflicts may have difficulties which originally arose from other sources such as (1) inadequate parent-child relationships, (2) poor marriage relationships between parents, (3) poor family attitudes toward sex, (4) personality-adjustment problems, (5) insufficient social learning opportunities, (6) misleading sex education, and (7) extremely disturbing childhood or early-adolescent sex experiences. Such occurrences can lead to inadequacy in later sex relationships. Strangely enough, feelings of sexual inadequacy can lead both to withdrawal from sex relationships *and* to unusually strong desires for sex relationships. The person who is not secure in his own sexual adequacy often feels the need for sexual exploits to prove to himself and to others that he is adequate.

Contemporary Sex Codes

Codes of sex behavior among college students have apparently changed substantially between the late 1950s and the present. On many campuses, students comment that the kind of sex behavior that alarms their parents and teachers has become so acceptable to students that it is no longer an issue. The evidence, however, is not completely clear. Some claims indicate that college students participate more freely and more frequently in intimate sexual relationships than they used to. Others indicate that the behavior has not changed—that sexual relationships have always been abundant—but that attitudes and values toward this behavior have changed. And some evidence still suggests that neither behavior nor attitudes have changed, but people are simply talking more about them.

Among the specific changes that have been mentioned are: (1) sexual experiences no longer lead to a bad reputation for college women; (2) college men no longer expect their wives to be virgins; (3) guilt over sexual intimacies is much reduced or completely absent; (4) discussion of sexual experiences is common and uninhibited, both in groups of men and of women and in mixed groups; (5) sexual promiscuity is still frowned upon, but sexual relationships based on love or deep affection are accepted for both men and women.

Is this picture accurate? If so, it means, among other things, that factors inhibiting sex behavior are disappearing, which may well lead to an increase in sexual intimacies on college campuses. We may then ask whether college students are setting the pace for the rest of the country, or following what others have set, or behaving relatively independently of what others are doing.

Opposing the idea that there have been changes in sex behavior among students, a recent study concludes that most college girls have never been sexually intimate and that they intend to restrict any premarital relationships to their future husband. According to this study, the sex behavior of college women has changed little over the past 20 years, but willingness to discuss sex values has become greater (Freedman, 1965). In any event, results of one survey indicate that students do not believe that their own standards for sex behavior differ much from those of their parents (Reiss, 1968).

Until very recently, sexual relationships outside marriage—and to some extent even within marriage—have been inhibited for some people by the fear of pregnancy. Today, however, knowledge about contraceptive devices and their relative availability have considerably reduced this concern. Many parents, including some who strongly disapprove of premarital sexual relationships, inform their sons and daughters about "the pill" and "the loop" and encourage them to use these devices, at the same time trying to discourage their participation in the intimacies that call for such use. Although clinical studies suggest that no artificial contraceptive, even when used correctly, is 100% safe, student use of contraceptives has undoubtedly increased greatly during the past decade, in spite of the opposition of some religious, educational, and legal authorities.

In the late 1960s, new forms of sociosexual relationships received attention. The most conspicuous of these evolved from the decision of young men and women to live together, either in small groups or as couples. Undoubtedly such relationships have always occurred; what was new was the openness with which these relationships were expressed. In one well-publicized case, a coed at an East Coast college forced her school's administration to admit that the fact that she was living, unmarried, with a young man was none of their business. Inevitably, such living together was roundly criticized by many community authorities, but the criticisms appeared to have little impact upon the participants. Several questions remain to be answered: How common are these relationships? Are they more common now than a decade ago or just more open? Are they an outgrowth of what has been considered "going steady"? Are they a transient phenomenon, or are they going to be with us for a while?

Most observers agree that sexual relationships are more open now than in previous years, but it is still uncertain whether there is also an increase in casual sex behavior, or whether, as one investigator stated, "Sexual intimacy . . . takes place in the context of a relationship that is serious . . ." (Katz, 1968). The evidence is obviously in conflict, partly because of inconsistent reports and partly because of our lack of knowledge about sex behavior 30 and 50 and 70 years ago. What hypotheses would you offer from your own observations?

Justifications for Sex Behavior

Students justify their sexual activities in many ways. Justifications include the belief that sex experience before marriage is an advantage for the marriage; the feeling that love is enough reason for sex, even without marriage; the desire to gain security by receiving physical as well as emotional closeness; the enjoyment of sexual pleasure; the attempt to hold on to a relationship through sex when it cannot be held together in other ways; the belief that prestige or daring is gained through sex; and "everybody does it—why not me?" An additional reason, although rarely expressed or even consciously felt, is the desire to punish parents. The student is, in a sense, saying to his parents, "I know how much it would hurt you to know what I am doing. I have so much power now to hurt you." There is also the belief that each person has the right to live his life as he wishes, assuming that he does not hurt others and that this relationship is what he wishes.

The reasons for opposing sexual relationships outside of marriage are also many. They include the possibility of pregnancy (which occurs even when preventive measures are used); the fact that many men, in spite of their willingness to "make out," still wish to marry a girl they consider "pure"; the fear that sex can lead to a one-sided relationship, in which the girl perhaps loves the boy and finds that only sex can hold him; the danger of drifting into a marriage neither wants; and the obvious fact that religious beliefs and the law both oppose such relationships.

From a psychological point of view, one additional problem in nonmarital sex is critical. Much **guilt** and **anxiety** can develop, not only for the girl but also for the boy. Whatever our present beliefs, almost all of us have been raised in an environment that condemned nonmarital sex, and we have internalized these values. Participation in a nonmarital sexual relationship, even though we may find many ways to justify it, still opposes the values we internalized as children and is very likely to arouse guilt feelings. Not only does each person feel guilt for what he has done, but he may feel doubly guilty about the fear and anxiety he has caused his partner.

Rick Kelley and Brenda Taylor met during their freshman year, and were soon deeply involved. A complete sexual relationship seemed quite natural, and—within a few weeks—they were making love regularly at Brenda's home, while both her parents worked. After eight months, they realized they had no intention of marrying each other— their love now seemed like infatuation, and they calmly and rationally decided to cut the relationship abruptly. On the surface, it seemed to be a good example of trying something out, then quitting before it was too late.

But it was too late. Rick and Brenda had planned their course schedule to have classes together, and they saw each other several times a week. Also, because of mutual friends, they continued meeting at parties. Each began to feel guilty about taking part in a relationship that, as they looked back, was not based on love but on physical appeal.

They made nasty comments about each other behind each other's backs. Then the whole thing erupted in a vicious argument when Rick criticized Brenda to her face.

They made life miserable for each other. Each felt the other had been the cause of the sex involvement, and each resented the other. At the same time, each recognized his own role and felt guilty. During the relationship, guilt had seemed impossible. Even their breaking up was done without anger. Everything seemed calm and sensible. But Rick and Brenda lived in a culture where their behavior was disapproved not only by others but, unconsciously, also by themselves.

It would be an obvious exaggeration to claim that every nonmarital sexual relationship ends unhappily. However, it would not be an exaggeration to state that things happen that the couple cannot anticipate and that affairs with unfortunate endings often have had apparently sensible beginnings. Too many people are confident that pregnancy, venereal disease, or reputation loss will not occur; they overlook the problems of guilt, anxiety, and remorse. In the final analysis, sex behavior, like all behavior, is the responsibility of the individual.

Courtship and Engagement

The term "courtship" is commonly associated with the period between the beginning of serious dating and either breaking up, engagement, or the wedding. For our purposes, we will consider courtship as meaning the same as serious dating.

Purposes of Courtship

The major purpose of courtship is for two people to get to know each other well enough to decide whether they wish to marry. If they decide they like each other well enough, they become engaged. If not, they can break off the relationship, which, as painful and embarrassing as it may be, is still far better than breaking an engagement, and infinitely better than breaking a marriage.

Evan Mann rarely dated until his senior year in high school. In the middle of his freshman year in college, he started going steady with Toni Bailes, a very attractive girl who was a senior at a local high school. They dated with increasing frequency for four months, and although Evan tried feebly to break up on two occasions, he always called Toni again. Suddenly Toni's parents began to talk about marriage, and the first thing Evan knew, he had proposed and had been accepted. Toni's father was going to take him into the retail clothing chain he owned, and Evan's parents were pleased with his opportunities. The wedding date was quickly set.

Evan had persuaded himself that he loved Toni completely. Toni knew she did not love Evan, but realized he would be an honest, faithful, hard-working husband, and she was not at all sure she could ever really love anyone. When Evan's mother became ill, he decided to transfer back to the community college in his home town. At first he missed Toni tremendously, but slowly it dawned on him that when he thought of Toni, he thought of sex, not affection. He began to notice other girls on campus and saw a couple for informal afternoon coffee dates.

Just five days before the wedding, Evan wrote Toni a long letter explaining that he could not marry her, and he willingly took the blame himself. Toni was at first heartbroken and embarrassed, then understandably bitter. Most of their mutual friends sided with Toni, and Evan faced great hostility when he returned for a final visit.

The courtship period may begin with the couple still playing games: both trying to impress each other, playing hard-to-get, trying to read deep meaning into innocent statements, hoping for flattery, and being on best behavior. Each is interested in the other but wants signs of returned interest and affection for assurance that the interest is mutual. (For an amusing and enlightening discussion, see *Games People Play*, by Eric Berne, 1964.)

As courtship continues, the couple usually become more relaxed with each other. Instead of keeping to the formal dating relationship, they spend a lot of time together informally. They behave with each other more as they behave in their parents' home, and thus more as they will behave in their own future home.

Problems in Courtship

One author has listed seven major causes of problems during engagement: (1) difficulty with families, (2) difficulty with friends, (3) conventions, such as manners and dress, (4) conflicting values, (5) the use of money, (6) religious differences, and (7) affection and sex (Merrill, 1959).

Difficulty with families. "I'm marrying you—not your family." This statement is very true, but families do come as part of the package. The importance of the family to a marriage is great, even if all the relatives live a thousand miles away—or even if no relatives are still alive. Couples can use the period of courtship to get to know each other's families, to spend time with them, and to learn to adjust to their habits and manners.

Parents will disapprove of a marriage for a variety of motives. Many parents become so attached to their children that they hate the idea of giving them up. Some parents need to have a child around who depends on them so they can feel that they have a place in the world. Others have difficulty in accepting the fact that their child is mature enough to leave home. Still others have such high standards for their children—after all, the person your child marries reflects credit or discredit upon you as well—that no one can possibly be good enough. Sometimes parents object to religious, social-class, or nationality differences. Although parents try to keep the happiness of their children in mind, the end result of their behavior does not necessarily promote that happiness.

However, parents can be correct. They can see the prospective mate more objectively. They know their child, and they may see trouble ahead. Particularly with teen-age courtship and engagement, parents are anxious to avoid letting anything become permanent too quickly. Our attitudes and aspirations at 18 often change by 22. The boy who seems so romantic at 19 may be unable to hold a job at 30; the girl who is so lovely at 17 may be more worried about getting to the beauty parlor than to the grocery store after she is married. (And these are things "your best friend won't tell you.")

There is another excellent reason to learn about the family of your prospective mate—after all, they are the significant others in the life of the person you are going to marry. A perceptive boy will learn a great deal about his girl by seeing the way her parents treat each other, by observing for himself the social and religious values in her home, and by looking for important little details. Do the parents bicker? Is her younger brother totally undisciplined? Are the parents gossips? Is the home always noisy? These behavior patterns provide indications of what might be expected later from the daughter. The emotional climate of your childhood home cannot help but affect the later emotional climate of your adult home after marriage.

Difficulty with friends. Since it is rare to meet anyone and like *all* his friends, it is rare that one member of an engaged couple does not dislike at least a few friends of the partner. Sometimes, rather than disliking any individual friend, the girl may resent that her fiancé spends so much time with "the boys," whereas he feels her girl friends are "just a bunch of gossips." These problems need to be dealt with early in the relationship.

Previous romances also intrude upon the couple. The newly engaged girl may be very jealous of all the dates her fiancé ever had, and his talking about them does not help matters, especially when the engagement is recent and both are insecure in their new roles. Nor does it help for either one to describe all previous dating relationships "because I want to be honest with you."

Adjusting to conventions.   Everyone has certain kinds of behavior that others might find difficult to accept on a long-term basis. Many of these actions are merely habits or manners and are so unimportant that they cannot interfere with an otherwise healthy relationship, but they can become a great annoyance far out of proportion to their real importance. For example:

> Claudia smokes two packs of filter cigarettes a day, and her fiancé cannot tolerate the smell of tobacco.
>
> Mac likes to sit on the front porch or walk to the corner drugstore in his undershirt. His fiancée finds this very irritating.
>
> Jonathan's mother is an immaculate housekeeper, and Jon demands that everything be neatly in its place. He acts like a hurt little boy when things are not just so.
>
> Marlene puts her hair up in curlers right after supper. Her fiancé cannot stand women with their hair in curlers. He argues that it is unfair to a husband to have to spend most of his life staring at his wife's bare scalp, so that she can look attractive for strangers the next day.

Courtship and engagement enable two people to learn each other's manners and habits and to determine whether their feelings of attraction are sufficient to overcome these irritations. Unfortunately, the effects of some such habits can often be understood only after marriage, at which point the couple must make the best possible adjustments.

Conflicting values.   No two people have the exact same values, and two people may be happily married with very different values. When important values are in direct conflict, however, both the engagement and the eventual marriage are troubled. If the man demands peace and quiet and the girl prefers noise and loud parties, their values conflict; if the girl insists upon owning a home and having a stable life but the man enjoys freedom from responsibility and wandering from town to town, their values conflict; if he favors leisure and she admires hard work and high achievement. . . .

The use of money.   How important is money? How should money be spent? In courtship and engagement, there is an increased feeling that the money is jointly possessed. When it is spent, even though earned by the man, the woman feels *her* money is being spent. How much should be spent, how much should be saved, and how much should be used as down payment on credit buying? In our society, disagreements over money can become a major problem for couples.

Religious differences.   Church affiliation and religious values can create two major types of courtship problems. First, you feel yourself a member of a particular religious group and have a sense of loyalty to that group. Therefore, you are likely to prefer the person you marry to be part of the same group and to bring up your children similarly.

Second, as a member of a particular religious group, you tend to internalize the group's values, some of which may conflict with values of other groups, for example, attitudes on birth control, church attendance, eating habits, or religious education. Two people who differ widely on these and other matters might find religious values somewhat of a barrier to a satisfactory marriage.

As old community ties become weaker and more students attend college, especially college away from home, they are bound to meet those of different religions. Also the general behavior and values and mannerisms of Protestants, Catholics, and Jews are becoming more similar, and there is less to restrain dating and subsequent marriage outside the religious group.

People often claim that those entering into interfaith marriages are neurotic or are trying to throw over the values of their parents. Recent evidence, however, shows there is no difference in emotional health between those who had intermarried and those who had not (Sklare, 1964).

Many parents would accept interfaith dating if they did not fear interfaith marriage. Ironically, even parents who do not personally attend church or follow religious rituals may object vociferously if their children date outside the religious group. Some of these feelings result from nothing more than prejudice. Many objections, however, arise because parents have developed a strong sense of identification or association with their own religious group, even if they do not follow its beliefs and rituals carefully. They wish their children to affiliate with the same group when they marry and especially when they bring up their own children.

At the same time, parents want their children to be as happy and successful as possible in their marriage. Interfaith marriages have consistently higher divorce rates (for example, Gordon, 1964), and you often hear the statement "Marriage is so difficult at best, why make it more difficult by marrying outside your own religion?" When religious values and habits are different, the relationship can lack an important basis for sharing. Students themselves indicate that marrying outside their religious group would be more difficult than marrying outside their educational, nationality, or economic group (Gordon, 1964).

Also, the general community may disapprove and bring pressure to bear. Since parents recognize that they are largely responsible for their children's values, when children marry outside their religion it seems to the parents as though they had failed by not being able to keep the children in the fold.

In spite of these potential problems, of a sample of 5,400 college students drawn from 40 colleges across the country, only 8% indicated that they would "break off at once" if they fell in love with someone of another faith; nearly half would continue to date. Perhaps these reactions occurred because 40% of the students had already observed an intermarriage in the family, and only one in ten had never dated a person of another religion; one-third of the students implied that they dated people of other religions as often or more often than they did people of their own religion (Gordon, 1964).

Many factors relate to the success of interfaith couples: the intensity of their identification with their church group; the attitudes of their community and their friends; the acceptance by their families; and—probably the most important—the similarity in their values and beliefs.

Marriage can be compared to a rope consisting of many strands of different thicknesses. Each strand represents some quality joining a couple, for example, educational background, food preferences, enjoyment of travel, liking each other's family. Religion is one strand. If religion is important to either partner, that strand is very thick; if it is unimportant, the strand is thin. If the strand is cut (that is, if religion is not shared), the rope is that much weaker. Cutting a thick strand would obviously be more dangerous than cutting a thin strand. For some couples, the rope itself is very thick, and a severed strand is not important; for other couples, so little is shared that the marriage rope is thin. When pressure is applied to a thick rope, little happens; when pressure is applied to a weak rope, it pulls apart (adapted from personal communication with Dr. Abraham Stone).

In other words, if the marriage is basically good and religion is unimportant to the couple, interfaith marriage is no problem. If the marriage is not secure or if religion is very important, the marriage will pull apart more easily in an interfaith marriage. If the marriage does occur, certain hazards may be avoided by the husband and wife who show special respect for each other's beliefs.

Affection and sex. See earlier discussion.

Love in Courtship and Marriage

Have you ever really loved someone in a man-woman relationship? How did you feel? What is love? Love is usually defined as a very intense affection or liking for a person or, sometimes, a thing. Love is an emotion or feeling that may be expressed through overt behavior or may, for many reasons, be kept unexpressed or even repressed. Healthy mutual love is likely to increase over the months and years and to help both parties grow as individuals *and* as a couple. It begins with mutual respect, a strong feeling of affection, the desire to be together, and the willingness to make more of yourself for the sake of the other person *and* to help the other person make more of himself as well. In order to lead to marriage, love should also include physical attraction, but physical attraction often grows from love.

Can everyone love? Some people claim not. They feel that those who were not themselves loved cannot feel love for others. It has also been said that you cannot love others unless you can accept yourself and trust others (Blood, 1955). These statements emphasize the importance of early experiences and relationships with other people, particularly with significant others.

In much popular fiction, in movies, and on the television screen, you find depictions of *romantic* love. The Rock Hudson type or the Pat Boone type meets the Doris Day type or the Ann-Margret type; they find themselves romantically, excitingly in love and overcome great odds in order to marry. You put down the book or leave the theater or turn off the television with a warm, happy glow, feeling that if you are lucky, something like this might happen to you. Not only does this sort of romance rarely exist, but even when it does occur, it is seldom a relationship that would last through 40 years of marriage. Romance and sex appeal are occasionally one part of love, but they are not the same as love.

Overly romantic love is not the only sort of misguided love. Some people persuade themselves they are in love, when they merely seek to marry for money, for status, for security, or to get away from an unhappy home situation. People who wish to marry for these reasons will often rationalize their feelings as being love, since their self-concept makes it unacceptable to marry without love.

Courtship and engagement allow two people to get to know each other very well before entering into the permanent relationship of marriage. During this period, both people have the opportunity to anticipate many of the problems their marriage might entail, such as uncooperative relatives or highly irritating mannerisms, and evaluate these problems in light of their feelings for each other. In the United States, we expect people to love each other before becoming engaged and most certainly before marrying.

Marriage

Marriage, for most people, leads directly to the most important human relationship of adult years. Only vocation can even begin to compete with the family in its impact upon a person's life. The success and stability of marriage influence the emotional health of all concerned, especially the children, and—as a result—influence the vitality of the entire country.

In the United States we believe that the goal of marriage is to make the two marriage partners happy—it should be a worthwhile, self-actualizing, enjoyable experience for the couple. Carrying on the family name or taking care of the parents in their old age or bringing a dowry are no longer important to most Americans. These values are quite different in other areas of the world.

Who Marries Whom?

What brings two people together so that they wish to marry? The immediate answer is *proximity;* that is, they live or work or go to church or do something near each other, so that the chances are high that they will meet frequently and have the opportunity to get to know each other.

Husband and wife tend to be similar in numerous characteristics, such as race, religion, education, intelligence, social class, age, previous marital status (that is, divorced people tend to marry other divorced people), attitudes toward drinking, and the number of children desired (Berelson & Steiner, 1964). Husband and wife also tend to have similar personality characteristics, although these similarities are not so consistent as those cited above. When people select the characteristics of an ideal mate, they select characteristics similar to their own (Prince & Baggaley, 1963). Thus, the old idea that opposites attract is not upheld.

Among college students, women prefer to marry older men, and men prefer to marry younger women.* One study revealed that all the college women wanted to marry men with more or at least as much education as they had; the men preferred the women to have about the same amount of education as they had themselves. College women wanted to marry when they were about 22 or 23; men selected 24 and 25 as the best ages for marrying (Goldsen, Rosenberg, Williams, & Suchman, 1960).

Certain types of individuals tend to marry early. For example, school dropouts, less intelligent girls, people who are not church attenders, and teen-agers from broken homes have been found more likely to marry early. In addition, the husbands of early marriages are less likely to have vocational training and job skills and are more likely to have an unstable work career (Havighurst, Bowman, Liddle, Matthews, & Pierce, 1962). How will these factors affect the success of early marriages?

---

* What effect does this preference, in combination with the longer life expectancy of women, have upon the family structure in later years?

What Makes Marriages Successful?

Successful marriage depends upon many factors, some of which are far from being understood. Nonetheless, research into this matter has been extensive, and psychologists can predict with some success which marriages will be happy and which will be unhappy. In reading the rest of this chapter, keep in mind that although evidence may show that being happily married is *related to* some factor, this relationship does not imply that a happy marriage is *caused by* that factor. Thus, happily married people have been found to be less likely to be depressed than unhappily married people (Renne, 1968), but it is not certain that depression led to marital dissatisfaction, since the cause-and-effect could be exactly reversed.

Background Factors in Happy Marriages

Many childhood experiences are found to be related to later marital happiness. First, if you were brought up in a home with a happy marriage, you will have better chances of having a happy marriage; if you had a happy childhood, your chances will also be improved. Second, good relationships with parents produce later happy marriages. Third, children receiving firm discipline administered without undue harshness or frequency make better spouses. And, fourth, if parents are frank regarding sex and communicate healthy attitudes toward sex, their children seem to have happy marriages (Terman, 1938).

In addition, a happy marriage is more likely if the partners have finished high school or gone further, are happy on their jobs and with their leisure activities, and are physically healthy (Renne, 1968). Social relationships are similarly related to marital satisfaction. Happily married couples are more likely to see close friends and relatives frequently, but are no more apt to join social, recreational, union, professional, or community organizations (Renne, 1968).

You have undoubtedly also heard that early marriages are less successful than later marriages. In one Midwestern city, 40% of those who married before 21 wished they had waited, compared to less than 10% of those married after 21 (Inselberg, 1961). The early life of the individual and his age at marriage are definite factors in his marital success; yet they are certainly not insurmountable barriers.

Personality and attitudes. Marital happiness is greater when both husband and wife come from emotionally stable families and are themselves emotionally stable (Burgess & Cottrell, 1939; Lippman, 1954). In addition to emotional stability, other personality characteristics have been found to be related to happy marriages: (1) consideration for others, (2) willingness to yield rather than insistence on dominating, (3) being a good companion, (4) self-confidence, and (5) being able to accept emotional dependence (Burgess & Wallin, 1953), but not necessarily becoming so dependent that nothing matters except the relationship—a good relationship should build people up, not reduce their effectiveness.

People who accept themselves and admire their spouses are more happily married than those who have low esteem for themselves and their spouses. Lower marital satisfaction is found when one or both parties see themselves as impatient, lacking self-respect, being distrustful, unwilling to accept help, uncooperative, lacking warmth, and being gloomy (Luckey, 1964a, 1964b). Whether or not the personality descriptions given by the subjects in this study were accurate was not learned —the important matter was what the subjects *felt* was accurate.

Husband and wife need not share everything—indeed, there is merit in being apart from each other occasionally—but enjoying many of the same things can enrich a marriage. Liking the same movies, the same sports, or the same books adds a common bond, as does having similar religious, social, political, and child-rearing values. It is interesting to note that not only do husbands and wives often share political attitudes, but each also assumes that the other agrees with him more than he actually does (Byrne & Blaylock, 1963). That is, husbands and wives overestimate the degree to which their spouses think as they do.

Complementary needs.   Married couples may have similar psychological needs; however, it is more important that their needs be complementary, that is, that the needs of each be satisfied by the other. Thus, if the husband has a need to be admired and the wife has a need to admire others, their needs are complementary. If the wife has a high need for achievement and the husband has a need to have an achieving wife, their needs are complementary. Good evidence exists that husbands and wives tend to have needs that are complementary (Winch, Ktsanes, & Ktsanes, 1954).

Betty Williams was 30 years old when she married. She was attractive, intelligent, and popular, and few people could understand why she did not marry sooner, especially since she had had many proposals. Her husband, Marv, did not share either her vivacious personality or her popularity. In addition, he had a lower income than her parents and most of her friends. Many of Betty's friends could not understand why she married Marv, since she had the opportunity to marry men with more money and status.

The answer can only be understood in terms of Betty's needs. Betty had no need for a talkative companion or for someone to keep up with a hectic social life. She enjoyed talking, and her husband enjoyed having a sociable wife. Also, Betty wanted a strong, dominating man like her father. Marv was strong to the point of being stubborn—so was

Betty's father. Betty had a need for someone to understand her as a woman, not a social companion. Marv recognized her femininity and paid no attention to her surface bossiness which had dominated previous admirers. All in all, Marv and Betty satisfied each other's needs, so that the prediction of future success was good.

Women and men often do not want the same things from each other. Women show more need for love, affection, sympathy, and understanding; men have a greater need for a mate who is neat and tidy, can adjust to routine, and is even-tempered and dependable (Langhorne & Secord, 1955). Thus, the woman who needs affection and can be neat will probably be happiest with a man who needs neatness and can be affectionate.

Role Behavior.   Each person enters marriage with a self-concept, an ideal self, and an idea of how he expects his mate to behave. Happiness in marriage occurs when you behave as you expect to and your mate also behaves as you expected (Ort, 1950), and when you assume your spouse agrees with you (Levinger & Breedlove, 1966).

The role of the husband has traditionally been the dominant role. Throughout history and in most societies, men have been the warriors, while women have cared for the family. Even the God of the Judeo-Christian tradition is referred to as *He*, rather than She or It.

One author states that marital happiness is related to role behavior in three major ways. The marriage is happier when: (1) the husband's self-concept and ideal self are similar; (2) the husband's self-concept resembles his concept of his father; and (3) the wife looks upon the husband as being like *her* father (Tharp, 1963). Also, when the concept each partner has of himself corresponds to the concept the spouse has of him, the marriage is happier. Thus, in a happy marriage, the husband is the sort of person he wants to be; he has internalized the masculine role from his father; his wife has learned to judge the masculine role from *her* father and finds her husband lives up to her father; and both husband and wife have a self-concept consistent with the concept the other has of him.

In the United States, marital roles are relatively *egalitarian,* which means that the husband and wife share the power to make decisions and are considered fairly equal in the marriage. In most of the world, marriages are husband-dominated. College men are, perhaps understandably, less favorably disposed toward egalitarian marriages than college women (Kalish, Maloney, & Arkoff, 1966).

In spite of this *relative* egalitarianism, each home has a division of labor. Wives usually are responsible for doing the dishes and the cooking; husbands take care of the lawn and home repairs. However, when the wife works, the husband must share some of the wife's tasks, and the wife finds that she has less time to help him with his (Blood, 1960).

To some extent, each person re-creates in his marriage the marriage he lived with in his parents' home. He will behave much as the parent of his own sex behaved and will expect his mate to behave much as his other parent behaved.

> Marcia Sohn was the daughter of an aggressive woman who pushed her to "go with the right people" and "do the proper thing." Marcia's mother pushed her father also, until he was wealthy and terribly unhappy. As a child Marcia swore to herself that she would never push her own husband to become wealthy. Marcia eventually married a very pleasant man who enjoyed building up his business. Marcia did not push him to become wealthy, but she did push him to become better educated. He tried, but he decided he did not like college. Unlike Marcia's father, her husband refused to be bullied beyond a certain point, and he suggested a divorce. The couple decided to see a marriage counselor, and through his help, Marcia realized that she had been repeating the same pushing pattern that her mother had shown, except that she had pushed her husband to improve his education rather than to earn money.

Obviously, the role behavior of children is not the same as that of the parents. Nonetheless, children tend to behave somewhat like their parents. Since we assume that role behavior is learned, largely through **identification** and **internalization**, the behavior of parents becomes a vitally important influence upon the role behavior of their children.

Behavior in Marriage

When two people enter into marriage, they usually have extremely fine ideals. In spite of good intentions, most newlyweds do not find adjusting to marriage easy, even when they know each other well, are well-suited to each other, and come from stable homes.

During the first several months of marriage, many unanticipated difficulties may occur, until the couple finally work out reasonably healthy life patterns. Love and willingness to make an effort can help produce a successful marriage and encourage personal growth.

Advice on Getting Married, from Several People Who Did

Real love and a good marriage do not make two people as one. Rather, they make two people more distinctly two by letting them become better individuals than they were before. (A mathematical physicist in California)

You should not marry until your love is so strong that you feel that you just *have to* get married. Marriage should never be based on "might as well" or "I think it's okay," but on "I feel I must." (A recent divorcee in Ohio)

I don't know if I really loved my husband when we married, although I thought I did at the time, but I let myself love him over the years, and I know I do now. Love must have a chance to grow, no matter what it is to begin with. (A teacher in Illinois)

Try to imagine yourself getting out of bed every morning, only half awake, and sitting down at the breakfast table, and across the table is this face, looking like hell. If you can still love that face, that's love. (A hospital executive in Texas)

The saddest thing in the world is to see someone get married with the idea of making over the other person. They are unhappy if they succeed and unhappy if they fail. (An Air Force sergeant in South Dakota)

How can you contribute to making your marriage successful? A few of the many possible ways are the following.

Recognizing the needs of the other. Two people who have spent a great deal of time together under a variety of conditions should know each other very well. In a good marriage, each party becomes increasingly sensitive to the needs of the other, until—after a time—each can understand his partner's feelings, even without being told.

Learning to communicate. Sharing thoughts and feelings is important in marriage. The strong, silent type may be romantic before marriage, but he can be a frustrating husband. Some men feel that expressing their fears and hopes is a sign of weakness, but the opposite is actually the case, since a man must feel secure in his masculinity in order to be able to express his feelings.

Communication is important on a day-to-day basis. When a problem arises, it is useful to be able to sit down and talk it out. A new husband who feels his wife is flirting too much may be reluctant to mention it directly, so he displaces his anger by sulking in the corner or criticizing his wife's dress. However, if he and his wife can discuss the problem later, it will normally become no problem at all. When a married couple lack the ability to communicate with each other, they lack an important quality that fosters marital stability and satisfaction.

Learning to compromise. The importance of compromise is stated so often that it may actually have become exaggerated. Some compromise is necessary, but we often learn that a little discussion and thinking will allow both husband and wife to have what they wish. For example, Wife wants to visit her parents, and Husband argues that they just spent ten days with Wife's parents and he does not have the money to make the trip again. However, instead of compromising, Wife agrees to visit parents when Husband is out of town on a business trip. Both get what they wish.

Willingness to compromise sometimes means a willingness to give in. In one study, the husband or wife who reported that he and his spouse both gave in were happier than the ones who stated that either he gave in all the time or he never gave in (Renne, 1968). Apparently even winning all the battles—at least on the surface—does not make a married person as happy as when an effective compromise is reached.

Respecting privacy. Although communication is important, so is the opportunity for privacy. Married couples have the right to keep certain thoughts and feelings to themselves. A husband need not mention that he was unpopular back in high school; a wife may prefer to remain silent when a brief visit with an old boy friend rekindles some flame. Each should encourage the other to talk freely about feelings and ideas, but each should also respect the need of the other for privacy. Married people not only have the right to psychological privacy, but to physical privacy as well. The opportunity to be alone upon occasion is very important to many people.

Maintaining individuality. Marriage, as stated before, should not make two people into one but should make them more distinctly two. Married couples tend to share similar values, attitudes, behavior patterns, and styles of living, but this is no reason to apply pressure when similarity does not occur. The husband or wife who wishes to make the other over in his own image should marry a mirror instead of a human.

Being faithful. Our society expects sexual faithfulness in marriage, and extramarital relations can easily be disastrous to the future of the couple. Faithfulness neither begins nor ends with the sex act. Teasing and flirting may be harmless, or they may be a type of unfaithfulness. The man or woman who gives all his attention to work, children, clubs, or hobbies, and none to his spouse is also breaking the faith upon which the marriage was based. Forgetting or ignoring the human relationship in marriage can be as psychologically damaging as sexual infidelity.

Expecting too much. In countries where marriages are arranged, the participants do not expect much companionship and affection from the marriage. The husband may expect his wife to maintain the home, care for the children, uphold the family reputation, be careful with his money, be pleasant to him, give some physical affection, and respect his family. The wife expects to be cared for, given an occasional luxury, receive kindness, and be allowed some pleasures.

In the United States, expectations are much greater. We not only anticipate all the above, but also much more. Both husband and wife expect the other to be a social companion, share interests and values, participate in activities with mutual friends, be sexually exciting, and be

Development of Human Behavior

intellectually stimulating. Expectations, often including impossibly romantic notions, are frequently greater than can possibly be met. Although
husbands and wives in arranged marriages may receive less, they also
expect less. Thus, less difference exists between achievement and aspiration, and frustrations are fewer. This factor, often overlooked in discussion of marital success and failure, is undoubtedly a vitally important
variable.

Marriage is probably the most rewarding and the most demanding
relationship during adult life. Research has shown that successful marriages can, to an extent, be predicted from a knowledge of background
factors, childhood experiences, personality, attitudes, and needs of each
partner. Marital roles and marital role expectations also influence the
happiness of marriage. An awareness of the importance of certain types
of behavior during the marriage may lead to the increased satisfaction of
security, love, and esteem needs.

**Figure
11–1.**

Although these data are more than 30 years old, the general relationship between
marital adjustment and length of previous acquaintance still holds. Source: Saxton
(1968), after Burgess and Cottrell (1939).

Divorce

Statistics show that divorces increased steadily from the beginning of this century until a few years after the end of World War II; since then, the divorce rate has dropped back to what it was in the very early 1940s. We hear many reasons for the high rate of divorce, but a high divorce rate may be inevitable in a culture that feels that marriage is primarily for the happiness of the two people involved rather than for pleasing their families. If marriage is primarily for the happiness of the partners, then unhappiness would logically lead to dissolution of marriage.

Several factors are related to divorce. For example, divorces are more common among less educated people, among children of divorced parents, in interfaith marriages, among nonchurchgoers, for those with brief engagements, and for those who did not know each other very long before the marriage (Berelson & Steiner, 1964; Merrill, 1959). Divorces are especially common among couples married when still in their teens —about six times as common as among the general population—according to the Purdue Opinion Panel (cited in the *Los Angeles Times,* May 25, 1961). Of every 100 teen-age marriages, 50 end in divorce within five years (Menninger, 1968). The high proportion of teen-age brides who are pregnant undoubtedly contributes to the teen-age divorce rate. One investigator learned that nearly half of the high school brides surveyed were pregnant on their wedding day (Inselberg, 1961).

The real picture of divorce, however, is not given through statistics, but by observing the individuals involved. Not only the divorced couple, but also their children are punished for whatever mistakes were made. These children face three difficult problems: (1) the months leading up to a divorce are usually months of tension and family disruption; (2) the process of the divorce is often upsetting for the children; and (3) it is difficult for the children to live with only one parent or with a step-parent and see the remaining parent irregularly.

It has long been debated whether the child is better off with his parents divorced or with parents who are unhappily married. The dispute cannot be settled, except for individual cases. One child may be better off living with only one parent, because family arguments are hurting him deeply; another child has parents who conceal their unhappiness with each other, and he is probably better off if the marriage stays intact.

Some Never Marry

Our society puts such a high value on marriage that we are often critical of those who do not marry. Some choose not to marry because they recognize they are unwilling to share their lives, or because they do not like any member of the opposite sex enough to live as man and wife. Others just do not find the right person at the right time.

Although unmarried people certainly miss much of the enrichment a marriage can bring, they gain in other ways. They can spend much more of their money on themselves and have less financial concern regarding the future. They can do things and go places as they please and travel extensively if they want, without worrying about anyone else. Often they have warm relationships with relatives, married couples, or children, and receive some of the enjoyment of marriage indirectly.

We often forget that certain people who do marry would have been better off to have avoided this relationship, but were pressured into it by well-meaning family and friends.

Summary of Important Ideas

1. Parents have always considered seeing their children properly married to be one of their most demanding responsibilities.

2. The new freedom in colleges requires of students a new willingness to accept responsibility for their sex behavior.

3. Evidence conflicts as to whether there has been a substantial increase in sex behavior among college students, or whether attitudes on sex are just more open than before.

4. Permissible sex behavior differs from culture to culture, but each individual must deal with his own personal values and with the values of the community in which he lives.

5. The pros and cons of nonmarital sex behavior are many, but the final decision and final responsibility must necessarily reside with the individual.

6. The purpose of courtship is to allow two people to get to know each other well enough to decide whether they wish to marry.

7. The families of both partners are an inevitable factor to be considered in a future marriage.

8. Marriage across religious lines increases adjustment problems and the probability of divorce, but can still be successful.

9. Other problems in courtship include difficulty with friends, agreement on conventions, conflicting values, use of money, and affection and sex.

10. Marriage leads to the most important human relationship of adult years.

11. Husband and wife share some needs and values and have other needs and values that complement each other. There is no evidence that opposites attract.

12. The success of a marriage is related to the marital success of the partners' parents, to the prospective couple's childhood happiness, and to other factors of their earlier years.

13. Self-concept and role are also related to marital success.

14. In marriage, husband and wife are encouraged to recognize each other's needs, learn to communicate with each other, respect each other's privacy, allow for individuality, learn to compromise, be faithful (and not just technically), and not demand too much of the other.

15. Divorce rates are high, but have remained roughly constant for about 25 years or more, except for a sharp rise during the immediate post-World War II period.

Chapter Twelve

The Mature Years

It seems a little unfair to spend five chapters discussing the first 25 years of life, and only one chapter discussing the subsequent 50 years. However, the principles discussed in the previous chapters, including the chapters on needs, perception, and learning, do not change merely because a person is married and has a family. Nonetheless, there are certain matters of particular concern in the middle and later years of life, and these will be discussed in the present chapter.

The early adult years are marked by new opportunities, new freedoms, and new responsibilities. The fight for emancipation from parents should now be over. Health is usually good; vocational skills have been recently acquired; social relationships may be enjoyed with fewer restrictions than ever before; and hopes for the future are high. The age 21, which technically begins the adult years, has a certain magic about it. You are now free in many ways—you can vote, order a drink, get married, or take a job without your parents' permission.

With these new freedoms come new responsibilities. The adult is expected to take full responsibility for his own behavior: he must organize his own time, learn how to be fully responsible for earning and spending money, seek advice when he needs it, and enter into much more mature and demanding relationships. He is also fully responsible legally for his own actions and is expected to participate in the community and contribute to it.

The Adult Life Cycle

The early adult years still involve experimentation. The individual may experiment with his new emancipation from his parents, perhaps carrying freedom to excess one time, then being afraid to venture forth another time. He tests out relationships with the opposite sex, but with marriage more likely the purpose than in earlier years. He tries different jobs, lives in different houses, participates in different activities. From the great range of possible behavior patterns, he selects those that satisfy him the most.

As he moves into his thirties and forties, he gains a better idea of where he wants to go and where he is likely to be able to go. Although some people do make substantial changes in their life patterns after 30 or 35, most have settled into a type of routine that they will maintain until retirement age.

Between 40 and 50 "should be the peak period in life, not only for financial and social success but also for authority and prestige" (Hurlock, 1959). During this period, the individual is still active, vigorous, and alert, and he has accumulated experience and knowledge. Identity, sex, emancipation, and finding a purpose in life are no longer such bothersome problems. They have been replaced, however, by the need to come to grips with the reality that time is not infinite and that what is going to be accomplished during the lifetime must be accomplished fairly soon.

The hopes a person feels in his twenties must, for the most part, be realized by the time he is in his fifties, or they will never be realized. This decade demands a painful personal re-evaluation. Some of his friends have surpassed him and are much more successful than he; the expensive home he had hoped he would own may be as much a dream as ever; his children are not the geniuses he had always desired. Retirement suddenly becomes a concern, and his health may no longer be so good. His level of aspiration must be modified in terms of the present reality.

However, maturation and personal growth do not cease when a person reaches 21; they continue throughout his life-span. There will be times when he will feel the great satisfaction of knowing that he has made effective use of his capabilities—that he has accomplished his goals on a work project or in preparing his children to meet the world or by giving enjoyment to others.

Even in later years, happiness, satisfaction, and self-actualization can continue. People then have much to look back on and still have much to look ahead to. Some, of course, psychologically curl up and wait for death, but others use their later adult years to do the things they had always wanted to do, but for which they had never had the time. Their old age is rich and exciting, filled with warm, human relationships and stimulating activities.

Changing Patterns of Behavior

Behavior changes during the years from childhood through maturity, because at each stage of development new roles become appropri-

Development of Human Behavior

ate. Nonetheless, certain consistent patterns do carry over from child-hood into maturity. The aggressive child is likely to mature into a competitive adult; the intelligent child becomes an intelligent adult.

One interesting study traced a group of people from their infancy into their early adult years. The investigators found that the need for achievement among children between 6 and 10 predicted their actual achievement in their twenties, and that this was especially true for intellectual achievement. In the same study, teen-age boys who did not date or show other typical masculine interests seemed to avoid contact with the opposite sex ten years later. Children who displayed no aggres-sion turned into adults afraid to express aggressive feelings, and boys who were aggressive and dominant became competitive as adults (Kagan & Moss, 1962). Another study followed adults from their engage-ment until nearly 20 years later. The religious values and vocational interests of this group changed relatively little, although their attitudes toward marriage and child rearing did show change (Kelly, 1955).

Although general personality characteristics and underlying values are resistant to change, change most definitely occurs. Caucasian women attending a South Carolina university were given an attitude test in 1935

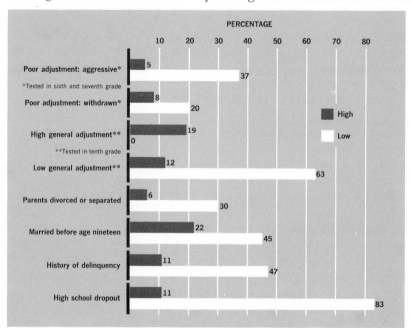

**Figure
12–1.**

Behavior in the early years can often predict later circumstances. This graph shows how family circumstances and adjustment during childhood and adolescence distin-guish high from low work-adjustment groups at a later time. The graph does not ex-plain *why* the relationships exist (Havighurst et al., 1962).

and were retested in 1965. The proportion of women who believed that Negroes should have equal rights increased from 8% to 56%; those believing that "militarism is necessary for proper defense and protection of individuals of our country" also increased by approximately the same amount (Capel, 1967). People's attitudes do change in time, often reflecting change in the attitudes of others and changing conditions.

An individual's intelligence relative to others of his age shows considerable consistency over the years. Those who were more intelligent than average when they were young tend to remain above average in intelligence in their mature years (Bradway & Thompson, 1962). However, although an individual's intelligence remains constant *relative* to others of the same age, changes in intellectual functioning do occur over the years. After the rapid increase from infancy through childhood, the growth of intelligence slows down during the junior high school years. Then, in the late teens or early twenties, performance on *some types* of intellectual tasks ceases to change until the later years, when performance begins to decline (Bayley, 1955).

At one time it was believed that general intelligence did not improve beyond the early adolescent years, but recent research has suggested otherwise. Certain groups, such as those who attend college and who go into more intellectually demanding jobs, increase their IQ scores, and their intelligence does not drop until they are well advanced in years (Bayley & Oden, 1955). Even then, the decrease in IQ test scores may reflect the reduced capacities of those who are physically ill or who have suffered strokes, rather than intellectual loss for all.

Evaluation of Changes Resulting from Age

Differences that result from age can be measured in two basic ways: first, by following the same group across a period of time and taking regular measurements; and second, by comparing groups of different ages at the same time, assuming that differences between them result from aging.

Both approaches have limitations. The first approach, termed **longitudinal** research, suffers from requiring much time to carry out. Also, it is greatly affected by what could be called accidents of history. For example, if we find that students who were tested in 1940 have different attitudes toward religion when retested in 1970, how can we know whether their religious attitudes changed because they aged 30 years or because of the specific events that took place between 1940 and 1970?

The alternate approach, the **cross-sectional** method, is also limited. Assume that you have found that the young and the elderly differ in vocabulary, with the young getting higher test scores. You might hypothesize that vocabulary skills decrease with age from youth onward. However, it is well known that the educational level of the elderly is far below that of the young, so differences might result from differential education. And how motivated are older people when they take tests? How much experience in being tested have they had? Thus, whether you are comparing vocabulary scores or attitude scores, it is very difficult to determine whether differences between age groups are caused by the process of getting old or by the fact that different age groups have had different life histories. Consider another example: Are generation-gap conflicts caused by the inevitable process of aging or because each generation has lived through different life experiences that are difficult to share with other generations?

Physical Changes and Psychological Reactions

Between early adulthood and old age, the body undergoes many slow changes. The hair thins out, especially for men, and the skin begins to develop wrinkles. Muscles tend to lose their tone, and an increase in weight is common. These changes, along with an increase in medical problems, usually do not make themselves felt until the person has approached or passed his middle forties; and they occur to different people at different ages.

During the late forties, many women go through **menopause**, a period during which the menstrual flow becomes less and less frequent and eventually stops. Menopause signals the end of the woman's potential for childbearing.

The impact of menopause is more emotional than physical, although many women describe disturbing physical symptoms also. Women often feel that they must be able to conceive to be truly women; when they lose this ability they feel they are also losing their femininity. Menopause is also a distinct and unavoidable sign of advancing age. These psychological problems, accentuated by physical discomfort, may produce feelings of depression and irritability.

The United States has been called a youth-centered society, because we place so much emphasis upon looking and behaving youthfully. Age means the end of youth, of its health and energy and physical attractiveness, of its hopes and opportunities and status. People resist the idea that they are growing old. Many men and women attack the most obvious symptoms of age through cosmetics, hairpieces, diets, and a variety of special treatments. Others participate in activities which appear out of keeping with their maturity level, such as the mother who insists upon being "one of the gang" at her 14-year-old's parties but refuses to spend time with her own age peers.

Although physical changes that come with age are rarely pleasing, people are certainly not equally bothered by them. Mature individuals who have built satisfying relationships and who have developed absorbing interests are likely to spend less time and energy worrying about physical changes. They are not so worried about looking youthful nor so frightened of seeming older, since other, more exciting ventures take up their days. They find their work challenging and their family relationships rewarding; home, friends, and enjoyable leisure, perhaps combined with political work or artistic endeavors, keep them busy.

New Opportunities and Responsibilities

Your life patterns change when you finish school and begin what you anticipate will be your career. Marriage and children produce another change in the life pattern and introduce new problems. As an adult, however, with increased knowledge, understanding, and maturity, you should be able to deal successfully with these problems. New opportunities and new responsibilities emerge through marriage and the family, financial considerations, interaction with the community, the mature sex role, the career, and enjoyment of leisure.

Family Responsibilities and Satisfactions

Your parents are likely to be the most significant others in your early development; your spouse and children will become vitally important to your adult years. Changes in your self-concept will depend to an appreciable extent on how these people look upon you and respond to you. The parent who is loved and respected by his family becomes a more complete person; the parent who is not loved or respected by his family becomes a less complete person.

Having a marriage partner and children not only offers opportunities for growth, but also adds demands and responsibilities. Your behavior, your health, your interpersonal relationships, and your happiness now affect not only you but also others. You can help others grow and mature effectively, or you can contribute to their having unfulfilled safety and love needs. How can you best help your family grow and make the most of their capacities?

Being a parent, particularly for the first time, causes great concern

---

Today's Family, Compared to the Family of 60 Years Ago

—They live in cities and suburbs, not in small towns or on farms.

—They commute to work.

—They move frequently (one out of five Americans moves each year °).

—They seldom live in the same home with grandparents; they often do not even live in the same community.

—They are less likely to have lost a parent by death, but more likely to have lived through parental divorce.

—Work is rarely a family affair.

—Education continues until the late teens or even later.

—The mother is more likely to be working or involved in social, political, or service activities.

Thus, at the very time that members of the family become more dependent upon each other because they are separated from family and childhood friends and the community, the realities of our society force them apart because work and education no longer occur within the family.

° Metropolitan Life Insurance Company Statistical Bulletin, April 1966.

---

for both husband and wife. They listen to advice, perhaps read books, and think back on what their own parents did that was right or wrong. Often they make great resolves about the wonderful things they will do with their children, but beneath everything is the question "Will I really be a good parent?" Some are undoubtedly better parents than others (see Chapters 7 and 8), but new parents should realize that "there is no such thing as a professional parent. We are all amateurs . . ." (Adams, 1968).

The purpose of having children. Do you want to have children? Why? For what purpose do you want children? At first, the idea of a purpose for children may seem absurd, since it seems natural to want children. Throughout history, however, children—especially male children—have had a very definite financial value: they were needed to help on the farm, to work in the family store, or to help support the family through some other form of work, and to take care of elderly and disabled parents and relatives.

Today, in the United States and in many other countries, children are needed neither to work for the family nor to care for the parents in their old age. As a matter of fact, having children is a great expense and responsibility. Nonetheless, people continue to have children. Married couples without children are considered unfortunate, and those who do not wish children are looked upon as peculiar.

The best reason for having children may very well be to enjoy them —enjoy watching them grow and enjoy helping them lead satisfying lives. Yet many foreigners observe that American parents do not really seem to love and enjoy their children. They remark that Americans worry about caring for their children, sending them to college, protecting them with insurance, and using good measures to protect their mental and physical health; but American parents just do not appear to others to enjoy their children. Does this relate to the often-heard comment that American parents push their children to grow up too fast? Why have so many foreigners felt this way? Do you feel that American parents are able to enjoy their children?

Some married couples do not want children, because they do not wish to expend the time, money, and personal involvement required by children. They can move around more easily and can devote full time and effort to careers or creative tasks that they find more fulfilling. Some adults do not particularly like caring for children, although they may be very fond of other people's youngsters. Although the traditions and values of our society place a certain amount of pressure upon married couples to have children, certain individuals recognize that—for them— the disadvantages of being childless are outweighed by the advantages.

Financial Responsibilities

In our society, finances are important. The ways in which you get money and the ways in which you spend it influence much of your behavior. What you buy is determined not only by your income, but also by your needs and self-concept, which affect both your expenditures and the conditions under which they are made.

Jack Valdez and Marty Keene were both recently married and in the market for a refrigerator, which each needed within a week. Marty, after a little shopping, bought a refrigerator "on time," since he did not have the money to pay outright. The initial price of the refrigerator was $212, but he ended up paying $263 through extra charges for the time payments. Jack was more frugal. Through newspaper advertisements, he picked up a used refrigerator for $50 from a person who was moving. Then he put $15 a month into a savings account at 5% interest. Ten months later, the $212 refrigerator was on sale for the special price of $172.95. Jack easily bought it for cash, then turned around and sold his old refrigerator for $45. By using a second-hand refrigerator for one year, Jack and his wife saved over $80.

Jack's approach seems to make sense, but it does not take into account Marty's self-concept. His self-esteem is based partly on his ability to buy things like a new refrigerator. Also, he feels that buying second-hand goods implies that he is not a good husband. He wants his wife to have "the best we can possibly afford." He knows his wife will entertain her friends in the breakfast nook, and he does not want them telling their husbands that he bought his wife a used appliance.

The same product is not worth the same amount to everyone. One couple give up new clothing in order to take a trip; another family puts a substantial portion of its income into the bank instead of buying a new automobile; a third couple prefer to eat at home unless they can go to an expensive restaurant. The wife of an extremely wealthy hotel executive was asked by her husband whether she preferred a yacht or an original painting by the great artist Pablo Picasso. She chose the painting and hung it in the bedroom. What do you suppose motivated her? What would you select if you were offered $200,000 to spend on any *one* thing?

What financial responsibilities does a husband have? What about a wife? How much of our income should be put away against future old age, illness, or some catastrophe? What kinds of insurance should you carry? What is a good investment: land? stocks? government bonds? Each of these questions can be answered only on an individual basis. How do you think you will answer them in ten years?

Money can buy money. When you borrow money or make a credit purchase, you are using money to buy money. Like anything else, buying money can prove very expensive. Sometimes, by the time the hidden costs are accounted for, you may be paying a true annual interest of 20% or more to borrow money. A simple 1½% per month charge is 18% per year; if there is a minimum interest or carrying charge payment of 50¢, the rate may easily go over 20%. Credit, like an attractive woman, is alluring; also, like an attractive woman, credit has been the downfall of many families.

Even though the wealth of the average American has never been greater, more people and more businesses are going bankrupt (*Los Angeles Times*, February 3, 1966), largely because people are buying more on credit than their income justifies. In order to maintain an adequate level of protection for emergencies, the American family is advised to have enough savings to live on for six months, but very few families have this amount of money available. What sort of personality is a "money saver" likely to have? What about an "overspender"?

Interaction with the Community

What responsibilities do you feel to your community? To your nation? To the world? You are a part of each of these, and you expect each to offer you something. What do you wish to give in return? One great American, Horace Mann, stated, "Be ashamed to die until you have won some victory for humanity." Do you feel you have any responsibilities to win some victory for future generations?

The work and the responsibility of supporting our community are always divided unequally, with some people doing much more than others. Those willing to put forth the time and effort, however, may have the satisfaction of seeing the effects of their work.

A person with a healthy personality wishes to participate actively in the democratic process. As an informed voter, he needs to know more than who belongs to what party or who is running for what congressional office. He also needs to know something about the men running for judge, for district attorney, and especially for the state legislature. It is at the local level that you can be most influential. Few people can affect national or statewide elections, but you can have some impact upon nominees from your district to the state legislature. By joining and working for a political party, you can find ways to present your own ideas directly to the men who represent you.

Using community facilities.   Every community offers many facilities in exchange for the money and energy its citizens supply. Some facilities and services, such as roads, schools, libraries, zoos, and police and fire protection, are supported by taxes. Entertainment and recreation are provided both by private businesses (movies, plays, bowling, golf, athletic contests, and concerts) and by public agencies (parks, tennis courts, museums, and swimming pools).

Local colleges offer educational opportunities, counseling, visiting speakers, and a variety of athletic and cultural programs. Formal education need not stop when you have obtained your degree. People trained in technical fields in college may return after some years of work to take refresher courses, to investigate a new career, to add to their human relations skills, or to satisfy their curiosity about literature or history. Someone who has studied liberal arts may want to learn data processing, electronics, or typing. The range of educational opportunities after high school is vast, particularly in urban areas and college communities.

The world community.   People can no longer shut themselves off from the rest of the world. The opposite ends of the earth are just a fraction of a minute away by radio, a few hours by jet airplane, and—sad to say—not very far apart for intercontinental ballistic missiles. Your life may be deeply affected by a tribal feud in Iran, an impoverished economy in Indonesia, or a political fight in Iceland.

The well-adjusted person recognizes that he is a part of the world, and he wishes to have knowledge of it beyond the slogans of propagandists. This means that he needs to know something about the historical and cultural backgrounds of other nations, as well as of his own. He needs to try to understand how people around the world think and feel and develop self-concepts and aim at self-actualization. The reactions of a soldier in Laos, a politician in Gambia, or a farmer in France can be understood only in terms of *his* background, *his* culture, and *his* individual development.

Mature Love

Love is a word used to describe a multiplicity of relationships, from the schoolgirl's crush on her favorite movie idol to the passion of young lovers to the warmth and serenity of the love of the no-longer young (see Chapter 11). Psychologist Erich Fromm writes that mature love lets a person remain very much an individual and retain personal dignity and integrity; it also helps break through the loneliness and isolation that so many feel. On the other hand, immature love requires that the other person offer love first (for instance, the infant's love for his parent is immature) and that love be based on a need for the loved one. Mature love follows the principle "I am loved because I love," and "I need you because I love you"; immature love says "I love because I am loved," and "I love you because I need you" (Fromm, 1956).

Love, in the sense the term is used here, is not limited to relationships between mature adults of opposite sexes. Love can occur between virtually any two people. However, love need not be "between." A human being may love another without reciprocation; for instance, he may love his month-old son, a political or religious figure he has never met, or his mother who died as he was born.

Love should help both the person giving and the person receiving to grow and to be better able to become what they wish to become. Although love, like friendship, has obvious hazards in that it opens the giver to the possibilities both of rejection by the loved one and of loss of the loved one, it should be enriching.

Consider the variety of situations to which the term "love" can be properly applied:

> A parent and his child may love each other, regardless of the age of either one. The love may continue long after one of them has died. Under certain conditions an individual may feel love for a parent of whom he has little or no memory.

A husband and wife may retain a very deep love for each other throughout their lives. And, after one member of the couple dies, the surviving spouse may continue to love the deceased mate, even though he or she loves another person and remarries. There is no principle of human behavior that prevents a person from loving both living and deceased spouses.

Sometimes a man and woman, not married to each other, develop a friendship deep enough to be called love, but without overt sex or romance. Sadly enough, complications can arise in such a relationship, especially if either is married to someone else and if the relationship encourages jealousy from those not included.

An individual may feel love for nonparental significant figures, such as a grandmother, a maid, or a teacher. Children who spend a long period in a hospital might direct such feelings toward a doctor or a nurse. You can undoubtedly think of other circumstances that would lead to a similar sort of love.

Unhealthy Expressions of Love

What is often called "love" can tear down an individual's self-concept instead of building it up. It can produce constant fear, anxiety, and pain; and it can lead to deficiency-motivation instead of growth-motivation. These things occur when love is rejected or in danger of being rejected, when it is too demanding, or when it is based upon psychologically unhealthy needs. Such love would appear inconsistent with the healthy personality; and we might even question whether the word "love" can properly be applied to such cases, but this is not the occasion to begin a semantic argument. Consider the following examples:

Bob Frand was very much attached to his mother, and he lived with her until she died, shortly after his thirty-first birthday. Up until that time he had never been involved with any girl for more than a few weeks. However, he was greatly upset by his mother's death and sought comfort with a woman at work, an attractive, very understanding 45-year-old widow. They began to see each other casually, until the woman decided to move to Florida, where a married daughter was living. At that point, Bob declared his love for her and, in a whirlwind romance, persuaded her to marry him. Once married, Bob immediately manipulated their relationship so that his wife did the same things for him that his mother had done, and he pouted and fussed like a child when the new Mrs. Frand tried to have him play the normal male role in the home. Bob had no interest in sex relationships, although he spoke very vaguely of having children "someday." When his wife decided to spend two weeks with her daughter and grandchildren, Bob complained bitterly that she did not love him. Then, the day before she was scheduled

242

Development of Human Behavior

to leave, he began to vomit and complained of terrible headaches. His wife canceled her trip. She never learned that Bob's mother became so concerned over his slightest sniffle that he could completely dominate her by pretending illness.

Joe Calvin came to Los Angeles with a high school diploma, an amazing memory, and tremendous motivation to get rich and be able to forget his poverty-stricken, rural Texas background. Maria Kent came to Los Angeles with a college degree, a great sensitivity to the arts, and a desire to make good on her own without the help of her family's money and status. They met, were strongly attracted to each other, and married. But the mild disagreements they had had before their marriage flared into a constant state of bickering and arguing after their marriage. Maria admired Joe's energy and ambition, but she resented his lack of sympathy for the arts and his lack of patience. Joe liked the idea of having a wife who dressed well, knew the right people, and enjoyed art, but he resented the way she nagged him to go to museums and concerts with her and to give more money to charities for the poor, which Joe felt was just money thrown away.

In her irritation, Maria began to criticize Joe for his manners, his speech errors, and his lack of education; she was particularly hostile when Joe's well-educated business associates and friends were with them. Joe reciprocated by withdrawing into his work. He explained that her clothes and other money demands forced him to expand his business and devote more time to it. As Joe withdrew into work, Maria withdrew into the community art league and a relief organization for American Indians. Tired of waiting until 9:00 for Joe to come home from work, Maria volunteered for evening activities, leaving Joe to return to an empty house. Joe so hated the empty house that he began to have his dinners downtown, and came home only after several after-dinner drinks. At that point, Maria announced that she had accepted a job offer working with American Indians that would require her to be away from home several days at a time.

Neither the Frands nor the Calvins were happy in their marriages. In the Frand marriage, the unhealthy needs that caused Bob to marry in the first place made him dependent upon his wife, yet very demanding of her. The Calvins' problem was much different: here are two basically well-adjusted people who are unable to communicate with each other; each frustrates the other, and each frustration leads to a new aggressive response which, in turn, leads to a new frustration. Slowly each tears the other down, leaving a less adequate person who becomes less able to respond to his spouse's needs. Would you apply the term "love" to the Frand marriage? How about the Calvin marriage?

Love is an enriching, enhancing experience when it is mutual, when it involves healthy, growth-directed motives, when the people involved can communicate with each other, and when it produces healthy interdependency, but not overdependency.

The Mature Sex Role

An individual's social roles change as he matures, but these changes differ considerably according to sex. Boys, for example, are given much greater freedom than girls, even though girls mature more rapidly. Boys can misbehave, fight, get dirty—or even smoke, drink, cut school, or miss church. Although they may be criticized or punished, their treatment will be much more lenient than what girls receive for the same offenses.

In our society and in most others, being a man is looked upon as more desirable than being a woman, and more American girls would prefer to have been boys than boys would prefer to have been girls (Brown, 1957). This sex preference stems from the greater freedom, the higher prestige, and the more exciting life (at least, so people think) of a man.

Throughout the life-span, the role of a woman is more restricted. She has less freedom to travel, to do things by herself, even to use the education she is now able to receive (given the choice between educating the son or the daughter, most families still would select the son). Even though the American woman is now recognized as having a potential for maturity, competence, and stability equal to men, she is treated differently because of her sex role.

Some Comments About the Role of Arab Women in the Middle East (Muhyi, 1959)

—Before marriage, the Moslem girl is "expected to stay at home, to help with the housework and . . . the younger children, to obey her father, mother, brothers, and . . . older sisters."
—In the very traditional families, the girl studies primarily household arts; she may even wear a cloak and veil. She has little voice in the selection of her husband, although she may refuse a marriage.
—The wife is not supposed to protest against anything her husband does.
—Most of the modern and better-educated girls disapprove of dancing or going to movies with boys.

A book entitled *The Feminine Mystique* (1963) struck at the heart of this issue. Author Betty Friedan reiterated that women are not really being treated as equal to men. Men, she felt, had persuaded women that self-actualization could be best attained through being a wife and mother, by learning to sew creative clothing for the children and cook exciting meals for "hubby." The author complained that women, in spite of more and more education, were wasting their training and intelligence on dull tasks. To keep women from competing with them on the job, men were trying to lull women into thinking that the home was really exciting, although these same men knew that this was not true. Miss Friedan urged women to get better training and education, to get interesting jobs, to make the most of their capacities and education.

Needless to say, the book caused a storm of controversy. Many women as well as men objected to the idea, claiming that Miss Friedan was out to break up homes. What she actually tried to do was alter the entire tradition of proper female sex-role behavior. Miss Friedan seemed to be saying, "Women have brains, education, and needs for self-actualization; the life they lead at home is not sufficient to satisfy their needs for self-actualization; their brains and training qualify them for more exciting work; they deserve it." The book may have oversimplified the solution, but the problem is an important one: When the traditional sex role for women is no longer adequate to the needs they feel and express, what should be done?

Many women have complained that their world is surrounded by the walls of the kitchen and is inhabited by creatures three feet high with runny noses. They may exaggerate the excitement in the lives of their husbands, but there seems to be no doubt that many women have been frustrated by the activities they are forced into. Volunteer work, an evening college class, a lecture series, PTA work, an art class—these things are not enough for some women, who may be skilled teachers, secretaries, nurses, or beauticians. More than that, it is certainly not enough for those women who would have wished to be engineers, business executives, physicians, or electricians, but were kept out because of job prejudices against women.

Is a woman's first responsibility to herself or to her family? If it is to her family, does this mean she must remain in the home? "No!" shouts Miss Friedan, who goes on to claim the woman is a better wife and mother when she is self-actualizing through worthwhile work. She is more interesting, better company, and more satisfied with her self-concept.

The Working Wife

More and more women have joined the work force in our country, and this trend will undoubtedly continue. In 1964, 37% of all females aged 10 and over were working—double the percentage working in

The Mature Years

1900 *—and one-third of all married women were working. Yet many married women who work are in conflict between wanting to work and wanting to spend more time at home.

There seem to be four major reasons why women work: (1) to add money to the family bank account; (2) to satisfy needs for accomplishment and self-actualization; (3) dislike of childcare (not necessarily of children) and of housework; (4) pleasure from the activities and relationships that occur on the job.

The woman who works to add money to the family bank account can do so if there are no major childcare expenses. However, working mothers often far overestimate the amount of money their work will add to family income because they underestimate the additional expenses: federal and local income tax, transportation (which sometimes includes a second car), housework help, lunches, clothing, cleaning and laundry, baby-sitting or nursery school, more frequent trips to the beauty parlor, not having time to shop at sales, and the extra recreation because "you're working so hard." One bank executive estimated that the average working wife with children has to earn three dollars to add one dollar to the family budget. To make matters worse, a married couple become accustomed to living on two incomes. If the wife should become pregnant, the loss of her income, even for a few months, could be disastrous.

If money is the only motive for her work, the wife is likely to feel guilty for taking time from her children and her home. However, if she dislikes taking care of children all day, or if she has a need to do something with her talents, she may consider the income as a bonus. In such instances, working may well make her a better wife and mother than staying at home.

In one survey, half the men disapproved of working mothers, and more than one-fourth of the women also disapproved (Goldsen, Rosenberg, Williams, & Suchman, 1960).

Because the traditional male role requires that he support his wife financially, and because her working may imply that he is unable to do so, the husband of a working wife must have a healthy self-concept in order to make a good adjustment to his situation. He must be secure in his feelings of masculinity and not be fearful of criticism about his wife's working. Rather than actually competing with men for jobs, most women enter fields that are not dominated by men; less than 10% select business, law, medicine, or engineering for a desired future profession (Goldsen et al., 1960).

Some light has been shed upon the effect working mothers have on

---

* *Information Please Almanac,* 1966.

Development of Human Behavior

their children, but the question is far from answered. One study showed that year-old infants whose mothers did not work were more emotional and more active, but also more dependent upon their mothers (Caldwell & Hersher, 1964). Among very intelligent children, those with working mothers are more likely to perform below their capacities in school (Frankel, 1964).

A more sophisticated study took into account not only working versus nonworking mothers, but also stable homes versus unstable homes. The results indicate that the working mother in an unstable home

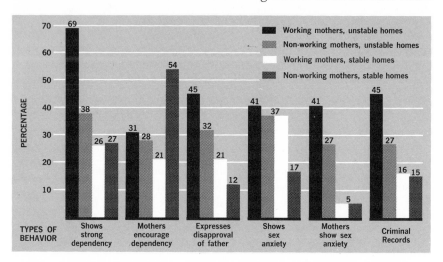

Figure
12–2.

Effects of maternal employment and home stability on boys (McCord, McCord, & Thurber, 1963).

had the most poorly adjusted children. However, the children of working mothers who provided stable homes were not much different from those of nonworking mothers (McCord et al., 1963). There is also evidence that the mother's attitude toward working or being a housewife is most important; that is, mothers who want to be housewives and are housewives or who want to work and are working have good relationships with their children. Mothers at the office who would rather be at home and mothers at home who would rather be at the office have child-rearing problems (Yarrow, Scott, deLeeuw, & Heinig, 1962).

The author would evaluate the working wife and mother as follows: the wife's working is appropriate (1) if the home is stable and can remain so, (2) if the woman has psychological needs that can be met by working or if the family's financial position requires it, and (3) if she and her husband can compensate for the time spent away from the

"Whatsamatter, Mac,—think my place is
in the home or somethin'?"

**Figure
12–3.**

Working women are sometimes a threat to the male's sense of self-esteem. Courtesy
Ed Fisher.

children and from each other by healthy love and attention when they
are together.

Use of Leisure

What do you like to do in your spare time? Sleep? Watch television? Tinker with an automobile? Listen to music? Read? Talk? Play
cards? The amount of leisure time available to the working man has been
increasing steadily over the years until, today, the average amount of

leisure per work week is three times that of 1850 (Kaplan, 1960), and the future will most likely see a continued reduction in work hours and increase in leisure time. You may see, during your lifetime, a standard three-day weekend, a seven-hour day, a three-month vacation every ten years. If these changes occur, what will you do with your vastly increased leisure time?

Leisure can be used for relaxation or for exciting activities, but it is usually a change from the regular daily routine. A strenuous camping trip is just as truly leisure as a week of loafing around the house. Surprisingly enough, a man who spends a week camping may return to work more refreshed than the man whose free week was just an overextended, loafing weekend.

Some forms of leisure may be financially rewarding. The person who writes or takes photographs in his spare time may eventually earn money with his efforts. Similarly, the person who fixes the car or sews for the children or paints the bedroom is saving money. If these tasks are enjoyable, they are leisure; if they are disliked, they are work.

Productive work as part of the American tradition can be traced back to our Puritan ancestors and the early days of Protestantism. Many Americans, perhaps without realizing it, look upon work as "good" and loafing as "bad." In casual conversation, you do not brag about how little you work, but about how hard you work. The emphasis upon productive work has become so much a part of the culture that you may find it difficult to relax without feeling you should be "doing something." Yet leisure, either relaxing or exciting, can be just as fulfilling as work. As a matter of fact, people who use their leisure effectively are likely to be able to work harder and get more done in the long run—and will probably live longer.

Educators are often very unhappy with the amount of time people spend watching television, the family television set being on an average of five hours a day, seven days a week, and even more than that in the winter (Bogart, 1962). Educators also point out that many programs that are thoroughly enjoyed by first-graders are also followed faithfully by their parents, which hardly speaks well for the maturity level of the programming.

Television is relaxing. It requires neither thinking nor bodily activity. As such, it has a definite appeal to people who want to be entertained without any effort. Watching television may help children from disadvantaged homes, by exposing them to new speech patterns and vocabulary, but it does little for the child or adult who has a stimulating home environment.

Claims are made that television reduces the time children would spend on more productive and stimulating activities, but the evidence does not fully bear this out. Watching television cuts most deeply into such activities as listening to the radio, going to movies, and reading comic books. In England, at least, it seemed to have little effect upon other activities; both book sales and library use, which dropped just after television first appeared, increased as people ceased finding the novelty of the home screen exciting (Himmelweit, 1962).

Leisure activities are influenced by many factors, including the time available, facilities available, finances available, personality and needs, and interests (adapted from Lehner & Kube, 1964). People fortunate enough to have the initiative find ways to spend their leisure time enjoyably and with profit to themselves. Others are bored with their spare time and end up killing time in any way they can, and some use increased leisure time for working at a second job.

The Elderly

Patterns of behavior change during the later years of adult life, and the elderly person must adapt himself to new activities, new expectations, and new opportunities and limitations. Over the past few years, the interest in geriatrics (the treatment of the aged) and gerontology (the study of the aged) has increased greatly, until now a much better awareness exists about the elderly and their concerns.

The proportion of the American population aged 65 or over has been steadily increasing. In 1900, under 5% of our population was in that age group, whereas over 10% will be in that group within a very few years. Americans seem to fear becoming old and try to appear youthful. One famous Japanese author wrote, "The sharpest difference between America and Japan is the truly inept manner of growing old demonstrated by the Americans and Europeans. . . . The sight of an old woman, decked in a sleeveless, short-skirted dress of a pink-flowered material, her face powdered a dead white, on the skating rink . . . is not objectionable, I suppose—but I . . . would not wish my grandmother to look like that" (Mishima, 1964).

In our society, the elderly person often feels that he is without a meaningful role. Because he is retired, he has no work role; because his children are grown and out of the house, his role as a parent has lost much of its importance; as his friends die, the attractiveness of developing new social roles diminishes. As a result, the older person is likely to *disengage.* Disengagement refers to a mutual withdrawal of the older person and of the community around him (Cumming & Henry, 1961). The older person finds the community more difficult to deal with and less appealing, and the community finds the older person less valuable; thus they pull away from each other.

Disengagement is not necessarily harmful. For some people, it actually provides a healthy basis for adjusting to age. Reducing community involvements may be essential for some older persons in order to maintain the energy and the money necessary for other activities. Older persons require more time to do things and can accomplish fewer things during the waking day. Older people, of course, vary as much as younger people; some 80-year-olds are still going strong, and others have slowed down measurably at 65. Also, behavior in old age is undoubtedly a continuation of earlier behavior, and the people who withdraw at 70 might well have given indications of withdrawal when they were 40.

The fear of anticipated dependency weighs as heavily upon the older person as any other matter. "I do not want to be a burden on my children" is a frequent statement. In many parts of the world, grown children expect to care for their elderly parents; in the United States, however, the desire to remain independent is strong in all age groups. Perhaps if more emphasis were placed upon mastery, that is, the ability to control the environment and the self, and less upon independence, problems would diminish. No one of any age is truly independent—we all depend upon others all the time. However, since our country values independence so much, children internalize its importance; then when these children grow up and become elderly, they resent their own dependence as a sign of inadequacy (Kalish, 1967).

Changes in the Aged

The elderly face many problems. Their changing physical appearance makes them less attractive in the eyes of the rest of society. They may begin to forget things quickly, even things told them a few minutes earlier; and personality and self-concept changes become evident. Just as the adolescent and the middle-aged person must learn new roles, the elderly also must learn new forms of behavior consistent with their age and situation.

Physical and intellectual changes. · In old age, bodily changes occur more rapidly than previously. The senses of sight, hearing, taste, smell, touch, and balance become less sensitive. Fortunately in a way, the sense of pain also becomes less acute. Strength diminishes, and reaction time becomes longer, so that responses are sometimes slowed down (Birren, 1964).

Physical appearance changes in many ways. The skin becomes loose and wrinkled; the body shape changes; and hair continues to thin out and changes in color to gray and white. Resistance to disease diminishes, and the bones become harder and more brittle.

Some types of intellectual abilities, for example, those involving memory or perception, decrease in old age. Other capacities, such as the

Figure
12–4.

Do you recognize these famous radio entertainers of the 1940s? What does the picture suggest about the aging process of an individual? What does it suggest about other kinds of changes that occur with time? Courtesy Columbia Broadcasting System.

---

ability to accumulate knowledge and information, show little or no decrease. When severe decrements in intelligence do occur, they may be the result of physical illness rather than of normal aging.

Individual differences among the elderly are great. Their previous history of health, nutrition, and care affect their vitality; their mental health and eagerness to live are also thought to be factors. Heredity and luck undoubtedly are also important. When death comes, it seems to be without pain in most cases, at least according to the words of the dying themselves (Osler, 1911).

Personality changes. The needs of the elderly are not met nearly so well as the needs of younger people. One psychologist has suggested five sources of frustration that restrict the satisfaction of both deficiency motives and growth motives.

1. *An age status that idealizes youth.* Since the attributes of youth are so admired, the aged often feel unwanted. Their self-esteem suffers, and they feel frustration, to which they respond in many of the ways described in Chapter 14.

2. *Pressures of time and money that lead to restriction of interests and activities.* The elderly have limited earning potential and often live on pensions, social security, and gifts from their children. At the same time, since they do not know how long they will live, they are forced to be cautious with their expenditures so that they can continue to support themselves.

The pressures of time operate differently for the aged. Since they recognize that the years ahead of them are limited, they may feel reluctant to begin any long-range projects. Some can no longer look forward to new accomplishments. The hopes and plans that have not yet been fulfilled may never be fulfilled.

3. *Physiological changes that demand attention.* Because of the increase in illness and the increased danger from accidents, the elderly become very much absorbed in their own physical problems. This restricts their opportunities to be concerned with other people and other things, and they may gain the reputation of being complainers.

4. *Technological changes that outdate their skills.* The world is changing rapidly, and new inventions and processes emerge constantly. Younger people can learn and become accustomed to these new ways, but older people have less opportunity and less motivation to do so.

5. *The feeling that there is less chance to move out of a frustrating situation.* Change is more difficult for the elderly, and many of their unhappy life situations, they realize, will never be changed. The elderly recognize that their physical and intellectual abilities are diminishing and will not return (Kuhlen, 1963).

Successful Adjustment

The picture of the aged described above is certainly not a pleasing one. Some aspects of it are inevitable, in spite of advances in the medical and social sciences. However, many elderly people remain very vital, productive, and active. What do you know about the lives of Albert Schweitzer, Herbert Hoover, Casey Stengel, Bernard Baruch, George Bernard Shaw, Grandma Moses, Amos Alonzo Stagg, Robert Frost, or George Washington Carver? Think of elderly people you know who lead

Figure
12–5.

Pablo Casals was 88 years old when this picture was taken. Despite his age, his cello performances place him as one of the world's greatest musicians. Courtesy Columbia Broadcasting System.

enjoyable and productive lives: what qualities do they have that enable them to live like that?

The elderly who do adjust well differ from the average older person in many ways. They gain satisfaction from their activities; they are able to accept the changes that come with age, rather than fight them; they seek, instead of avoid, social relationships (Terman & Oden, 1959). People who have established healthy relationships with their children are more likely to enjoy these relationships in their later years.

Successful adjustment to old age is partly the result of proper planning. Men who plan for retirement and who want to retire remain happier and healthier, and they also are busier; those who do not plan or do not want to retire become bored easily (Thompson, 1958; Thompson & Streib, 1958).

Retirement can be distressing. It connotes reduction in income, loss of social contacts and of meaningful roles, and lack of having time structured by the work schedule. However, for many people retirement is the beginning of a long and rich life. Social contacts once found on the job can be found through organizations, including—but not limited to—senior citizens' clubs. Many older people find their services useful in political organizations, through volunteering for work in hospitals and social agencies, and in providing care for those elderly who are unable to take care of themselves. One of the more innovative programs for the elderly is the Foster Grandparent plan. Through this plan, young children in institutions (for example, the mentally retarded, crippled, or parentless) are assigned foster grandparents who spend several hours every week with them. Both the child and the older person are given a meaningful relationship, and the older person is provided a small income to supplement his social security pay. (In 1967, half the older couples in the country had an income of under $3900, although the comparable figure for younger persons was well over twice as high, and the discrepancy appears to be increasing.)

Social relationships for retired people are more readily available if there are many other older people around. Although you hear claims that the elderly really need to be surrounded by the young, evidence exists that people in general do not establish many friendships outside their age group, and that living near other retired persons offers a more fruitful opportunity (Rosow, 1967). Those who move to retirement communities express slightly higher life satisfaction than those who remain in their own community. They are also likely to have more friends, but they tend to regret lack of contact with children and grandchildren (Wilner, Walkley, Sherman, & Dodds, unpublished data, 1969).

When do you begin planning for old age? The answer is "Yesterday." Financial planning begun during the early adult years will increase the chances of financial comfort during the later years. Physical health in later years is partly the result of diet, exercise, and other patterns begun today. Having interests and activities in the early adult years will mean a better chance of being interested in life in the later years. Such activities as travel, reading, music, certain types of mechanical work, painting, woodcraft, camping, and fishing can be begun in early years and easily carried over into later years.

People whose entire existence is centered exclusively around their family or their work find they have nothing with which to occupy themselves when their children are grown and independent and the retirement period begins. They feel useless and bored.

When death becomes imminent, only about 10% of the elderly will admit a fear of it, another 30% express mixed feelings, and the remainder state they are able to accept the inevitability of death (Jeffers, Nichols, & Eisdorfer, 1961).

Recently, increased attention has been given the aged. Community activity centers have been established. Physicians, psychotherapists, and social workers have become more responsive to their psychological and medical needs. We recognize now that they are likely to wish to discuss the coming of death instead of avoiding it (Feifel, 1959). Institutions for the elderly are becoming oriented toward keeping their patients active and involved in the world, rather than merely maintaining them as bed patients. Perhaps most important of all, there has been an increase in the demand that the elderly be able to live and to die in pleasant surroundings, with ample opportunity for activities and warm, human relationships, and in dignity.

Summary of Important Ideas

1. Maturity demands increasing responsibility and offers new opportunity.

2. The life cycle provides an ever-changing pattern of demands, responsibilities, roles, activities, and problems.

3. Certain patterns of behavior and certain capabilities remain relatively consistent from childhood to maturity.

4. Changes that occur as a function of age are measured by the longitudinal method and by the cross-sectional method.

5. Family responsibilities are characteristic of the mature years in Western societies. Being able to give and to receive a mature form of love is one of these responsibilities; financial awareness is another.

6. Differences between male and female sex roles are evident in all cultures. In the United States, the male role tends to be more prestigious.

7. Many people feel that the sex role of the woman is unnecessarily inhibiting.

8. The proportion of women, including married women, in the work force is much higher today than 60 years ago.

9. Working wives and mothers are often not approved of by the community. However, research suggests that the stability of the mother, rather than whether or not she works, is the major influence upon the children.

10. The mature individual has a responsibility to his community, which—in turn—offers him many opportunities.

11. Leisure can be used for relaxation or for exciting activities. The proportion of time available for leisure has increased steadily over the years and is likely to continue to increase in the future.

12. The proportion of Americans over 65 has nearly doubled since 1900.

13. The elderly person often feels that he lacks a meaningful role in the community. Sometimes disengagement occurs, as the older person and the community move away from involvement with each other.

14. Fears of dependency are great for many elderly people.

15. Many physical, intellectual, and personality changes occur in the later years.

16. Proper planning can help make retirement a very rich period of life.

Part Three

Development and Effects of Stress

Chapter Thirteen

Emotions and Stress

Perhaps you just read Chapter 12; perhaps your instructor decided to follow another plan and asked you to read this chapter immediately after Chapter 6 or 7. Both approaches—or, indeed, several other approaches— make sense. Thus, if you have just finished the material on human development, you have learned about inadequate parent-child relationships and poor marital adjustments, but you may have noticed that the responses of the individual to these stress-provoking situations were not explored fully. If you have just finished reading Chapter 6 or 7, you have probably spent several weeks studying the human being under normal conditions, but not under stressful conditions. The present chapter starts with a discussion of normal emotional responses, and then begins to view the effects of stress.

Humans are capable of feeling and displaying a wide variety of **emotions**, from the greatest glee and happiness to the most miserable sorrow, from the heights of elation to the depths of depression, from extreme contentment to extreme agitation. If people felt no emotions, the world would be a much duller, although probably a more peaceful, place.

An emotion may be thought of as a feeling or a state of arousal that stirs an organism to observable action or to internal change. The similarity between the words *emotion* and *motivation* is obvious—they both evolved from the same Latin word meaning "to move." In addition, *emotions* (joy, hatred, jealousy, fury) can serve as *motivation* for behavior.

Try to recall the last person who spoke to you. What emotions was he feeling at the time? How do you know? Determining whether a particular person is feeling a particular emotion at a particular time can be very difficult, perhaps impossible. However, we usually will accept the idea that an emotional state exists if one or more of the following criteria can be applied: (1) certain physiological changes have taken place which, by common agreement, indicate an emotional state; (2) the person reports that he is feeling one of the emotions; or (3) observers report that the person displays behavior commonly believed to be caused by an emotion. Although psychologists assume that physiological changes underlie all emotional responses, it is rarely possible to investigate such an assumption; therefore, we must rely on the report of the person himself or of an observer.

You might say, "When I'm angry, I'm angry, and that's all there is to it!" By saying this, you are neglecting the changes that are going on while you are feeling the emotion of anger. Your heart is beating faster, your breathing has changed, your mouth may be dry, your pupils might have enlarged, your system is infused with adrenaline and noradrenaline (hormones secreted during anger), and you may feel a pounding in your stomach. Your body has assumed an alert posture in an effort to meet the stressful stimuli. Beyond these observable bodily changes, you are experiencing a subjective feeling that you yourself identify as anger. What is *anger?* It is a word, a learned label, for certain physical and psychological sensations that occur in certain kinds of social situations—it is something you perceive. Aside from the obvious physical changes and your subjective understanding of these changes, the emotion called anger also involves very complex chemical and electrochemical processes in your brain and body.

Certain physiological changes accompanying anger also accompany fear. On the other hand, evidence exists that different emotions are related to different physiological change patterns (for example, Ax, 1953). These change patterns may serve to motivate the organism into behavior, or they may produce an emergency store of energy to facilitate such actions as fighting or running away.

Examples of emotions that motivate behavior are numerous. Mild fear of failure, for example, may cause a student to study harder; moderate anger may induce a policeman to run faster when chasing a suspect. Extreme emotional states have been known to make possible amazing acts of strength and endurance, such as the instance reported several years ago of a small woman who lifted an automobile that had fallen on her son. Normally, she probably had trouble lifting a tire. Under emergency conditions, however, her emotions not only motivated her to lift the car, but also produced bodily changes that enabled her to lift the car.

Intense emotional feelings may not always motivate or facilitate behavior. Blushing or fainting result from physiological changes brought about by emotion, but they certainly do not facilitate behavior; anger or fear can cause stuttering when verbal fluency is needed or "freezing" when quick action is necessary. Strong feelings can also motivate impulsive behavior rather than appropriate behavior. The fear that leads to driving away from the scene of an accident or the anger that causes an employee to shout his resignation at the boss are two examples.

Development and Expression of Emotions

The range of emotional behavior that a person is capable of displaying is extremely great during maturity, or even during childhood, but observers report that young infants respond in similar fashion to all emotion-arousing stimuli. Thus, at birth, the only emotion shown is *excitement* or *arousal*. Before the infant is 2 months old, a pleasant state of excitement and an unpleasant state of excitement, often called delight and distress, can be distinguished. A few weeks later, anger, disgust, fear, and elation are identified, followed by most of the remaining emotions, all of which appear within the first 18 months (Bridges, 1932).

Both learning and maturation influence emotional development. Some emotional responses occur almost inevitably, with no opportunity for learning to take place. For example, an infant does not need to learn to smile when he is pleased—it happens inevitably—but he does need to learn to smile at the sight of his mother standing in the doorway with his bottle in her hand. He learns that this picture is soon to be followed by the opportunity to drink milk; using technical terms, we might describe his smile as a conditioned response to the stimulus of the image of his mother with a bottle. (See Chapter 4.)

Other emotional responses are learned. People learn to love their parents (and a few learn to dislike their parents). Children learn to fear the dark, snakes, and the bully down the street. Later, fear may be aroused by the sight of a motorcycle policeman in the rearview mirror, by the news that surgery is needed, or by hearing some politician claim that war will begin within the year. Human emotions can be aroused by anticipation of the future or recollection of the past.

Expressing Emotions

Sometimes it is simple to recognize the emotion another person is feeling. He may laugh or cry or show his feelings by the expression on his face. Defining the emotion is helped by knowing the entire situation, since facial expression alone can be misleading. In general, the more you know about the situation, the better you can judge what emotion is actually felt.

In every society, people learn what emotions may properly be expressed under what conditions. Little boys are repeatedly told, "Don't cry—don't be afraid—be a man," until they feel that being afraid and being masculine are contradictory. Thus they may become reluctant to show any signs of fear and may also believe they have failed as men if they even feel fear. Sometimes such people make a great show of bravery in order to prove to themselves that they are not afraid. One young man from the Union of South Africa joined a band of soldiers paid to fight in the Congo in 1964, because, he said, "I had to prove to myself that I was a man."

Children are discouraged not only from expressing fear, but also from expressing anger, especially anger toward adults. Children will often shout, "I hate you!" at their parents, long before they have any accurate idea what "hate" means. If their display of anger is strictly punished, they learn not to express their anger directly; however, they cannot be stopped from feeling anger, which may then be expressed indirectly. Many emotions occur that our society does not allow to be expressed directly.

Anger that cannot be directed toward parents can be redirected toward some handy object. After getting an undeserved scolding from his father, a student stormed out of the house, drove off in the family car, and—for the first time in his four years of driving—drove well over the speed limit and was ticketed. Through **displacement**, he redirected his anger to the automobile.

Many people who feel anger because of some frustration take out their feelings on minorities, such as Negroes, Mexican-Americans, Indians, Jews, Catholics, or Southerners. They are displacing aggressions upon a **scapegoat**.

During the early 1930s, the fortunes of Germany were extremely low. The country had to repay massive debts for the war it had lost; the money system was so unstable that people did not know from one day to the next what the prices would be; international esteem for the country was very low. Hitler, recognizing that the German people could not make effective use of their capabilities in the absence of national self-esteem, found a scapegoat in the Jews. Instead of directing their anger at themselves for having lost World War I and for being unable to control their own economy, the Germans readily displaced their aggressions away from themselves and onto the Jews, who were thereby held responsible for all of Germany's ill fortune.

In major-league baseball, when a team does not do well for a year or two, the owners often fire the manager. Although the team's inability

Emotions and Stress

to win may actually result from the unwillingness of the owners to obtain good players, it is easier and cheaper to use the manager as a scapegoat.

When feelings of anger or fear are not expressed directly or displaced in some fashion, they may be repressed. Everyone has feelings he is unable to admit, even to himself (for example, you may be so furious with your parents that you may, for a moment, wish to do them violence;

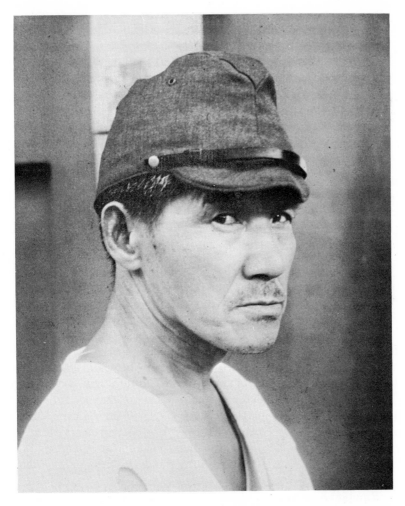

Figure 13–1.

This man is a Japanese war veteran who was spending his life on the streets of Tokyo as a licensed beggar. What feelings do you believe he has at the moment? After you decide how this photograph affects you, turn the page. Photograph and concept by Mark Davidson.

Figure 13–2.

This is the same Japanese war veteran as in Figure 13–1, photographed only a second later. Now what feelings do you think he is expressing? Is your present judgment consistent with your previous one? Photograph and concept by Mark Davidson.

---

or you may be fearful of not being truly successful on a future job), and these feelings become unconscious. However, even though you are not consciously aware of them, such feelings still influence behavior. Can you think of examples?

Different societies teach different forms of emotional expression. Affection between an adult man and his father may be expressed by kissing and hugging in France, Italy, Israel, or Iran, but Americans usually just shake hands. In Japan, a son would rarely talk back in anger to his father, but such behavior is not uncommon in the United States. Englishmen have the reputation of showing their enthusiasm at athletic contests by clapping their hands; Americans at a baseball game may shout, cheer, threaten the umpire, or even tear their programs and throw them onto the field; in Latin American countries, the response may be much more violent.

Emotional restraint, although certainly necessary in many instances, can be carried too far. Americans are probably more likely to inhibit the expression of their emotions than people in most countries. "Play it cool" is an attitude encouraged among many Americans of all ages. Many college students do not want to be involved in anything that arouses deep emotions and deep loyalties.

Emotions and Stress

People who allow themselves to feel things deeply, instead of insisting upon playing it cool, find life more exciting. They are not dominated by deficiency motivation, which calls for the reduction of tensions, but by growth motivation, which enables them to be open to new experiences. They have sufficiently accounted for their physiological, safety, love, and esteem needs to be able to become emotionally involved, even though involvement exposes them to the possibility of emotional pain and failure.

Examples of Emotions: Fear and Anxiety

Two familiar emotional states are fear and **anxiety**. Feelings described as fear occur when a person responds with alarm to an actual stimulus he can identify. He may feel fear if he stumbles across a rattlesnake, when he sees a snarling dog racing toward him, or when a drunk approaches him with threats of violence.

Anxiety, an emotional state closely related to fear, occurs when a person worries about what *might* happen in the future, or when he is fearful about some vague or unknown thing, which he cannot explain.

Watch airplane passengers when the plane begins to take off. Notice

Figure 13–3.

Three well-known professional actors (Eli Wallach, Rosemary Harris, and Pernell Roberts) enact a tense scene in a drama of marital conflict. What emotions do you see them exhibiting? Courtesy Columbia Broadcasting System.

their variety of reactions, such as gripping their armrests, closing their eyes tightly, staring straight ahead. These are signs of normal anxiety, of people anticipating future possibilities.

Some other examples of anxiety-provoking situations are:

Your professor asks you to drop in to see him after class. You have no idea what he wants, but you did copy part of your homework directly from an encyclopedia.

You have been driving about 20 miles an hour over the speed limit on a deserted country road, and you see automobile headlights flashing on and off in your mirror.

About three weeks after applying for a job with a Chicago company, you find a note in your mailbox stating that the post office has a special-delivery letter from Chicago for you. Unfortunately, today is Friday, and the post office is not open again until Monday.

You have just been informed that you will need an operation early next month. The operation is a routine one, resulting in complete success 97% of the time, and only one person in 200 dies as a result of the operation. But there is that 3% failure and that one death. . . .

When you feel anxious, you are strongly motivated to reduce the source of tension. Sometimes the reduction of anxiety is so rewarding that you would rather know the worst than remain uncertain. Doctors report that patients who have been anxious about whether they will need an operation are relieved when the decision is made, even when the decision is that the operation will be necessary. Anxiety tends to be deficiency-motivating rather than growth-motivating.

Sometimes it is difficult to relieve anxieties. Some people seem constantly anxious, to the point of disregarding the real world around them. The basis of their anxiety, then, arises from their own feelings of inadequacy, not from what is happening in their environment. You frequently meet students who are constantly anxious about their grades, even though they do well in all their classes. In one such instance, the student's anxiety resulted from his being compared to an older brother who was always at the top of his class; no performance of the younger brother could surpass that of the older, and parental praise was reserved for the older.

Tension-reducing behavior is very reinforcing, and a person may repeat such behavior on later occasions when he feels anxiety. Thus, if a freshman's anxiety concerning dating is relieved by avoiding dates (and assuming this solution does not produce even greater problems), he is likely to continue to avoid dating, even if it means missing some fun and making up some strange excuses.

Because feelings of fear produce discomfort, many people do their best to reduce fear in others. At times, these attempts are misdirected, since fear, like other emotions, will often motivate adjustive behavior. In one study, hospital patients about to undergo an operation were asked whether they were afraid; the degree of fear they expressed was found to relate to postoperative difficulties. Those who indicated very high *or* very low fear displayed more trouble in subsequent adjustment than those in between. In a follow-up study, some patients were told exactly what to fear in a forthcoming operation, but others were told very little. The former were not only better off psychologically, but also their medical condition improved more rapidly (Janis, 1968). Patients who lack normal fear may be unprepared for the pain and subsequent discomfort of operations. They also lack the opportunity to anticipate and, thus, rehearse for the future. In a way, objective fear may serve as an inoculation to prevent worse fear, disappointment, and frustration after the event (Janis, 1968).

Violence and the Emotions

"Violence," claimed a leading militant of the 1960s, "is as American as apple pie." Is this true? Is the violence of assassinations and street riots and widespread ownership of firearms the result of American traditions, the outcome of the actions of a few disturbed people, or the result of chance circumstances? To what extent can violence be prevented? Can this prevention be brought about through the crackdown of power, through psychiatric treatment, or through biological changes?

The rage that leads to violence is undoubtedly associated with frustration, but not all highly frustrated people become violent and not all violent people are visibly frustrated. Violence seems to run in families, but again we cannot determine the degree to which it is transmitted to children through the genes or instilled through learning experiences in the environment (Rosenfeld, 1968).

Some studies offer a possible key. Rage and violent behavior have been produced in animals by electrical or chemical stimulation; they have been stopped by drugs or radio signals. "The doctor can, by pushing a button and sending a radio signal, induce a peaceful monkey to go into a rage and attack other monkeys. When he releases the button, the monkey is peaceful again" (Rosenfeld, 1968).

The evidence certainly suggests that violent behavior is caused, at least in part, by human physiology, resulting from genetic conditions or

Development and Effects of Stress

from later injuries, or perhaps both. Does such evidence mean that environmental influences have little to do with violence? The answer seems to be "No." People with a predisposition to violence seem to be readily aroused by their fantasies. Thus, movies, television, and even newspaper articles may stir them to violence, although without these sources of excitation, they would remain relatively calm. Even the sight of a gun can increase the tendency to act out violent and angry behavior (Berkowitz, 1968).

Figure 13–4.

Violence or the threat of violence elicits feelings of fear or anger. Courtesy Columbia Broadcasting System.

None of us are immune to rage and violent behavior. Overcrowded living conditions may reduce the **threshold** for violent behavior. Constant exposure to violence in entertainment, in the news, and in political speeches may also reduce the threshold. Given sufficient stimulation, almost anyone might feel rage (Rosenfeld, 1968). Violent behavior appears to be the result of a dynamic interaction between the chemistry of the brain, the general environment, and the motivating properties of the specific situation. What implications does this conclusion make for the claim that a political assassination is the responsibility of the entire population?

The Nature of Stress

Stress is a strong, unpleasant emotional force or pressure that produces feelings of **tension** or strain. The term *stress* is frequently used in physics and in biology to refer to pressure, such as the stress of a weight resting upon an iron bar or the stress of a bone pressing upon cartilage. Stress in physics and biology implies that the resulting tension is accompanied by the possibility of distortion.

The term is used in a similar fashion in psychology. We talk about stress associated with academic pressure to succeed, which causes tension and, perhaps, distortion in the person's normal functioning. Driving on a crowded freeway while trying to get to an appointment on time is a stressful situation that leads to strain, distortion of normal driving habits, and possibly a traffic ticket.

Stress is most definitely motivating, with the resulting behavior largely directed at reducing the stressful conditions and the accompanying tension. The greater the stress, the stronger the motivation for its reduction. Stress can occur through frustration, conflict, anxiety, and guilt.

Frustration

Have you ever gotten a flat tire while trying to get to a very important exam on time? That is an excellent example of a situation that may produce **frustration**. When a person cannot reach the goal he desires, when the demands are greater than his ability, frustration occurs. Frustrations may be caused by personal inadequacies, natural conditions, or man-made conditions.

Personal inadequacy. Most girls are not going to win a beauty contest. No matter how intelligent or charming, no matter how clever in dressing and using makeup, they simply are not going to win. If such girls are really motivated to win a beauty contest, they are doomed to frustration.

Fortunately, failing to win a beauty contest is not frustrating for many people, but other types of personal inadequacies are. Limited intelligence can keep a person from entering college; limited height can keep a competent soldier from being an officer; limited knowledge of English may cost a person the chance to get a good job. Limited social skills, limited business experience, limited funds, limited technical skills, limited strength, all these and many more can lead to mild or extreme frustrations.

Natural conditions. Conditions beyond your control can keep you from achieving a desired goal. A long period without rain will lead to limited food and water, destruction of farmland, and, often, the death of animals; a fire started by lightning can destroy hundreds of acres of timberland and homes; fog can delay the return home of thousands of airline passengers. A delayed flight may not be so critical as the destruction of a home; however, both can frustrate people.

Man-made conditions. Man is often his own worst enemy. Man creates wars and the resulting death, pain, and frustrations. Professors create frustrations for students, who, in turn, create frustrations for professors. Parents can provide great frustrations for children, who may not realize the frustrations they bring their parents.

Not all man-made frustrations are bad. The man-made law against my stealing your car may frustrate me, but it is very much in your interest. Restrictions on hitting a person when you get angry with him may be frustrating, but not to the person about to be hit. Some drivers are frustrated by speeding laws, but this is no reason to discard the laws.

Conflict

Conflict occurs when an individual is motivated by two or more needs, and the satisfaction of one causes the denial of the other. The old saying "He has the tiger by the tail and can't let go" is a good example of a conflict.

A conflict will occur only if the alternative goals are fairly equal in importance. Confronted with the choice between a delicious hamburger and a $20 bill, you would rarely be in conflict, no matter how much you loved hamburgers. However, if you had not eaten anything for two days and the hamburger was the only food available, a conflict might well exist.

There are four categories of conflict: **approach-approach**, **avoid-**

ance-avoidance, approach-avoidance, and multiple approach-avoidance.

Approach-approach. Two desirable and mutually exclusive goals create an approach-approach conflict. Examples of an approach-approach conflict would be deciding between two good jobs, having to choose between buying a new suit and taking an exciting three-day trip, voting for a close friend or voting for someone else who is much more competent.

Avoidance-avoidance. Being forced to choose between two unpleasant alternatives leads to an avoidance-avoidance conflict. A few examples are getting a painful tooth pulled or having it continue to hurt, going on a date with a dull escort or staying home, studying a very difficult and tedious textbook or risking an F.

Approach-avoidance. Often one goal involves both pleasant and unpleasant features. A part-time job provides necessary spending money, but cuts into free time and social life; joining the Navy for four years is patriotic and will enable you to visit exciting places, but it might do little for your career.

Multiple approach-avoidance. Most real situations involve a complex combination of pleasant and unpleasant factors, as exemplified in the following hypothetical case.

> George is a college student, but he does not enjoy college; neither is he doing especially well. If he leaves school, he will be drafted immediately, and he does not wish to go into the Army. College will increase his lifetime income, give him a better understanding of the world, offer him enjoyable social activities, and may allow him to escape the draft altogether. On the other hand, he is likely to flunk out, he is bored with his courses, and he can take over his father's hardware store whenever he wishes. In addition, he is not so certain he wants to marry his steady girlfriend, although her father owns a chain of hardware stores and has no son to take into the business. Service would be an easy way to get away from his girl, but it would not help him in the hardware business; besides, he hates marching and gets irritated when people give him orders.

George will have a difficult time making a decision. Settling conflicts becomes even more difficult because of the influence of unconscious motives. Part of George's motive for not wanting to get married is that the girl reminds him too much of his mother, who has made life miserable for his father by pushing him to be successful. Taking orders in the Army is too much like taking orders from his mother. Working in a hardware store symbolizes the life his father led, which frightens George because he does not wish to live like his father. However, George is not aware of these feelings, even though they do influence his behavior.

Development and Effects of Stress

A study of real-life conflict resulted from a series of disastrous explosions that rocked the town of Texas City. People were caught in the conflict between wanting to see what happened to their families and wanting to do what they could to stem the terrible destruction, between wanting to save their own lives and property and wanting to help others (Killian, 1952).

Some people find making a decision very difficult. They cannot decide which movie to see, and so they end up missing the beginning; they cannot decide which job to accept and finally find that both have been filled; they cannot decide where to vacation and then learn that there are no more reservations. Such people may have weak self-concepts and may be very much frightened of making an error. They do not feel adequate in making decisions and are unwilling to accept the consequences of making the wrong decision.

Anxiety and Guilt

The discomfort caused by anxiety about the future and the discomfort caused by guilt over the violation of internalized standards of behavior in the past are both forms of stress. The tension that results from anxiety is particularly disconcerting because the specific source is vague, and therefore difficult to deal with or to dismiss. Some people suffer from varying degrees of anxiety all the time. Termed **chronic anxiety**, this condition causes a continuing tension that constantly interferes with effective behavior. Guilt tends to be associated with a particular situation, although a few people do seem to experience a chronic sense of guilt, so that virtually any occurrence will elicit guilt feelings.

Joseph McArthur had internalized his father's value that any form of disobedience of parental authority was evil. When he was 16, all his friends were actively dating, but Joe's father would not allow him to date or to attend house parties. One morning he felt so frustrated that—for the first time in his life—he argued with his father. The discussion became increasingly heated, until Joe finally yelled, "Oh, drop dead!" and stalked out of the house. That afternoon, Mr. McArthur was killed in an automobile accident.

Joe felt that the death was God's way of punishing him for his disobedience, even though he knew that logically this was impossible. He began to have frightening nightmares in which his father came back as a ghost to threaten to kill him in revenge. For weeks Joe was unable to sleep until thoroughly exhausted, because he had a fear (which he again recognized as illogical) that he would die in his sleep. His guilt and his anxiety were slowly destroying his physical health and his emotional stability, until he finally sought help through a psychologist associated with his school.

Internalized values become very much a part of us, and when our behavior violates these values, guilt and anxiety are common responses. Joe had internalized the value that disobedience was improper, and when it seemed to him that his disobedience and his hostile statement were related to his father's death, he felt very guilty. No matter how hard he tried to persuade himself that there was no cause-effect relationship between his outburst and his father's death, he continued to feel that his sin was going to be punished, and his dreams were an expression of the fear that the punishment would be his death. Guilt and anxiety worked simultaneously.

Frustration, conflict, anxiety, and guilt occur constantly in the lives of all people. Sometimes stress becomes too great for the self-concept to maintain itself in the face of this stress. Then, instead of being able to work toward utilizing his abilities to the fullest, the person consumes his time and energy in dealing with the stress.

Some Factors Causing Stress

Innumerable situations, incidents, relationships, and conditions are stressful. Those that affect children are not necessarily those that trouble college students, and those that disturb college students may differ from those that concern middle-aged people. Some types of situations, however, may be stressful for most age groups.

Family relationships. Even in emotionally well-adjusted families, stressful situations frequently occur. Frustration occurs when the parents need the car the evening of an important college dance; conflict is felt when the 17-year-old daughter wants to get married and her parents are violently opposed; guilt and anxiety result when a youngster tries to cover up for smoking pot by burning incense.

Some families attempt to work out their conflicts and frustrations together, perhaps through sitting down and discussing the problem and working out a solution agreeable to all. Other parents put their foot down and demand complete and immediate obedience—which they may or may not get. The reactions of most families fall between these extremes.

In a few families, stress seems to be present all the time. Perhaps the parents fight with each other, placing the children in conflict; perhaps the father has such a great need to assert his own power that he constantly criticizes the children; perhaps the older brother has been so successful that other children are pushed to do as well, despite their interests and abilities.

Jean, Mike, and Will Lambert ranged in age from 15 to 19. Their parents demanded that they be excellent students and also that they be socially active. The children were intelligent, but not so brilliant as their parents assumed. Will, by studying very hard and not dating, got grades good enough to satisfy his mother, but was criticized by his father for being a sissy and an egghead. Mike was very popular, but did poorly in school. Jean, who was encouraged by her mother to be like Will, and by her father to be like Mike, was in such conflict that she did poorly in school and was too anxious over her low grades to be popular. When she began to show an interest in becoming a nurse, Mr. Lambert became angry because the pay was so low, and Mrs. Lambert was upset "because nurses have to do all those dirty jobs—like emptying bedpans." The children left home as soon as they could. The boys both entered the Army, and Jean married just before her nineteenth birthday. The parents then accused their children of being "hard-hearted and forgetting all about your parents, who love you so much and who did so much for you."

Love and affection. Important human relationships occur not only with parents, but with a great variety of people. Marriage, going steady, dating, and good friendships between people of the same or of opposite sex are all sources of great satisfaction and great potential stress. You become anxious (Does he really love me?) or guilty (I shouldn't have gone out on that late date) or frustrated (I love her so much, but she says I'm like a brother to her) or in conflict (I wish he'd ask me out, but I can't flirt too much when he's dating my best friend).

Some individuals refuse to risk the possible unhappy consequences of love and affection. In order to receive full satisfaction from a human relationship, you have to take a chance that the relationship will culminate in an unhappy separation. Any true affection means that you become dependent upon the other individual and upon the continuation of the relationship. In loving, you open yourself up to possible emotional pain, and—because of previous unhappy experiences or because of an inadequate self-concept—certain people are not willing to take this risk. They prefer giving little to a relationship, even if they get little in return, because they feel safer that way.

Opposing group standards. The ability to adhere to what you think is right when the entire group opposes your position is not only very difficult, but also very stressful. Everyone has defied certain groups on minor matters—perhaps standing up for a friend the others were disparaging, expressing your admiration for a movie the others disliked, or defending a political candidate no one else voted for—and each of these little acts caused a certain amount of stress.

Opposing group standards on important issues opens a person up to various types of stress. He may endanger his status in the group; he may be threatened with property loss and even bodily injury or death; he may be isolated from all his friends. At the very least, he must face the conflict between remaining faithful to his values and making a major sacrifice.

Consider the stress and other forms of pressure that the following individuals face:

The student who is known to have reported the star quarterback for cheating.

The coed who makes no secret of her belief that men are basically less intelligent than women and that she has no intention of ever becoming a slave to a man through marriage.

The politician who exposes congressmen in his own party for having taken graft.

The minister who advocates suicide as a proper act for an extremely elderly or painfully ill patient.

Sex-role demands. Every society has forms of behavior that are acceptable for members of one sex, but not for the other. In our culture, women take care of the home while men produce the income; women are talkative, and men are silent; women like romance movies, and men prefer westerns. Men are expected to be taller, better educated, and more interested in "things" (as opposed to people).

Stress can occur when behavior contradicts the expected sex role. Men in college feel frustrated because they are not supporting themselves financially; college women rarely feel guilty about having their families pay their way. The girl who telephones men and hints that they ask her out learns eventually that her behavior is considered improper. Both husband and wife may feel uncomfortable if the wife is more successful in her job than the husband is in his, and the discomfort is intensified if they are both in the same field.

Expression of sex behavior and hostile-aggressive behavior. Most Americans have internalized the values that sex behavior and **hostile-aggressive** behavior should not be expressed openly. Hitting someone when you get angry or "making a pass" when your sexual needs are aroused is certainly forbidden by custom, and often by law. Even the thought of sexual or hostile-aggressive behavior may be considered improper (recall Joseph McArthur, page 270).

But, even though you cannot express these feelings, you continue to feel them, and the frustrations caused by not being able to act according to your feelings can be very stressful. After being teased by his younger sister for failing English, Jerry exclaimed, "I wanted to hit her so much I could feel my fist tingling."

When sexual or hostile-aggressive feelings are expressed in a socially or personally unacceptable fashion, guilt and anxiety ensue. If

Jerry had hit his sister, his guilt and anxiety would have caused more stress than expressing his feelings would have settled.

Problems with authority figures. Ask any policeman, teacher, minister, or parent about the resentment some people have toward authority. We have all had to work toward being independent, and most adults have succeeded. However, some people find themselves unable to accept any authority or sign of not being independent. Many who fight authority the hardest have either had unpleasant experiences or are unable to feel secure in their independence.

Academic and vocational success. Even though definitions of "success" might vary, most people consider academic and vocational success important. Pressures to succeed come from all around. The family, friends, the general community, and—usually—the self-concept all encourage a high level of academic and vocational achievement. Frustrations are acutely felt by those who do not measure up to their own standards of success. Perhaps even more stressful are the fears and anxieties that "I may not make it." Such anxieties are likely to be stronger in the United States, which might be termed an achievement-oriented society, than in countries where greater importance is attached to success in having many children or in being recognized as a good wife and mother, a valiant warrior, or a cooperative member of the community.

Financial pressures. No matter how wealthy a person appears, he may not have enough money to satisfy himself. As income and financial worth increase, the level of aspiration tends to rise proportionately. Ask someone who has been working for ten years whether he could

Figure 13–5.

What sort of trouble with authority figures does this character have? Courtesy Columbia Broadcasting System.

get along on what he was earning seven years ago. Then ask him whether he had fewer financial problems seven years ago or today. People all over the world envy the material possessions and financial opportunities of Americans, but Americans themselves are not necessarily satisfied.

Money is a source of stress between husband and wife, parent and child, employer and employee, and occasionally between college and student. Cheating, stealing, lying, and killing have often been the result of pressure to obtain money. The love of money may not be the root of all evil, but it is most certainly the root of some.

Although having money certainly causes conflict and anxiety, having very little money can lead to great frustration, especially if the economically deprived individual sees others around him living much better. The misery of poverty is bearable until the impoverished suddenly decides that lots of people are much better off than he and that he deserves to have a better life than he has been living. This is an example of what has been called the law of **relative deprivation.**

Think of the stress caused by not having enough to eat, not being able to keep warm, not having the skills necessary for a job, not being able to live without worrying how you and your family will eat or where they will sleep tomorrow or next week, or not being able to have occasional entertainment. These instances illustrate absolute poverty, not relative deprivation.

Health problems.   As long as health is good, people seldom think about it. When health is poor or as people grow older, health worries increase. Poor health or physical defects or limitations can cause great stress.

Death and bereavement.   Although the idea of death is unpopular and many individuals attempt to deny its reality for themselves or for their loved ones, we all eventually encounter death. The comment made to a friend of the author's by a fellow airplane passenger is especially indicative of the way many people feel about death; he began a conversation by saying, "If I should ever die. . . ."

When someone you feel close to dies, you are sad because of the loss of friendship, companionship, and love; but sadness is not the only way to respond to grief. You may also feel guilty for the arguments you had, for not having been nicer than you were, or for having been neglectful. You may find that the image of the dead person is constantly in your mind's eye and that you continue to think of him, even when you wish to do other things. You may even show physical symptoms, such as loss of appetite, having an empty feeling in the stomach, or lacking your usual muscle power (Lindemann, 1944).

The mentally healthy response to the stress caused by bereavement is complex. People who try not to show grief or who try to avoid thinking of the deceased person often take longer to recuperate from the loss. Crying and unhappiness are normal grief reactions, and tension is often caused by trying too hard to avoid displaying emotions (Lindemann, 1944). Once the grief is expressed, the person can begin to adjust to a life without the deceased and can begin to enter into new relationships.

Stress is inevitable in our daily living. Even young children meet frequent stress in their interactions with adults, with other children, and with their physical environment. Experience in meeting and dealing with normal, day-to-day stressful situations is not unhealthy for young children, assuming the stress is neither too heavy nor too frequent. As children learn to cope with mild stress, they gain in ability to cope with greater stress and are able to develop a self-concept of being competent and potentially independent.

A stable, secure childhood with loving, understanding parents seems to enable children to satisfy most of their deficiency motives and to build a sound self-concept. When stress does occur, such children are emotionally stronger and better able to call upon their resources to deal effectively with the stress. In the same way that a physically healthy person can recuperate from flu more rapidly than a physically ill person, the mentally healthy person can withstand emotional stress better than a mentally unstable person.

When you confront stress, whether it takes the form of frustration, conflict, guilt, or anxiety, you become uncomfortable and wish to reduce the effects of the stress. Stress arises from a great variety of situations in interaction with your own personality and needs, and can also have a great variety of effects.

Summary of Important Ideas

1. Humans are capable of feeling and displaying a great range of emotions.

2. An emotion is a feeling or state of arousal that stirs an organism to observable action or to internal change.

3. When an emotional state occurs, the body undergoes certain internal physiological changes; since these changes are usually difficult to observe, we often need to accept the report of the individual that he is feeling an emotion.

4. Emotions can be motivating. On occasion, emotions can reduce the effectiveness of behavior, but they are more likely to increase the effectiveness of behavior.

Emotions and Stress

5. At birth, the only emotion expressed is excitement or arousal.

6. Some emotional responses occur almost inevitably; others occur as the result of learning.

7. In every society, people learn which emotions may properly be expressed under which conditions.

8. Anger and other emotions may be displaced upon scapegoats.

9. Emotional restraint, although often necessary, can be carried too far.

10. Anxiety, an emotional state similar to fear, results from worried anticipation of the future or concern over some vague or unknown and unexplainable possibility.

11. Violent behavior appears to be the result of a dynamic interaction between the chemistry of the brain, the general environment, and the motivating properties of the specific situation.

12. Stressful conditions include conflict, frustration, anxiety, and guilt. Stress is inevitable in day-to-day living, but not all individuals have an equivalent ability to cope with stress.

13. Specific factors leading to stress include family relationships, love and affection, opposing group standards, sex-role demands, sex behavior and hostile-aggressive behavior, problems with authority figures, academic and vocational demands, financial pressures, health problems, and death and bereavement.

Chapter Fourteen

Reactions to Stress

You have just finished reading about the nature and causes of stress. The present chapter discusses the variety of responses that stress elicits. Since every individual finds himself having to cope with stress throughout his life, many of the behavior patterns mentioned in this chapter may be familiar to you. You may even have noticed some of them in yourself, which is, of course, to be expected.

The architects who planned the Egyptian pyramids designed them with a strong, solid base, and the structures have withstood the punishment of many centuries. Men who design today's long-span bridges allow for some swaying in strong wind, because bridges with "bend" are less likely to break. If psychologists could design personalities as engineers and architects design structures, they would specify a strong, solid base, and enough flexibility to prevent breaking.

The impact of stress upon human beings, just like the impact of stress upon buildings, is less if a firm base exists. For humans, the base would be the strength of the self-concept, which is directly related to the **stress tolerance** of a particular individual.

Flexibility, or adaptability, is also needed to withstand stress. Rigid people who are unable to modify their behavior in the face of stress are more likely to be harmed by the stress. In a violent storm, a thin bush with deep roots will neither break nor blow away, but a tall, rigid tree may break, and a bush with shallow roots may be pulled out by the force of the wind. (However, a bush that is too flexible bends and twists in the slightest breeze, and no one ever knows its real form.)

The specific response of any given individual to stress depends upon his self-concept, stress tolerance (or frustration tolerance), and methods of adjustment, in addition to his previous experiences, the specific nature of the stress, and the immediate situation. Some major categories of response include bodily changes; rigidity, withdrawal, aggression, and disorganization; defense mechanisms; and new growth motivations.

Bodily Changes in Response to Stress

Every change in behavior involves a pattern of physiological changes. The brain, the **nervous system**, the **receptor** and **effector** organs, the voice box, and many other parts of the body must work together when you touch a hot stove, yell "Ouch!" and pull your hand away. More complicated forms of behavior involve more complex patterns of bodily change.

According to one theory, the body undergoes three stages of physiological change in response to stress. At the initial sign of stress, the *alarm reaction* occurs, at which point the body rapidly organizes itself to get ready to cope with the stress. The second stage, *resistance,* describes the continued attempt to cope with the problem. The final stage, *exhaustion,* comes after the body has used its resources in fighting the stress. This pattern of responses, termed the **general-adaptation syndrome**, describes the physiological workings of the body, which in turn determine much observable human behavior (Selyé, 1956).

Psychosomatic Problems

If the tension produced by stress continues for a long period of time, the resulting bodily changes will continue also. Unfortunately, these bodily changes, which initially protect the individual against stress, may have a harmful effect if extended too long and may contribute to such physical disorders as ulcers, asthma, and skin problems (recall the discussion of acne in Chapter 10).

Physical disorders arising from stress are termed **psychosomatic** disorders. They are real physical problems (not imaginary, as some people think), but, instead of resulting from germs or a blow to the body, they result from physiological changes induced by stress. A psychosomatic headache is very painful; a psychosomatic asthma attack is extremely disruptive.

Ulcers, for example, may be caused by emotional tension that leads to an unusually heavy and long-term flow of chemical secretions produced by the body. Under normal circumstances, these chemicals are manufactured for only a short time, and the body's defenses can cope with them. With certain types of emotion (for example, chronic resentment) or as the result of extremely intense emotions, the chemicals are produced over a longer period of time or in greater quantity, and the body cannot maintain its defenses. Eventually the chemicals overwhelm these defenses and cause sores, or ulcers, on the inner walls of the stomach (Wenger, Jones, & Jones, 1956).

Psychosomatic disorders, unlike faked disorders, are very real. Unlike conversion reactions (discussed in Chapter 15), they produce recognizable **organic** symptoms that may require medical treatment if they become incapacitating. Like other reactions to stress, these disorders appear both in mild and in severe forms.

One young college couple ran into a psychosomatic problem that finally ended their romance:

> Ed Bradford and Rita Alonzo met during tennis class, had their first date that evening, and were going steady by the end of the week. They clicked. After a few weeks of exciting romance, Rita became a little worried. She felt she was not ready for marriage, and Ed had begun to "hint around." She seriously considered breaking up with Ed, but finally decided to continue to see him.
>
> On the way home from a party one night, Rita began to sneeze. Her eyes teared, her nose got extremely red and runny, and she sneezed and sneezed and sneezed. This, of course, spelled the end of the evening, and the usual parking period was called off.
>
> Their next date ended the same way. The date after that, Ed was on guard, and arranged the evening so as to get to Rita's house early, supposedly to watch television. Rita's parents were there, and Rita showed no sign of a cold. Her parents usually went to bed about 11:00. At 10:45 Rita's eyes began to cloud, and she started to sniffle. By 11:00 her cold was going full blast.

Many other psychosomatic symptoms come to mind: the headache the night before a difficult examination, the nausea after seeing the mutilated victim of an automobile accident, or the rash that develops during especially anxious periods. These, however, are not particularly damaging psychosomatic disorders, unlike ulcers or asthma, which build up over a long period of time and produce serious medical symptoms.

That stress is associated with the onset of disease is well established, but the mechanism-through which the stress operates is not fully understood. Studies have shown that the death of a spouse can cause an increase in illness (Parkes, 1964), and that an accumulation of life crises (for example, divorce, loss of job, or being imprisoned) may be followed by much more frequent illness than would be anticipated by chance

(Rahe & Arthur, 1968). Perhaps these illnesses are of psychosomatic origin. On the other hand, the crises might have brought about a change in behavior patterns and personal care. A woman whose husband has just died or a man who is suddenly unemployed may alter his way of living so that his health deteriorates. Psychosomatic change and behavior-pattern change very likely interact dynamically with each other to produce the increase in stress-caused illness.

Other Bodily Reactions to Stress

Psychosomatic disorders are not the only bodily reactions to stress. Fatigue and bed-wetting are other frequently observed occurrences. Emotional tension over an extended period of time can be very tiring. Three hours of a difficult examination may be more fatiguing than three hours of physical labor; driving a dynamite truck is usually more tiring than driving the same truck loaded with wooden crates. The body mobilizes its energies to cope with stress, but the expended energies must be renewed through sleep or rest.

Fatigue and the resulting sleep can also be a form of escape. How often have you had the following type of experience?

8:00 P.M. You sit down to study. Tomorrow you have an examination, and even though you are not fond of the textbook, you feel hopeful and almost enthusiastic.

9:00 P.M. You have read one chapter and now feel impossibly sleepy.

10:00 P.M. You cannot keep your eyes open any longer. You have read only a few pages during the past hour, and you remember little of what you read because of the brief naps you took between sections. You decide to watch television, since you are not getting any real work done.

11:00 P.M. After an hour of television, during which you are not in the least sleepy, you return to your studies.

11:10 P.M. You decide that, since you are too sleepy to study, you might as well get a good night's sleep before the examination, so you go to bed.

1:00 A.M. You are still tossing and turning in bed. You have not been at all sleepy since you put your book down.

Fatigue has served to remove you from the unpleasant or stressful situation of studying a course you do not like or for an examination that causes you to feel anxious.

Bed-wetting that continues beyond the age of 5 or 6, or **enuresis**, as it is technically called, is usually a reaction to stress rather than the result of muscular immaturity, and is more common than generally supposed. One out of 40 young soldiers reported at least occasional bed-wetting after the age of 18 (Thorne, 1944). Psychologists consider most bed-wetting to be an indication of some emotional problem that may need to be resolved before the bed-wetting will cease. However, devices are available that use classical-conditioning methods to cure bed-wetting: the moisture triggers an electric connection that sets off a buzzer and wakens the child. Eventually he learns to wake up by himself in response to pressure upon the bladder, which is the stimulus that precedes the sound.

Rigidity, Withdrawal, Aggression, and Disorganization

Stress not only produces biochemical changes, but also many overt behavioral changes. Some of the more familiar patterns of stress-induced behavior include rigidity, **withdrawal**, aggression, and disorganization.

Rigid Behavior

People, like bridges and bushes, need some flexibility in the face of stress. They need to be able to re-evaluate their behavior and their beliefs, not at the slightest pressure, but when the situation is appropriate. However, certain individuals become extremely rigid when faced by stress. When the situation causes them to feel anxious or confused, they fall back on previous forms of behavior, rather than investigate new possibilities.

Some people appear to behave in a rigid fashion much of the time. They may see only black or white, rather than shades of gray; they may prefer a strong leader telling them what to do, rather than the freedom to decide their actions for themselves. The world of today is a fantastically complex place, and some of its problems seem almost impossible to solve, but these rigid individuals continue to believe in simple, clear-cut solutions.

Because rigid people need something definite to cling to, they are said to have **intolerance of ambiguity**. Such individuals become unhappy when uncertain. They feel cheated by the psychology professor who cannot give them exact rules for "psyching out" their friends; they resent the artist whose painting can be interpreted in numerous ways; they become suspicious of the mechanic who cannot guarantee whether regular or premium gasoline is better for their car; they distrust the minister who feels that different religious views might be equally truthful. When they go on vacation, they need to know exactly where they are going, when they will arrive, how long they will be there, and what they will be doing. Complete flexibility, if such is possible, is not necessarily desirable, but in the long run, rigidity is not an adaptive response to stress.

Withdrawal

Withdrawal as a response to stress can be either physical or psychological. An example of the former would be the student who, facing an examination he expects to fail, does not show up; then he becomes afraid to see the professor again, and he eventually gets a failing grade for the course. The soldier who knows he will be disciplined for some minor offense may decide to pretend he is sick, or he may go AWOL.

Some people resort to alcohol to withdraw psychologically from stress. After a few drinks, the world seems to be a more pleasant place again. The self-concept, which might have suffered because of guilt or frustration due to failure, is temporarily adequate, and the threatening future looks rosy again. When the heavy drinker becomes sober, his problems return, so that being intoxicated becomes more rewarding than being sober, and drinking may become more frequent. Heavy drinking does nothing to change the actual environment, but only temporarily changes the outlook upon the environment. To make matters worse, few people do anything to change their situation when they have been drinking; so their problems only become worse, which may lead to more drinking, and a circular frustration pattern of drinking → withdrawal → more drinking → more withdrawal is established.

Tranquilizers and sleep are two other ways of withdrawing temporarily from stress. Physicians may recommend tranquilizers to help a person feel better during a particularly tense situation. Sleep is not only a type of retreat, but the person may wake up feeling better equipped to deal with his problems. (In Russia, sleep is used as a form of psychotherapy.) Both types of withdrawal are useful, but both may be abused through overuse, and neither deals directly with the tension-inducing problem.

People can even use recreation, hobbies, television, schoolwork, sports, or their jobs as ways to withdraw from the demands of the world around them. Have you ever known anyone who withdrew into a world of "things," such as mechanical activities or books, in order to withdraw from the world of people?

Aggressive Behavior

Stress, especially frustration, elicits feelings and expressions of anger and aggression. You may direct the aggression toward the cause of the frustration, toward another source (displacement), or toward yourself, or you may attempt to ignore the feelings and not act upon them at all. Have you ever become so frustrated by pounding a nail crookedly that you smashed at it with your hammer, missing the nail (but not your thumb)? Have you ever forgotten that you parked your car in a tow-away zone, then "cussed yourself out" for being so stupid?

Figure 14–1.

Frustration often leads to aggression. Courtesy Columbia Broadcasting System.

Chapter 13 discussed violence as a response to emotion-arousing stimuli. Such violence is a form of aggressive behavior and often arises from frustration. Whatever other causes might have contributed to the racial riots of recent years, the high level of frustration in the minority communities has certainly been a—and perhaps *the*—major source of aggressive behavior. Have you ever felt so frustrated that you were ready to turn your aggression into violence? Have you ever become violent as the result of frustration?

Disorganized Behavior

You may have heard the expression "He got on his horse and went galloping off in all directions." The implication is that the person de-

Figure
14–2.

Her mother has just yelled at her for standing on the edge of the crib and rocking back and forth. Note the aggression in her response to frustration. Photograph by Albert Kallis.

scribed is disorganized, a common reaction to stress. Frustrations, conflicts, and anxieties can become so great that an individual is no longer able to function effectively. He vacillates back and forth between one decision and another; he makes foolish errors on simple tasks; he forgets to do things that he normally never forgets. These are all forms of disorganization resulting from stress.

Rigidity, withdrawal, aggressive behavior, and disorganized behavior are all basic reactions to stress. These reactions may also be expressed through defense mechanisms.

Defense Mechanisms

The need for self-esteem—and a resulting healthy self-concept—is very important. If you do not respect yourself, your energies are expended in justifying your own behavior to yourself, and little effort can be channeled into developing your potential capabilities. When frustration, conflict, anxiety, or guilt threaten your self-concept, you tend to defend yourself and to try to retain your satisfying self-concept.

In his attempts to maintain and improve his self-concept, especially in the face of stress, each individual utilizes certain types of behavior, termed **defense mechanisms**. These mechanisms operate unconsciously and automatically, so that he is not aware he is using them (Coleman, 1964). For example, the fox who could not reach the grapes decided they were sour. He defended his self-concept against having to accept failure. If he had said to himself, "I'll pretend they are sour," he might have fooled others, but he would not have been able to fool himself and thus could not have defended his self-concept.

Probably the most basic of all defense mechanisms is **repression**, which was discussed in Chapter 2. Repression is a process that occurs when an individual is unable to recall or recognize something because of unconscious needs to deny the awareness. The concept of repression is at the core of the psychoanalytic theory of personality, as described by Sigmund Freud.

> Sid Janson was an effective campus politician. He managed to win every time he ran for office, except the time he lost the election for vice-president of the senior class. Many years later, when he bumped into an old friend he had not seen since graduation, Sid's politicking career was brought up. "I wasn't too bad," Sid said, "I never lost an election." His friend mentioned that he had lost his campaign for vice-president of the senior class, but Sid shook his head. He was able to name six or seven offices he had won, including that of treasurer of the German Club, but he could not recall losing any.

If Sid was able to recall winning the relatively unimportant German Club office, it is unlikely that losing the senior class vice-presidency would have been forgotten. Rather, he had repressed this blow to his self-esteem.

Not only memories, but also ideas and feelings unacceptable to the self-concept are repressed. A child who is deeply resentful of some parental behavior may repress his resentment, since to recognize it would cause him to direct anger against the parent, an act unacceptable to his self-concept. The entire process, of course, is unconscious.

A conscious attempt at forgetting or ignoring something is called **suppression**. When a favorite uncle of yours is very sick, you may try to forget about his illness by going to a movie; when you are very angry with your closest friend, you may decide to work your anger off through a hard game of tennis. In these instances, you are not fooling yourself, but you are making an effort to ignore the anxiety you feel, and perhaps you may find it easier to hide your worry from your uncle when you visit, or your anger from your friend when you see him next (assuming, of course, you want to hide your feelings from them). Suppression, under the definition used in this book, is not a defense mechanism.

Many sorts of defense mechanisms have been observed. Some mechanisms redirect responsibility from yourself to other people or things; some allow you to withdraw either psychologically or emotionally; still others enable you to gain support for your self-concept by affiliating with those recognized as more capable. The following discussion covers only a portion of the possible categories of defense mechanisms.

Redirecting Mechanisms

Sometimes a person seems to be trying to say, "Not me. I didn't do it. I couldn't. I'm not that type. It must have been two other guys." Of course, he does not actually make such statements, but his behavior implies that, unconsciously, he wants to redirect responsibility away from himself.

A very common redirecting defense mechanism is **rationalization**, which is the attempt to make behavior or feelings seem rational, sensible, and consistent with the self-concept, when they really are not.

Here is a list of common rationalizations for low examination grades. Remember that the students expressing these ideas actually believe their statements to be true.

"There were too many tricky questions." (That may be true, but it does not explain why the other students were not tricked.)

"All the questions came from the one chapter I hadn't read." (This also may be true, but a careful check usually shows it is not.)

"You never knew what the professor really wanted to know." (But the other students apparently did.)

"I'm not interested in the course—the teacher is boring." (This may be true, or it may be a rationalization by a student who is afraid he will fail.)

"I didn't study." (Why? Is this a rationalization by a student who unconsciously felt he did not understand the course well enough? Was he afraid to try, because if he did try and then failed, he would have no excuse left?)

Each of these rationalizations explains failure in such a way as to protect the self-concept. It redirects the cause of failure to sources outside the self.

Projection is another way of redirecting responsibility. Two types of projection occur: first, denying your own thoughts and feelings and attributing them to someone else; and second, justifying your own behavior by claiming that others feel the same way.

A 4-year-old had just been bawled out by his teacher for socking another child. "I had to do it," he sniffled. "Why?" asked the teacher. "'Cause he wanted to hit me, so I hit him." "How do you know he wanted to hit you—he was playing with the blocks." "I just knew."

In talking to his 16-year-old son, a father said, "All men want money and power. Those are the only real goals in life."

The 4-year-old is transparent in his use of projection (although nations have used the same defense mechanism for going to war), but the father's statement is less obvious as a projection. Whether or not he is correct, he is very probably projecting his own attitudes toward money and power onto "all men."

Sometimes people feel so guilty or anxious about their unconscious feelings and motives that they lean over backward to deny them. They say, in essence, "I'm not the one you mean; look—I'm just the opposite." This is an example of **reaction formation**. The self-concept is protected by an exaggerated display of behavior indicating feelings opposite to those actually felt.

Jay Laub was the most aggressive, girl-hungry fellow on campus. He had dates three or four nights a week and talked freely, although vaguely, about his supposedly active sex life. Still, he had a reputation among girls as being easy to handle. His conscious self-concept was a reflection of his behavior: popular, aggressive, debonair. Unconsciously, however, Jay was afraid of girls, but he could not admit this fear to anyone, especially to himself. He was saying, unconsciously, "I'm the fastest, most popular, most aggressive guy around—it's obviously impossible even to consider that I'm afraid of girls." Jay had been engaged five times, but had not married, by the time he was 36.

Movie and book censors, who reserve the right for themselves to see or read what they want to forbid others, may be using reaction formation. They seem to be saying, "Look how moral I am—I not only oppose seeing such terrible movies, but I keep other people from seeing them. Of course, I have to see them myself, but don't get me wrong—I don't really enjoy it."

Often people have feelings and needs, especially of an aggressive or sexual nature, which cannot be expressed directly. When you feel extreme anger toward authority figures, such as policemen, parents, or teachers, you are often frustrated in your attempts to show anger. Since in all likelihood you would be punished for expressing such feelings, you redirect the anger through the defense mechanism of **displacement**. Instead of expressing anger toward the person or thing responsible, you direct it at someone or something else. You cannot kick the teacher or yell at the traffic policeman; so you kick the wastebasket and yell at the clerk in the store—they are your scapegoats.

Rationalization, projection, reaction formation, or displacement occurs without your realizing that something other than objective perception and appropriate motives elicits your behavior.

Withdrawal Mechanisms

Rather than face a threat to the self-concept and the resulting discomfort, people may withdraw. Withdrawal might be into **fantasy**, the defense mechanism through which people create their own world rather than face the conflicts, frustrations, and anxieties of the real world. Although the content of the fantasy is conscious, the ways in which the fantasy protects the self-concept are not conscious.

John Malcolm has just been bawled out by a neighbor for playing his hi-fi too loud late at night. Slowly John recalls that this is the neighbor with three noisy dogs. Now he is fantasizing the retorts he should have made, and in his fantasy, he is making the neighbor feel very foolish.

Portia Gregg had been hoping against hope that Brad Meinicker would ask her out, but Brad dated her roommate instead. When her roommate and Brad leave the dormitory, Portia fantasizes herself as Brad's date and mentally enacts the entire evening.

Fantasy is not the only type of withdrawal. Rather than withdraw into a dream world when the present is too filled with anxiety and frustration, you can unconsciously withdraw into the past. An older child may demand to drink from a bottle and begin to wet his pants when his baby brother is born, although he had been weaned and toilet-trained two years earlier. He is using the defense mechanism of **regression** to return to an earlier form of behavior. In the face of frustration, adults will often regress to name calling, threats of violence, and other forms of childish behavior. When people long for the good old days, they are, in a way, expressing a desire to regress from the stress of the modern world.

People also withdraw from the emotional impact of frustration or anxiety through **intellectualization**. One student with a religious conflict undertook an intellectual study of religion and tried to bury his conflict in an intellectual explanation. Another student, whose fiancée broke off their engagement just three weeks before the scheduled wedding, devel-

**Figure
14–3.**

Top: A new infant in the family elicits a variety of responses from the older children. What do you think Marni and Dan are feeling as they look at their new brother? *Bottom:* Although Marni has shown nothing but love for her little brother, she has resumed thumbsucking since his birth. This is a good example of regression under stress. Photographs by Albert Kallis

oped a lengthy explanation for his ex-girl friend's behavior, using all sorts of psychological terms.

When a person is apathetic, we usually assume he is just not interested. However, **apathy** can be a defense mechanism used unconsciously when frustrations or conflicts are too great. Removing oneself completely from the situation reduces the threat to the self-concept. "I don't really care if I make the team or not" protects the speaker's self-concept. If he does not make the team, his self-concept is not greatly damaged; if he does make the team, it is all to the good. Some students claim they are bored or apathetic about college when they are unconsciously trying to withdraw from a tension-provoking situation.

Affiliating Mechanisms

Identification is the unconscious act of taking for oneself the attitudes, values, and behavior of a person or a group. As such, it is very important in the socialization process, and parents are often very much concerned about those with whom their children identify. A boy will identify with his father, and perhaps with a popular television hero as well. Such identification adds to the boy's feelings of self-adequacy, because he feels, to some extent, that their abilities and positive traits are now his. The young child is expected to identify with the parent of the same sex, and behave like that person at least in regard to sex role. The concept *identification* is very similar to *internalization* (see Chapter 9), which refers more specifically to values and attitudes.

You might say, "I identify with Americans." Not only are you saying you are an American, but also that you feel associated with your country. Some people identify strongly with certain regions of the country; inhabitants of New York City, Texas, San Francisco, and Hawaii often have a strong regional identification. Some people also identify with a college (school spirit depends upon identification), with a church group, a social club, or an interest group. When you identify like this, the success of the group is felt as your success, and its failure is felt as your failure. The real baseball or football fan feels wonderful or miserable, depending upon whether his team wins or loses—his feelings could not be stronger if he were on the field playing.

Defense Mechanisms as Crutches

We use most defense mechanisms to fool ourselves about ourselves. They function much like a psychological crutch to support an anxious self-concept. Like every crutch, they are necessary at certain times. You do not remove a person's crutch until he can walk without it; if you try to do so, he will either reject your offer or will fall and hurt himself.

To carry the analogy further, when a person on crutches reaches a

**Figure
14–4.**

A royal identification. Courtesy British Information Office.

certain point in his recovery, he can begin to walk for short distances without them. However, premature removal of the crutch will cause the patient to fall and will perhaps worsen his condition.

If the doctor forces the patient to discard the crutch before the patient is ready, the patient may find a cane that is lying around the house; he may become angry and get another doctor; he may not use the crutch when the doctor is around, but continue to use it at other times. Sometimes, when the patient is nearly ready to walk without the crutch, the encouragement from the physician is just what is needed to get him back on his feet, especially if the first trial steps are firm and not painful.

The parallels between the physical crutch and the psychological crutch become more apparent through the experiences of Lorne Kunin.

> Lorne Kunin was a very mediocre artist, but every time his painting was not given an award or not exhibited, he claimed that "this proves how little people know about art." His fiancée tried to point out to him that he did not have enough artistic ability to become a success-ful painter and that he was constantly rationalizing his failures. At first Lorne was deeply hurt, but he soon decided that his fiancée was "just as stupid as the others," and he broke the engagement. After several years, Lorne became a successful businessman dealing in artists' supplies. He came to know many artists quite well, and in the small city where he lived he was considered an expert in his knowledge of art. With his business success and his expertise in art recognized, his self-concept became sufficiently strong, and he slowly accepted the idea that he could never have been a successful painter.

When Lorne was young, he needed the rationalization crutch to maintain his self-concept, and he totally rejected the help of those who tried to get him to discard it. At one point he tried to take a few steps without the crutch, but preferred getting rid of the "doctor," that is, his fiancée. When time and success had improved his ability to function, he was able to maintain his self-concept without the crutch.

Professionals in psychology, psychiatry, and social work are ex-tremely cautious in their attempts to get people to throw their crutches away, and they prefer to try to reduce the need for the crutch in other ways. Eventually, when the self-concept no longer needs defending, the use of the crutch ceases without resistance.

Defense mechanisms of many varieties occur in normal (and also non-normal) behavior. All of them are alike in that they occur automati-cally, are used unconsciously, cause us to look good in our own eyes, and make our behavior appear consistent with our self-concept. These mech-anisms serve an important purpose for the individual using them, and mental health goals are not served by premature attempts to persuade people not to use them.

Growth Responses to Stress

The previous discussion has implied that the effects of stress are always negative, but this is not necessarily the case. People have the capability of dealing with stress through positive action. Stress can lead to increased motivation to learn and to achieve, to new insights and more appropriate levels of aspiration, and to new approaches to old problems.

Increased Motivation to Learn and to Achieve

Stress is often caused by lack of learning or lack of accomplishments, and the stressful situation motivates increased efforts and increased learning, which lead to increased self-esteem and opportunity to use available talents. If your frustration stems from being unable to dance, you can learn to dance; if you feel anxious about talking in groups because your vocabulary is limited, you can find numerous sources of help; if you feel guilty because you have not written your grandparents in nearly a year, you might write them.

Classroom exams provide stress that motivates learning; competition for the girl you are dating motivates you to try harder to win her; the possibility of not getting a promotion may motivate a higher level of achievement. In each of these instances, the resulting behavior may be deficiency-motivated or growth-motivated, depending upon the specifics of the situation and on the individual.

New Insights and New Levels of Aspiration

Colin was a very competent engineer who desired to move into a management position in his company. He received numerous salary increases, but never the supervisory job he wanted. Finally, the frustration of being passed over so often forced him to re-evaluate his own limitations, and he began to observe the way he treated his secretary and his assistant, the only two people working directly under his orders. Slowly he gained insight into the reasons for his not being promoted.

Sometimes the **insight** produced by stress may require a new **level of aspiration**. A politician is subjected to so much stress after losing the nomination for mayor three times straight that he decides to run for another, less important post. A student who tackles an advanced mathematics course and does poorly decides to take a refresher course at a more elementary level. A salesman becomes frustrated because he is bored with his work and finally recognizes that he needs a different sort of challenge in his occupation.

If stress provides you with a better understanding of yourself or with a new, more appropriate level of aspiration, it has served a useful purpose.

New Approaches to Old Problems

Stress often causes rigid behavior, leading the individual to repeat previously unsuccessful acts.

> You have misplaced your house key, and your ride to campus is about to leave without you. You are looking frenziedly for the key. Where?—in the same drawer you have already examined thoroughly and emptied out twice.

But the stress of the situation may force you to revise your morning habits, and you begin setting the alarm a little earlier, to allow for emergencies. In the same way, the physician is frustrated because of innumerable encounters with patients suffering from an illness he cannot cure, and so he devotes some of his time and energy to finding a cure. A group of students, frustrated by the level of creativity in the movies, evolves new techniques in film-making.

Learning to Live with Stress

Sometimes there is nothing you can do to eliminate stress; for example, you have an ill parent, or the draft board is going to re-evaluate your deferment, or you have had a recent traffic accident and the hearing is next Monday. Such stressful situations do occur, and you are powerless to affect them. Thus, all you can do is try to deal with your reactions to the stress. Perhaps talking to a professional counselor or close family friend or personal friend will help. Sometimes you can only try to ignore the stress or live with the stress, and put additional effort into the tasks that the anxiety has disrupted. When stress and anxiety become greater than the defenses can cope with, the resulting behavior may be seen as non-normal.

What happens when the stress you face exceeds your level of stress tolerance? What happens when frustration, conflict, anxiety, or guilt become greater than your ability to handle them? What happens when defense mechanisms can no longer protect your self-concept from threatening attack?

People must find some way of adjusting to stress, and under the usual conditions of living, most individuals will make an adequate adjustment. Some will adjust more effectively than others. However, when the demands of stress are greater than the individual can deal with, the result is often faulty or disordered behavior. The degree to which behavior becomes faulty is determined by the degree of stress in the situation and the individual's personal background and resulting ability to cope with stress.

Who Is Normal?

Have you ever worried that you "weren't all there"? Did you ever do something "a little nutty"? Is it possible that you are not normal? What is *normal* behavior?

The last question is not easy to answer. First, keep in mind that "normal" and "average" are different concepts. Average height, for adult American males, for example, is about 5 feet 10 inches, but normal height would probably range from about 5 feet 3 inches to 6 feet 4 inches. Student grades may average a little above a straight C, but normal people receive grades of straight F and straight A, although both of those extremes are unusual. The average person does not play chess, but chess players are certainly normal. Normality, then, is a wide range of possible behavior, not just an average.

Second, what is normal in one society or in one time period is not normal in another society or another time period. In 1750, it was normal to believe that witches could destroy your cattle by putting a curse on them; today, we would not consider such a belief to be normal for American college students. In Nepal, many citizens believe that smallpox is the "kiss of the gods," but that idea would not be considered normal in our country. So, to some extent, normal behavior depends upon the time and the place.

This book will use another definition of normality: a normal person is one who knows the difference between what is real and what is not, who does not use defense mechanisms to excess, who is able to get along satisfactorily outside an institution, and whose day-to-day behavior is not dominated by *excessively* rigid, irrational, or self-defeating actions. According to this definition, a person may be far from average, yet still be normal.

Symptoms of the Non-normal

There is no particular point at which a person moves from normal to non-normal. Certain types of behavior are, at least in our society, clearly normal; certain types are clearly non-normal; certain types are borderline. Consider a simple rationalization for not getting a job, as expressed by four different people:

"I didn't get the job, even though I'm qualified, because I don't have a college degree." (Probably normal rationalization; perhaps true statement.)

"I didn't get the job, although I'm qualified, because the supervisor is afraid to hire someone smarter than he is." (Probably normal rationalization; probably not true statement.)

"I didn't get the job, although I'm well qualified, because the personnel director is part of a secret ring of scientists who are trying to get control of the company, and they know I will expose them." (Most probably no longer normal; most probably not true statement; person may be mentally ill.)

"I didn't get the job because the president of the company is under the control of the devil, who has eaten away his brain and now wants to take over the plant to control the world." (No comment necessary.)

Many deeply disturbed people behave normally most of the time, and almost all normal people have some mannerisms or ideas or behavior that might be considered non-normal. The sniffles share certain symptoms with pneumonia; a student after drinking a bottle of beer shares certain characteristics with an alcoholic. Yet no one would claim that the sniffles *is* pneumonia, or that behavior after one drink *is* alcoholism.

Emotional disturbance is not an all-or-nothing happening, but a matter of degree. The following are examples of some symptoms of emotional disturbance that are often found in normal people but may occur in exaggerated form in very deeply disturbed individuals:

Depression—feeling that everything is going wrong, that nothing matters.

Inappropriate worry and fear—constantly worried or afraid about one thing or another, far out of proportion to the actual cause; chronic anxiety.

Suspicion—inability to trust others, feeling that others are deceitful.

Inadequate emotional control—crying, being frightened, getting angry far out of proportion to actual stimuli.

Overly strict emotional control—not showing emotions, even when appropriate circumstances occur.

Fantasy—daydreaming so much that little gets done.

Rigidity—difficulty in behaving or thinking in new ways, tendency to follow rituals in behavior.

Organic symptoms—fatigue, illnesses, and ailments that occur without medical basis.

Hostility—undue readiness to fight, argue, or verbally attack others.

Ineffectiveness—inability to make decisions, dislike of taking responsibility for own behavior, behaving in immature fashion.

Unhappiness and tension—seeing the world as a difficult, tense place.

Inadequate interpersonal relations—contacts with other people marked by hostility, arguments, tension, suspicion, overdependence, and other signs of inadequacy.

From time to time, everyone exhibits behavior patterns like those described above, and exaggerated worry about them may be labeled *symptomitis*, a common disorder of college students, especially those in medicine, nursing, and psychology.

Webley R. Confused had a classic case of symptomitis during his freshman year. When his psychology professor talked about rationalization, Webley knew he himself rationalized all the time; when he heard about sibling rivalry, he recalled how much he disliked his brothers; the study of religious values reminded him that he had a religious conflict. When the professor lectured on mental illness, Webley panicked—he had every symptom the professor described, and the more he heard, the worse they became.

People who overestimate the importance of some insignificant example of unusual behavior are creating unnecessary stress. People who underestimate the importance of consistently unusual behavior are ignoring a potentially real problem.

The final evaluation should be left to professionally trained people. Very few untrained people consider themselves competent to diagnose cancer, to construct a skyscraper, or to program a computer. Unfortunately, many untrained people feel competent to diagnose and even treat serious emotional problems. Trying to determine who has received adequate training is a more difficult matter. Teachers, ministers, lawyers, policemen, and physicians are constantly placed in the position of being asked to help people with emotional problems. How should they respond in such situations? The validity of advice rendered through newspaper and magazine columns appears especially open to question. It is implausible that even the most capable individual can learn enough about the writer of a brief letter to offer him valuable advice. These columns probably do no harm, as long as they are read for fun.

"I don't know exactly why, but people always seem to come to me with their problems. I guess I'm that sort of person." When did you last hear someone say something like that? When did you last say something like that? What are your responsibilities when people bring their problems to you? How should you respond?

Behavior Under Severe Stress

The person under severe stress is in a bind. As feelings of frustration, conflict, guilt, or anxiety build up, he finds it more and more difficult to respond effectively and within the range of normal behavior. He may need to turn to highly exaggerated forms of behavior or, eventually, to behavior considered non-normal. The situation forces him to adapt to extreme stress, and he learns ways of doing so. However, the behavior he learns is likely to disrupt other aspects of his life. When he does find a way of behaving that enables him to avoid the stress-produced feelings, this behavior is reinforced because it reduces his discomfort, even though it may be destructive in the long run. A person learns that living in a world of fantasy is less painful than facing reality; he learns that attributing his own sexual impulses to the forces of Satan is less painful than accepting himself as he is. And just as the student learns the correct response through having the teaching machine reinforce his response with the word "Correct," the person suffering greatly from stress learns the "correct" response through being reinforced by tension reduction.

As the situation becomes more stressful, the faulty adjustment becomes more obvious, and the resulting behavior becomes more rigid, more irrational (from the view of the observer), more confused and disorganized, and less in touch with reality. If the stresses are moderately severe, the person will find great difficulty in being successful or happy in certain phases of his life, but will be able to function in the day-to-day world. If the stresses are very severe, the person may need protective services or hospitalization, since he can no longer care for himself or be responsible for some of his actions.

Why are some people able to withstand stress better than others? Psychologists believe that those who can satisfy their physiological, safety, love, and self-esteem needs are better able to withstand stress than those who cannot. They have established a strong and secure base, so that the world is not interpreted as threatening or disturbing. These people tend to come from homes in which the family relationships enabled them to feel loved and wanted, so that they could develop a concept of themselves as individuals of value and worth. They feel that they are likable because they have been liked; they feel respected because they have been shown respect; they feel secure because they have been given security. In essence, normal, effective, perhaps self-actualizing behavior has been possible, and it has been rewarded. Since they do not need to direct their efforts at warding off anxiety and other outcomes of stress, these people have been able to satisfy their needs and have developed healthy self-concepts. They approach their problems realistically, and the world seems a relatively understandable and friendly place.

After so much discussion about environmental stress as a cause of disturbed behavior, you may wonder whether genetic inheritance has any influence on stress at all. The answer is necessarily incomplete, but many psychologists, including the author, would agree with one authority who says that genetic factors can have an influence in two ways. First, people have differing degrees of stress tolerance at birth; second, inherited differences may help determine the particular type of personality disorder that occurs (Coleman, 1960). We would not state that a person has inherited a particular **mental illness**, but that he might have inherited a predisposition to that disorder. Thus, if three different individuals were subjected to exactly the same environment and exactly the same stress, one might develop a personality disorder of one type and severity; the second might develop a disorder of another type and severity; and the third might show no signs of behavior disturbance whatsoever. However, keep in mind that the evidence for this point of view is still incomplete (see Chapter 7).

Perhaps by now you have asked yourself, "But what is it that's disturbed? Is it behavior or feelings or body chemistry or what?" The answer is complex. We talk about disturbed *behavior,* because we recognize that the behavior is faulty and nonadjustive; we talk about disturbed *feelings* or *emotions,* because we assume that underlying the behavior is the subjective feeling of great discomfort; we talk about disturbed *body chemistry,* because we have learned that biochemical changes influence the subjective feelings and the behavior (see the section on violence in Chapter 13). And sometimes we refer to the disturbed or disordered *personality,* a term that encompasses a variety of aspects. When we want to alter the disturbed condition, we can attack it through behavior, through the underlying emotions, or through body chemistry. Each approach has its proponents and its opponents.

Summary of Important Ideas

1. The degree of stress tolerance is related to the strength of the self-concept and the flexibility of the individual.

2. Physiological changes occur in response to stress.

3. A psychosomatic disorder is an organic problem induced by stress.

4. Other bodily reactions to stress include fatigue and bed-wetting.

5. Overt behavioral reactions to stress include rigid behavior and intolerance of ambiguity, withdrawal, aggressive behavior, and disorganized behavior.

6. Defense mechanisms are unconscious reactions that serve to protect the individual's self-concept and enable him to interpret his behavior as being consistent with his values and self-concept.

7. Defense mechanisms may redirect responsibility (rationalization, projection, reaction formation, displacement), allow for withdrawal (fantasy, regression, intellectualization, apathy), and produce feelings of affiliation (identification).

8. Defense mechanisms often function as psychological crutches. There is danger in using them longer than necessary, but removing them too quickly can also be dangerous.

9. Responses to stress may produce growth, for example, increased motivation, new insights and new levels of aspiration, and new approaches to old problems. Sometimes, the individual needs to learn to live with the stress in his life.

10. When the demands of stress are greater than the individual can deal with, the result is often faulty or disordered behavior.

11. Normal behavior falls within a wide range of possibilities, and it varies with cultures.

12. Basically, a normal person is one who knows the difference between what is real and what is not, who does not use defense mechanisms to excess, and whose behavior is not dominated by excessively rigid, irrational, or self-defeating actions.

13. Faulty adjustment becomes more obvious as the stress in a situation increases, and the resulting behavior becomes more confused and disorganized, more rigid, and more (apparently) irrational.

14. Genetic factors can probably influence mental disorders by producing a predisposition to mental illness and by helping determine the type of disorder.

Chapter Fifteen

Behavior Disorders and Their Treatment

When stress becomes so great that the individual can no longer cope with it through the normal defense mechanisms and other response patterns described in Chapter 14, the result may be faulty or disordered behavior. The degree of disturbance may become so extreme that the person requires professional help or even hospitalization. On the other hand, the behavior disorder may be of such a nature that he can care for himself and continue a relatively normal life, although certain aspects of that life may appear strange or self-defeating.

The two major classifications of severe emotional disturbances are **neurosis** and **psychosis**. Both neurotics and psychotics may display exaggerated forms of behavior patterns, described on pages 297–298. Neurosis is considered a relatively mild personality disturbance that usually does not incapacitate the individual nor demand his hospitalization. Psychosis is a very severe personality disturbance that may necessitate hospitalization. The differences between neurotic behavior and psychotic behavior are not always clear-cut, but the following may serve as an acceptable guide:

1. Psychosis is more severe and implies greater personality disorganization.
2. Psychotics are often dangerous to themselves or others and may destroy property; neurotics rarely are dangerous in these ways.
3. Psychotics usually need hospitalization both for care and for protection; neurotics can usually get along without special care and without hospitalization.

Behavior Disorders and Their Treatment

4. Psychotics rarely recognize that they are emotionally ill, but neurotics are often aware of their symptoms, although they still cannot change their neurotic behavior.
5. Psychotics may show intellectual deterioration, but neurotics can function at or near their normal intellectual level.
6. Psychotics are out of touch with reality in some way; neurotics can differentiate reality from the nonreal, although they are unable to control the aspects of their own behavior that are affected by their neuroses.
7. Neurotics are much more likely to respond to psychotherapy than are psychotics.
8. Psychotics often exhibit **delusions** and **hallucinations**; neurotics do not.

Prison-brig Euphemia, and Store-ship Apollo.

Figure
15–1.

The brig *Euphemia* was California's first mental hospital. It also housed convicts. Courtesy California Department of Mental Hygiene.

A delusion is a false belief, for example, the belief that "people over there are talking about me," or that you are the ruler of the universe, or that you are being slowly eaten up by invisible insects. Hallucinations are perceptions that occur without external stimuli, for example, hearing voices inside your head or tasting poison in your food. (See Chapter 3.) The following case provides examples of both delusions and hallucinations:

Jackson Wade was an intense young engineering student who worked hard at his studies and rarely socialized. He had been brought up on a small farm and had developed amazing physical strength. The day after the Thanksgiving holiday, Mrs. Wade telephoned the college vice-president to warn him that Jackson believed that the vice-president had been plotting to have him expelled from college, and that he was planning to kill the vice-president to prevent his putting the expulsion into effect.

Jackson drove back to campus with a shotgun and a rifle on the back seat of the car. Somehow he managed to elude the three-man campus police force, and he returned to his dormitory parking lot, but slept in his car for two nights. On the third day, two of his friends asked him to accompany them to breakfast, which Jackson did without protest. On the way, they had to pass the police station, and Jackson walked in and asked the officer in charge to help him. He explained that his voices had initially commanded him to kill the vice-president, but later new and stronger voices insisted that he confess his intended crime to the police.

The delusion in this instance was Jackson's false belief that the vice-president was plotting to have him expelled from college; the hallucinations were the "voices" that commanded him first to murder the official and, later, to give himself up instead. Check the factors differentiating neurosis from psychosis to determine how many of them described Jackson. Was he neurotic or psychotic at the time?

Neurosis

Neurotics, or psychoneurotics, are individuals who exhibit relatively mild personality disturbance in the way they handle stress. Although they can get along without hospitalization or constant supervision, they display certain forms of disordered behavior marking them as neurotic.

The classifications of neurotic behavior include **anxiety reactions**, **conversion reactions**, **dissociative reactions**, **phobic reactions**, **obsessive-compulsive reactions**, and **depressive reactions**. However, keep in mind that real people do not fall into the neat pigeonholes described below. Not only do many individuals display symptoms from more than one category, but symptoms also do not remain static; disturbed people change their behavior patterns just as normal people do.

Anxiety reactions.   Anxiety is a fear of something vague, uncertain, or nonexistent. A person suffering from anxiety reaction feels great

Behavior Disorders and Their Treatment

fear or anxiety with no apparent immediate cause. Bodily changes such as rapid heartbeat and extreme perspiring often accompany these feelings of anxiety. Both the subjective feelings and the bodily changes are likely to become chronic in a person suffering from neurotic anxiety reaction. They are influenced less by the external environment than by the emotional state of the individual.

Conversion reactions. A *psychosomatic illness* is a real physical illness caused by emotional stress. *Malingering* refers to purposely faking some type of medical problem. Conversion reaction, which is sometimes confused with the other two, describes sensory or motor functioning that is defective without apparent physical damage. Unlike psychosomatic problems, no bodily changes are found; unlike malingering, no conscious faking is involved.

The term **hysterical** is used in connection with conversion reactions. A person is said to have hysterical blindness when he cannot see, but no damage has occurred to his eyes, brain, or nervous system. Medical treatment is often useless, because no physical problem is present. Despite the lack of actual organic symptoms, however, the hysterical symptoms appear to be real and do share certain characteristics with normal medical problems.

> A woman of 50, plastered heavily with makeup in a useless effort to look 30, attended one of the author's lectures. During the question period, she told the following story: "About three years ago, I woke up one morning to find I just couldn't straighten my back. At first I thought I had slept in a draft and that a hot bath would help, but it didn't. Then I became afraid and called my physician. He took X rays and did other tests and finally told me that he couldn't find anything wrong. Well, that really got me—here I couldn't straighten up and this idiot doctor couldn't figure out why, so I really told him off. I had seven weeks' sick leave coming from my company, and I phoned a friend whose brother was a doctor and would verify that I couldn't work. After about six weeks, I was getting pretty sick of being at home, when a friend dropped in one Sunday. I told him what had been happening, and he just looked at me and laughed. He said, 'That's the poorest excuse for staying home I've ever seen, you faker. *Stand up straight!*' When he yelled at me, I was so startled that I guess I stood up straight, and I haven't had any trouble since."

It later turned out that the woman's hysterical paralysis began on the anniversary of the death of her father, who had a severe spinal condition in his last few years.

Dissociative reactions. There are several types of dissociative reactions. The **multiple personality**, a very rare occurrence in real life, seems popular in fiction. This disorder refers to the condition in which one person exhibits two or more distinctly different personalities. Several years ago, a book (later turned into a film) appeared describing a true instance of multiple personality. The book was *The Three Faces of Eve,* by Thigpen and Cleckley (1957). The original Eve was a quiet, sweet woman with few bad habits, and the second Eve was a fun-loving, sexy creature who hated the first Eve. Later, a third Eve emerged who, with the aid of a psychiatrist, managed to eliminate the other two Eves and turn the woman back into one personality again. The different personalities had different values, different handwriting, different IQs, and different ways of talking. Finally a fourth Eve emerged with mature values, eventually becoming the only Eve.

Another dissociative reaction is **amnesia**, also very popular with writers of fiction. Amnesia is the total or partial blocking of memories concerning certain past events or periods of time, usually assumed to result from emotional stress working through the mechanism of repression. When this memory blocking occurs over an extended period of time, the condition is termed a **fugue state**. Some fugue victims will actually begin a new life with a new identity, although such cases are rare.

Phobic reactions.   From time to time, a person will exhibit a dread or morbid fear of some object, some person, or some situation. This morbid fear, or **phobia**, is much stronger than the situation normally calls for. Perhaps you occasionally feel a little uncomfortable in a small elevator, but the person with claustrophobia (fear of enclosed places) might perspire, shake, or even faint in the elevator. Whatever produces the phobic reaction is often interpreted as a symbolic substitute for the real cause of fear and anxiety.

Obsessive-compulsive behavior.   In the very famous sleepwalking scene in Shakespeare's *Macbeth,* Lady Macbeth, some time after Macbeth has killed the king, wanders through the halls of the castle muttering, "Out, out, damned spot." She is attempting, symbolically, to rub her hands clean of the blood of the king whose murder she encouraged, but she cannot do so. Lady Macbeth is obsessed with the idea that she has the king's blood still upon her and feels compelled to continue rubbing and cleaning her hands. The obsession is the idea, and the **compulsion** is the hand rubbing. Obsessions and compulsions are usually considered "a single . . . behavior pattern" (English & English, 1958).

In obsessive-compulsive behavior, a person's thinking is dominated by a feeling, an image, or an idea—he is obsessed by it. The compulsive behavior is an attempt to cope with the obsession through some ritualistic act, which seems to be a symbolic attempt to ward off the "evil." The compulsive behavior often seems irrational not only to observers but to the person himself.

Rocky Prater went to college only because of pressure from his older brother. Unfortunately, he got into several courses he hated, so that the entire school day seemed difficult and dull. Shortly before midterms, Rocky developed an obsession that he had not set his alarm clock. He would lean out of bed to check, but it was always set. Sometimes he would wake up in the middle of the night with the terrible feeling that the alarm was not set, but it always was. Still he compulsively continued to go through this alarm-checking ritual at least once every night and often more frequently.

Finally his counselor helped him realize that his obsession was based on his unconscious desire to sleep through his morning classes, and that the compulsion was his unconscious method of counteracting these unrecognized feelings. After his talk with the counselor, his obsessive-compulsive behavior began to fade away.

Rocky was certainly not seriously neurotic, in spite of his exhibiting this particular obsessive-compulsive behavior pattern. As a matter of fact, his specific symptom is not unusual in college students. Rocky's case is an excellent example of how a normal person can have one non-normal pattern of behavior that interferes only slightly with day-to-day effectiveness. What other examples of obsessive-compulsive behavior have you observed?

Depressive reactions. Some people have the constant feeling that nothing is going the way it should, that life has little fun or pleasure, and that the future appears bleak. If a person maintains such attitudes far in excess of what the conditions justify, his symptoms are those of a neurotic depressive.

Psychosis

By and large, human beings can deal with stress well enough to avoid becoming psychologically incapacitated. Occasionally they use neurotic defenses to cope with the stress in their lives. Sometimes, however, for reasons not fully understood, the person under stress will not use neurotic defenses, but will respond by losing touch with reality, that is, by becoming psychotic.

Much mental illness results from **organic psychosis.** This term refers to behavior disorders induced directly by brain damage caused by conditions such as brain tumors, syphilis of the brain, brain injuries, lack of blood supply to the brain, or chemical changes affecting the brain. Organic psychosis often takes the form of **chronic brain syndrome,** which cannot be reversed through psychotherapy or other environmental changes, although its impact may sometimes be lessened. The brain change producing behavior disorder, memory loss, and confusion sometimes found in the elderly, usually called **senile psychosis**, is one of the two major types of chronic brain syndrome; the other is brain change resulting from overuse of alcohol (Morgan & King, 1966).

The second major category of mental illness is **functional psychosis**, which occurs when the stress in the environment becomes greater than the person can tolerate and overwhelms his defense mechanisms. The real world becomes too painful, and the person retreats into a world he has created for himself, where he has learned he can avoid the extreme discomfort of the stress. This does not imply, by any means, that mentally ill people are happy. The general opinion of ex-patients and of professionals working with the mentally ill is that they are extremely unhappy, fearful, anxious, suspicious, and—for the most part—unable to enjoy work, human relationships, or anything else, no matter how they might appear to a casual observer.

Recent thinking and research have led to the belief that the body chemistry of functional psychotics differs from that of normal people. One hypothesis is that many functional psychoses will occur only when both a disorder of the brain chemistry and the necessary level of environmental stress are simultaneously present (Morgan & King, 1966). An oversimplified example would be: If the environmental stress is fairly high, functional psychotic reactions will occur with X level of brain chemistry disturbance; however, if the environmental stress is extreme, the same psychotic reaction will take place with a lesser amount of brain-chemistry disruption. If this hypothesis turns out to be true, then all psychoses have a biochemical basis; the term *functional psychosis* could then be used to refer to forms of mental illness requiring environmental stress as a trigger. Also according to this hypothesis, functional psychoses are affected and perhaps altered completely by environmental changes and by changes in the self-concept, whereas chronic brain syndrome requires biomedical intervention. However, it is already known that the specific symptoms that chronic brain syndrome generates depend not only upon the disorder itself, but also upon the unique history of the individual. An understanding of both biochemical and environmental factors is necessary for a full understanding of mental illness.

The following classification system has been widely used to describe psychotics:

Schizophrenic Reactions

Schizophrenia is the most common form of psychosis. Several types of schizophrenia have been described, although the types often overlap and differences are not always clear in real cases.

Behavior Disorders and Their Treatment

The person suffering from **simple schizophrenia** shows a loss of interests, loss of ambition, emotional indifference, and withdrawal from social relations (Coleman, 1964). Situations that would arouse deep emotional feeling in a normal person receive only a casual shrug. This schizophrenic copes with stress by withdrawing from most of the world, but often remains sufficiently adjusted to avoid hospitalization.

Perhaps the most dramatic form of mental illness is **paranoid schizophrenia**. This schizophrenic has bizarre delusions (false beliefs) and frequent hallucinations (false perceptions). His behavior is often extremely unusual, and he will almost inevitably come to the attention of the medical authorities.

Barney Hauser was from a very strict, devoutly religious family and had been brought up with a strong sense of the horrible price a person paid for sin, whether actually committed or committed through fantasy. During his senior year in high school, his parents decided to obtain a divorce. Shortly after they separated, Barney had a dream which recurred frequently in later weeks. In the dream, Barney was told that he was a re-creation of Jesus Christ, and that "the Son of God would be thrown out of the House of God."

As the dream was repeated again and again, he came to believe it was true, and he thought of a way to test the dream's truth. In the poorest section of his city was an old church called the "House of God." Since this was the phrase that turned up in his dream, Barney visited the minister of this church to ask his advice. The minister quickly realized how disturbed Barney was and asked him to leave, but Barney refused and began to pound on the desk in his excitement. The noise brought some men from the store next door, and they held Barney while the minister called the police. Barney was taken from the church to the nearest psychiatric hospital. However, the entire occurrence only confirmed his dream: the Son of God (Barney Hauser) was being thrown out of the House of God.

Barney remained in the mental hospital about a year, but was released in 1963 and, as of this writing, has not needed further treatment. Since his release, he has completed college, where his performance was adequate, and he has begun to establish friendships. Barney's experience shows how hallucinations (the voice in his dreams) and delusions (the belief he was the re-creation of Jesus) form a pattern of behavior of the mentally ill.

A person is considered to have paranoid delusions when he feels people are always talking about him, plotting against him, trying to kill him, or ready to ask him to conquer the universe. One Navy veteran integrated his work assignment with his paranoid pattern when he believed he was receiving radar signals from Mars that controlled his thinking and forced him to think "strange thoughts."

The person suffering from **catatonic schizophrenia** may spend days, weeks, or longer in an apparent stupor. If his hands are placed upon his head, they may remain there for hours (try it for a few minutes). He needs to be dressed, bathed, and fed. In spite of his apparent withdrawal, the catatonic is often very much aware of what is going on, and his passive behavior occasionally changes into violence, probably accompanied by hallucinations and delusions.

Confused, immature, and often silly, the person with **hebephrenic schizophrenia** has strange ideas and responds inappropriately to emotional situations. He uses words incorrectly and sometimes makes up his own. The hebephrenic frequently regresses to childish behavior.

Several other classifications of schizophrenics have also been described: the childhood schizophrenic (some young children show psychotic symptoms, particularly involving extensive fantasy behavior); the chronic undifferentiated schizophrenic (in certain cases, a variety of schizophrenic symptoms may be observed, often on a mild level); the acute undifferentiated schizophrenic (similar to the previous type, except that the symptoms come suddenly and may disappear or change suddenly); the schizo-affective schizophrenic (such individuals show considerable depression or elation, along with their other schizophrenic symptoms); and the residual schizophrenic (those who have recovered sufficiently to leave the institution but who still exhibit mild schizophrenic symptoms).

Affective Reactions

The second major grouping of psychotic characteristics refers to patients whose major disruption is in mood. They may exhibit extreme depression or extreme elation, often accompanied by delusions and hallucinations. Some patients alternate between a depressed state and an elated or **manic** state. In between the two psychotic conditions such a patient may function normally in the community for months or even years. This condition is termed **manic-depressive psychosis, circular type.**

Most manic-depressive patients, however, display only manic or only depressed symptoms. The manic is, in varying degrees, joyful, boisterous, and excited; he claims that everything in the world is just wonderful. He talks rapidly and constantly and is very optimistic, although these attitudes may be interpreted as camouflage for low self-esteem.

The depressed patient is just the opposite. If he is inactive, sad, pessimistic, and prone to delusions about being dead or rotting away, he is suffering from **retarded depression.** If, on the other hand, his depression involves much activity, rapid walking, and talk about how terrible he is, the symptoms describe **agitated depression.** (White, 1964). Both groups display considerable self-hatred and frequently discuss suicide.

Two other types of affective disorders may be briefly mentioned. In both **psychotic depression** and **involutional psychosis**, depressed behavior is exhibited. The former is similar to the depressed condition of the manic-depressive disorders, although the symptoms seem to be more directly the result of the immediate environment. The latter is a disturbance that typically occurs around the age of 45 to 55 for women and 50 to 60 for men and often involves agitation, anxiety over approaching old age and loss of vitality, and feelings of guilt and hopelessness.

Paranoid Reactions

Paranoid (as opposed to paranoid schizophrenic) symptoms include the development of a system of delusions that are consistent, seem to make good sense, and are often persuasive to others. The delusion often centers around persecution or grandeur, but the rest of the individual's behavior seems relatively normal. Some paranoids have hallucinations but do not discuss them, because they know they will not be believed.

The two classifications of paranoid reactions are *paranoia* and the *paranoid state*. They differ only in that the latter is a little more confused, less seemingly logical, and more likely to be temporary.

Peter Beschwan, a competent engineer, was fired from his job with a missile-research company. The reason for his being fired was a book outlining a new theory of aerodynamics that he had written and had published at his own expense. When the company's senior engineers read the book, they expressed great doubt that Peter had any idea of what he was talking about, and they felt that his statement that his theory "outshone both Einstein and Newton" was—to say the least—a little far-fetched. When Peter learned that he was being fired, he immediately sent a letter to the company president in New York City, and when he received a brief, unsatisfactory answer, he wrote protests to several top state officials, including the attorney-general and the governor. His letters were so well written and made so much sense to anyone who did not understand the technical problems under consideration that one state legislator demanded a legislative investigation of the missile company for incompetence in the use of tax funds for research. At that point, Peter wrote a follow-up letter to the legislator, thanking him for his interest. He added a note that the suicide of a well-known nightclub singer was actually murder. She had spoken up for him after her performance one evening, and Peter's employer had ordered her killed.

In every other respect, Peter remained a competent, well-functioning individual. He had no hallucinations, got along well with his fellow-employees on his new job, was a good husband and father, and lived a sensible and rather conservative life. As long as the topic of his book and his old job are avoided, you would never know he had any psychotic symptoms. Even if he did tell you about his troubles, you might be inclined to believe him—at least until he told you about the nightclub singer.

Everyone must cope with stress, and you inevitably find that, at various times and in various ways, your life is made less pleasant and less successful as a result of stress. Most people are able to develop adequate methods for dealing with the stress they encounter. It is only when the individual is unable to handle the stress that he employs neurotic defenses or finds the real world so emotionally painful that he must retreat from it with psychotic symptoms.

Personality Disorders

Instead of exhibiting neurotic or psychotic symptoms, some people handle disruptive stress by heavy use of alcohol or narcotics, through sexual deviation, by suicide, by gambling, or by criminal behavior. The particular form or forms employed are influenced by the person's attitudes, values, self-concept, and previous psychosocial and, perhaps, medical history, as well as the characteristics of the immediate situation. (Criminal behavior will not be discussed in this book, because it receives such thorough coverage in other courses.)

Alcoholism and Drug Addiction

"One drink is too many and one hundred is not enough." That expression, which is a basic belief of members of Alcoholics Anonymous, states the major problem of the true **alcoholic** (many very heavy drinkers are not true alcoholics). Once he begins, the alcoholic cannot stop.

Although many people turn to liquor during times of stress, only a portion of them become compulsive drinkers. Compulsive drinkers *must* have a drink—and another and another. Once they become alcoholic, they eventually lose their jobs, their friends, and their money. Even after the initial stress has disappeared, alcoholism and the tragedy it brings produce their own stressful problems. Recent estimates by the National Council on Alcoholism indicate that alcohol produces serious behavior and adjustment problems for 6,500,000 Americans. In addition, the death rate from alcoholic disorders rose by more than 50% between 1950 and 1964.

In comparison, the 60,000* **drug addicts** in America seem like a very small group. Yet, even more than alcohol, some narcotics create an extreme craving that can be satisfied only by more narcotics. Drugs, like alcohol, temporarily produce a wonderful feeling of well-being, but the same stressful world is there when the drug wears off. The world seems so much more pleasant to the person under the influence of drugs that the desire to escape the real world plus the habit-forming effects of the drug motivate another try.

Often, a person insists that he will have no trouble kicking the drug habit when he is ready. The evidence does not bear this out. Those individuals who become addicted to drugs (not all drugs, of course, are addicting) find it overwhelmingly difficult to overcome their obsessive desire for more. Since most drug addicts do not have the funds to pay the high prices demanded by drug peddlers, they often turn to crime and prostitution for the money needed to satisfy their addiction.

Treatment for both alcoholics and drug addicts has included psychotherapy, medication in a hospital setting, vocational rehabilitation, and membership in such organizations as Alcoholics Anonymous, Addicts Anonymous, and Synanon. Alcoholics seem more amenable to treatment than addicts, and Alcoholics Anonymous, with hundreds of chapters around the country, has had conspicuous success in helping alcoholics remain sober. AA's program includes social activities, regular meetings with explanations from members about how the organization has helped them remain sober, and—as one member phrased it—"a willingness to sit up all night and hold the hand of any member who has either had too much or thinks he will." Synanon provides a large house —the original one is in Santa Monica, California—where narcotic addicts and others live together in a relatively normal social setting and try to help each other overcome their addictions. (For college student alcohol and drug problems, see Chapter 19.)

Sexual Deviation

Many forms of sexual deviation occur in our society, the best known probably being **homosexuality**. Both male and female homosexuals prefer sexual relationships with their own sex, rather than with the opposite sex.

Several beliefs concerning homosexuals are totally lacking in evidence. For example, there is no good evidence that homosexuality is determined genetically or that it results from an imbalance of biochemicals, although some data suggest such a possibility (Kallmann, 1953).

* Some estimates of drug addiction run much higher, but none are remotely close to the estimates for alcoholism.

Also, it is a mistaken notion that the effeminate man and the masculine woman are homosexual, whereas the masculine-appearing men and the highly feminine women are not; physical appearance and mannerisms can be very deceiving here. A third incorrect belief is that homosexuals have found a method of adjusting to the world that makes them happier than most heterosexuals.

Both laws and social values are strongly opposed to homosexual behavior in America today. As a result, both male and female homosexuals are fearful of police interference with their activities and, simultaneously, may feel guilty for having participated in homosexual acts. Even a normal attraction, without sexual implications, to someone of your own sex may produce such guilt that an adult man finds it difficult to kiss his own father or embrace his own brother, although such affection is displayed freely in many nations of the world.

The difficulties of the homosexual do not stop with legal restrictions and social disapproval. Some psychologists and others claim that the homosexual, both male and female, has very low self-esteem and is unable to enter into satisfying love relationships, even through homosexual "marriage" (Buxbaum, 1967). If homosexual behavior is actually a way to avoid the anxiety of a heterosexual relationship, then the behavior pattern obviously has rewarding elements, since it provides companionship and sexual release without involving the opposite sex. One psychotherapist told the author that he had helped men overcome their homosexual behavior by associating discomfort with their homosexual acts and rewarding signs of accepting heterosexual involvements (Joseph Cautela, personal communication).

Most people take the position that homosexual behavior is inappropriate and that homosexuals need help in altering their behavior. However, homosexuality is found among various species of animals, and is reported in societies throughout the world, some of which regard it with extreme tolerance (Ford & Beach, 1951). How do you look upon homosexuality?

Suicide

In the United States, suicide is an illegal act, and is also considered by many as an act against God. However, in some countries, killing oneself is considered appropriate under certain circumstances. Recently, suicide has been interpreted as a sign of extreme stress and, in most instances, of mental illness. Although the person who fails in his suicide attempt is liable to criminal prosecution, he is more likely to receive psychiatric help in our country today. That suicide *may* result from emotional disturbance is evident; that all suicides *must* be caused by emotional disturbance is far from established.

According to folklore, people who threaten suicide will not actually kill themselves. This belief is completely untrue. A suicide threat or attempt is definite basis for concern and, perhaps, psychological treatment. Many people who threaten or attempt suicide may not really wish to die; they may be calling for help, using the suicide threat or attempt as a way to attract attention. One recent theory suggests that suicide occurs when people feel helpless and hopeless, and the suicide effort is their way of getting others to recognize their plight and rescue them from helplessness and hopelessness (Kobler & Stotland, 1964). Even unsuccessful suicide attempts may be injurious to health, and there is no way of knowing in advance whether the attempt will be successful.

Recently, much attention has focused on the problem of suicide, which ranks about tenth in causes of death in the United States and third among those of student age (Dublin, 1967). One major effort to reduce suicides has been the establishment of Suicide Prevention Centers, patterned after the one in Los Angeles. These agencies encourage potential suicides to contact them to discuss their difficulties. They also offer psychotherapy to people who have failed in their suicide efforts. They are answering the suicide's cry for help (Farberow & Shneidman, 1961).

Compulsive Gambling

The attitudes of Americans toward gambling are amazingly contradictory. You may find, for example, that horse racing is legal in your state, but that you cannot legally play poker for money on your front porch; bookies may be prosecuted by state law, but they are supposed to purchase a federal license nonetheless; one church condemns gambling, and another raises money by sponsoring bingo games. Gambling laws are inconsistent from state to state or even from town to town and are very difficult to enforce.

Gambling is common in many colleges, and the stakes range from penny-ante to several dollars a chip or a point. As stakes go higher, the game attracts people who have developed elaborate systems of cheating. One university student, who worked his way through college by gambling, admitted that he was proficient at stacking the deck, slipping in marked cards, cutting as he wished, and using other tricks. "Hell, no, I don't feel sorry for those guys. They're a greedy bunch anyhow, or they wouldn't be gambling." A professional gambler once remarked to the author, "When I was a kid (about 1915), gambling depended upon skill. Now it's just a matter of who cheats best."

A study of gamblers shows them to be rebellious and unconventional people who describe themselves as "hating regulations." The problem gambler, however, like the problem drinker, is the *compulsive gambler*—the man who *must* gamble. He may or may not enjoy gambling, but he cannot stop. About 10 years ago an estimated 6 million compulsive gamblers in the United States lost an estimated $20 billion a year (Rosten, 1961). For comparison, the entire cost of *all* education in the United States was only about $28 billion a year (*Statistical Abstracts,* 1965).

To show the power of the gambling compulsion, the following story is often told:

> Joe Doakes, a compulsive gambler, comes into a new town for a sales convention. As soon as business is over, he asks a taxi driver where he can find a game. "There's only one game in this town, Mister, and that's at Sharkey's Bar, but I'll warn you—it's as crooked as they come." Joe thanks the driver and gets out of the taxi. The next morning, he bumps into the driver again. "What did you do last night, Mister? Catch a movie?" "No, I thought I'd try the game at Sharkey's—I lost about $400." "But I told you it was crooked." "Yeah, but it was the only game in town."

Help for the Troubled Personality

Neurotics, psychotics, and individuals with personality disorders often wish help in dealing with their difficulties. Even people without severe or obvious problems may wish help in handling the stress they face, so that they can expend less time and energy on the stress and more toward being themselves and using their capacities.

Just like the best treatment for medical and dental problems, the best treatment for psychological problems is prevention. There is good reason to believe that better parent-child relationships, fewer unhappy homes, and less poverty would all lead to fewer emotional problems and personality disorders.

However, we do not really know the best way to achieve these goals. More than that, we do not know why some people from apparently good homes and healthy family situations still become neurotic or alcoholic, whereas others brought up in seemingly inadequate homes turn out to be well adjusted and able to self-actualize. Much work remains both in determining effective methods of prevention and in persuading people to apply them.

Help for disturbed people ranges from tranquilizers to psychotherapy to hospitalization. Each approach has its place, depending upon the individual and the circumstances.

When a person seeks help for an emotional problem, he is trying to unlearn attitudes and feelings that took years to learn. These attitudes are very much a part of him. They form part of his self-concept, are built into his defense mechanisms, and have greatly influenced his internalized values and social relationships. Thus, although a brief period of psychological help may make a person feel better and behave more effectively, any deep-seated problem may necessitate longer treatment. Fortunately, the improvement of day-to-day behavior through psychological methods does not always require a long time.

Trends in Mental Health Care

The awareness that the community shares a responsibility for mental health care and treatment is relatively recent. Up until 175 years ago, mental patients and others unable to care for themselves were housed under conditions as bad as the worst prisons of the time. At various times in history, they have been tortured and killed for being witches and helpers of the devil. Conditions in mental hospitals in the United States have slowly become better over the years, but even today many are overcrowded and understaffed.

Recent criticisms of mental hospitals have gone beyond their physical conditions. Many mental health experts feel that the "hospital routine tends to reinforce (submissive) behavior and dependence . . ." (Bandura, 1967). These experts have suggested that mental hospitals be more than custodial institutions where patients can avoid some of the stresses of the community; instead, hospitals should prepare patients for return to the community.

Part of this preparation for community living would be to reduce the hospital atmosphere in mental institutions. When you ask a physician to cure your stomachache, you usually follow his advice without much questioning, take the prescribed medicines, and assume you will feel better as a result. However, emotional problems do not readily respond to advice and medication. For functional mental disorders, the person in treatment needs to become personally active in the treatment process. Psychologists have advised that all treatment programs for mental disturbance, including hospitalization, offer the patient the opportunity to make decisions and to take responsibility for matters involving daily routine, coming and going, and long-range plans. When they are placed under strict routines with no decision-making opportunities, mental patients realize they are looked upon as mentally ill and incapable of caring for themselves, and "if people are *expected* to act crazy, most of them will" (Smith, 1968).

As was mentioned at the beginning of this chapter, much disturbed behavior results from learning, particularly learning to avoid stress and the anxiety that stress produces. If this is the case—and there are many who would disagree—then the way to alleviate the disturbed behavior is to arrange unlearning, relearning, and new learning opportunities. As one prominent psychologist has put it, "the institution developed to deal with these conditions may well be educational in nature" (Albee, 1968).

Figure 15–2.

One ward at an overcrowded mental hospital. Courtesy California Department of Mental Hygiene.

Perhaps in the future, psychological disorders will be treated in "learning centers" rather than hospitals or clinics, and those coming for help will not be looked upon as patients who must receive help, but as "responsible people who participate actively in developing their own potentialities" (Bandura, 1967).

Not only is the mental health treatment process undergoing change, but its relationship to the community is also being re-evaluated. The community mental health programs now being initiated around the country are attempting to provide mental health facilities right in the community where the emotionally disturbed person lives and where he will continue to live after completing his treatment. Some of the aims of these programs are:

Behavior Disorders and Their Treatment

1. Move patients away from old, factory-like mental hospitals in isolated areas to smaller, community-based facilities;
2. Give patients as much freedom as possible to come and go;
3. Make it easier to enter hospitals voluntarily and to leave voluntarily;
4. Reduce the waiting time before treatment is available; and
5. Integrate the services for patients living in the facilities with services for outpatients (Smith, 1968).

Another arrangement provides institutional care on a part-time basis. The patient may spend evenings or weekends in the hospital, but work at a regular job during the day; or he may live at home, but come to a mental health center during the day (Wechsler, 1960). Behavior disorders are seen as the outcome of faulty learning arising from the need to avoid stress and anxiety. Therefore, the treatment must focus upon correcting the faulty learning and getting the person back to full-fledged membership in his own community as soon as possible.

Major problems still exist. First, it is very difficult to get help to all who could profit from it. Many people will not use the help that is available, and others are unaware that they can receive help or are unaware that they need help. Also, mental health facilities are not available in all communities.

Second, new ways of staffing the mental health facilities are required, since there are not enough professionals to go around nor enough money to hire them, even if there were. This problem is being handled by hiring people with less formal training, but whose personal sensitivity and awareness of the community qualify them as *subprofessionals*. Frequently they are given a special training course. The use of subprofessionals has been accelerated by observations that mental patients and others needing help often respond more successfully to help from people of similar backgrounds to their own (Rioch, 1966). Thus, well-educated mental patients felt that the psychiatrists and psychologists were most helpful, but less educated patients stated that the aides and fellow patients did the most for them (Keith-Spiegel & Spiegel, 1967).

Third, the problems that exist in the community or in the family are not necessarily going to disappear just because the individual has sought mental health help. The patient still has to be able to function in the community and with the family. Involving the entire family in the program seems to be a partial answer, but it is only a beginning (Smith, 1968).

Perhaps, at this point in your reading, you have asked yourself why the author places so much emphasis on mental health as it relates to the community when, in an earlier section, he suggested that mental disorders had a biological base. Why not just work to find the right pill or injection? The answer is not simple; neither is it final. At present, we can merely say that pills and injections seem to work only as long as the person continues under medication. They help only in the short run. Although the biological base of personality is important, it is environmental stress that sets off the functional disorder. The individual must learn to deal effectively with the environment to avoid future behavior disturbance. If he can do this, the impact of the environmental stress is reduced and ceases to be a disruptive force.

The trends in mental health treatment have been summarized thus:

*Figure
15–3.*

College students participating in Project Weekend, an educational service project of the Mental Health Association of Los Angeles County, converse with patients in a ward of a local state mental hospital. Courtesy Mental Health Association of Los Angeles County.

(1) from emphasis on the person to emphasis on the person-in-the-environment; (2) from facilities offering partial services to facilities offering comprehensive services; (3) from complete domination by professionals to much involvement by subprofessionals; (4) from simple custody to correction of the problem to prevention of the problem to enhancement and enrichment, that is, from doing nothing to satisfying deficiency motives to satisfying growth motives (Arkoff, 1968).

Psychotherapy

Psychotherapy is the process through which a person trained in psychological treatment techniques applies these techniques, using personal consultation, to help another learn to handle his problems more effectively. Psychotherapy is not limited to emotionally disturbed individuals, but is frequently used by normal people with normal problems who feel that help will be valuable. Although most psychotherapy involves one therapist and one client or patient, group psychotherapy has been shown to be effective also.

Many psychotherapeutic theories exist, and psychotherapists argue over which is best. However, the different approaches have much in common:

1. Each theory makes use of a therapist who shows interest, trust, and respect for the client. The therapist may or may not offer obvious encouragement, but the mere fact that he listens carefully and responds with understanding and patience is reassuring.

2. Each theory includes the opportunity for the client to express his feelings. In the therapy situation, the client can usually discuss his most personal fears, desires, hates, and his most embarrassing and guilt-producing behavior and fantasies. Once they are expressed by the client and accepted by the therapist, the client often feels less anxious and his self-concept achieves a new sense of adequacy. We cannot express all these feelings to those we love, nor to a casual stranger, but we can reveal them to a person who shows he is interested in us and respects us.

3. Each theory encourages the client to increase his insight into his own feelings and motives. Although insight itself is no guarantee of improved self-concept, insight in combination with the opportunity for self-expression and a healthy client-therapist relationship seems helpful. If the therapist tries to force the client to understand himself too quickly, the client may quit therapy—he will feel that the therapist does not really understand him. Insight must come gradually.

4. Each theory attempts to teach new forms of behavior, new attitudes, and new self-concepts, which are aimed at enabling the person to function more effectively in society *and* to recognize himself as an adequate and worthwhile individual.

The individual schools of therapy, in spite of sharing many basic characteristics, also differ in many respects. Some emphasize the need for lengthy treatment, and others try to provide treatment in a brief period of time. Some require that the therapist keep his own values divorced from his therapy, but others allow the therapist to include his values. Some insist that the person in therapy remain responsible for the pacing and the direction of the therapy; others give the therapist more freedom to control the therapy. Some include the use of psychological tests, and others reject these devices. Some assume sex to be the usual source of difficulty, but others emphasize the self-concept, encounter with death, personal identity and meaning, or inappropriate social learning.

During the past several years, a form of psychotherapy called **behavior therapy**, based on operant learning methods, has developed. Therapists using this approach try to get the people they work with to relax their muscles as they think about matters that distress them. They begin with the least distressing stimuli related to the problem under attack, and the client (a term used instead of "patient" with many forms

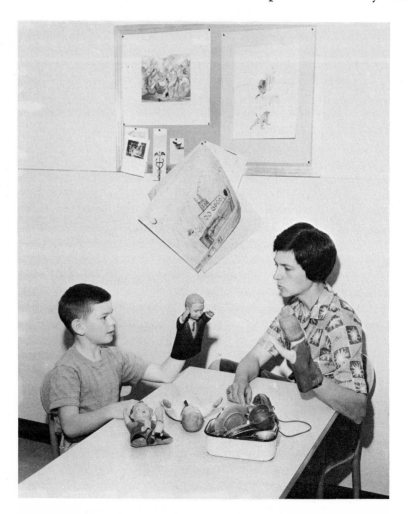

Figure 15–4.

Expressing one's feelings through puppets or other forms of play can be therapeutic. Courtesy Reiss-Davis Child Study Center.

Behavior Disorders and Their Treatment

of psychotherapy) dwells on this stimulus until he can be completely relaxed at the same time as he imagines the stimulus to be present—until it no longer produces anxiety and tension. Then the therapist goes on to a slightly more disturbing stimulus and repeats the process. This sequence is continued until the therapist has enabled the client to relax even while thinking about matters that were extremely upsetting on previous occasions. According to some criteria, this form of therapy has been shown by research to be more effective than more traditional psychotherapeutic approaches (Eysenck, 1967). However, much more evidence needs to be accumulated before a final judgment is possible.

Another important aspect of behavior therapy is the use of reinforcement for appropriate behavior. Whenever the client does or says something that suggests he is behaving more effectively, the therapist rewards him, often only with a smile or a word of approval, following operant learning techniques. Although a smile may not sound like much of a reward, approval by those we respect is very meaningful, and people respond to these slight reinforcements more readily than they often realize themselves. Think of the times when you watched a friend, a teacher, or an employer for the slightest sign of approval or disapproval; recall the hours that you would spend attempting to interpret a few words, a meaningful glance, or a pat on the arm from a person of the opposite sex whom you liked very much.

As the therapist reinforces certain statements and acts, he ignores others. The client repeats the reinforced statements more frequently, and performs the reinforced acts more frequently. Eventually the person learns to stop behaving inappropriately and to behave in ways that will satisfy growth needs. Behavior therapists are most concerned with the change of ongoing behavior, assuming that underlying feelings will also change when the new forms of behavior are found to be more effective than the old. You may have noticed that there is little emphasis on insight, although the other three approaches held in common by most therapies are used.

Evidence on the effectiveness of behavior therapy is far from complete. Much research still needs to be done before deciding whether behavior therapy is really better than more traditional approaches, whether it uses the same principles but without realizing it, or whether it works best only for those who feel more comfortable with it. In any event, its emphasis on producing fairly rapid change in behavior through rewards and reinforcement is compatible with the community mental health programs, whose main purpose is getting people to function effectively in the community as quickly as possible.

Also consistent with community mental health concepts is the use of *crisis intervention*. At various times in a person's life, crises arise. They may be set off by the loss of a job, death or serious illness of a loved one.

reaction to a divorce, or an accumulation of frustrations leading to great depression, and, perhaps, a suicide attempt. At these times, the person needs immediate help. Once he is helped through the crisis, he is able to carry on by himself with little or no additional professional help. Crisis intervention aims at preventing the build-up of behavior disorders that might otherwise occur through learning faulty behavior patterns—by providing immediate help directed primarily at the problems brought on by the crisis. A person facing a crisis might attempt suicide, ignore his own health needs, remain away from work until he lost his job, drink heavily, or ignore important responsibilities. Each of these forms of behavior would set off additional inappropriate behavior until the individual's problems would become substantially greater and his behavior substantially less effective. Crisis intervention attempts to stop this chain of events before it begins, but stops short of dealing with long-term problems.

Psychologists and others in the community mental health field are not ignoring the deeper underlying problems. However, they place major emphasis on helping people deal with the here and now and on influencing the interaction between the person and his environment to improve life for everyone in the community.

Summary of Important Ideas

1. The two major classifications of severe emotional disturbances are *neurosis* and *psychosis*. Among the many differences between them are the following: neuroses are milder, less likely to require hospitalization, and more amenable to psychotherapy than psychoses.

2. Among the symptoms of neurosis are extreme anxiety, defective sensory or motor functioning without organic cause, dissociative reactions, extreme fears or phobias, obsessive-compulsive behavior, and chronic depression.

3. Among the symptoms of psychosis are hallucinations, delusions, inappropriate emotional responses, withdrawal from social relationships, feelings of persecution and other paranoid feelings, physical immobility, regression to earlier stages of development, extreme depression, and extreme elation.

4. There is very likely a biochemical basis to all psychosis. However, those disturbances that are directly induced by brain damage are referred to as *organic disorders;* those that are triggered by environmental stress are termed *functional disorders.*

Behavior Disorders and Their Treatment

5. Some people handle disruptive stress by heavy use of alcohol or drugs, sexual deviation, suicide, or compulsive gambling.

6. Alcoholism occurs when "one drink is too many and a hundred is not enough."

7. The best-known form of sexual deviation is probably homosexuality. There are many untrue stereotypes regarding homosexuals, including the idea that homosexuals are always easy to spot by their behavior.

8. The causes of suicide and attempted suicide include extreme stress, emotional disturbance, depression, and feelings of helplessness and hopelessness.

9. Gambling, although illegal in many communities, is very common. There are many compulsive gamblers.

10. Although mental hospitals have improved greatly over the years, the community mental health movement is now urging that the mental patient be brought back to the community, where he will learn to get along in his normal environment.

11. Mental health experts also emphasize the need of the patient to learn to make decisions and to respond actively rather than passively. He needs to be given freedom, and he should be approached as a responsible person.

12. Subprofessionals are becoming an important addition to community mental health programs.

13. The various schools of psychotherapy have much in common, for example, the desire to teach new forms of behavior to the client and to have the therapist show interest, trust, and respect for him.

14. Behavior therapists believe that inappropriate social learning is the basis of behavior disorders. They make use of operant-learning theory in their therapy methods.

Part Four

Man and His Society

Chapter Sixteen

The Individual and His Groups

*This chapter represents a substantial break with the materials of the previous chapters. Until now the emphasis has been on the individual; here the focus shifts to the social environment. The field of sociology deals with the same topics as psychology, but in a different way. The present chapter describes the **groups** with which people identify, such as social-class groups and ethnic groups. Chapter 17 will discuss values, which are largely determined by the groups to which a person belongs.*

Man is a social being. He has developed an extremely complex network of groups, ranging from a small, face-to-face group like the family, to large, impersonal groups like the political party or religious denomination.

Could you get along without groups? Obviously not. Your food, clothing, transportation, social life and entertainment, education, religious observances, and safety are possible only because of groups. Consider each of the motives in Maslow's hierarchy of motives: (1) the physiological need of hunger is satisfied, in our society, because numerous groups grow, process, transport, distribute, and sell food; (2) safety needs are met through such groups as the family, the police force, the courts, and the military; (3) love needs are gratified through friendship and family groups; (4) esteem needs often receive satisfaction through the family group, social groups, and work groups; and (5) self-actualization for many people occurs through accomplishments in a group setting.

The groups you belong to have a major influence on your self-concept. People identify the success and failure of their groups as their own success and failure. When an American wins an Olympic medal, when a graduate of your college is elected assemblyman, when a girl from your home town is elected Miss America, you feel a sense of pride from belonging to the same group. Similarly, you feel embarrassed when a fraternity brother is arrested for hit-and-run driving or a member of your church is accused of bribery.

Man and His Society

Group loyalties can be amazingly strong. People will sacrifice their lives for their family or their country. Smaller, face-to-face groups seem to command even stronger loyalties than larger, less personal groups. The Chinese Communists, recognizing such group loyalty, did their best to breed suspicion within their Korean War prisoners' groups (Schein, 1958). During World War II, both American and German soldiers felt as much or even more loyalty to their own units than to the country as a whole (Shils, 1950; Shils & Janowitz, 1948). Workers will often perform below their capacity if their best performance exceeds the expected performance set informally by their work group (Roethlisberger & Dickson, 1939).

Although most people find great satisfaction in being with a variety of groups, some people prefer only occasional group contact. Healthy needs may keep an individual from groups; for example, he feels that he works better alone or that his leisure-time interests can be pursued better without others around. However, a person's needs for solitude may be unhealthy ones, for example, the feeling that he is socially inadequate. Whether you are a joiner or a loner, you are still part of some groups, and these groups do have an influence on you.

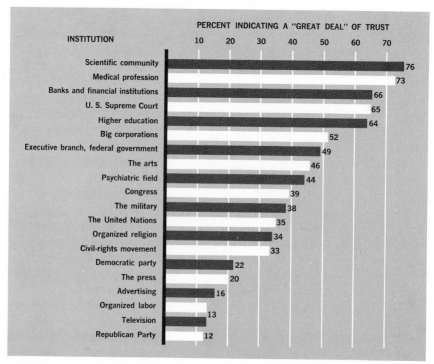

Figure 16–1.

How students view the world around them (*Newsweek*, 1965).

In 1965, *Newsweek* surveyed hundreds of college students at more than 50 colleges to see how students felt about the world, their colleges, their future, and themselves. One of the questions asked was "How much confidence do you have in these institutions?" Figure 16–1 shows the percentage of students who indicated a "great deal" of trust in each institution mentioned.

As you read this chapter, keep in mind that groups are made up of individuals, each of whom behaves in ways discussed in earlier chapters.

Group Pressure on Group Members

Because groups are so important in satisfying needs and because a person does build extensive group loyalties, he becomes dependent upon groups and is deeply concerned about how their members feel about him. As a result, individuals often receive considerable pressure to conform to group demands, a pressure made very difficult to resist by an understandable reluctance to risk being forced out of the group or losing **status** in the group. Even the disapproval of other group members is carefully avoided.

In extreme situations, the punishment for disobeying the demands of the group may be death or complete isolation. Usually such measures are unnecessary because people do not violate the standards of groups they join, since the act of joining implies acceptance of the values of the group (when joining is not voluntary, the situation may differ). On the whole, the longer they remain members, the more will people internalize the values of the group as their own. The American Medical Association, for example, wields considerable power, and most physicians must join. However, most of them prefer to join, not because of pressure but because the AMA represents their interests and satisfies many important needs. Labor unions function in the same way. Some doctors and some workers prefer not to join, and only a few of those who do join would agree with every action taken by their organization.

Conformity

Conformity refers to behavior, including attitudes and judgments, that is intended to live up to the expectations of a particular group; the behavior may or may not be consistent with the values of the person who is conforming.

Man and His Society

Two types of conformity have been described: conventional conformity and yielding conformity. *Conventional conformity* alludes to behaving in a fashion similar to others from a similar background. It refers to being conventional in behavior, or at least conventional in terms of the group with which the person identifies. Conventional conformity implies that the behavior occurs without being evaluated; it has been internalized. Examples would include dressing in the same style as the other students or accepting the belief that members of your preferred political party are more ethical than the party's opponents.

Yielding conformity involves giving in to immediate social pressure, which implies responding in a particular fashion, even if the person's values are opposed to it. Taking a particular stand on a political issue, while actually feeling otherwise, in order to be accepted by a social group is one example; pretending to agree with the philosophy of a work organization in spite of feeling quite different is another (Beloff, 1958).

An extreme example of conventional conformity is the **other-directed** person. As the name implies, he has such a strong need for approval by one or more of the groups with which he associates that he internalizes their values as being his values without any critical evaluation or concern with his own long-range value system (Riesman, Denney, & Glazer, 1950). As a child, the other-directed individual internalized one important value from his parents and society: gain approval and acceptance of the group. Therefore, his conscience reflects the group attitudes of the moment, not his own personal commitments.

Yielding conformity was exemplified by the study of the group of students who were asked to judge the length of a line while the psychologist arranged to have other members of the judging group falsify their judgments (see page 54). Opposing demands to yield can produce a high level of worry or anxiety. Those who "called them as they saw them" indicated higher anxiety as measured by physiological changes (Bogdonoff, Klein, Estes, Shaw, & Back, 1961). In one demonstration, a subject who disagreed with the group on every occasion (and was correct on every occasion) was dripping with perspiration by the end of the session. Remaining independent of conformity pressures to yield is neither psychologically, socially, nor physiologically easy, but it can be personally very satisfying.

Use of the term "conformity" presents a problem, because people tend to apply it to behavior that they disapprove and to say "he was persuaded" when they approve. Thursday's newspaper will editorialize that students conform too much; Friday's edition will complain that students do not do what they are told. The real complaint is not that students conform, but that they do not conform to the desires of the newspaper.

Conformity obstructs self-actualization, because the conformist is not expressing his own feelings or doing what he feels is correct. Rather, he responds to the pressures of the social environment. The anticonformist, who is rebelling against society, is not self-actualizing either; like the conformist, he is merely responding to social pressures, only his response is negative instead of positive. The true individualist neither rebels nor gives in, but acts according to his own values. He is himself and is able to develop his talents without fear that society does not admire or pay those talents sufficiently. But how does the observer decide who is an individualist and who is a conformist or anticonformist?

Many sincere people believe they have the right to decide what forms of individualism are permissible in what others think, speak, read, and view. Through censorship and various forms of group pressure, they attempt to control what can be said and written. There is a point, we all would probably agree, at which irresponsibility can occur, but we would have trouble agreeing about where that point is. Do you believe, for example, that strong group pressure should be brought to bear to restrict the freedom of speech of Americans? What if they use this freedom of speech to advocate Communism? Revolution? Slavery? Murder? Or, to use a less serious example, what sort of group pressure should exist in the area of student dress in class? Should students be allowed to come to class barefoot? With shorts? With no clothes at all? How do you decide where group pressure should take over? What freedoms are you willing to give others?

Many people we consider heroes today were violently criticized during their lives for not conforming. The best known of these people is undoubtedly Christ, who was nailed to the Cross for not conforming. Others from more recent times include Henry David Thoreau, Voltaire, Samuel Gompers, Mark Twain, Martin Luther, Patrick Henry, and Martin Luther King, Jr.

Recent research on obedience to authority has led to some extremely thought-provoking results. In one study, the subject was directed by the experimenter to administer electric shocks to another person as punishment for making incorrect responses on a simple learning task. Each time the other person, who was supposedly strapped in a chair behind closed doors, made a wrong response, the subject was ordered to increase the intensity of the shock. This procedure continued until the person being shocked began to shriek and beg to have the project stopped, but the experimenter demanded that the subject continue. In about half the cases, and with a variety of types of subjects, the shocks were continued in spite of evidence that they were causing great pain and were perhaps having dangerous effects. The subjects appeared to continue administering the shocks (though with great hesitancy and unhappiness) largely because they were being ordered to do so—and they were obedient.

Man and His Society

In actuality, the person supposedly being shocked was an actor, and his entire role was faked. However, none of the subjects realized this, and many seemed willing, although tense and fearful, to extend the shocks as long as the experimenter ordered (Milgram, 1965). What does this study imply about the possibility of countries being taken over by dictators? What does it suggest about the Nazi regime in Germany and

"Damned radicals!"

Figure 16–2.

New ideas are often disturbing to the group. Courtesy Ed Fisher.

Adolph Eichmann's claim at his war-crime trial in Israel that he was only acting under orders?

Obedience to an individual and conformity to a group have much in common. Those whose needs for security, love, or esteem are inadequately met are probably more likely to give in to others or to accept uncritically the ideas of others. To be a true individualist is to accept ideas on a basis *you* feel adequate and to think and behave as *you* feel proper. You will take what others think into consideration, but will not let it become the basis for your own thoughts and behavior.

The effects of group membership vary depending upon the particular group. Since almost everyone is influenced by **social-class-identification** and by **ethnic-group identification**, we shall explore these in more detail.

Social-class Groups

In a democracy that emphasizes equality, as in the United States, the idea of social class is unpopular. After all, social class implies that there is a recognized hierarchy in which people are ranked according to respect and status. What does such ranking do to the idea that everyone is created equal and that no one is better than anyone else?

The answer is simple: social class is not a moral judgment but a description of how a person acts and how others react to him. As you move up in social class, you find an increase in income, education, influence, and status, among other things. This suggests that people in the higher-social-class groups are more fortunate or *better off* than others, but certainly not that they are *better* than others.

Would you be pleased if your sister married a physician? What if she married a union carpenter? Or a bartender who just won $100,000 in a contest? How hard would you try to avoid a fist fight? Would you prefer to fight with words? Your answers will be based on values that are partly the result of social-class associations. No answer is right or wrong, except in relation to values.

A person's social class is evaluated primarily by his attitudes, values, and manners (Krech, Crutchfield, & Ballachey, 1962). Other factors include the use of language, formal education, job status, income, neighborhood, family background, and even child-rearing techniques. Although we divide people into social-class groups (a very common division is upper class, middle class, working class, and lower class), these groups are not separated by distinct boundaries, but are on a continuum. Nor do people *always* behave as a "typical person" of that class is expected to behave; most exhibit nontypical behavior at times.

A person's friendship group directly affects his social-class values and behavior, and his social values also inevitably affect his friendship group. Most friendships, especially dating friendships, are between people of the same or similar social-class background (Hollingshead, 1949). The reasons are many: (1) people of the same social class tend to share the same interests and values; (2) they are likely to be at, or aspiring to, the same level on their jobs; (3) they live in the same neighborhoods and, therefore, attend the same schools; (4) many people feel that a

Belief	Preferred by Working Class	Preferred by Middle Class
Children should be toilet-trained casually.		x
Children should not play "Doctor" and other games involving nudity. Modesty is important.	x	
Masturbation and sex play with other children must be avoided.	x	
Children should be neat and clean.	x	
Spanking and other physical punishments are effective discipline methods.	x	
Threats of withdrawing love should be used in disciplining children.		x
Children must obey their parents.	x	
Children must be considerate of others.		x
Children should never talk back or show aggression toward parents.	x	
Children should not fight back or defend themselves against other children.		x
Both fathers and mothers should show children affection, including physical affection.		x
Children should be dependable and use self-control.		x
Children should be curious about things.		x
Parents should exert pressure for children to do as well as possible in school.	x	
Parents should exert pressure for children to complete all the schooling they are capable of.		x
Parents should use reason in handling children.		x

Figure 16–3.

Child-rearing methods among middle-class and working-class parents (abstracted from Kohn, 1959; Maccoby, Gibbs, et al., 1955; Newson & Newson, 1967; and Sears, Maccoby, & Levin, 1957).

friendship with a person lower on the scale is not a good idea; (5) they may also feel that people higher on the scale are snobbish.

As one interesting example of how social-class association affects behavior, note Figure 16–3. A comparison of middle-class with working-class mothers indicated that child-rearing practices differentiate the two groups. Obedience and neatness are considered more important by working-class parents; dependability and self-control are stressed more by middle-class mothers. Middle-class mothers also rely more on reasoning than do working-class mothers, and reasoning indirectly reinforces verbal behavior (Newson & Newson, 1967). Thus, middle-class children become accustomed to dealing with problems through words and reasoning, whereas working-class children are more likely to receive physical punishment or demands for obedience. Which group do you feel uses more effective punishment? Which group do you feel follows more correct practices?

Another characteristic distinguishing social-class groupings is the attitude toward physical aggression. Actual physical fighting is more common among lower-class children and adults; the middle class expresses aggressive feelings through words or other less direct methods. Does this mean that middle-class people are cowardly? Does it mean that lower-class people, who want to settle matters right away rather than wait and cool down (Schneider & Lysgaard, 1953), are tough?

Educational and Vocational Goals

Nowhere is the importance of social-class values better exemplified than in the pursuit of educational and vocational goals. Even the use of education as a means of achieving goals is a value acceptable primarily to the working class, middle class, and upper class. Lower-social-class people seldom consider education as proper *for themselves*. They may dream about being famous doctors or astronauts, but they rarely contemplate ways to achieve these goals.

To draw a parallel: You might feel that you could write a good movie script; you tell others how you feel, and you think a lot about it, but you never *do* anything about it. The whole business is just a hazy dream. It never occurs to you that books have been published about writing movie scripts or that courses are available in some colleges; you know you need an agent, but you do not know how to try to get one; you know nothing about the instructions to the cameraman. So it all remains a dream, until you are about 50, when you begin to tell people, "Oh, I could have written a movie script if I had wanted to, but I never had the time." Many children from the lower social class have the same hazy dream about college, because they understand very little about college and just assume that college is for other people. Since their parents, often through conditions beyond their control, did not advance far in school, they are less familiar with the purpose or the methods of formal education and less effective in encouraging their children to succeed in school.

Although lower-class children are much more likely to come from financially poorer homes, the family income has less to do with their social-class values than the ideas expressed by their parents and other relatives and friends. Many poor families sincerely encourage their children to do well in school, and these parents do all they can to help their children succeed. Immigrant parents often bring with them a tradition of admiration for education, and their children internalize these values and succeed in school and in work, although the parents always remain poor.

Social class is self-perpetuating from generation to generation. For example, lower-social-class parents do not know how to encourage education, but education is the best way for young people today to move up in social class. Since lower-class children, for a variety of reasons, do not do as well in school as children in the higher classes, they are not eligible for good jobs; thus their incomes are restricted, they live in lower-class neighborhoods, and they marry and have children who mature into the same pattern.

To accentuate the problem, lower-class people are less likely to internalize the value that immediate satisfactions should be sacrified for long-range satisfactions (Gross, 1958). College education means sacrificing immediate income for a long-range better job; savings in the bank mean sacrificing immediate pleasures for a nicer home or investment or retirement security in the future; working extra hours on the job means having less fun now, but increasing chances of promotion. College education, savings in the bank, or working extra hours are all ways to move up the social-class ladder; but lower-class people may not recognize these ways as relevant, and they frequently ignore them.

School dropouts very definitely reflect social-class differences. Middle- and upper-class children rarely drop out of school. Not only do their parents encourage them more, but their teachers are also middle class and understand them and appreciate their problems more (Ausubel, 1954). The middle-class teacher and the middle-class student speak the same language. Also, lower-class parents are more concerned with salary, whereas middle-class parents emphasize the enjoyment received from work (Hyman, 1953). Thus, lower-class children are more likely to want to see an immediate relationship between their schoolwork and their anticipated future job, which often does not appear to require an academic background. Middle- and upper-class children see more relationship between their future job success and job satisfaction and such courses as English or history. Lower-class children, not finding any meaning in education for them, tend to drop out of school.

Yet, in spite of this picture, some lower-social-class children break the pattern, get a good education or training, and obtain a job which is generally regarded as a working-class or middle-class position. These people have received help and encouragement from a teacher, a minister, a parent, or a family friend. Maybe they found something exciting in a book they read, or perhaps military service opened up a new world to them. In 1963, college students all over the country began to volunteer to spend a couple of hours a week tutoring children who came from culturally deprived backgrounds; a year later, the federal government began to set up training programs for school dropouts to learn job skills. Most definitely, the present trend is to recognize the problems of lower-social-class people and to try to alleviate them. However, as problems are alleviated, the values of lower-social-class people seem to undergo change. Do you see any moral or psychological problem that may arise when one group tries to change the values of another group?

Of course, you might say: "Lower-class people are lucky—they aren't worried about education or jobs. They're happy, maybe even better off than I am. Leave them alone." Or you might say: "There's nothing wrong with these people—they're just lazy; they want to be poor and avoid responsibility; if they don't have the initiative to do something about themselves, I don't want to bother helping them." The author disagrees with both of these points of view, but they should be discussed and understood.

Social-class Mobility

The social-class structure is not permanently fixed. People constantly move up and down. Marriage offers one way to change social-class association, although merely marrying a person of another social class will not be sufficient; one's values and behavior must also change. Today, increased educational opportunities have enabled a great upward movement in social class, although becoming part of the true upper class is still very difficult.

The person with **social-class mobility** has two types of problems. First, he is entering into social relationships with people whose values and manners he may not fully understand and who might have low regard for his background. Second, he is leaving an old group of friends whose resentment of his desertion might induce feelings of guilt. Many college students have had the experience of meeting an old high school friend, who now seems to live in a totally different world. Some old friends seem to have made no progress since high school, but others have advanced tremendously.

The socially mobile person must adapt himself to the different manners, speech patterns, and values he encounters. Those who make the transition most successfully have begun to internalize the values of the new group even before they have moved into it (Krech et al., 1962). Those socially mobile individuals who have difficulty internalizing these values often feel uncomfortable in the company of their new friends. To make matters worse, their children frequently take on the values of the new group very quickly and feel resentful that their parents are not truly of the group. The person moving down the social scale seems less happy and adjusted with his new role than does the person moving up (Douvan & Adelson, 1958); he even shows more racial prejudice (Adorno, Frenkel-Brunswik, Levinson, & Sanford, 1950). Although many people move along the social-class ladder with little or no problem, others pay a psychological penalty. Perhaps the most difficult move to make is into the true upper-social-class group. This population segment wields great decision-making power in the country and cannot be entered merely with money. Entrance into the group requires association with acceptable private schools, belonging to recognized social clubs, and—often—active participation in charitable and cultural projects (Domhoff, 1967).

People usually internalize the values and behavior of parents, friends, family members, and neighbors. To some extent, these values are also shared by others in the community, who, as a result, are assigned a particular status or class position by the community as a whole. Such values as vocational and educational goals and such behavior as methods of expressing aggressive feelings are indications of the class with which you identify. Social class should not imply a moral "good" or "bad" but a place in the status system of the community.

Ethnic Groups

Numerous religious, racial, linguistic, and national-origin groups live in the United States. The term *ethnic* is applied to a group whose members share one or more of these qualities. What ethnic groups do you belong to? Catholic? American of Irish ancestry? Negro? Jewish? American Indian? American of Mexican ancestry? American of Armenian ancestry?

Ethnic-group membership affects personality in two major ways: first, different ethnic groups maintain somewhat different values, which are communicated to each new generation (divorce, suicide, and crime rates, for example, differ greatly from ethnic group to ethnic group); and, second, people are evaluated partly in light of how their ethnic-group affiliations are perceived.

The self-concept, which depends so much on how you feel others look upon you, is inevitably influenced by how you feel others look upon the ethnic group to which you belong. If you associate yourself with an ethnic group commonly regarded as inferior and inadequate, your self-concept and resulting behavior cannot help but be affected. Perception of an ethnic group is often reflected in everyday expressions ("jew" him down), in laws (some states forbid marriages between people of certain differing ethnicities), in fiction and movies (how often do popular books or films show an American of Mexican ancestry as the handsome hero who wins the beautiful girl?), or in customs (most cities and towns have districts that exclude certain ethnic-group members as residents, without regard to their other characteristics). Under these circumstances, members of the particular group often internalize these attitudes as part of their self-concept.

Membership in an ethnic minority group may affect an individual's personality in six ways, according to one source: (1) possible reduction in normal and casual contacts and communication with members of other groups; (2) increased importance of his own ethnic-group membership; (3) increased effort for acceptance by the majority group; (4) development of hostile and stereotyped attitudes toward other groups; (5) possible negative effect upon self-esteem and self-concept; and (6) increased acceptance of violence if directed at the majority group (Berelson & Steiner, 1964).

The Black Community

Of all ethnic groups in the United States today, the black Americans appear to be the most harshly treated (although American Indians probably have the lowest standard of living of any ethnic group). Consider some of the problems the black person meets:

—Certain jobs are closed to him, regardless of ability and training; advancement is slow or impossible elsewhere.

—Certain social relationships are not easily available.

—He is often refused the opportunity to rent or purchase a home that fits his family's needs and finances.

—He has evidence that he does not receive equal treatment before the law.

—In order to be permitted to vote, he has had to fight through the courts; and when he tried to exercise his voting rights, he was often met with threats of violence.

—Many of the professionals supposedly helping him, such as teachers, policemen, and social workers, admit to prejudices against his ethnic group.

—Restaurants, hotels, and similar facilities frequently offer him inferior service or reject him altogether.

—Medical and educational facilities available to him are often less adequate, sometimes much less adequate, than the facilities available to others.

—The educational system reminds him that his origins were in slavery, ignoring the fact that the ancestors of most other Americans were poor, illiterate farmers 300 years ago.

Can you think of other problems faced by blacks? How would you deal with these problems? What forms of discrimination and prejudice do *you* face because of your ethnic background?

Black children gain an awareness of their ethnic identification, and to some extent their ethnic role, when they are as young as 3 or 4 (Clark & Clark, 1958). Many of their parents admit having difficulty explaining to their children what it means to be a black American (Pettigrew, 1964), and these children find disturbing contradictions in what happens

Figure 16–4.

Restoring ghetto homes provides job training and income, as well as an important service to the community. Courtesy Columbia Broadcasting System.

to them each day. They learn that their uncle, while waiting for a bus in a Los Angeles suburb, was told by a policeman to "get out of town before sunset, if you know what's good for you"; they learn that their cousin in Alabama was beaten up when he tried to vote; or they learn that their parents were refused service at a dumpy hamburger joint while driving through Indiana.

So many things occur to these children just because they are black, that they develop different self-concepts than a nonblack ordinarily would. Some of them turn their resentment onto themselves: they resent being black and, perhaps, internalize the value that blacks are inferior.

Others respond by withdrawing; they do not exert a maximum effort and seem to be saying, "If they don't think I'm any good, they might be right. So I'm no good and I won't work very hard at trying to be." Others do increase their efforts, but often with the frustration that being black means they must work harder to get the same things.

The family also suffers. The male is hired less frequently than others with equal qualifications and is fired with less reason, making it very difficult for him to keep a job. The black woman, on the other hand, can usually get employment, although not necessarily well-paid employment, and is not likely to lose her position. Thus, the usual sex roles are reversed, and the woman is the stable breadwinner in the black home. This circumstance has two significant, deleterious results: first, the male children do not so often have in the home a man whose behavior they could internalize to learn the proper male role; and, second, the black male, unable to live up to what is expected of him in the male role, feels inadequate and may not try as hard as necessary, again increasing the difficulty for his sons to learn proper male behavior patterns. This family situation leads to an increased number of broken homes, which again accentuates problems of sex-role development and other family problems. Even social-welfare regulations that govern aid to dependent children often require that in order to receive funds a home be without a healthy adult male. Thus a financial reward is given to the family that either has no adequate male figure or at least pretends that one does not exist; either circumstance would be damaging to the healthy growth of the children in that home.

The black man as seen on television, in movies, and in books and newspapers perpetuates the stereotype. Until very recently, blacks were very rarely pictured in advertisements for general consumption. Although many Western cowboy heroes and villains were black (Durham & Jones, 1965), this was not shown on the movie or television screen until the late 1960s. Up to then roles for blacks were limited to servants and uneducated people.

Interestingly, blacks who are proud of their own ethnic status are also more satisfied with the behavior of others (Noel, 1964). The blacks who dislike whites are also likely to be less proud of being black. You might hypothesize that their resentment of themselves is redirected as resentment of others, or that resentment of others, being difficult for some people to express openly, is turned inward as resentment of self.

The Black Militants

For many years, the black community consisted of two major socioeconomic groupings: the Elitists who had "made it" in terms of middle-class achievement, and the Survivalists who were struggling for food. The former group has grown rapidly in numbers, although it has remained a much smaller portion of the black community (perhaps 15–20%) than its counterpart is of the general community. Those struggling for survival are an estimated 40–45% of the black community. Whereas the Elitists are frustrated because they have been unable to gain status equal to members of the general community, the Survivalists have suffered frustration by simply not having sufficient money for a minimal standard of living (Cohen, 1968).

Recently a third group has made its weight felt: the *Militants*. Unlike the Elitists and the Survivalists, the Militants did not see integration with the white community as the answer to their problems. Rather, they demanded better conditions for and more control by the black community. They emphasized pride in being black—"Black is beautiful" became a slogan—and pride in black history and black art and other achievements. Moreover, they blamed white racism for their problems. Their success came about for several reasons: (1) Many poor—and about 25% of these were black—realized that they were not to be included in the growing American affluence. (2) Peaceful demonstrations and sit-ins, although making some gains, did not achieve the desired goals quickly enough. (3) Hopes that had risen with the 1954 Supreme Court decision requiring integrated schooling and the subsequent passage of many civil rights laws were not being realized. (4) The violence that did occur in black communities brought the hatred of many whites into the open; conflict and suspicion became intense, to the point that both residents of the black communities and the nonblacks venturing into them were tense and ready for fighting.

Much of what took place can undoubtedly be related to the self-concept of many of the blacks. For 300 years of their history in America, they had lived in a society that constantly communicated to them the feeling that being black was equivalent to being inferior. They were treated as children, and, as is so often the case under such circumstances, they frequently found themselves responding as children. At the present time in our history, they are rejecting the idea that being black is inferior or that they need the kind of patronizing care that has been given to them. Thus, the leaders of today's black communities insist that they be permitted to direct their own affairs (for example, increased autonomy of local schools) and that they be neither ordered about nor patronized. Since up until very recently the behavior of most blacks did not suggest the intensity of the anger many of them felt, large numbers of whites could not understand the new mood. Much of the change in mood can be understood in terms of the desire of blacks to develop a much more positive self-concept for themselves both as individuals and as members of an ethnic group.

As the new mood intensified, anger mounted and the demands of the Militants became greater. Some of their demands were met, for example, teaching black history in the schools and opening up new jobs, but others were rejected or ignored. Frustration frequently leads to aggression, and aggression often leads to renewed frustration, particularly for the victims of aggression. Such was the situation in the black community during the last half of the 1960s.

The Black Middle Class

The rapidly growing black middle class, that is, the Elitists, maintain values and manners similar in almost every way to others of the same class (Parker & Kleiner, 1964). Unlike many Survivalists, the fathers in this group do support the family, and the sons do not have difficulty learning masculine behavior patterns. They dislike violence as much as their Caucasian equivalents (remember that attitudes toward physical fighting develop through social-class associations, not race), and they value education greatly.

The black schoolteacher shares as little with the black domestic as white teachers share with the white domestic. The blacks who want to move to integrated areas desire less crowded neighborhoods, newer houses, and better schools. They are willing and anxious to help maintain the attractiveness of the neighborhood and the standards of the schools. However, as they are refused housing and equal job opportunity, they may come to view the Militants as offering more hope for their future than the Elitists. At least during the later 1960s, one segment of Elitists, black college students who wished to be active in ethnic matters, were virtually all Militants.

Some people feel that the Elitists, or even the Survivalists, have so many advantages over the Russians or the Chinese that they should not complain. However, blacks do not develop their self-concepts and self-esteem in comparison with Russians and Chinese, but with other Americans. The past ten years have seen greatly increased opportunities for blacks, resulting from changes in laws and changes in people, but have seen little change in the black standard of living as compared to the white. The next decade may well see a continuation of this pattern, along with a continuation of the occasional violence of the past few years. Resistance to social change is always great, and violence is no newcomer to conflicts between those desiring change and those preferring things as they are.

The Spanish-speaking Communities

The United States population includes several groups with recent origins in Spanish-speaking areas. These include Americans of Mexican

Figure 16–5.

For the first time, in 1965, a black man played a sustaining lead role on a network television show. By 1969, several shows provided major parts for blacks. *Top:* Courtesy Columbia Broadcasting System. *Center* and *bottom:* Courtesy National Broadcasting Company.

and Cuban ancestry, most of whom live in Florida and the Southwestern states from Texas to California, plus the extremely large Puerto Rican community in New York City.

Apparently black militancy has proven contagious, for members of the Mexican-American community are also speaking out, demanding increased opportunities and a greater decision-making role for themselves. Although sharing certain social and financial difficulties with black Americans, the American of Spanish-speaking background has been brought up in a home that emphasizes somewhat different values.

The family structure in Mexico stresses (1) father domination of the family and general masculine superiority; (2) strict disciplining of children; (3) distinct separation of sex roles; and (4) strict obedience to authority figures (Ramirez, 1967). A comparison of Mexican-American and Anglo college students—all of them middle-class and all Catholic—showed that students tended to agree with the values of their country of origin, except for attitudes regarding masculine superiority and separation of sex roles. The continuing obedience to authority may explain why the Mexican-American community did not enter the fight for civil rights as early as the black Americans did (Ramirez, 1967).

Other ethnic groups share some of the concerns of the black American and the American of Mexican ancestry, and also have unique problems of their own. A discussion of the related topic of prejudice is offered in Chapter 17.

Leadership Roles

Almost every group distinguishes between the role (or roles) of **leader** and of follower. The leader "by his actions modifies, directs, or controls the attitudes and actions of one or more followers" (English & English, 1958). Leadership, thus, stems from the influence or power one individual has over others.

Have you ever been a leader, as defined above? What did you do to become a leader? From the definition, it is obvious that everyone exerts leadership on some occasions, but a few people seem to be leaders under a variety of circumstances.

Different situations call for different leaders. Each group has its unique membership, goals, organizational structure, and immediate circumstances. The qualities needed to influence one group are not necessarily good for influencing another group, or even for influencing the same group at different times. The man who makes an excellent chief of police may be unable to lead a group of Sunday School children; a school principal might do well as a leader under normal conditions but fail miserably under stress. The more similar two situations are, the more likely will a leader in one situation become a leader in the other.

A leader must be able to satisfy the needs of his group, but groups are not always stable in terms of membership, immediate circumstances, or needs and goals. Therefore, the demands a group makes upon its leader change constantly. If one leader cannot keep up with the changes, his influence will diminish and the members will seek another leader. Although leaders certainly do influence groups, people often underestimate the necessity for leaders to be responsive to the needs of the group.

Types of Leaders

Arguments over who is really the leader of a particular group are often impossible to resolve, unless the possibility is recognized that more than one person at a time may function as a leader. Consider the following types of leaders and the hypothetical situation created to show how several different people can be leaders simultaneously, without conflict.

1. *Popular leader*—selected by voting or expressed approval of group members.
2. *Appointed leader*—group has little or no voice in selecting the leader, for example, a work group or a military group.
3. *Emergent leader*—as the group operates, a member becomes the leader because group members turn to him for leadership.
4. *Subject-matter-expert leader*—someone with expert knowledge on an important topic will exert considerable influence, although often only for a brief time.
5. *Figurehead leader*—someone who does not play the role of leader, but is presented to the public as a leader, perhaps for public relations purposes.

A group of students wished to organize a new political party on campus. After looking around, they selected Gordon Baines as their chairman, not because he was competent, but because he was a star athlete and was well liked by everyone. He was a figurehead leader. The new political party quickly realized that Tim Malley was the most able member, but he had a bad temper and irritated people. Without ever officially saying so, they turned to Tim for advice and usually followed his plans; Tim controlled the group as an emergent leader, but had no title. Fred Balzer was elected vice-president because everyone in the group liked him, and he became the popular leader. Pete Jablockski, who had been student-body president two years earlier, agreed to lend his advice in running the election campaign, thus becoming a subject-matter-expert leader. However, Pete had already graduated, so Tom Rice was appointed chairman of the Campaign Committee, which decided that Fred Balzer was their most likely candidate for student-body president.

Qualities of Leaders

Although leadership roles change as the situation changes, a person who is leader under one set of conditions has a better-than-average chance of becoming a leader in another situation. After all, leadership roles, even of different groups, do share certain elements. Many qualities have been found with greater frequency in people identified as leaders than in those identified as nonleaders (Gibb, 1954), even though no two leadership situations demand the exact same qualities.

For example, leaders have outdone their followers in

—physical health (Izard & Manhold, 1954),
—intelligence (Stodgill, 1948),
—grades and ability to communicate (Gowan, 1955),
—awareness of who in the group is popular and who is not (Bugental & Lehner, 1958),
—numerous personality measures, such as good adjustment, self-confidence, dominance, sociability, cheerfulness, sense of humor (Mann, 1959), and responsibility and tactfulness (Tarnopol, 1958).

Most important, leaders must have certain qualities that advance the purposes of the group. Physical attractiveness would more likely be found among leaders of college sororities than among female business executives; one sort of skill and daring will contribute to leadership in a delinquent gang, and different sorts will produce a military leader or a business leader.

Leadership Methods

Successful leaders must appeal to the needs of their followers in order to get things done. By and large, the leader who tries to take the membership in directions it opposes will either lose his leadership position, be unsuccessful, or cause the disintegration of his group. Some leaders have obtained their position by anticipating what the group's needs will be and finding a way of helping them achieve their goals. Many political leaders owe their success to anticipating what the voters will want in the future and taking a stand on those issues.

We often talk about three kinds of leadership: democratic, authoritarian, and laissez faire. The democratic method allows each member of the group to express his ideas, and the democratic leader tries to be friendly and to respect all members. The **authoritarian** leader attempts to run things strictly, without giving his followers much voice in how things are to be done. The **laissez faire** leader is casual and easygoing, and lets things run themselves.

When groups of boys under the democratic, authoritarian, and laissez faire methods were compared, the democratically led boys appeared to be the friendliest, the most independent of the leader, and the least discontented. Nonetheless, some of the boys appeared to prefer a nondemocratically led group (Lippett & White, 1958). Democratic leadership produced the sort of behavior we in the United States consider important; but people in some other countries, as well as some Americans, might consider obedience to be more important than independence, and would prefer a nondemocratic group experience.

Effective Group Discussion

In some instances, a group is formed to make a decision, provide advice, or perform a task by general agreement rather than by voting or through the power of a leader. For example, an advertising agency has just obtained a new account, and the director has assigned the account executive, the staff artist, the staff copy editor, a representative of the manufacturer, an accountant, and a package-design expert to plan advertising strategy. The committee is instructed to work together and obtain general agreement for all major decisions. A member of this group who is adept at functioning in such discussions may exert considerable influence over the other individuals, and may help guide the way to a group decision, without haggling or hurt feelings.

The process of group decision making is often slow and frustrating, but it has been found to be successful for several reasons. First, more often than not, group decisions turn out to be better than decisions made by one person (Argyle, 1957). Second, a group decision means that the entire group has participated in the decision and, therefore, has given it at least passive acceptance. Third, group members are more likely to abide by a group decision and not attempt to make it ineffectual at a later time. Being allowed to discuss an issue openly appears more persuasive, assuming ample evidence is available, than a well-planned lecture would be (Lewin, 1958). Fourth, an effective group discussion allows for the interplay of ideas, so that each person can build on the contributions of others, and the group often ends up with a decision that no one individual would have arrived at by himself.

Group discussions are not influenced equally by all members. One important type of discussion group, the jury, is more influenced by men

---

A Few Guidelines to Effective Behavior in Discussion Groups

1. Present information and ideas to the group, but do not try to impose them on the group. The more you argue, the more you force others to argue back, until they will refuse to be budged.
2. Avoid dealing in personalities or playing politics. You are not trying to win a point, but to find a solution.
3. Consider the ideas of others carefully.
4. Let the discussion move along. Once all ideas have been aired, let a decision be reached. Then let the group move on.
5. Be brief and to the point.
6. Keep the group on the topic. It is amazing how frequently a group discussion becomes involved with irrelevant points.
7. Remain alert to those who are not participating. The silent ones may be agreeing, or they may merely be unable to get a word in edgewise. Make certain everyone has a chance to say what he feels.
8. Help the group understand its goals and help everyone move toward those goals. Try to define the issues, if they need defining.
9. Try to summarize the progress from time to time. A summary will draw attention to how much has been accomplished and will also startle a few people who were under the impression that something entirely different had been agreed upon.
10. Try to clarify the meaning of others, if there is any doubt. "What you are saying is . . ." or "Is this what you really mean: . . . ?"
11. Reconcile differences instead of arguing them out. Reconciliation may result in a compromise or a totally new idea.

---

and by those in higher-prestige jobs (Strodtbeck, Simon, & Hawkins, 1965). Nor is participation equally distributed: those who talk more in groups also have more education, higher income, more frequent attendance, and more memberships in other groups (McGinnies & Vaughan, 1957).

Whether a group is directed by a formally designated leader, an emergent leader, or no leader at all, each member is able to assume the leadership role at times and to make important contributions to the progress of the group.

Summary of Important Ideas

---

1. Man has developed an extremely complex network of groups, ranging from small, face-to-face groups to large, impersonal groups.

Man and His Society

2. Groups have an important influence on the personality and self-concept of their members; the amount of influence varies greatly according to the particular individual and particular group.

3. Group loyalties can be extremely strong.

4. Although most people find satisfaction in being with a variety of groups, some people prefer only occasional group contact.

5. Because groups are so important and loyalties are so strong, it is easy to become dependent upon groups and upon the ways other members feel; pressure for conformity to group values is common.

6. Conformity refers to behavior, including attitudes, intended to live up to the expectations of a particular group. This behavior need not be consistent with the values of the conforming individual.

7. Many people respond submissively to authority, even when authority demands behavior they disapprove of.

8. Social-class identification is important in determining behavior. A person's social class may be evaluated by his income, his ancestors, his job, or his education; but psychologists and many others tend to feel that the most important criteria are attitudes, values, and manners.

9. Educational and vocational goals are related to social-class identification.

10. Social-class identification tends to be self-perpetuating, although people can become socially mobile through marriage, education, vocational achievement, fame, and changes in attitudes and values.

11. Socially mobile persons face some problems of acceptance in the new group, as well as conflict over leaving the old group.

12. Ethnic-group membership affects personality in two key ways: by influencing attitudes and values through internalization, and by producing an evaluation of the individual as a reflection of his ethnic group.

13. The black Americans appear to be the most harshly treated ethnic group in the United States.

14. The black Militant has recently emerged as a third force in the black community. His emergence is partially a reaction to the anger and frustration felt within the community.

15. Spanish-speaking communities face many of the same difficulties as black communities, but their backgrounds are very different.

16. Leadership is the result of the influence or power one person has over another.

17. Different situations call for different leadership qualities. In the United States, democratic leadership seems the most successful approach.

Chapter Seventeen

The Importance of Values

This look at values and attitudes may remind you of closely related materials in the discussion of human needs, of the development of the sex role, or of the process of internalizing feelings of guilt. The emphasis in the discussion presented here is upon values as related to the group identifications that lead to the formation of these values. Although the focus on values has been largely fostered by social psychologists, the topic is now under scrutiny by psychologists with a variety of interests.

What do you value?—life? happiness? freedom? health? money? fun? achievement? travel? How much do you value each of these things? Do you value fun more than money in the bank? Do you value freedom more than security? Do you value your religious beliefs enough to give up your life for them? Do you value a college degree enough to postpone purchasing a new automobile for two years?

Values are **beliefs** about what are desirable and undesirable goals and about ways of reaching goals (after English & English, 1958). They serve as guides to action; they form the basis for attitudes; they structure the way we judge others and ourselves; and they provide a standard by which we try to influence others, for example, our children (Rokeach, 1968). Also, values refer to beliefs that are maintained for long periods of time—they are not subject to sudden shifts. When you value something highly, you are strongly motivated by it. If you place a high value on money or new cars or grades, you will be strongly motivated to gain these goals.

Values, like needs, may be consciously or unconsciously held. People recognize their conscious values and can think about them and discuss them with others, but they also have values that influence their behavior without their conscious awareness. A person may place great value on being thought good-looking without being aware that he has such a value. He might even deny that he values good looks; but the value would show through in his behavior, the way he dresses, the way he always asks whether others think he is good-looking, or the way he worries about the slightest mark on his face.

There are two basic kinds of values. The first kind are those related to your present conduct. You might value honesty, courage, wealth, or intelligence. The second kind of values involve what might be termed "ultimate concerns," such as religious salvation, freedom, equality, and peace. Each person has a hierarchy of values, with certain ones being more important than others. Thus, when the individual is faced with a conflict between producing wealth or being honest, he will normally express the value that is higher in the hierarchy.

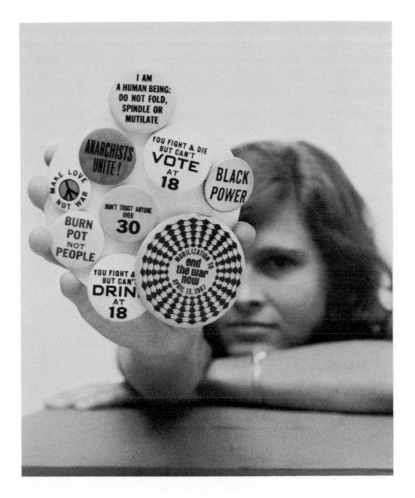

Figure 17–1.

People find a variety of ways to communicate their values. Courtesy Columbia Broadcasting System.

The Importance of Values

The values of any given person often conflict in ways that the value hierarchy cannot easily resolve. A soldier places high value on patriotism and being a hero, but he also desires to stay alive. A student esteems honesty, but he wishes the friendship of his roommate who wants to copy from his exam paper. A coed seeks popularity, but not at the price of a series of affairs.

Value differences frequently lead to misunderstanding and disagreements between individuals. The hippie (see Chapter 10) values "doing his own thing," but his parents value academic and vocational achievement. Recent research has shown that, of 12 "ultimate" values, the police ranked freedom first and equality last, whereas unemployed blacks ranked equality first and freedom tenth (Rokeach, 1968). The recent clashes between police and unemployed blacks may be partially explained by their differing values. In terms of housing, for example, the policeman sees his freedom to sell his house to whom he wishes as of primary importance; the black man views equal opportunity to buy as more important than the policeman's freedom to sell. Even when two people seem to agree on the verbal labels of what they value, for example, freedom, achievement, or equality, they may be far apart on what they believe constitutes an expression of that value. For example, freedom to carry a gun is most important to one person, and freedom of speech is primary for another.

Values shape behavior in many ways. The man who places a high value on earning money will behave differently from the man who places a high value on being of service to other men. These two men will probably enter different vocational fields, vote for different political candidates, join different clubs, and try to teach their children different values.

People seek friends whose values are similar to theirs. The college student who is satisfied with a C average usually makes friends among others with similar values; the political liberal or conservative becomes friendly more easily with others of similar political beliefs; the accounting major tends to have relatively more friends interested in business than in teaching. (There are many exceptions, but the tendency to select friends with similar values exists.)

Sometimes a person is not even aware that he does join groups and make friends who generally accept his values. Some of you are proud of having "all sorts of people" for friends. However, if you stop to think, you will usually find that most (not necessarily all) of your friends share many values with you. You are likely to have relatively similar values regarding such subjects as moral and immoral behavior, religion, politics, school, money, the meaning of freedom, the purpose of work, and the place of athletics on campus.

For evidence of the way values help determine friendship, notice the seating at your college cafeteria. At one table will be those who value athletics; another table will be filled with girls from the most popular clubs; at a third table will be seated students with artistic interests; and the science majors will fill a fourth table.

Some Basic Values

The best-known test of values is undoubtedly the Study of Values, constructed by Professors Allport, Vernon, and Lindzey (1960). This questionnaire investigates the relative importance of six categories of values that the test's designers felt were the most basic.

Theoretical—values the discovery of truth; critical, rational, intellectual; oriented toward the sciences or philosophy; systematic.

Economic—values the useful and the practical; emphasis on money and material goods; similar to stereotype of businessman.

Aesthetic—values form and grace; artistic.

Social—values social relationships, particularly giving to people in a psychological (not necessarily financial) way.

Political—values power and influence (not necessarily in politics).

Religious—values unity; mystic; wants to understand the meaning of the world.

Values are not isolated but occur in patterns, often called **value systems**. For example, students who favor the principles in the Bill of Rights of the United States Constitution also show less prejudice toward minority groups (Robin & Story, 1964). What other values would you guess these students held?

How Values are Formed

Parents and Other Significant Figures

Parents and other significant figures probably have the greatest influence on the formation of values and attitudes. First, they reward the attitudes and values they like, leaving the others unrewarded or perhaps punished; second, they provide models that their children consciously and unconsciously copy; and third, they live in such a way that the children, as they develop their self-concept by internalizing what their

The Importance of Values

parents think of them, also internalize the parental values regarding education, God, humanity, or work. Since the child hears his parents' ideas and relatively little else in his first few years, he internalizes them without much conflict.

Even in later years, children maintain much the same values as their parents. With few exceptions, studies have shown that children's values and **attitudes** resemble those of their parents in such areas as politics, economics, or religion (for example, Hyman, 1959; Newcomb & Svehla, 1937).

"Well, you were the one who said we shouldn't force religion on them—that they'd find it for themselves."

Figure 17–2.

Children usually internalize their parents' values. Of course, they must first grasp what those values are. Courtesy Ed Fisher.

However, children's values are not exact duplicates of their parents' values. Occasionally, adolescents and young adults will even rebel aggressively against their parents' views, although this rebellion frequently disappears after they leave home, marry, and achieve a sense of emancipation from their parents. Sometimes a child develops such an intense dislike for his parents or their values that he will discard parental values permanently.

Values are also influenced by the self-concept and by needs, both of which are, of course, greatly influenced by parents. People maintain values that are consistent with their self-concept and expressive of their personality characteristics. People who are rigid and inflexible tend to value cleanliness and orderliness, rather than casualness and informality. People who are anxious and fearful may prefer a strong, perhaps dictatorial, leader they feel will protect them. If you conceive of yourself as studious and serious, you will likely place a high value on these characteristics.

Parents and the home are not the only influences on values. As children mature, other factors, including direct experiences, friends, the school, the community, and the vocational field begin to have an effect.

Direct Experiences

Strangely, direct experiences are probably less important in affecting values than are the ideas internalized through parents, friends, and groups. If you have internalized the belief that prayers are answered or football players are stupid, an unanswered prayer or a bright football player will rarely change your mind. You merely admit that one prayer was not answered, or one football player was not dumb. If, on the other hand, a particular prayer is answered or a particular football player is stupid, you accept this as evidence for your belief.

People often find it so important to maintain their values that they do so, even in the face of much contrary evidence. A devoutly religious student commented to an agnostic friend, "You don't really take your own experiences into consideration. If Jesus ever did appear to you in a real vision, you would probably put yourself in a mental hospital rather than admit He truly existed." The agnostic admitted that his friend was correct.

However, personal experiences can change values, as the following story illustrates:

"One summer I joined the staff of a summer day camp in Gates Mills, a very wealthy community close to where I lived. I had been raised in an average sort of home, and I felt that these rich kids would give me a lot of trouble—I just *knew* that they would be snobs. To make matters worse, most of the other counselors were also from wealthy homes. Much to my surprise, this was the best bunch of kids I ever worked with. They were creative, interested in camp, bright, and reasonably well behaved without being goody-goody. Of course, a similar camp in another wealthy community might have been altogether different, but I certainly changed my attitude about children from wealthy homes."

The Friendship Group

You tend to make friends with people who have certain values and interests similar to yours. Once you have become friends, however, pressure is put on you to accept other values of the friendship group. Thus an amateur actor joins the college dramatic club because he enjoys theater and likes to be with others who also value acting and the arts. At this school, however, the college dramatic club also places high value on good grades and on drinking wine. The amateur actor meets subtle pressure to change his behavior, and he is likely to begin working for better grades and drinking more wine. As he does so, any success he shows will be reinforced by approval from the other club members. Even if his behavior does not change, he is not likely to brag about low grades or criticize wine drinkers.

The values of your friends interact dynamically with your own personality and values and affect your value system, while simultaneously your values influence theirs. Parents, aware of this interaction, encourage their children to develop friendships with playmates having values the parents approve.

Education

The process of formal education affects values in many ways. Values are influenced by the books you read, the teachers you listen to, and the other students you meet. You learn about the values of other countries and of earlier periods in your own country. You study the values of the men who began the American Revolution, the French Revolution, the Russian Revolution, and the many South American and Asian revolutions. You learn from teachers who place a high value on being creative, from those who stress memorization, and from those who emphasize proper manners and good behavior.

The first year in college is often disturbing because you are told so many things that appear to contradict not only what you learned in high school, but also other things you are learning in college. You are told that human behavior is determined by climate, body chemistry, love, hunger, traditions, society, money, religion—the professors cannot seem to get together. Are these professors actually disagreeing?

Temporary confusion regarding certain values may not be bad. As students form new values—often similar to the old ones but usually more carefully thought out—they may go through a period of confusion, an experience that frequently contributes to their maturity and self-understanding. The person who has never been confused has never had to think through what he believes.

"I never realized how much I was an American and a capitalist until I spent a year in another country. Having to live with new values made me examine my own values very carefully. I had seen the Statue of Liberty many times before, but on the trip home I cried when I saw the 'Lady.' "

"When I finished high school, I had pretty strong religious convictions—I figured I knew what was right, and no one was going to change me. By the middle of my second semester in college, what with philosophy and psychology and history courses and all, I doubted everything—I didn't know what was 'truth' any more. Somehow—I really don't know exactly how—about a year after I finished college, I realized I knew what I believed again. I still had occasional doubts, but these didn't bother me any more. My views had changed somewhat from when I was in high school, but—more important—I knew why I believed what I did."

These two students were involved in situations in which doubt and confusion led to growth and maturity.

The Community

Every society, through its unique circumstances of history and geography, has developed its own values. Even two towns or two cities located an hour's drive apart may emphasize different values: people in one will work hard to provide money for an art museum, and residents of the other will work just as hard to raise funds for a ball park.

Values held by the general community need not be rigid. A variety of types of behavior may be allowed. Our society, for example, considers college success to be a positive value, yet many in our country do not feel college is worthwhile. They are not put in jail or whipped, although they are punished in milder ways. Others in the community may criticize them, and they are likely to be turned down for jobs that require some college education.

The penalty for violating certain other values, however, is severe. In Texas in 1950, a white man bragged to the author that he slammed a bus window down on the hand of a black man who disobeyed the values of that community by sitting in the front section of the bus. In Russia today, church-going Christians suffer from job discrimination. In Pasadena, California, a high school teacher was dismissed when he rejected the principal's demand that he shave off his beard.

Values held in one place and at one time will differ from values held in other places and during other times. In Pasadena, Christians do not suffer job discrimination; in Russia, a teacher can grow a beard; in Texas *today,* blacks can ride in the front of the bus. As the world changes,

The Importance of Values

values change. The conditions of the community today are different from those faced by the parents of today's college student when they first looked for work. These parents faced a war and military service, with a good possibility of going into combat, or an uncertain postwar period. Today, although tensions still exist, they result from different problems,

Figure 17–3.

These two scenes were photographed within a few miles of each other in Brazil. How would the values of the inhabitants of the two types of buildings differ? Courtesy Columbia Broadcasting System.

and these problems produce some of the changes in the community's values.

A serious student of human behavior will wish to learn the historical origins of the values of the general community and of the subgroups within this general community. How did unions begin, how did they rise in power, and what are they like today? What is the recent history of the American Indian, and what is his life like today? What was the beginning of free education, and how has it affected our country? Understanding such historical problems will help you understand the values and feelings of the older union member, the American Indian, and the schoolteacher who is extremely dedicated to free education. In the same way, to understand the values of people in other countries, you need to understand their history and traditions.

It is impossible to live in a community ("community" is used *in this case* to refer to either a village, a city or a part of a city, or a country) without being influenced by the values of that community. If the values of the parents are similar to those of the general community, the children are more likely to internalize these values than if only a minority of the community members agree with the parents (Berelson & Steiner, 1964). Although parents cannot shield their children from the general community values, they can make an effort to provide their children with their own values before the children have much community contact. Parents who do not wish their children to smoke or drink, for example, cannot wait until the children are 16 before teaching them about tobacco and alcohol. Such values should be learned at a much earlier age, if the children are to ignore the general community attitudes.

Vocation

Your vocation also influences your values and attitudes. You may be influenced by those with whom you work, or by your supervisors, or by the management philosophy or union philosophy prevailing in your company.

In addition, the type of work itself influences attitudes. A policeman spends so much time with the least pleasant elements in society that he may develop the belief that people cannot be trusted. A minister, partly because of the respect people have for his position, is much more likely to see people at their best—even the same people that the policeman sees at their worst. Thus, the type of work you do and the work relationships you enter into help form some of your values.

Of course, both the policeman and the minister bring their own experiences and personalities to the situation. Each may have entered his vocational field to help people, but each has elected a different way of going about this job. The very values that prompt one person to become a representative of the law, and another, a representative of God, will also affect the ways in which each looks upon others and interprets their behavior. Your needs and your attitudes draw you to certain types of work; the work influences the nature of your contacts with people, which is, in turn, interpreted through your unique personality. Your attitudes and values are affected accordingly.

How Values Change

Values and attitudes, like other elements in the personality, undergo continual change, even though these changes are often slight and occur slowly.

As your roles and self-concept change, your values change also. The adolescent may value popularity with his own group, whereas the adult values being liked by the boss. The worker places greater value on his union, until he becomes a supervisor, at which time his values emphasize the success of the company. The professor who now values hard work valued "living it up" as a student. A freshman girl does not place much value on avoiding a fellow with a "fast" reputation, but when the same girl becomes a mother and *her* daughter wants to date in the "fast" crowd, she finds she has a strongly negative attitude.

Changing the Values of Others

It seems logical that a good sound argument would be sufficient to change someone's values. That is, assuming you had supreme powers of logic and a pile of evidence on *your* side, you should be able to convince any normal person that you are correct and that his values are wrong. Try it. It does not work very often.

Values and beliefs are closely related to needs and motives and are often learned very early in life. Attacking them with logic merely forces the person to try to defend them with logic. Soon, he is so deeply involved in justifying his views that he finds arguments he had never considered before. Often the best way to make certain a person *never* changes his values is to argue vociferously against them. Attacking strongly held values can cause them to be still more firmly maintained (Kelley & Volkart, 1952), often with the support of defense mechanisms.

However, values and attitudes can be changed. The professions of advertising and public relations are devoted to changing people's attitudes and their resulting behavior. Salesmen, teachers, ministers, and clinical psychologists also find that much of their working time is spent changing attitudes and values, including people's attitudes toward themselves, that is, their self-concepts.

Occasionally, one dramatic event can alter an attitude or value. In one such case, an English professor was drowning, and he swore to return to belief in his religion if he lived. He did live and became a devoutly religious man. More commonly, however, values change slowly, as the result of many things, and people who wish to persuade others must take this into account.

Thus, advertisers establish continuous campaigns, instead of just offering an occasional advertisement; psychotherapists meet continually with their patients, not just once; ministers have learned that the over-night convert usually becomes a backslider (in spite of occasional real conversions as described above).

Changing people's values is only the first part of the story. Most frequently, the purpose of producing such change is to alter behavior affected by the values. The political candidate wants to change voting behavior, or the teacher wants to change classroom behavior. A recent study shows how difficult the changing of behavior can be. A program was undertaken to alter the behavior of 109 street-gang boys. The professional staff used individual counseling, group work, and a variety of other approaches over an extended time period to help the boys learn to be fully independent, self-sufficient members of the community. The boys responded well through each step of the program until the time came to cut their contacts with the professionals. This step produced failure—and the more the workers increased their efforts, the worse the failures became (Caplan, 1968). Apparently the professional workers had succeeded in enabling the boys to adjust well to living with the protection of the professionals, but not to assume an independent role in the community.

Changing long-term behavior is a very difficult task, and behavioral scientists need to learn a great deal more about such planned interventions. You need only ask yourself how successful you and your friends have been in such comparatively insignificant behavior as stopping smoking, cutting down on calories, sticking to the study schedule you set up for yourself, or not losing your temper, to know how limited the effectiveness of attempts at change can be.

Value Change and Needs

Since values are closely related to needs, the self-concept, and other personality characteristics, value change can be produced by changing the needs or the self-concept. Although this change is difficult, it can occur. One commercial firm used this principle when they learned that housewives were reluctant to buy instant coffee because they held the attitude that using instant coffee was a sign of poor planning and laziness, and they had the need to have the self-concept of hard-working women (Haire, 1950). The advertisers then changed their approach from emphasizing the convenience of instant coffee to emphasizing its taste and aroma, thus playing up to the needs of the housewife. Similarly, politicians attempt to persuade people that their election will satisfy the needs of the voters, that is, needs for better schools, lower taxes, better military protection, less air and water pollution—whatever the voters perceive as their needs. In the same fashion, the values children hold regarding school may improve if the children overcome fear of school or feelings of inadequacy in school.

The success of attempts to change attitudes and values is partly the result of the personalities of those under pressure to change. At one interracial summer camp, some of the campers became more prejudiced by the end of their camp experience, but others became less prejudiced. Compared to the latter, those who became more prejudiced were more aggressive and more afraid of punishment, yet they also felt more picked on (Mussen, 1950). The same camp environment led some white children to develop better attitudes toward blacks and led other white children to learn more negative attitudes—depending upon their personality and values.

Personality is related to value change in another way. Since people appear to have the need to believe that their values and their behavior are consistent, if something changes their behavior, they are also inclined to change their values accordingly. Thus, two groups of people were paid to lie about some relatively unimportant matter to their friends. One group was paid $20 each, and the second group was paid only $1 each. A later inquiry found that those paid the smaller amount of money had changed their attitudes somewhat about the matter concerning which they had lied; they had—to some extent—come to believe what they had said. The other group did not change much at all. Apparently the higher-paid individuals could justify the lie by having received so much money, but the group that told a falsehood for so little money had behaved inconsistently—they could not justify having lied, so they altered their values to reduce the significance of the lie (Festinger, 1957). Perhaps you have had a similar experience. Have you ever purchased something you could not really afford and then tried to convince yourself that you had made a wise purchase? This pattern helps salesmen immeasurably, since people who buy things tend to justify their purchasing behavior and are not likely to return the goods, even if they did not get a good buy.

In college, Jack Trevor prided himself on wanting to be of service to humanity, particularly by using his writing talents to improve the conditions of the economically impoverished. After graduation, he found he could not make a living through free-lance writing, so he took a job with a magazine that published stories emphasizing murder, lust, and crime. Five years later, he had become editor of the magazine and was earning a substantial income. However, his values had changed. When he first began with the organization, he claimed he would only stay long enough to "get me started, because this magazine really puts out trash." Now that he had given up his mission to help the poor, he justified his behavior by stating that the magazine was important because many poor people read it and received great enjoyment from it; therefore, he was really providing an important and useful service to the poor. His values and attitudes had changed in order to become consistent with his actual behavior.

Value change does not necessarily precede behavior change. When conditions cause people to behave in certain ways, their attitudes and values may change so as to support their new behavior, much as Jack Trevor's values changed during his job with the magazine.

Persuasion and Propaganda

Situations calling for effective persuasion often arise. We may wish to talk someone into agreeing with our values, buying our product, or changing his behavior in the direction we wish. Advertisers, politicians, social workers, policemen, and parents are all constantly involved in persuasive activity.

The task of persuasion involves four considerations: the message itself, the source of the message, the audience, and the specific situation (Ruch, 1967).

As editorialist for the campus newspaper, you wish to write an article persuading students to demand more participation in decision making at the college. You know you need to consider your audience, in the same way that television commercials selling used cars are geared to a different audience than those selling new cars. You finally decide to direct your effort at the uncommitted, although you might have tried to propel your supporters into action or to change your opponents to a neutral position. You do hope, however, that your article will affect all your readers.

You also need to know something about the group loyalties and the personal needs of your audience. How do the social clubs line up? Can you appeal to the special-interest groups, such as commuters, social club members, athletes, or social science majors? Do you focus on people's needs for power, for wanting to feel important, for dealing with feelings of alienation, or for fighting authority?

The message itself is of primary importance. How should you present your issues? Should you be emotional or use the soft-sell? Should you attack your opposition directly or not? Should you give statistics or refer to success on other campuses? Should you admit some of the disadvantages of your position before your opponents can use them to attack you, or should you remain silent on them?

Since you are already marked as a strong supporter of student participation in decision making, your credibility as a source of information is not high. You find a six-year-old speech by your college president supporting your position, and you quote from it freely. You also collect statements from professional educators and national figures endorsing student involvement in campus decisions, and you use these sources to bolster your case.

You need to recognize the unique qualities of your situation. The college president has been regarded as fair and honest, and you do not wish to antagonize him. Also, the year is almost over, and the graduating seniors are not particularly interested in campus affairs any more.

In writing your persuasive message, you might think of yourself as providing educational information, but others claim you are a propagandist. Both education and propaganda are aimed at changing values

Figure 17–4.

Changing the values of others takes many forms. This photograph was taken in Communist China, where everyone, including the visiting Canadian news correspondent, is required to read the thoughts of Chairman Mao twice a day. Courtesy Columbia Broadcasting System.

Some Propaganda Methods

Appeal to Authority. The claim that a particular authority favors the behavior considered. An expert, a respected textbook, or a prestigious person are all considered authorities.

Bandwagon Effect. The attempt to persuade people by claiming that everybody is doing it.

Big Lie. An obvious untruth told so often that people begin to believe it. Some people, for example, feel that "where there's smoke, there's fire."

Guilt by Association. The suggestion that a person has done something wrong because he has had some association with another person who has done something wrong. "Dr. Carr was seen with Mr. Holt, who is known to be a Fascist." They might have attended the same college and have been seen in different parts of the same room at an alumni meeting.

Image. The picture held by the public, or segments of the public, regarding a person or a product. The common image of the United States in Communist China is "Imperialist" and "Colonialist."

Plain Folks. The attempt to persuade people by causing them to believe that the attitude or behavior is similar to that of "just ordinary people." The implication is that the opposing views are held by snobs.

Snob Appeal. The attempt to persuade people by causing them to believe that the attitude or behavior is similar to that of the wealthy or the famous.

Transfer. The opposite of guilt by association, transfer is the suggestion that a person is good because he is associated with something good.

---

and at getting across new information. The differences between education and propaganda are fewer than many people think, since propaganda may be educational and education may include propaganda. Propaganda to persuade people to donate to the National Heart Association may include much educational material; education in a psychology class may include some propaganda regarding the professor's viewpoint.

However, education and propaganda have different purposes. The purpose of education is to provide information and understanding, then allow the student to make up his own mind. It is directed toward increasing personal growth. Propaganda is concerned solely with changing values, attitudes, and behavior *in a particular direction,* and any learning involved is only incidental. Propagandists may purposely distort the material they present, but educators are supposed to be as objective as possible.

To a large extent, whether you believe something is education or propaganda depends upon how you feel about the issues. The Democratic candidate for Congress insists that the newspaper articles he writes are educational, but his Republican opponent claims that they are mostly propaganda. The Democrat believes that what he is writing is true and gives his readers a better understanding. The Republican believes that his opponent has omitted important facts and misinterpreted important events. Strangely, both men are being sincere. Is there propaganda in the present book? How is it introduced? Is it also educational?

The factors that produce changes in attitudes and values are very complex and differ from person to person and from time to time. Short-term changes, especially on issues that are not considered very important, may occur without too much difficulty. However, it is much more difficult to produce long-term changes, changes in values considered important, or changes in values that are part of a value system and related to the needs of the person.

The Meaning of Prejudice

To have a **prejudice** is to make a "pre-judgment," or to make a judgment or hold an attitude before all the necessary information is available. Being prejudiced also implies that the attitude or feeling is held with some degree of emotion and cannot be readily altered.

Everyone holds prejudices that lead either to favorable or unfavorable reactions toward people, things, and ideas. You may be prejudiced against a western on television without even seeing the show. You may be prejudiced against women who lisp or in favor of men who smoke pipes.

Although everyone has prejudices, this is not to say that any particular prejudice is either natural or inevitable. As with any attitude, belief, or value, prejudices are learned largely through interaction with significant figures and tend to fit in with personality needs and the self-concept. They are then reinforced by approval from friends and from the community, by personal experiences, and by reduction of anxiety. Also, like other values, prejudices are difficult to change. They resist logic because they satisfy needs that may be more important than being logically consistent, or because they were so effectively internalized that they are stronger than logic. Research has shown that people have trouble with simple problems in logic if their prejudices become involved (Sells, 1936).

Prejudice, Discrimination, and Segregation

Prejudice is an attitude. **Discrimination** is a form of behavior that usually arises from prejudice. Discrimination refers to treating people unequally. Prejudice against women leads to discrimination against hiring women for certain jobs. Prejudice against adolescents leads to discrimination against them by some adults. Prejudice favoring well-behaved students leads teachers to discriminate in their favor by giving them better grades than they deserve. What groups do you discriminate for or against? Why?

Discrimination arises from prejudice, and—in turn—increases prejudice. As children grow up observing women being discriminated against, they tend to internalize the value that women really are inferior, thus leading to prejudice. Prejudices and discrimination interact dynamically.

You may recall that the term *discrimination* occurred with a slightly different meaning in the discussion on learning in Chapter 4. The original meaning of discrimination was "to distinguish" or "to recognize a difference between." It is obviously necessary for a child to learn to discriminate *between* his mother and his teacher, or between the street and the sidewalk. However, discrimination is also used in the sense of discrimination *for* or *against*. The real problem of discrimination in the area of racial prejudice is that it is not used appropriately. For example, instead of discriminating between Jews or teen-agers who have good qualities and those who have poor qualities, some people lump all Jews or all teen-agers together *indiscriminately,* and then endow all members of these groups with the characteristics of the worst members of each group. Proper discrimination is vital in gaining a realistic view of the world, but discrimination *for* or *against,* when based on previous biases, reduces the ability to see the world realistically. Do you know of people who do not sufficiently discriminate *among* different college students?

Since attitudes and values, when deeply felt, resist change, it is almost impossible to alter already formed prejudices by passing laws. However, laws can affect discriminatory behavior, which, in turn, will help create situations in which prejudices may be more easily changed and in which prejudices will not be so effectively passed on from generation to generation. Would you prevent women from voting? Your great-grandparents did, but laws were eventually passed that gave women the vote and other forms of legal equality. There is a definite tendency to accept *what is* as being *what is right.* Few Americans wanted women to vote 80 years ago, yet few Americans would deny women the right to vote today.

When prejudice and discrimination become severe, **segregation** often results. Segregation is the act of isolating members of certain groups. At various times in history, the Jews in Europe were segregated and were not allowed to live anywhere except in small, overcrowded ghettos.

Groups may segregate themselves. People try to live near others whom they consider similar. This similarity may be based on race, religion, age, national origin, or social class. Self-segregation or "clannishness" may result from a dislike for others. It may also be caused by **in-group** preference, which occurs when members of a particular group feel more comfortable with others in their group and feel uncomfortable with those who are not members of their group. The elderly living in retirement communities are not prejudiced against younger people, but they may feel more comfortable and more accepted in a community of the elderly. Americans of Armenian origin often live close to each other, not because they dislike non-Armenians, but because they want to share traditions and customs with each other, and because they are more comfortable in their group. (To observe a good example of in-group preference, notice how faculty chaperones stick together at student dances.) When segregation results from prejudice, it cannot be considered primarily the result of in-group preference.

Ethnic-group Prejudice, Discrimination, and Segregation

Is prejudice against ethnic groups appropriate? How about discrimination or segregation? What rights do you have to avoid members of certain groups if you wish? Would it be right for your club to blackball someone because his ancestors were born in Africa? In Greece? In Sweden? If you do not wish a member of a particular group to live near you, what action is justified? Economic pressure? Social avoidance? Threatening telephone calls? Damaging his property? Physical violence? What are the financial costs of discrimination? What are the psychological costs to the victim of discrimination and to the discriminator?

The Irish immigrants who settled in New England and New York during and shortly after the potato famine of the 1840s were the object of much prejudice and discrimination. They were accused of being drunks, of fighting, of ignoring laws, of neglecting education, of being involved in improper sex acts, and of being traitors to the United States (*Newsweek*, 1964). They could get jobs only as maids and unskilled laborers, and many employers refused to hire the Irish at all.

As a result, the Irish clung together, rarely pursued higher education, and developed self-concepts somewhat similar to what they were told about themselves. Their frustrations eventually burst through during the 1870s with a group called the Molly Maguires. The Mollies "struck back with incredible savagery, total terror—murdering, dynamiting, burning, pulling out tongues and slicing off ears" (*Newsweek*, 1964). Of course, such behavior only increased the hatred and fear others had of the Irish.

Over the years, the Irish changed this image people had of them. As time passed, their position improved financially, educationally, and politically. Today, the picture of the Irishman is substantially different. He is still seen as a strong person who will not back away from a fight, but he now is the hero, rather than the villain. The self-concept of the Irish has changed also, and the term "shanty Irish," common even 40 years ago, is rarely heard today. In 1960, a man of Irish descent was elected President of the United States. However, for nearly a century, the Irish in the United States suffered prejudice and discrimination. The cost in money, in human suffering, and in progress for the country as a whole was tremendous.

A second example of the wastefulness of prejudice is the feelings expressed toward Americans of German ancestry during World War I, and toward Americans of Japanese ancestry during World War II. In 1918, Americans of German background were subjected to many forms of name-calling and hatred, and were accused of being sympathetic with the Germans who were fighting the Americans at that time. During World War II, Americans of Japanese ancestry met with an even more obvious form of prejudice and discrimination. It was more obvious for two reasons: first, it came directly and officially from the United States government; and second, although almost all Americans of Japanese ancestry were affected, almost none of German ancestry were similarly affected.

The Japanese-Americans were removed from their homes on the West Coast and placed in what amounted to prison camps scattered around the country. They were often pressured into selling their property, usually at a fraction of its true value, giving up their businesses, and living under worse conditions than we often demanded of enemy prisoners. As one Nisei social worker stated, "I lived in the stable next to Sea Biscuit's for two months. Of course, they had only put one horse in that stable, but they put four Japanese into it." It is ironic that the 442nd Division, made up primarily of Japanese-Americans, suffered an extremely high casualty rate and earned one of the highest proportions of awards of any American military unit in World War II.

Once again, the cost of prejudice in money and in human misery was overwhelming, and—in looking back—few, if any, reputable Americans feel that the Japanese Relocation Centers achieved anything to help the war effort.

Many groups have suffered from prejudice and discrimination in the past or at present in the United States. The following are just a few examples of discriminated-against groups drawn from our history: union members, Americans of Mexican ancestry, policemen, blacks, Roman Catholics, Masons, Southern whites, Jews, soldiers, Socialists, poor people, American Indians, atheists, wealthy people, actors, Americans of Greek ancestry, and Mormons.

Prejudice against racial and religious groups is not limited to the United States. Citizens of countries highly critical of prejudices in the United States display strong prejudices themselves, although usually they are not so violent or so well publicized as American ethnic prejudices.

England, for example, has recently been the scene of considerable prejudice and discrimination against nonwhite people from the West Indies, Pakistan, and elsewhere. The tiny South American country, Guyana, has been in turmoil for several years because of fierce prejudices of the residents of African and of Asian background against each other. In India, the Untouchables are still subjected to discrimination, although laws officially forbid it. Communist Russia has shown prejudices against both Jews and Christians, and Canadians of French origin claim that British-Canadians discriminate against them.

Prejudice does not result from one simple cause, but is brought about by a combination of several. Consider the problems of Theresa Guerra:

> Theresa was brought up by affectionate, loving parents who accepted the values of their homeland, Mexico, as to the proper role for a woman: getting married and having children. Since Theresa had little contact with children outside the Mexican-American community, she never questioned her future role. Also, since neither parent was especially concerned about having their daughter educated beyond ninth grade (in their village in Mexico, women rarely had gone beyond the sixth grade), they gave Theresa no encouragement in her school achievement. Little English was spoken in the home, and English-language books and magazines were never available. One of eight children, Theresa received relatively little time and attention from her parents, both of whom worked.
>
> However, one of her high school teachers felt that she did have the potential for college. Unfortunately, when she spoke to the assistant principal, he checked Theresa's IQ scores (administered when she barely spoke English) and claimed that she "wasn't too bright—just like the rest of *them*." The teacher then spoke to the school counselor, but the counselor did not wish to be bothered with anyone who could not go on to college, and he insisted that girls from that kind of background were hopeless.
>
> The teacher persevered and decided to wait for the PTA open house to talk with Mr. and Mrs. Guerra. However, the Guerras both

worked hard all day, and had little energy or interest to visit the school when they did not really care if their daughter continued in school or not. Finally, in frustration, the teacher telephoned Mrs. Guerra to ask her to make an appointment. Mrs. Guerra was doubly embarrassed: she was reluctant to admit that she worked in a bar, and she was ashamed to meet with a well-dressed, well-spoken "Anglo," when her own dress and speech were so inadequate. Although she was pleased by the attention Theresa was receiving, she was afraid to ask her husband for help, since she was positive he would get angry with her for suggesting their daughter should go to college when none of their sons seemed to have such an inclination.

Mrs. Guerra made one appointment and did not arrive; she made another one and called in to break it. She then said she would call the teacher for a third appointment, but never did. The teacher finally decided that perhaps the assistant principal and the school counselor were correct in their appraisal of Mexican-Americans.

Prejudice, Personality, and Needs

Certain personality characteristics and needs are associated more with highly prejudiced individuals than with others. People who are rigid and not open to new ideas or ways of thinking, for example, tend to be more prejudiced than average (Rokeach, 1960). Prejudiced individuals also demand an extremely high level of neatness, cleanliness, and sex morality, insisting upon very severe punishment for those who do not live up to their standards. Such people also like things to be clear and obvious, and they dislike art or writing or even ideas they cannot understand. They frequently insist that all problems should have simple, neat answers (Allport, 1954).

Human beings have a need for self-esteem, and ethnic prejudices can sometimes help maintain this need. Thus, the individual who looks upon himself as highly competent, but is unable to get a job he feels he qualifies for, may rationalize that "The Jews are trying to destroy the job market," or "The Mexican-Americans will work cheap, so there's no place for me." Either claim explains his own failure in such a way that he can retain his self-esteem.

Prejudice and discrimination are obviously not limited to ethnic groups. Elsewhere in this book you have read about the difficulties that discrimination causes for women, teen-agers, the elderly, people on low-status jobs, and people of lower social-class background. Prejudices regarding ethnic, age, social-class, sex, and vocational groups are found throughout the world and throughout history, although they are learned and are far from inevitable. Prejudice can be created by any one, or several, of many factors, and each specific prejudice fits into the general value system of the person holding the prejudice.

Summary of Important Ideas

1. Values are beliefs about what constitutes worthwhile and not worthwhile goals and about methods of reaching goals.

2. Values may be consciously or unconsciously held and may conflict with each other.

3. Values shape behavior in many ways, for example, through vocational selection, choice of friends, and leisure activities.

4. Values are formed through the internalization of parents' values and those of other significant figures, through reward and punishment by parents, and through imitation of parents.

5. In spite of the influence of parents, children's values are not exact duplicates of their parents' values.

6. Values are also influenced by personality, personal experiences, the friendship group and other groups, education, the community, and vocation.

7. Values can change, although the changes occur slowly.

8. Changing the values of others is a very difficult task.

9. Persuasion involves four considerations: the message itself, the source of the message, the audience, and the specific situation.

10. Propaganda and education differ in purpose, but not necessarily in content.

11. Prejudices, or "pre-judgments," may be positive or negative.

12. Prejudice is an attitude; discrimination is a form of behavior that often results from prejudice; segregation is an act of physical isolation that often results from prejudice and discrimination.

13. Prejudices are learned, and although everyone has prejudices, there is no evidence that any particular prejudice is "normal" or inevitable.

14. Ethnic prejudices exist all over the world but differ in intensity and content.

15. No one factor can explain all types of prejudice.

Chapter Eighteen

The Role of Religious Values

This chapter has been included for two reasons. First, since everyone has had some form of personal experience with religious groups and religious values, they provide a framework for the study of groups and values in general. Second, the author feels that religious groups and religious values are underestimated as forces both in this country and in the world in general. Before evaluating the author's assertion, study the numerous definitions of the term "religious" given below so that you can interpret the term in its broadest sense.

No discussion of social behavior would be complete without a consideration of the role of religion, which has been so vitally important throughout the history of humanity. Religion has influenced human behavior both through the effects of religious beliefs and through the effects of religious-group memberships.

To find a universally agreed-upon definition of religion is impossible. The definition of religion most commonly accepted by Americans would undoubtedly resemble that in *Webster's Intercollegiate Dictionary* (Fifth edition): "The service and adoration of God or a god, as expressed in forms of worship." Or, "An awareness or conviction of the existence of a supreme being, arousing reverence, love, gratitude, the will to obey and serve, and the like." Other types of definitions are also possible; for example, religion might be considered as man's relationship to other men, man's method of explaining the unknown, man's ultimate concern (that is, whatever he is primarily concerned with or whatever he would be willing to die for), or man's ethical and moral guidelines.

Each person has a set of values and beliefs that affects his feelings about and behavior toward a supreme being, his relationships with people, his definition of his ultimate concern, and his method of explaining the unknown. These values may emphasize the sacred, such as a strong belief in an all-good, all-powerful God, in afterlife, and in the effectiveness of church ritual and prayer. They may emphasize secular

The Role of Religious Values

values, such as improving relationships among men, helping achieve peace, and improving physical and emotional health. The values may be strictly followed or frequently violated, relatively stable or in a state of change, carefully thought about or learned from parents and never questioned. They may motivate him to join a religious group or to remain

Belief in God?	Yes		Belief in the Devil?	Yes
United States	98%		Greece	67%
Greece	96		United States	60
Austria	85		Norway	38
Switzerland	84		Netherlands	29
Finland	83		Finland	26
W. Germany	81		Switzerland	25
Netherlands	79		W. Germany	25
Great Britain	77		Austria	23
France	73		Great Britain	21
Norway	73		Sweden	21
Sweden	60		France	17

Belief in Hell?	Yes		Belief in Life After Death?	Yes
United States	65%		United States	73%
Greece	62		Greece	57
Norway	36		Finland	55
Finland	29		Norway	54
Netherlands	28		Netherlands	50
Austria	26		Switzerland	50
Switzerland	25		W. Germany	41
W. Germany	25		Great Britain	38
Great Britain	23		Austria	38
France	22		Sweden	38
Sweden	17		France	35

Figure 18–1.

A Gallup Poll of religious beliefs in the United States and ten European nations found that Americans adhere most strongly to traditional beliefs (published in the *Los Angeles Times,* December 28, 1968, p. 19).

apart from any religious group, to mature and use his capabilities or to become narrow and limit his thinking.

The concern of this chapter is not to evaluate the validity of religious values or the adequacy of religious groups, but to discuss such psychological matters as the development of religious values, the religious beliefs and problems of college students, and the relationship between religion and mental health.

Development of Religious Beliefs

People learn religious beliefs and values, as they learn all beliefs and values, primarily through interaction with significant others, although the school, the general community, and the mass media also have an effect. The unique personality of the individual is another obvious influence on the system of values each person evolves.

Development in Childhood and Adolescence

Young children usually internalize the religious values of their parents and other significant figures in their environment. They almost always attend the church selected for them by their parents, usually without much question. Children tend to look upon God as a person and accept literal interpretations of what they are told: one girl who had been told "God is in you" was afraid He would leave when she had her tonsils removed. For young children, prayer is very self-centered and primarily an expression of wishes for things such as candy or toys. By age 11 or 12, prayer is associated with morals and ethics, and children ask for peace and human betterment (Long, Elkind, & Spilka, 1967). In essence, the child's concept of prayer, like many of his other concepts, develops from a vague idea to concrete expression to an abstract concept.

In adolescence, questioning of certain aspects of religion begins. This questioning may also involve criticism, although criticism tends to be leveled at ceremonies and rituals, rather than at the basic beliefs. Undoubtedly many adolescents (and many adults) never see religion as being more than rituals and ceremonies. Doubting and questioning do not necessarily indicate loss of faith and can actually be a sign of maturity, since childish concepts of God may need revision (Hurlock, 1959).

A study of religious experiences of ninth-graders had interesting results. When asked, "When do you feel closest to God?" most of the respondents referred to some activity related to the church, and many reported having had this feeling at a time when they were alone. The personal experiences which made them feel "especially close to God" occurred most frequently when the student himself or a close friend or relative narrowly escaped death or injury; the second most common situation was again when the student was alone (Elkind & Elkind, 1962).

The importance of privacy and solitude in the religious feelings of these students is significant.

Toward the end of high school and during the years immediately following, young people increase their religious criticisms and doubts (Kuhlen & Arnold, 1944). Although this is often interpreted as a period of antireligious feelings, young people in the 16–25 age range are rarely atheistic or agnostic, unless their parents are. Their criticisms of religion probably stem from a combination of two factors: first, they are seeking to understand their religious values better and must test them in discussion, even argument, with others; and second, they are made unhappy by some of the behavior they observe in people who are, or claim to be, religious. Numerous studies have shown that 90% or more of the adolescents surveyed believe in God and that a large proportion also accept the ideas of a Christian afterlife, of the value of prayer, and of the need for ritual and ceremony (for example, Kuhlen & Arnold, 1944).

The changes in adolescent religious attitudes that occur with age seem to be the following: (1) from a literal interpretation of the Bible to a symbolic interpretation; (2) from an almost complete acceptance of religious rituals, prayers, and ceremonies to some doubt; (3) from a strong belief that only "my" religion is correct to a feeling that all religions have something to offer; (4) from a virtually total belief in the existence of God to some questioning (for example, Kuhlen & Arnold, 1944).

Church attendance in adolescence typically drops off. Whereas part of this decrease may be due to increased doubting, most of it probably results from reduced family demands for attendance. Many parents insist that their young children go to church, but are more lenient with their teen-agers.

Development in Maturity and Old Age

The man who is 20 years old today has lived through a world quite different from that of the person who was 20 years old in 1947 or the person who will be 20 in 1981. It would be strange if they had identical values concerning religion. Parents of the present generation of college students should not expect their children to agree with them any more than the next generation will agree with this one. Yet people accept the religious values of their parents to a higher degree than they accept most other types of values (Fisher, 1948). When a shift does occur, it is usually away from the traditional beliefs.

Once the person is married and away from his parents' home, antagonisms to parental values often fade away. By the time his own children begin to arrive, and especially when they reach Sunday School age, he is likely to join a church again. Thus, from age 35 on, religious activity and traditional beliefs increase (Argyle, 1959). Religious conflicts tend to disappear during these middle years and church attendance is high.

As people move from middle age to old age, they state that religion becomes more important to them and that they hold their religious beliefs more firmly, although their church attendance and church activities diminish (Moberg, 1965). This apparent inconsistency is caused by health problems and transportation difficulties as well as by the orienta-

Figure 18–2.

Older people adhere more closely to the traditional religious values than do younger people. Whether this fact is due to changes that occur with age or to differences arising from the values of the generations in which they were born is uncertain. Photograph by John G. Warford.

tion of most church programs toward satisfying the needs of children, adolescents, and young adults, rather than the elderly.

Many religious viewpoints, including atheism, exist in the United States. The mature individual can evolve a set of his own religious beliefs that he has thought through and found appropriate; the beliefs may be closely related to a particular denomination or may be highly secular.

Religious Beliefs of College Students

Religious beliefs of college students vary greatly from school to school. In some colleges, almost all students attend church; only a small fraction will go to church at other schools. All in all, about one in four college students attends church regularly, and about one in four does not attend at all. Attendance increases after graduation (Jacob, 1957).

One large study investigated the attitudes of many high school graduates, then requestioned them four years later. Those who completed college were more likely to reject religious faith (13%) than those who went directly to work (4%). At the same time, workers were much more likely than college graduates to state that religion had become more important to them during the four-year period under study. In general, college students seemed to move away from traditional religious values (Trent & Medsker, 1967), particularly when compared to nonstudents.

A major investigation of college student religious attitudes included 4,600 male students, primarily in East Coast colleges. Although this group is certainly not completely typical of the country (for example, mostly nonchurch schools were included), their responses are worth considering. Half of these students accepted the traditional view of God, fewer than 20% discarded the idea of God, and most of this latter group said they believed in man, in science, or in natural law. Over one in four believed in "a power greater than myself which some people call God and some people call Nature." Only 1% claimed to be actual atheists (Goldsen, Rosenberg, Williams, & Suchman, 1960). Those students who practiced their religion were more likely to feel that cheating is wrong, but were also more likely to agree with the statement "If everyone else cheats, why shouldn't I?" They were less likely to be nonconformists and were less likely to believe others should be allowed to express nonconforming ideas.

The results of two more recent surveys support the above data, with some qualifications. *Newsweek's* campus poll indicated that three out of four college students believed in God, but that "in many cases the belief was highly tenuous." Also, almost 40% of all students interviewed felt that their college experiences had caused them to question their faith (*Newsweek*, 1965). An earlier study (Gallup & Hill, 1961) showed two out of three college students displaying a "very firm" belief in God and only about 7% disbelieving in God's existence.

Putting the above studies together with other information, a picture emerges of religious values among college students. By and large, they believe very firmly in the traditional God; and when they do not, they are either uncertain or have accepted science, man, or nature as their "ultimate concern." In later years, many of them will slowly move back to the values they internalized in their earlier years and will undoubtedly join some church group, probably the same one their parents belong to or one slightly less traditional in its views. A small portion will retain agnostic or atheistic beliefs into maturity and throughout their lives.

Some Religious Problems of College Students

Religious conflicts occur throughout mature life, but the period between the middle teens and the middle twenties is often considered the most difficult, perhaps because so many people begin to consider the more complex problems of life at this point. Among the problems college students commonly confront are the science-versus-religion controversy, learning about other religions, defining the place of religious freedom, considering the purpose of life, and understanding the meaning of death.

Science and religion. Scientific and technical achievements have become so important in our world today that some people claim they have been made a substitute for religion. In addition, *certain* scientific findings appear to conflict with *certain* beliefs held by *some* religious groups. For example, the scientific assumption that the world is millions of years old conflicts with the belief that it is only a few thousand years old; the scientific approach to mental illness conflicts with the idea that disturbed people are inhabited by devils.

Nonetheless, the vast proportion of scientific findings do not conflict with the religious beliefs of any group, and many religious denominations find nothing in science to conflict with their teachings. However, scientific thinking and religious thinking each demand different sorts of faith: scientific thinking demands a faith in the scientific method and the potential ability of man to comprehend the universe, and traditional religious thinking demands faith in an unseen supreme being.

Students are taught to think scientifically, to demand to see results,

The Role of Religious Values

to insist upon observing variables, and to be able to predict what will happen if compound A is added to compound J. Such learning may cause them to distrust thinking that does not operate scientifically and to cast aside traditional religious beliefs because they cannot be tested scientifically. Thus, the beliefs of science and religion do not conflict, but the methods do. These same students, however, recognize that not all decisions require scientific proof, for example, political beliefs or the choice of a date for Saturday night.

Figure 18–3.

In India, the cow is a sacred animal. Devout Hindus will consume neither milk nor meat of the cow, and cows roam freely through city streets. As strange as this custom may seem to you, can you think of any of your religious beliefs that would strike a Hindu as peculiar? Photograph by Mark Davidson.

Learning about the religions of others. Many students receive little or no religious training before college; others receive good training in their own religion but learn nothing of other philosophies or customs. In either instance, college life can be upsetting, partially because courses discuss numerous religious ideas and partially because contact with students of other religious backgrounds is often inevitable.

John Holdren grew up in a small town where people believed the theory of evolution to be the work of the devil. The state constitution restricted the way evolution could be taught, and all his childhood was spent with people of similar religious values. "I even felt a little brave when my Boy Scout troop visited a Catholic church once a year."

Will Gilberg was raised in a section of a large city where almost all his neighbors were Jewish, and well over 80% of his high school was Jewish. He had never had a non-Jewish close friend.

When John and Will were assigned as roommates at college, they liked each other, but with reservations. John was astounded that anyone in America could deny the divinity of Jesus without being struck dead on the spot, and Will was dismayed that anyone in America could deny the truth of evolution. John began to worry that Will would not go to heaven, and Will began to worry that John was really anti-Semitic. John's religion taught him that drinking was sinful, and Will's religion included wine in its ceremonies.

Both took a philosophy course taught by a visiting professor from India. Since they had both always taken their own religious views for granted, learning how Christianity and Judaism looked to a scholar from Asia was very disconcerting. John firmly believed that Jesus walked on water, and Will firmly believed that Moses parted the Red Sea; yet both were shaken when they realized how strange such miracles sounded to a person from a totally different culture.

The place of religious freedom.   When asked directly how they felt about religious freedom, over 90% of the students surveyed expressed their belief in "unrestricted freedom to practice one's own religion." However, nearly one in four felt that religions preaching "unwholesome ideas" should be suppressed, a direct contradiction of the first belief. Another 17% were uncertain (Goldsen et al., 1960).

Not only students, but adults of all ages are similarly uncertain about how much religious freedom they wish to allow. When asked directly, they always favor religious freedom. However, notice that in the above survey fully 40% of the students refused to support the idea that all religious ideas should be expressed. Thus, they did not truly favor complete religious freedom, but only freedom for those religions that did not make them unhappy. Are there any religions whose freedom you might not approve?

The purpose of life.   College students are sometimes disturbed by the question "What is the purpose of life?" Students have heard the explanations of others—that the purpose of life is to serve God, or to serve fellow men, or to enjoy life, or to be successful, or to serve one's country. But many students come to doubt that any of these purposes is *the* purpose of life, yet they cannot find an adequate substitute.

These students may go through a period of confusion and even depression. Life has no purpose; life seems vacant and meaningless. By reading, talking, and thinking, they begin to formulate what they feel to be the purpose in life. This formulation is not static, and is likely to continue to develop and change during their mature years, but the confusion and depression that they may have felt as students will probably not recur.

The meaning of death.   Although the life expectancy of college students is many decades and although their death rate is very low, they are still very much aware of death and are very much concerned as to what it means for them. Most major religions offer an explanation of why death occurs and what happens to the self (or the soul) after death. Some college students, however, reject the traditional view of soul and afterlife and claim that the end of life on earth also marks the end of existence of the self anywhere. Confronting your own death or the thought of death is distressing, and it is extremely difficult—some contend, impossible—even to conceive of the idea that the time shall come when you will no longer exist on earth in any form. Religious explanations of the meaning of death and existence after death offer comfort to many people, who thereby no longer need face the prospect of nonexistence. Those who cannot accept these religious explanations need to work out some other fashion of coping with the reality of death.

According to one study, deeply religious people fear death least, and nonchurchgoers have a medium fear of death. Those who attend church irregularly have the greatest anxiety over dying (Kalish, 1963); perhaps they lack both the devotion to believe fully and the self-confidence to reject belief fully. Many people attempt to deny the reality of death for themselves and others. They refuse to discuss it, or else they talk about it in terms that remove the meaning. Physicians and other hospital personnel frequently avoid the subject completely, even when talking with a person who is known to be dying and who may even recognize his condition. If, as is often expressed, the only inevitabilities in life are death and taxes, it is interesting that taxes are spoken of so freely, but death is approached almost as though it were pornographic.

Religion and Mental Health

Like other values, religious values can offer opportunities for growth and increased self-esteem and stability, or they can lead to intense conflict and limit the possibilities for growth motivation. Also, a church group may be warm, friendly, and emotionally satisfying, or cold, demanding, and emotionally punishing. The degree to which any college student finds religious conflicts upsetting undoubtedly relates to his general emotional stability. Among the most important elements of religion in its relationship to healthy adjustment are faith, rituals, guilt, and church affiliation.

Faith

An individual can have faith in any one of many religious value systems or in some combination of several. He may have faith that God exists or that no God exists, that the soul goes to heaven or hell after death or that neither the soul nor heaven and hell are real, that prayers are answered or that prayers are a waste of time. He may place more faith in science or technology than in the traditional religious values. When you view the behavior of peoples throughout the world, you can see that some have more faith in an ideology, such as Democracy or Communism, or in money or power than in a personal God.

Faith implies acceptance of a system of religious beliefs based upon what the individual feels is sufficient evidence or authority. It can be supported by logic, but it does not depend upon logic. You have faith when you say, "I don't know exactly why, but I feel that my concept of a supreme being is correct—it just has to be—I just know it is." Or you might have faith in the accuracy of a particular authority, such as the Bible, your parents, a minister, a philosopher, or a friend. Perhaps you believe you have come to your religious values through a process of reasoning; in that case, you have faith in your ability to understand religious ideas with your own reason.

A person cannot consciously decide to have faith. Faith can occur in many ways, but not through your saying, "I think I'd better get faith." Faith is a set of beliefs and values and is acquired just as other values are.

In order to be faithful to their religious values, people have faced many hardships and even death. Anyone rejecting the religious values of the great majority of his cultural group faces prejudice and persecution. Basic needs, such as hunger and safety, often go unsatisfied in order to maintain religious values.

The specific religious values are probably less important to healthy adjustment than the degree to which the values are consistent with the person's daily behavior and acceptable in the surrounding society. As mentioned elsewhere (page 330), opposing the standards of the group increases stress; also, behaving inconsistently with the self-concept can produce conflict and guilt. For example, the person who firmly believes that cursing is wrong, yet curses anyway, will feel a conflict between his values and his behavior. He may eventually change his behavior, alter his values, or justify swearing in some fashion, but he will be motivated to reduce the tension-producing feeling of conflict.

The Role of Religious Values

A few people maintain religious values that are helpful neither for healthy adjustment nor self-actualization. They may interpret their religion, often incorrectly, as unforgiving. They may have an "evil" thought and feel they have committed a terrible wrong; or they may feel that their religion requires that all who disagree with it are inferior and should be eliminated, with violence if necessary. Those faiths that are unforgiving, that demand an impossible level of "pure thinking," or that encourage disrespect or violence are not conducive to healthy emotional development.

Rituals

Rituals are important or meaningless, depending upon your religious feelings and your previous experiences with those rituals. Certain rituals are beautiful and add richness to life—many non-Catholics, for example, can enjoy the color and excitement in a Roman Catholic High Mass. Other rituals, such as the Catholic ritual of kneeling before entering and leaving the church pew, may be very meaningful to a Catholic, but have little significance to a non-Catholic.

"I don't believe in it any more, either, but I think it's a beautiful old cultural ritual which should be preserved."

Figure 18–4.

College students are often impatient with religious rituals—especially those they perceive as hypocritical. Courtesy Ed Fisher.

Students are often searching for religious values and are very much aware of inconsistencies. They are looking for meaning in religion and criticize rituals that seem impractical or so automatic that they appear meaningless. Also, students live in the present and often have little patience with the past; rituals usually have evolved over years, perhaps centuries, and have meanings that are often traditional rather than contemporary.

Rituals become very familiar and may be comforting and satisfying, particularly in times of stress. They frequently occur in a group setting and give those who participate a feeling of belonging to the group and a way of expressing their associations. On the other hand, a ritual can become a meaningless chore or habit that people continue to perform because of some vaguely felt belief that ignoring it will bring bad luck. When neglect of this type of ritual causes guilt and anxiety, the ritual is not only meaningless but potentially harmful emotionally.

Guilt and Relief from Guilt

Religious beliefs can contribute both to increased feelings of guilt and anxiety and to decreased feelings of guilt and anxiety. Religion creates guilt when it is interpreted as overly demanding and overly punishing. When a young child fears he will go to hell because he sneaked a candy bar from the drugstore, and when he wakes up shrieking from a nightmare of burning in hell, the guilt has progressed too far. When a college student cannot sleep at night because he fears he will be punished by God for harboring some slight religious doubt, anxiety has progressed too far. Religion sets up standards for behavior and feelings, but most religious leaders are aware that not all people can live up to these standards at all times.

Since people often find they cannot live up to religious standards, they feel the need for being forgiven. This can occur through prayer, through contemplation, and through devices such as the confessional. Not only can these methods be used to reduce the guilt and anxiety brought about by religious standards, but they can occasionally reduce guilt that originated in ways having little or nothing to do with religion.

> Martin Marcus and his brother did not get along as children, and, unlike most brothers, had even more difficulty as adults. When he was only 31, Martin's brother was killed in an airplane crash. Martin had so often thought about how good it would be to get his brother out of the way, that, in a sense, he felt responsible for the death. Martin finally undertook a lengthy period of prayer and contemplation, in the hope that he could gain a feeling of having been forgiven.

Martin's guilt feelings resulted from having *wished* that terrible things would happen to his brother, for he had nothing to do with his actual death. Martin could not apologize and be forgiven—his brother was dead and could not forgive him; nor could Martin admit to anyone else why he felt as he did. What if he had not believed in God? Then, in some fashion, he would have had to arrive at the belief that his brother would have forgiven him, had he actually understood.

Religious beliefs exert a great influence upon behavior through inducing or reducing guilt and anxiety. Do you think that the feeling of having been forgiven can go so far in reducing guilt as to encourage irresponsible behavior?

Church Affiliation

Motivation for church attendance varies. Some people go to church because they think it looks good to friends and neighbors; others have been persuaded that it aids peace of mind; still others attend with the vague feeling that they can "stay on the good side of God, just in case there is a God." Other motives include business contacts, social contacts, seeing who else is going, and looking the minister over.

Nonetheless, most church attendance is probably motivated by a sincere desire to join with a community of others to express deeply felt spiritual beliefs. In this seemingly impersonal world, many feel alone and vulnerable. Church membership not only gives spiritual satisfaction, but also provides the important feeling of belonging to a group that has similar beliefs and performs similar rituals. For some, unfortunately, church affiliation leads to such extreme loyalties that they look down upon or discriminate against other churches and their members. There are people who believe that certain religious views mark a person as inferior or immoral.

The Nonbeliever

"People who don't believe in God are lucky—they can do anything they please, and they don't have to worry about being punished."

"People who don't believe in God are in a miserable state—they must always be scared that something terrible will happen to them when they die."

The difference in behavior between believers and nonbelievers is much smaller than many people think. Nonbelievers neither do anything they please nor are they fearful that something terrible will happen. The nonbeliever is not without problems, since he has taken an unpopular position and may be criticized for his views. However, there is no evidence that his emotional health or self-actualization suffers for not believing in God. Although evidence does establish that the churchgoer drinks and smokes less than the nonchurchgoer (an expected relationship), the churchgoer does not seem to be more honest (Goldsen et al., 1960) or more concerned with the value of human life and of mankind (Kirkpatrick, 1949). As a matter of fact, although those who attend church regularly seem less racially prejudiced than those who attend sporadically, nonchurchgoers have less prejudice than either (Allport & Ross, 1967).

More important than the frequency of church attendance is the meaning of religion to the person. The study cited immediately above revealed that those who *live* their religion are much less ethnically prejudiced than those who *use* their religion. The former group consisted of sincere, devout, concerned people. The latter included people who used religion to advance their personal security, their status in the community, or their social contacts. Apparently, individuals who use religion for personal advancement have developed a set of values that cause them to reject people who differ from them, but those who live their religion tend to accept the concepts of brotherhood and love of mankind (Allport & Ross, 1967).

The nonbeliever often maintains humanistic values and activities instead of the church-oriented values of his more religious peers. Usually believing that the present life is the only one he will ever have, the nonbeliever may feel under more pressure to produce a high quality of life for himself and for others while on earth, since he is not consoled by the thought of the next life compensating for what he and others do not have during this life. Also, because he does not believe that his life should be wholly or in part dedicated to a supreme being, the nonbeliever appears to be better able to dedicate himself to improving the lot of other people.

Social Action by Religious Leaders

In recent years, many religious groups have begun to show increased concern for some of the social problems that have long involved the nonbelievers. Clergymen of all faiths have taken strong positions on war, poverty, the draft, and racial discrimination; and they have backed up their positions with action, often militant. Much criticism has been directed at these religious leaders for participating in antidraft or open-housing demonstrations. It would appear that many parishioners prefer that their clergy not become too involved with controversial social issues.

Although often accused by the more militant of moving too slowly, church leaders among the blacks and the browns have been very active in demanding civil rights and better living conditions for their followers. The outstanding black leader Martin Luther King, Jr., was a minister, as is Adam Clayton Powell. Cesar Chavez, leader of the movement to unionize Mexican-American (and other) migrant farm workers, received strong support from the Catholic clergy; and priests and nuns have taken part in many antiwar and antidiscrimination marches and programs. Such increased involvement with humanistic issues is a relatively new occurrence for many religious leaders. Whether this involvement represents, as some claim, an undue concern for secular matters, or whether it implies a new direction for America's churches remains to be seen.

Summary of Important Ideas

1. There are many possible definitions of religion: "the service and adoration of God or a god, as expressed in forms of worship," or man's relationship to other men, or man's method of explaining the unknown, or man's ultimate concern.

2. Young children usually internalize the religious values of their parents and other significant figures. They rarely resist their parents' requests regarding prayer, church attendance, or ritual adherence.

3. Adolescents feel close to God in situations involving privacy and solitude.

4. During adolescence religious values undergo some change: a diminishing acceptance of the Bible in literal terms, some doubts concerning ritual and prayer, more tolerance for other beliefs, and some questioning of the existence of God.

5. Religious values and activities continue to change after adolescence. In middle age, religious conflict seems to disappear; in old age, beliefs are held more firmly, although religious activities diminish.

6. Most college students believe in God, although some define their belief as being in "a power greater than myself that some people call God and some people call Nature."

7. College students face certain religious problems, including the possibility of conflict between science and religion, confusion from learning the religious beliefs of others, deciding upon the place of religious freedom, determining the purpose of life, and thinking about the meaning of death.

8. Religion affects mental health both through religious values and through religious group membership; either may lead to better emotional health or may precipitate mental health problems.

9. The degree to which a person's life is consistent with his religious values probably contributes to mental health.

10. Religious rituals are important or meaningless, depending upon the individual's feelings, previous experience, and the context in which the ritual is conducted. College students often attack rituals because rituals seem to lack contemporary meaning.

11. Religious values may increase guilt feelings and may also relieve guilt feelings.

12. People who *live* by their religion seem less ethnically prejudiced and more sincere and devout than those who *use* their religion.

13. In recent years, religious leaders of all faiths have shown increased involvement in controversial social issues.

Chapter Nineteen

Higher Education and the Student

The role of higher education has become increasingly important as knowledge and technology advance, and the role of the student in college has become increasingly difficult and demanding. For many students, college provides freedom and responsibilities that are new, often exciting, and sometimes frightening. Unlike the high school student, the college student can drop out of school whenever he—or his college—sees fit. At the same time, his close, warm relationships with significant others have changed considerably, and dating, marriage, and work relationships move into the limelight.

Make the most of your capabilities! It is easy to say, but its actual accomplishment takes more than good intentions—it demands that certain skills and knowledge be acquired. While offering one excellent source for obtaining some of these necessary skills and knowledge, college simultaneously opens up new opportunities and helps develop interests and capabilities you may not have realized you had.

Higher education is receiving increasing recognition from students and prospective students, from parents, from employers, and from politicians. Its achievements and its shortcomings are written up in books, newspapers, magazines, and highly technical reports. In 1966, over 6,000,000 students attended college, with the number expected to rise to over 8,500,000 by 1975.* Enrollment more than doubled between 1955 and 1965. The percentage increase is particularly dramatic in two-year colleges that award an Associate of Arts or comparable degree. These schools enroll approximately one in five college students, and new two-year colleges are coming into existence at the rate of roughly 50 per year (Lynes, 1966).

* Metropolitan Life Insurance Company Statistical Bulletin, September 1967.

Two-year colleges and four-year colleges are only two of the many types of institutions offering education and training beyond high school. Others include business colleges, technical institutes, art and drama schools, secretarial schools, and schools to educate nurses, morticians, keypunch operators, photographers, and a host of other specialists.

What Is a College?

Is a college just a group of buildings? Is it the students? The faculty? The administration? The spirit? Is it all these things together?

Try thinking of college as a community of scholars who come together to share their learning and to try to learn more. Students learn not only from the faculty, but also from other students; faculty members not only teach students, but also learn from students and from each other. The learning occurs through the formal channels of textbooks, lectures, library assignments, audiovisual aids, teaching machines, and demonstrations. Learning also occurs informally, such as in conversations in a faculty office or over a cup of coffee, in hearing a faculty member or student talk of his original project or research, or in disagreeing so violently with a professor that you search for some additional information yourself (Kalish, 1969).

In this community of scholars you can be like the gas tank of a car: you can sit back and let information be pumped into you, then run on it for a while, and eventually return for more. Or you can be active in seeking information and understanding: you can go beyond the formal part of college education and enter into the spirit of the community by reading on your own, by seeking new ideas, by evaluating what is told to you and relating it to your own experiences, by questioning faculty members, by learning from other students, and by being alert to the meaning of your own experiences.

The variety of learning tasks that are part of college education include developing the ability to

1. Express your own ideas and understand the ideas of others through effective and meaningful reading, writing, talking, and listening.

2. Understand human behavior, including your own, through a knowledge of historical and cultural traditions and human motivation.

3. Prepare yourself as a future citizen, a member of the work force, and a spouse and parent.

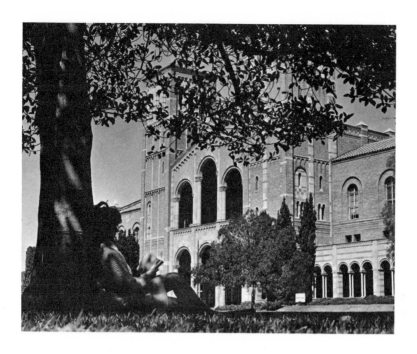

---

4. Familiarize yourself with the physical world, technology, and the scientific method.

5. Understand good mental and physical health practices, and apply them to yourself and in dealing with others.

6. Enjoy social relationships in the neighborhood, on the job, and with the family, and be able to give to and receive from these relationships.

7. Appreciate the artistic and creative contributions of others and receive satisfaction from your own creative and artistic talents.

8. Recognize the problems of the local community and of the world and determine the type of contribution you can make.

9. Evaluate ethical principles and develop your own.

10. Think, solve problems, and plan for the future.

11. Evaluate your own behavior and be self-critical.

12. Gain knowledge and understanding in a wide variety of areas, so that you can evaluate critically what others say and reach your own independent conclusions (suggested by a similar list by Bennett & Lewin, 1957).

In describing what the college student should be, one psychologist has suggested a combination of "College Chap," "Vocational Man," "Scholarly Student," and "Intellectual Rebel" (Wrenn, 1962). What sorts of attitudes and behavior do these types represent? If you had 100 points to describe yourself, how many points would you allocate to each type?

The Student Looks at College

What do the students themselves say about college? A number of colleges, scattered all over the country, participated in a study to answer this question. Although all the responding students were male, their answers are relevant to everyone. The following are the reasons they gave for going to college; the numbers in parentheses indicate the percentage believing each statement to be "highly important" (Goldsen et al., 1960):

1. To obtain a good general education and be able to appreciate ideas (74%).

2. To be better able to get along with others (72%).

3. To acquire necessary vocational skills (60%).

4. To become a better citizen (50%).

5. To acquire information helpful in determining "right" from "wrong" (45%).

6. To contribute to a happy marriage and a pleasant family life (22%).

However, a more recent study of 640 middle-class high school students indicated that both self-actualizing and financial aspects of work were equally desired from college education, although girls placed less emphasis on income. In the study results given below, the first numbers in parentheses indicate the percentage of boys identifying each reason for going to college as "very important," and the second numbers indicate the percentage of girls (Johnstone & Rosenberg, 1968):

The Chance to . . .
1. Discover a line of work that would really interest me (86%, 89%).
2. Prepare myself for a job with a really good salary (85%, 65%).
3. Learn more about subjects that really interest me (61%, 75%).
4. Meet new and interesting people (59%, 85%).
5. Develop my personality and become a more interesting person (59%, 83%).
6. Make my parents proud of me (58%, 61%).
7. Be stimulated by new ideas (44%, 73%).
8. Prepare myself to make a real contribution to mankind (38%, 54%).
9. Gain the social standing that comes from having a college degree (34%, 23%).
10. Take part in campus activities and social life (31%, 45%).
11. Get away from home and be on my own (30%, 34%).
12. Find a mate (27%, 29%).

The differences between the findings of this study and the one cited above could have resulted from the age of the respondents, the values of the community in which they lived, the year the study was conducted, or the wording of the statements.

When they talk more informally, students mention other reasons for college attendance, including avoiding arguments with parents, staying out of the military, postponing the need to get a job, having fun, finding a husband, and "because all my friends are going." Middle- and upper-class students receive strong parental pressures to attend college, although students from all social-class groups find that their parents encourage additional education.

Some students find college dull—just another obstacle to overcome before they can get a job. Others find excitement in the learning process: they see new potential in a creative approach to law enforcement; they watch their typing speed jump suddenly ahead; they gain new understanding of the principles of the stock market; they see new meaning in a poem or painting; or they achieve new insight into their own behavior.

Who Goes to College and Who Graduates?

Not everyone goes to college and, of those who do go, not everyone graduates. Going to college is associated both with academic ability and with social class (Trent & Medsker, 1967). Social class seems to affect college attendance in several ways. Students from middle- and upper-class families have the money to go to college; their friends and relatives are going and probably assume they will also; they have already developed the value that college attendance is important; they are more likely to have attended a high school that prepared them for college; and their parents were much more likely to have encouraged them to continue their education.

In essence, the basis for the motivation to attend college frequently comes from the family, and "aside from adequate intelligence, the factor most related to entrance and persistence in college is motivation. . . . motivation is formed early in life, probably largely in response to parental influences and early school experiences" (Trent & Medsker, 1967).

A substantial number of extremely able high school students never enter college. The reasons are numerous: financial pressures, early marriage, desire for independence, lack of awareness of abilities, inadequate counseling, and a number of personality characteristics that make college seem inappropriate. A person's definition of success is also relevant, since not all people define success in the same way. Success is so often assumed to refer to things that are available through work that we often tend to forget that some people see success in completely different terms. The hippies exemplify one such form of thinking.

Succeeding in College

What is college success? How is it measured? Is it getting high grades? Getting a degree? Learning about the world? Obtaining job skills? Getting married? The answer obviously varies from person to person. Just as the definition of a successful life varies, the definition of college success varies also.

For the purposes of this book, college success will be assumed to mean good grades and getting a degree, even though the shortcomings of such an approach are apparent. What is your measure of college success? How successful have you been, assuming your definition? Research has shown that a college education is seen as "acquiring greater self-esteem and a feeling of personal power. Not acquiring an education is perceived as being quite a deflating experience" (Sinnett & Stone, 1964). Do you agree?

Grades and Graduation: An International Comparison

Grades as measures of college achievement do not have the same meaning in all countries. In some European universities, grades are not given. Instead, students must pass lengthy, two- or three-day oral and written examinations to receive their diplomas. If the student fails these exams, which cover his entire course of study, he must wait six months or a year to try again.

In Japan, high school students are under tremendous pressure to get into good universities—much greater pressure than students in the United States. However, once they have been accepted, they worry less about grades, since almost no one leaves college because of low grades. College graduation occurs when the student has passed all his required courses and the necessary number of electives. If he fails a few courses along the way, no one cares much.

One Japanese student commented, "I think the American university system is cruel. It forces so much competition that students come to dislike each other. Our Japanese system is much better—students do not need to be afraid they will have to leave the university. When they have learned enough, they receive their degree. In America, if I take a very difficult course and get a D, the grade hurts my record, and no one cares if I learned anything from the course—it would have been better if I had not taken it. But in Japan, no one cares if I get a D, and I may learn a great deal."

In spite of her complaints, however, this Japanese student admitted that American university students study harder than Japanese students, although she felt Japanese high school students studied harder than Americans in order to get into college.

Each of these three systems, the American, the European, and the Japanese, has a method of determining whether a student has learned enough to deserve a diploma. Which system do you feel uses the most valid measurement system? How much tension is produced by each system?

As has been already mentioned, college success is based on a number of factors, including measured ability and motivation. One recent study investigated 10,000 high school graduates shortly before graduation and then four years later. Although academic-ability test scores in high school clearly differentiated those who completed college from those who entered but dropped out, a very high proportion of students in the upper one-third in test scores did not complete college. Some undoubtedly returned to college later, but the study makes clear that more than ability is needed to finish college (Trent & Medsker, 1967).

The best *single* method of predicting college success is to examine high school performance (Lavin, 1965), since the tasks to be accomplished in college are similar to those in high school. The second best single method of prediction is to examine scores on academic-ability tests (Reiter, 1964). The relationship between academic aptitude and college success is not, however, a simple one. Other factors, such as personality and adjustment, attitudes and values, study methods, social activities, and parental influences, all interact dynamically to influence college success.

Personality and adjustment. Results of research indicate that the successful student is more self-confident, more mature, more dependable, better able to overcome his personal problems, more efficient, and more realistic in his future goals than the unsuccessful student (Lavin, 1965; Taylor, 1964). He also has a higher need for achievement and is more curious and flexible (Lavin, 1965).

Personal-adjustment problems reduce study effectiveness, and the success or failure of poorly adjusted students often depends more upon the method they use to deal with personal problems than upon their academic aptitude (Malnig, 1964). Strong resistance to authority, inability to function independently, and inability to accept responsibility have all been associated with lack of college success (Trent & Medsker, 1967).

Attitudes and values. The purpose of college as seen by the individual is related to college success. Students who see college primarily as a source of vocational training are much less likely to succeed than those who emphasize general education (Trent & Medsker, 1967). Similarly, students who have a goal in college do better than those who do not (Wrenn & Crandall, 1941). These studies suggest that many students expect college to lead directly to job skills, and they are disappointed when they find so much emphasis on courses not directly related to jobs. Are these students in the wrong programs? Are they in the wrong colleges? Should they assume that their desires are inappropriate and go along with the demands of the college? Should the college assume that its demands are inappropriate and go along with the desires of the students? Perhaps these questions add up to three general questions: Is college relevant to the student's needs of today and tomorrow? Who decides? What are the bases for the decision?

Although having a goal, even a very much desired one, does not ensure college success, the person with no goals at all has no real motivation to succeed. As one wise Indian philosopher said, "If you don't know where you are going, any road will take you there." However, goals set by parents and accepted without evaluation can be worse than no goals at all. In this discussion we are assuming that college can help the student attain his goals, although many other goals (that is, many kinds of success) exist that are not met through college:

Susan Clay had wanted to be an actress since she was a young girl. After a year at Santa Monica City College, she dropped out to attend acting classes.

Marty Erikson thought an Air Force career would offer him the excitement that he needed, along with job security. He finished two years at the University of Maryland, enough to qualify him for flight school.

Phil Hernandez became increasingly involved with his work in the Spanish-speaking community. Eventually he left Miami Dade, hoping to return later, because he felt his community needed his services more than he needed an education.

Study methods. The use of good study methods, although less important than attitudes toward college or motivation to succeed, is definitely related to college success (Brown & Holtzman, 1955). The application of the SQ3R method (see page 74), for example, was shown to benefit a large proportion of students who used it seriously, and it helped the better students more than it did the poor students (Robinson, 1961).

Social activities. One study showed that for those who entered college too much social life was more predictive of future dropping out than either financial problems or academic problems (Trent & Medsker, 1967). It is difficult to determine, however, whether the unduly active social life might not have resulted from low academic motivation rather than high social motivation.

Parental influences. Throughout this book the role of significant others has been emphasized. In appraising college success, we again return to the importance of parents. Students who as high school seniors reported that their parents wanted them to attend college and often discussed college with them were much more likely to enter college and to finish (Trent & Medsker, 1967). Compared to college dropouts, those who completed college were more likely to seek occupational advice and general advice from their parents, suggesting that they had closer family relationships (Trent & Medsker, 1967).

Personality, attitudes, study methods, social activities, and parental influences are not isolated factors, but are part of a total picture. Good study methods seldom occur in conjunction with poor attitudes, and a student suffering from anxiety may have difficulty concentrating on his studies. Success in college results from a combination of intellectual and personal elements.

How Does College Change a Student?

What should happen to a student during the years he is in college? What does happen? We can probably assume that college graduates have learned a certain number of facts and concepts, but what else should they have learned? Should they have learned new ways of thinking? New ideas about society? New reactions to change?

College seems to find acceptance among those who finish it. A study of new college graduates, undertaken about 20 years ago, found that only 2% felt college did not help them vocationally, whereas 70% stated that it helped "a lot" (Havemann & West, 1952). When the subjects were asked if they would do it all over again, a resounding 98% said they would, and 84% said they would even attend their previous college (Havemann & West, 1952). Of course, the fact that recent graduates approve of having gone to college does not prove that anything happened to them during college. Fortunately other information is available.

College has been shown to help increase critical thinking ability and to decrease rigid and inflexible thinking. Interestingly enough, most of the changes occur during the freshman year (Lehmann, 1963). College students become more tolerant of ambiguity, but nonstudents become less so (Trent & Medsker, 1967). Also, "college seems to foster the growth of autonomy and intellectual disposition, whereas early employment and marriage seem to retard and even suppress development of these traits" (Trent & Medsker, 1967).

Whether college causes these changes to occur or whether it merely offers an encouraging environment to those about to change is not known. It is also not known why some students change in the directions indicated above, where as others do not change or even change in the opposite direction.

Jerry Towner's father was transferred from a small Louisiana town to a New England city just in time for Jerry to enroll in a large state college near his new home. Always politically active, Jerry caught on to city ways quickly and was elected to several campus offices. Having been brought up in a very conservative community, Jerry expressed the political and social philosophy of that community, and he became the rallying point for the campus conservatives. Yet less than four years later, Jerry was State Chairman of Youth for Senator X, a dynamic liberal political figure running for President. When asked about his change, he commented, "Where I came from, my position was liberal, but I guess

401

Higher Education and the Student

that being around here for four years opened me up to a much broader
point of view."

Not all students become politically liberal in college. Most follow
the party preference of their parents, and most register as Republicans
upon graduation (Trent & Medsker, 1967). Whatever their political
preference, there is a definite move in the direction of independent,
critical awareness and thought.

Sometimes the increased critical thought and awareness can be
troublesome to the very college authorities who offer the climate in
which such independent thinking can occur. In recent years, many
campuses have seen student demands for greater participation in the
decision-making process at the colleges. Although numerous motives
were behind these movements, a primary concern was that the administrations were not permitting sufficient student autonomy. An equally
important complaint was that faculty members were not "tuned in" on
what was happening in the world and that their classes were not relevant
to the world the student would face after graduation. Both faculty and
administrators responded that they, being older and more experienced,
were in a better position than students to judge what would be relevant
in the long run and how much autonomy was appropriate. College
trustees, local police, and many politicians became active in the campus
unrest in one way or another, and confrontations became explosive.

Issues concerning the ethnic minorities and the peace movement
became entwined with the students' rights movement. Violent encounters
with police and forceful student occupation of campus buildings occurred at many colleges and universities. Some community leaders sym-
pathized with the student protests, although usually not with their
violent methods; others demanded that the students return to their class-
rooms. College campuses in the middle and late 1960s were a far cry from
the passive, job-oriented campuses of the previous decade, even though
only a minority of students were involved in the protest movements.

New Freedom, New Identity, New Relationships, and New Responsibilities

As little as three months or even less may separate the high school
senior from the college freshman, but the change in freedom and respon-

sibility can be immense. College life requires increased self-discipline and responsibility.

Freedom from Supervision

While the student was still in high school, parents and teachers kept a close eye on him, but this supervision—of academic activities and of personal life—diminishes considerably in college. Students who miss a class must learn for themselves what they missed. Although most professors are happy to talk to students after class to explain some point in the lecture more thoroughly, the student must take the initiative for these conferences himself. Attendance is not always taken, and there is little—other than his own planning and motivation—to keep a student from falling impossibly far behind in his studies. Even parents do not supervise their college-age children so closely as previously, partly because they feel their children must now use their own initiative and partly because parents usually do not understand college assignments and demands as well as they had understood those from high school. College students are expected to be responsible for their own behavior without constant parental and professorial reminders.

In her first semester at junior college, Helene Gould signed up for an average load of courses and a heavy load of social activities. Although many of her professors did take attendance, her instructors in English and in psychology did not bother. Her psychology professor stated at the first class meeting, "Attendance is strictly up to you; you are in college because you choose to be, and your success depends upon your performance. If you decide something else is more important than class, that is up to you, but it is your obligation to make up what you missed." Since English and psychology classes were held on Monday, Wednesday, and Friday afternoons, Helene found that cutting these classes gave her a great deal of free time. At first she cut only Friday classes, but then she began to cut Monday and Wednesday occasionally. Neither professor said anything to her, so she felt safe—especially since she had low-C grades going into the finals. The ax fell when she received her final grades: a D in psychology and an F in English. She visited her psychology professor, tears in her eyes, and asked whether she could do extra work to bring her grade up. He listened patiently but said "No." Then Helene told him it was his fault that she had gotten the low grade, because, she said, "you should have insisted that everybody come to class every time."

Helene had not learned in time that college students are expected to be responsible for their own success. Since students are not forced by law to attend college, and since colleges are not forced by law to keep students who do poorly, the situation in college differs considerably from that in high school. The student is expected to solve problems and to gain knowledge and understanding on his own. When he needs help, he is expected to seek the help, not to wait for the help to find him. The watchful eye and commanding voice that Helene had been accustomed to in high school were lacking at college.

Even the scheduling of classes places a greater demand upon students to organize themselves. After a high school schedule of five days a week from 8:30 A.M. to 3:00 P.M., the college schedule of 15 to 20 hours a week in class seems "a breeze." Knowing that the week has many free hours reduces any sense of urgency, and assignments may be all too easily postponed.

The independence demanded by college is too much for some students, even though they live at home. Those who live in dormitories may have still more difficulty. They need to contend with all-night bull sessions (often valuable, always interesting, but rarely substitutes for study) and noisy roommates, and they have no one to remind them that work must be done. Some students thrive on such freedom; they work better and mature more than when closely supervised. Others simply cannot manage this much freedom.

A Continuing Search for Identity

The adolescent wish to answer the question "Who am I?" often continues through the college years. Large, impersonal colleges with student identification numbers, interminable lines to wait in, computerized advising and grading, and large classes may only intensify the confusion about identity. Because he is not treated as a meaningful individual, the student may become anxious about whether individuality still exists.

Even the student's role as a student is uncertain. In high school, he had been high man on the totem pole—a graduating senior. He knew his way around, had many friends, and was proud of his future status as a college student. Three months later, he is low man on the totem pole—a college freshman. He is new, does not know his way around, and is probably not especially proud of his status as freshman.

Perhaps more important, the college freshman does not know exactly how to act. He wants to behave like a college student and to have an identity as a college student, but he is a little unsure of what this means. The author had the following experience as a freshman:

> During high school, I had learned to smoke a pipe. I rather fancied myself with it, and the girls I dated in high school seemed to admire my pipe. Knowing that college men smoked pipes, I was puffing

around campus during my first week, rather pleased that I was able to present such a mature and scholarly picture: Young Man With Pipe. Then, at the Coffee Shop one evening, I overheard one of the older students, a veteran just out of the Navy, comment to his friend, "You know, you can always spot a freshman—they're the ones who smoke pipes." And they both laughed. I packed my pipes and tobacco away that evening and did not dig them up again for two years, when I was secure enough in my status not to fear being considered a freshman.

The author was extremely deflated to learn that what he thought was mature, typical college student behavior merely marked him as a naïve young freshman. His identity as a college student had not yet been established. Each freshman must learn for himself what it is to be a college student.

At the same time, college studies may open new and exciting, sometimes frightening, avenues for consideration. What is your relationship to God? To the universe? To nature? To other human beings? Who are *you* in relation to these phenomena? Here again the problem of identity becomes important. These are problems that cannot be answered in a lecture or through a textbook, but only through living and thinking and feeling and experiencing. These words may seem strange and confusing. What do you think they mean? How do they apply to you?

New Social Relationships

High schools draw students from the surrounding community. Thus, students at any particular high school are likely to share common interests and backgrounds, especially in urban and suburban communities, where large areas of similarly priced homes are found. Attending college often changes these circumstances. College students usually represent a wide variety of races, religions, social classes, and nationalities, so that any one student has an excellent opportunity to meet others from diverse backgrounds.

Some students have difficulty in being with those whose backgrounds are different and whose behavior may, therefore, not be so predictable. They may feel socially inadequate or fearful of making blunders, so they avoid stress by returning to more comfortable ground:

Mel Peterson lived within 20-minutes' drive of a good state college, and he decided to enter there, along with many of his old friends. However, Mel felt lost among the 14,000 students attending. To get a date, he returned to his old high school, where he felt more comfortable. Being a college student gave him new prestige, and he was soon dating the most popular cheerleader on the squad. The next year she also entered State, where she quickly started dating the men on the football team, so Mel returned to his high school again for dates. This continued for four years, until all Mel's prestige and glamor wore off, and he gained a reputation as a person who could not make the grade with college girls.

In a sense, Mel was unable to establish his identity as a college student. His behavior was obviously not in response to growth motives. He lacked self-esteem and feelings of security. Little growth can occur in a person who does nothing but repeat over and over again his earlier experiences.

The college student needs to gain a sense of identity as a student both in on-campus relationships and off-campus relationships. Many parents and friends, unfamiliar with the actual situation at colleges, may have inaccurate perceptions of college students; and students find themselves treated in terms of stereotypes that may be upsetting and discouraging. For example:

Spoiled. "Kids in my day didn't have it so good. College kids today got it easy. Easy life, good job, lots of money. They don't know what real work is."

Wild. "Boy, the things I've heard about you college people—Wow!! I was just reading that every college man has at least two girls just aching for loving."

Snobbish. "You guys aren't as good as you think you are. You're no better than anyone else, so don't put on airs with me."

Brilliant. "I know how hard you have to study to stay in college. You must be real brilliant."

Hippies. "All you college guys with beards and those girls with long hair and no makeup. Nothing but oddballs."

Rich. "I guess you have to have real money to go to college."

Radical. "You guys are mostly Commies, aren't you? Always yelling about peace and equal rights and stuff."

Only when a student is secure in his identity as a college student can he interact effectively with those who maintain these pictures-in-the-mind regarding college students. Although the new social relationships on and off campus can be somewhat difficult at first, they eventually become more satisfying and allow for personal growth and maturity.

Challenges to College Success

Although students are expected to be much more independent in college than they were in high school, personal and academic growth may be limited by numerous factors. Among the most common of these are academic problems, social and emotional problems, financial difficulties, and health problems. These areas are not isolated, but interact with each other. What is originally a financial problem might lead to a health problem, which, in turn, produces an achievement problem that subsequently aggravates the health problem.

Fortunately, many colleges are well equipped with sources of help for the various problems. These sources include counseling facilities, faculty advisers, the library, and medical facilities (see Appendix I).

Academic Difficulties

For many students, the most difficult task in college is adjusting to the academic demands (Will, 1957). Because of the grading system, particularly in large classes, some students will inevitably receive low grades. Poor grades, particularly for those accustomed to being among the better students, can lead to irrational, self-defeating behavior. The student blames everyone but himself, and he becomes bitter. Or, he may feel inadequate and decide to give up. On the other hand, low grades affect some students like a cold shower on a sleepy person—the shock jolts them back to reality.

Although academic aptitude accounts for a substantial proportion of one's level of achievement, many good students never finish college, and some poor students with low aptitude scores do receive degrees. Students who achieve at a higher level than their test scores predict are characterized by having high self-esteem, realistic goals, academic (rather than social) interests and activities, good relationships with peers and authority figures, and anxiety that—although not absent—is under control (Taylor, 1964).

What alternatives does a student have when his academic achievement falls below par? Assuming he does not understand where his difficulties are, his first step should normally be to see his instructors.

An analysis of a student's errors on a multiple-choice sociology exam turned up evidence that the student was not paying close enough attention in class.

A look at a student's textbook showed that he was underlining too much and was therefore unable to review his reading effectively.

A brief discussion with a student of American Indian background indicated that her knowledge of slang and idioms was limited, and she did not fully understand the class lectures and discussion.

When the instructors cannot help, the college counselor often can. Low grades can result from inadequate high school background, poor study methods, physical illness, insufficient motivation, personal problems, or lack of the necessary academic aptitude. College counselors, through tests and interviews, can usually determine the basis for low grades.

If nothing seems to work, the student must re-evaluate his college goals. Perhaps he needs to shift from one major to another or from one college to another. Perhaps the answer is to leave college and enter business school or a hospital training program for nurses. In some instances, it might be better to take a job or enlist in the armed forces, with the idea of returning to college at a later time with a more realistic and mature set of goals.

However, any major change should be undertaken only after all other possibilities have been eliminated, that is, after the student has tried to study as hard as he can, after he has eliminated poor study methods, when he believes that personal or health or emotional problems are not producing his difficulties, and when he is certain that neither outside work nor social obligations are robbing him of needed time.

Social and Emotional Problems

Life is not divided into neat, isolated compartments. Whatever affects one phase of living also affects other phases. When a marriage is unhappy, more than the family life of the couple is disturbed: their job effectiveness may be reduced; their children may become anxious; even their physical health may be disrupted. In the same way, academic success and failure do not stand in isolation. An unhappy family situation, an unfaithful fiancée, or an undue amount of suspicion can all reduce study effectiveness and deprive the student of his opportunity for optimum use of his abilities.

Mike Minton's childhood had been secure and happy, but his father died when Mike was 12, and his mother eventually married a man of modest means with children of his own. The insurance money left by Mike's father gradually went to pay living expenses, although it had originally been earmarked for Mike's college. In the meantime, the relationship between Mike's mother and her new husband had deteriorated, and sometimes their arguments became so violent that blows were exchanged. At this point, Mike began his freshman year as a dormitory student at a junior college about four hours' drive from home.

Man and His Society

Because of his limited funds, he had to work 30 hours a week to support himself. Letters from home were far from happy, and the combination of physical fatigue from his heavy load of work-plus-study and his anxiety regarding the situation at home caused Mike to flunk out of college by the end of the second semester.

In studies comparing underachieving students with overachieving students, personal problems are consistently shown to affect academic

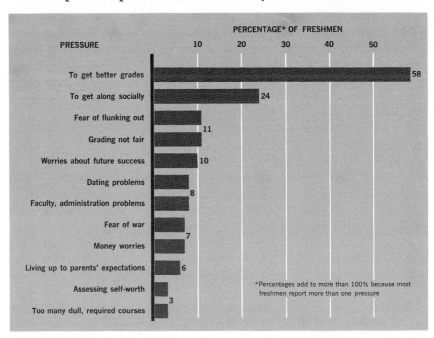

Figure 19–2.

Problems college freshmen feel depress them most. Courtesy the *Harris Survey*, by Louis Harris, published in the *Los Angeles Times*, March 18, 1965.

performance. The underachiever, for example, tends to lack confidence and to be somewhat depressed; he shows signs of maladjustment more openly, thus indicating that he lacks control; he is less likely to have a good relationship with his parents and is less likely to like his instructors; with other people, he tends to be withdrawn, uninterested, apathetic, and dependent; he is also more likely to resent authority figures. The low-achieving student may also be uncertain about his goals in college, or else he tends to set goals for himself that are beyond his level of ability (Taylor, 1964). These personal problems do not inevitably cause college problems, nor do college problems inevitably produce personality problems. However, students who are not living up to their potential in college tend to be the same ones who have difficulties in nonacademic areas. Since personal problems imply that the individual has not adequately satisfied needs lower in the hierarchy, he is unable to make the most of the capacities he does have.

Financial Problems

The man with all the money he wants is a rarity anywhere in the world. In college, students with financial difficulties often seem to outnumber those without such difficulties. Some students find that their success, even their ability to remain in college, is threatened by money problems.

Student funds come from two major sources: family funds and personal earnings. (Of course, students pay only a portion of the cost of their education; the rest is borne by the taxpayers or donors.) Estimates indicate that over half of American college students earn a large part or all of their college expenses (Gallup & Hill, 1961).

To intensify the problem, college students like to be independent, and their independence is curtailed when they are supported by funds from home. In order to be independent, some students reject family offers of support and take part-time jobs. Occasionally the work-plus-study load is more than the student can handle, and he either must quit work, leave school, or risk physical illness.

Students whose living costs are greater than their available funds plus earnings from part-time work have several alternatives:

1. Scholarships and grants are available for students with good academic records or with a background of participation in campus activities.

2. Today's generation of college students has an opportunity to obtain low-interest loans. The federal government, state and local governments, as well as banks and college authorities, have made funds available.

3. A compromise measure is to work full time and attend classes on a part-time basis. Although it postpones completion of college, such a procedure is usually better than carrying a full academic load while trying to hold a full-time job.

4. Often overlooked is the possibility of reducing expenses, which may be simpler than increasing earnings. In today's wealthy society, people feel entitled to luxuries. However, certain items can be readily eliminated from the budget if necessary. Have you ever made out a budget, then kept a day-to-day expenditure log to see how to cut your expenses?

Since students are often unaware of all the potential sources of financial help, those who have extremely restricted financial support are usually encouraged to make an appointment at the campus scholarship and loan office, with a college counselor, or with some other adviser.

Physical Health Problems

Students are more likely to neglect their physical health than their automobiles, their appearance, or their social activities. Fatigue and poor diet are common on college campuses. Physical problems inevitably reduce study efficiency. Although obvious physical problems, such as a high fever or stomach cramps, usually receive attention, many students ignore the need to maintain a good day-to-day program of physical care.

Most readers of this book will take a course that covers physical health and hygiene in considerable depth, so this discussion will be restricted to a brief outline of the requirements of a good personal health program and a consideration of problems involving tobacco, alcohol, and drugs.

A brief outline of a personal health program. Physicians are agreed that preventive medicine and good personal health care would reduce the rates of illness and death by a considerable degree. The following are some of the health procedures they suggest:

1. Maintain an effective and well-balanced diet. No one is harmed by missing one meal or spending one day stuffing himself with milk shakes and hot dogs, but some students make a career of such diets; others take great pride in avoiding vegetables and keeping breakfast down to the barest minimum.

2. Get adequate exercise. Once the required courses in physical education cease, the majority of students obtain their exercise in walking to and from the parking lot.

3. Get sufficient sleep. Sleep needs differ from person to person, but students tend to pride themselves on how little sleep they had the night before.

4. Have regular medical and dental examinations. Dentists usually suggest two visits a year; physicians recommend annual checkups after age 30 or 35, and one thorough check every two years before then.

5. Take care of minor medical and dental problems before they become major ones. A good night's sleep and a day in bed may prevent a cold from turning into something more serious; cleaning a bad scratch with soap and water can avoid infection.

6. Avoid medication without the approval of a physician, and do not make excessive use of alcohol, tobacco, or such drugs as the numerous pills that guarantee to keep you awake.

A good friend of the author's learned about the effects of extreme

Figure
19–3.

Exercise is a vital part of a physical fitness program for people of all ages. Courtesy Columbia Broadcasting System.

---

fatigue when he and the author were taking freshman economics together:

> The economics midterm was scheduled for 10:10 Wednesday morning, and Ralph Zeff closeted himself into a study room at 6 the evening before to begin reading the semester's assignments, which his active social life had previously prevented. Sixteen hours, three packs of cigarettes, 12 cups of black coffee, and five stay-awake pills later, Ralph walked into the classroom, satisfied with his all-night job of cramming. When I left the exam room, about ten minutes before the bell, I had to walk past Ralph's chair. I noticed his head was resting on his left hand, which was also being used as an eye-shield. Since I had already turned my paper in, I looked to check Ralph's answers, and I was startled to see only about one-third of the questions completed. At that point I pulled his arm away from his forehead, and he woke up with a snort that caused everyone in the room to snicker. P.S. He flunked the exam.

Alcohol and tobacco. In spite of religious, family, legal, and medical objections, drinking and smoking are very popular throughout our country, including our colleges and universities. The moral aspects of drinking and smoking are matters each person must interpret in view of his own personal beliefs. Medical and psychological evaluation, however, may be made here.

Man and His Society

In recent years, careful compilation of statistics has shown that smokers have a briefer life expectancy than nonsmokers, even when comparing people who live under comparable air pollution conditions and function under comparable degrees of stress.

Alcohol can be consumed in moderation with no permanent damage, although it may cause temporary loss of judgment, of visual ability, and of inhibitions (all very dangerous to automobile drivers). After sufficient time has elapsed, the alcohol is absorbed into the body, and normal behavior will recur. Because alcohol reduces inhibitions, some

Figure 19–4.

"I've quit smoking."

The relationship between smoking and cancer has caused many people to give up the habit. Courtesy Ed Fisher.

people feel freer in their sex behavior after several drinks, although the actual capacity to enjoy sex is reduced (Leuba, 1961). Chronic heavy drinking can lead to inability to perform effectively in class, on the job, or in social situations.

Smoking and drinking are two symbols of the adult world forbidden to children and adolescents. Thus, the adolescent who takes a beer or a cigarette is also partaking of a symbol of the society into which he desires entrance. His self-concept may be bolstered by the change in his picture of himself.

Smokers and drinkers seem to differ in several ways from abstainers. Heavy drinkers in college are less ambitious, less effective in planning and organizing, and less certain of their goals (Kukuk, 1960). Problem drinkers are more anxious and depressed than nonproblem drinkers. After a few drinks, their depression and anxiety leave, which may well explain why they use alcohol as much as they do, but these unpleasant feelings return if drinking becomes heavy (Williams, 1966). A thorough review of recent literature on smokers shows that they are more outgoing, more willing to take risks, and more interested in stimulation, but they are less dependable, less stable, and less agreeable than nonsmokers (Perloff, 1968).

The pros and cons of smoking and drinking make a good topic for class discussion, but underlying such a discussion must be one major question: Are the satisfactions received worth the risk of permanent health damage (from tobacco) and temporary reduction in judgment (from alcohol)? Most people who do stop smoking cite their health concerns as the major factor (Perloff, 1968), and the main reason given by teen-agers for substantial reduction in smoking in that age group is similarly health (Medical Bulletin on Tobacco, June 1968).

Drugs. Numerous hallucinatory drugs are available on college campuses, but those eliciting the most controversy have been marijuana and lysergic acid diethylamide (LSD-25). More recently, student attention has turned to hashish and a variety of other psychedelic drugs, such as peyote and THC, a derivative of marijuana. Initially, drug users were relatively few, but increasing numbers "turned on," and some campus estimates and surveys have set the percentage of drug users as high as 40–50%. Usage among students at some high schools is believed to be equally high.

Those who take LSD experience strange, usually exciting, occasionally terrifying, perceptions and feelings. They claim to feel "at one with mankind" and "wish nothing but peace and brotherhood." Ordinary stimuli take on new and deeply significant meanings: "That apple might look like an ordinary apple to you, but to me it was the reddest, the sweetest, the loveliest apple I had ever tasted." Or, "The flower was reaching out to me, saying something to me." Obviously the drugs affect the brain chemistry, although the particular mechanism is not fully understood.

Since legal sanctions were quickly applied to the sale, purchase, possession, and use of LSD, good research became difficult to accomplish. Nonetheless, over the years a few studies were conducted and reported. Studies with animals showed that changes did occur in ability to learn, in ability to make difficult visual discriminations, and in measure of brain waves. However, except for those taking extremely large doses, all animals returned to normal functioning after a period of time, although sometimes as long as several months. (See McGlothlin & Arnold, 1969.) Two studies involving human subjects showed the possibility of temporary reduction of abilities involving visual perception and spatial orientation, as well as temporary reduction of abstract abilities. No generalized brain damage was shown. The investigators have emphasized that their research is only preliminary and that much more work will have to be done before they can draw more than highly tentative conclusions (McGlothlin & Arnold, 1969).

Whatever research might eventually show, some LSD users had "bad trips," and a few ended up in mental hospitals, usually for brief periods of time. Claims were made that people under the influence of LSD committed acts of violence against themselves and others, and some of these claims were well substantiated. Eventually the use of LSD—and its publicity—tapered off. Some of the reduction in LSD trips stemmed from the strict laws and severe punishments involved, but the fear of genetic damage was probably a more important factor.

Marijuana produces much milder effects, and its potential for long-term harm became a medical controversy. The American Medical Association and many other medical, legal, and law enforcement groups strongly condemned its consumption. An AMA committee, while attacking its use, also attacked the penalties for violation of the marijuana laws as "harsh and unrealistic" (*Los Angeles Times*, June 20, 1968). Some foreign investigators claimed that they found evidence that marijuana, even when taken in moderation, did serious and permanent harm, but the general medical and psychological opinion was that the evidence was not sufficient. Two experts in the field, one a psychologist and the other a physician, state that "no physiologically addictive qualities" have been found in marijuana and that "no long-term physical effects of marijuna use have been demonstrated in this country, although more current studies are needed before this issue can be resolved . . ." (McGlothlin & West, 1968).

Psychological dependence on marijuana undoubtedly occurs to the extent that users come to like the mood that "pot" produces, and they desire the opportunity to repeat the experience. Heavy users experience mild irritability when they cease to use marijuana, but very few Americans are heavy users. It is not known whether withdrawal from marijuana is as difficult as from cigarettes or, for that matter, from frequent consumption of coffee. African and Asian reports of very heavy users indicate that physical health may suffer, and there is evidence that mental illness may also result; however, these studies refer to people who consume several times as much marijuana as is generally the case in the United States (McGlothlin & West, 1968).

Good research into the effects of marijuana on those who have recently begun to take it is not yet available. However, observations do suggest certain personality changes. Marijuana users appear more passive, more likely to turn inward, and less likely to be strongly motivated to achieve. Other changes include "apathy, loss of effectiveness, and diminished capacity or willingness to carry out complex long-term plans, endure frustration, concentrate for long periods, follow routines, or successfully master new material. Verbal facility is often impaired. . . . Such individuals exhibit greater introversion, become totally involved with the present at the expense of future goals, and demonstrate a strong tendency toward regressive, child-like magical thinking" (McGlothlin & West, 1968). The claim that marijuana leads to crime has received no acceptable evidence; in fact, the use of pot tends to produce passivity —unlike alcohol, which often leads to aggressive behavior.

One recent study of adults who had used marijuana for several years obtained the following results. Of the 32 reporting, 28 stated that their driving competence was impaired, due to perceptual distortion, speed distortion, slower reaction time, less alertness, and poorer judgment. Only seven of the 32 reported long-term effects, and six of these felt the effects were positive, while the seventh felt they were mixed (McGlothlin & West, 1968).

The use of marijuana and LSD was associated with hippies, militantly liberal students, and promiscuous sexual relationships. The police and community leaders often conflicted with drug users, not only regarding drugs but also regarding social, political, and religious views and behavior. Both advocates and opponents of drug use have made extravagant claims for their points of view, and communication between the two sides became extremely difficult.

In the past, the use of such drugs has been associated primarily with low-income, unemployed persons. This time the users were largely young people, primarily from the middle class. Thousands of students have been arrested and many convicted on misdemeanor and felony charges as a result. This situation has intensified the resentment between the police and young people, already aroused by clashes growing out of student rights, peace, and civil rights movements.

From a health point of view, the following can be said about drug use, as of this writing: LSD and some of the other psychedelic drugs definitely have dangerous short-term effects and may have dangerous long-term and permanent effects. These latter involve possible damage to the nervous system and to the brain, and the familiar occurrence of functional behavior change. Marijuana has the same kind of potential for dangerous short-term effects that alcohol has, because of the behavior changes it produces, but its long-term effects are at present unknown. Since we lack good long-term studies of "pot" use, it is possible that ten or 20 years from now cumulative changes or a "sleeper" effect will be observed. A similar possibility exists that research will conclude marijuana to have no long-term impact.

Throughout the controversies on the effects of drugs, good experimental evidence has been lacking. At the end of 1968, a report appeared of a study that used careful documentation, good experimental controls, and proper scientific reporting. Its major conclusions can be summarized as follows:

1. Subjects who have never smoked marijuana previously rarely have strong subjective experiences after smoking either low or high doses of the drug.

2. Regular users of marijuana do not show much impairment on simple intellectual and psychomotor tests after smoking marijuana, but nonusers exhibit readily observable performance decrement lasting as long as 90 minutes or more.

3. Marijuana use increases heart rate moderately and causes some dilation of blood vessels. It does not affect respiratory rate, blood-sugar levels, or size of pupils.

4. The effects of a single inhaled dose of marijuana "appear to reach maximum intensity within one-half hour of inhalation, to be diminished after one hour, and to be completely dissipated by three hours."

5. The setting in which marijuana is taken and the attitudes and expectations regarding its effects probably do influence the changes that occur.

6. Apparently both psychological and pharmacological influences contribute to the effects of marijuana upon performance and upon organic changes (Weil, Zinberg, & Nelsen, 1968).

Many more studies will need to be done to determine both longrange and short-range influences of drugs such as marijuana, but at least a start has been made.

Summary of Important Ideas

1. Higher education is receiving increased recognition from the entire community. The number of college students is expected to reach 8,500,000 by 1975.

2. A college can be looked upon as a community of scholars who come together to share their learning and to try to learn more.

3. Students see the main purpose in college as acquiring a good general

education, getting along better with others, and learning skills that would qualify them for a job that offers both stimulation and good income.

4. Going to college is associated with academic ability and social class. Social class affects college attendance through such factors as motivation, high school preparation, and peer-group pressures.

5. The best single predictor of college success is high school success; the second best predictor is scores on academic-ability tests.

6. Also related to college success are personality and adjustment, attitudes and values, study methods, social activities, and parental influences.

7. Besides accumulating information, students also experience other changes in college. Students who finish their education seem to increase their critical thinking ability and autonomy, and decrease rigid and inflexible thinking.

8. College requires that the student deal with freedom from supervision, with problems of his own identity, with new social relationships, and with new responsibilities for participation.

9. Among the most common challenges to college success are academic difficulties, social and emotional problems, financial restrictions, and health problems.

10. Users of alcohol, tobacco, and drugs risk the possibility of short-term, and perhaps long-term, ill effects to their physical and mental health.

Chapter Twenty

Career Planning
and the World of Work

The previous chapter discussed the student in college. This chapter, the final one in the book, carries the student from his present role to one of the most important of his future roles, the work role. Once again, you will read about human abilities, about personality and needs, and about self-actualization, but this time in the context of career planning.

What career field are you planning to enter? Why? How much do you know about this field? Do you know what is required to enter the field? The nature of the work? The working conditions? The opportunities for advancement? In what ways will the work satisfy your needs? We can assume it will earn you enough money to pay for food and shelter, but will it help you satisfy your security or self-esteem needs? Will it offer you the possibility for self-actualization?

Answers to these questions cannot be given on the spot, but such answers are very important to career planning and subsequent satisfactions during the adult years. After all, for better than two-thirds of your lifetime, for more than one-third of your waking hours, you will be engaged in activities related to producing income. Except for the retired, the disabled, and the housewife (whose working hours may be longer than her husband's), almost all adults work for financial return. Your career and your vocational success and satisfaction are highly significant in many ways. Inevitably, your job determines your income and thus affects what you buy and your standard of living. Your job also is a measure of your status and that of your family, a status only partially related to income. Thus, a teen-ager complained to "Dear Abby" that her parents pressured her to break up with her boy friend only because his father was a garbage collector, although the incomes of the two families seemed comparable (*Los Angeles Times*, December 31, 1965).

Your job reflects your educational level, your past achievements and future prospects, your values and attitudes, your self-concept, and—at least for some people—your means of personal growth and self-actualization.

Job success and job satisfaction (although related, they are not the same thing) can support an already healthy self-concept or help bolster low self-esteem. They can lead to great satisfaction, the feeling of accomplishment, and self-actualization. Lack of job success and low job satisfaction can have just the opposite effects.

Because the importance of work is generally recognized, most college students have already given considerable thought to their careers before their freshman year, and some have already worked out a thoughtful, sensible career plan.

Too often, however, students' vocational planning is unrealistic in light of their abilities, interests, and personality. A girl who played the lead in the high school play is confident she will be a movie star; a boy wants to be a lawyer because he enjoys arguing; another wants to study personnel management because he likes people; and invariably there are students who have had stories rejected by *Playboy, The New Yorker,* and *McCall's.*

Frequently the student's vocational plans result from family pressures to enter a career that satisfies the parents but may be unrelated to the student's goals and values. Sometimes a student plans an unrealistic career because parents, teachers, and friends demand his decision before he is ready to make one. Those who can make a proper vocational choice before beginning college are fortunate, but students who are pressured to make their decision too quickly will regret their hurry in later years.

Some of the major sources of confusion regarding vocational fields include the requirements for entering the field (for example, education, skills, health, or union membership); potential income (a large majority of college students anticipate an unrealistically high income after ten years of work—Goldsen, Rosenberg, Williams, & Suchman, 1960); the amount of work and time necessary for success and advancement; and the availability of openings at the managerial and professional levels for which the individual is qualified (there are ample openings today, but few people can meet management demands). Effective career planning demands a knowledge both of yourself and of the nature of jobs and the job market.

Personal Characteristics in Career Planning

How well do you know yourself? What should you know about yourself when you begin your career planning? Does it matter whether you are aggressive or shy, adept with your hands or clumsy, interested more in earning money or more in helping others? Of course it matters. Some of the more important personal characteristics in career planning include interests, needs, values, personality, abilities, education, environmental pressures, and characteristics such as sex, age, and ethnic background.

Interests, Needs, Values, and Personality Characteristics

If you are interested in your work, if the tasks you perform help satisfy your needs, if the purpose and methods of your organization are consistent with your values, if your personality characteristics are appropriate for the work, then you are very likely to be successful on the job. You will readily spend extra time on the job, and the time will pass quickly. You will not have the feeling, when you get up in the morning, "Nuts, another day of work. I'll sure be glad when it's over."

Unfortunately, not everyone is interested in his work or satisfied with what he does or with the organization for which he works. His work bores him. He spends each day looking forward to going home; each week, looking forward to the weekend; each year, living for the vacation.

Why do some people end up in a career they dislike? Perhaps they lacked the training or competence to do what they wanted; or else they misjudged their own interests and personal attributes; some may have wrongly estimated the degree to which they valued money or status or working conditions; and others have simply yielded to the demands of family and friends. Inevitably, there are those who never really planned their careers, but suddenly found themselves in the middle of a career before they ever stopped to figure it out.

Each individual has a unique pattern of interests, needs, values, and personality characteristics. Any one pattern is appropriate for certain careers but not for others. Police applicants, for example, have higher than average needs for achievement, dominance, and exhibitionism; they are also very masculine, but not especially interested in independence (Matarazzo, Allen, Saslow, & Wiens, 1964).

One recent investigation tried to determine what basic factors relate to career choice. The investigators found that a person's selection of a vocational field depends largely on the degree of importance he places upon the following: (1) having a good self-concept (desire to be popular, emotionally stable, or influential); (2) being personally comfortable; (3) enjoying artistic and creative tasks; (4) desiring prestige; (5) enjoying scientific and technical tasks; (6) being able to help others and to become personally mature. Students majoring in business placed above-average value on personal comfort; clergymen stressed the value of helping others; both nurses and secretaries indicated above-average

Figure 20–1.

Career fields differ in terms of both personal and training requirements. Can you see yourself as an automotive mechanic, personnel interviewer, or computer specialist? *Top:* Courtesy Parks Job Corps Center, Litton Industries. *Center:* Courtesy United States Steel Corporation. *Bottom:* Courtesy UCLA Public Information Service.

value on both personal comfort and helping others (Astin & Nichols, 1964). How much importance do you attribute to each of these six values?

Abilities

As the result of the dynamic interplay between heredity and environment, each person develops a unique pattern of **abilities** and potential abilities. Since different careers emphasize different ability patterns, an effective career plan tries to match the abilities of the individual to the requirements of the field. Both automobile salesmen and bank managers need to have good verbal ability, but the automobile salesman should have a different type of persuasive ability. A carpenter and a nurse both require a minimum level of ability with numbers, but the carpenter needs the ability to turn a blueprint into reality, and the nurse must be able to deal with ill patients.

How successful are you in maintaining good relationships with other people? Almost every job depends to some extent upon this ability, and some jobs—like that of a salesman, social worker, minister, or union organizer—depend greatly on human-relations skills. However, even skill in human relations has many facets, and much more than the ability and interest in getting along with people must be considered in career planning. The following hypothetical case combines several actual occurrences:

Evelyn Darcieux came to the counselor's office to discuss her career plans. "I don't have much of an idea of what I want to do, except I want to work with people." The counselor grinned a little. "Okay, if that's all you care about, you could be a missionary in Africa, or a policewoman on the narcotics squad, or a lifeguard, or a nursery school teacher. All these jobs involve the ability to work with people." Evelyn laughed, and the counselor continued, "Of course, the most important thing is to decide what kind of relationship you want with what kind of people. Very few of us have the ability to get along with all people under all conditions. Do you want to be in charge of people or work under people? Do you think you have the ability to persuade others or to learn to see through others when they try to persuade you? Do you have the ability to make decisions and risk being unpopular? Or do you prefer to carry through someone else's decision? Does your ability extend to all age groups equally? To normal people, to emotionally disturbed people, or to lawbreakers? Do you prefer a few people at a time or many? The same people every day or new people all the time?" Evelyn cut in as the counselor paused a moment, "I see—let me think about it."

When she returned a week later, she had given the matter much thought. "I think I know what I want, although, of course, I might change my mind later. But I think I want to work with adults, normal people. I'd like to work with the same people, rather than different ones; and I want to be in charge of people, even if I do become unpopular. Also I'd prefer to have close relationships with a few people, rather than more casual relationships with a large number."

Can you suggest some vocations that would meet Evelyn's criteria? Each individual has job-related abilities, but—like Evelyn—many people need help in relating their abilities to vocational fields.

Education and Training

Although many organizations give some on-the-job training, schools and colleges are responsible for teaching most job skills. Traditionally, colleges and universities trained managerial and professional personnel, and high school marked the end of training for everyone else. Today the junior colleges supply a stream of students not only to four-year colleges, but another stream directly into the job market. Careers in such fields as engineering, teaching, forestry, library science, or city planning require four years or more of college. Other careers are open both to junior college and to four-year college graduates, with sometimes the one and sometimes the other being favored. Such careers include: insurance salesman, police officer, free-lance writer, X-ray technician, dental assistant, auto mechanic, electrician, stenographer, nurse, printer, stockbroker, office manager, commercial artist, and television repairman.

Environmental Pressures

Although many people do not realize it, career planning is strongly influenced by several sources of environmental pressures, including family and friends. These pressures often operate unconsciously because they stem from values the student has internalized before entering college.

The son of a soldier killed in the Korean War has internalized the value that a professional Army career is dignified and worthy.

A young girl watches her mother wait tables in a restaurant and internalizes her mother's beliefs that office work is far preferable.

A young father, together with his son, spends hours working happily to keep the family car clean, efficient, and comfortable. The son grows up feeling that being an auto mechanic would be getting paid for having fun.

Pressures may be more obvious, for example, the father who offered his son a new sports car if he decided to study accounting, or the girl whose parents would not finance her college education if she majored in journalism.

Friends can also influence vocational choice. A person whose friends are all entering college is reluctant to admit that he has no intention of going. If everybody in a group of college women expects to become a career girl, their one friend who is interested only in marriage and a home may feel inadequate.

Sex, Age, and Ethnic Background

In certain vocational fields, success depends not only on ability, or even ability plus luck plus pull. Other factors, often having little or nothing to do with ability, are related to getting jobs and must be considered in career planning. These factors include sex, age, race, religion, and nationality.

Sex. In the United States, certain vocational fields are looked upon as being largely or strictly for men; these include engineering, medicine,* physics, construction work, radio announcing, and many factory jobs. Other careers, such as elementary school teaching, nursing, and many secretarial jobs, are thought most appropriate for women.

A person can, of course, enter a career traditionally associated with the opposite sex, although he may face discrimination both in receiving training and in getting jobs. Nonetheless, anyone who feels he will receive important satisfactions from such a career has the opportunity to prepare for it, and in spite of difficulties, openings are available.

Age. Some positions are closed to those who are too young, and others are closed to those too old. Even looking too young may be a problem. A competent personnel interviewer had difficulty getting a job, because he looked much younger than his 26 years, and the personnel director felt that prospective workers would take him for a teen-ager and be resentful. Looking older is an advantage for young people; looking younger may be an advantage for those in the latter half of their working careers.

Ethnic background. Members of certain groups find work unusually difficult to obtain, even when they have the necessary qualifications. The black American is probably the most severely punished by job discrimination, but Americans of Mexican, Puerto Rican, Italian, Greek, and Asian ancestry also meet frequent hiring and promotion problems.

* In Russia, over half the physicians are women.

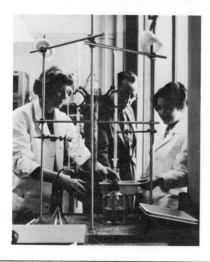

**Figure
20–2.**

Some women seek careers in
keeping with the traditional
feminine role, such as the job
of social worker or receptionist;
others achieve success in traditionally masculine fields such as
the natural sciences. *Top:* Courtesy Crippled Children's Society
of Los Angeles. *Center:* Courtesy
Office of Public Information,
Health Sciences Center, UCLA.
Bottom: Courtesy Antioch College News Bureau.

Jews, Catholics, and American Indians have similarly suffered from job discrimination.

A large portion of the difficulties faced by the black man, like those faced by women, result from a long history of being considered inferior. Because of economic and cultural deprivation, limited educational opportunities, and highly discriminatory hiring practices, many blacks have not seen education and training as relevant in their own job careers. Of course, they have been told of the importance of education, but being told by others and seeing the relevance yourself are different matters.

Americans of Mexican and Puerto Rican backgrounds have to overcome stereotypes, held in many communities, that they are not competent workers. Since many of these individuals have not been in the United States a long time, they may maintain somewhat different values concerning work and success and appropriate work habits. They were usually good workers in their own lands, but adapting to new styles of living and of working is often troublesome. In addition, their English is frequently poor, and they have lacked opportunity for job training. However, the discrimination they face in seeking jobs goes beyond what might be justified by these problems and can only be considered as, at least partly, the result of ethnic prejudice.

For a number of environmental reasons, many Mexican-Americans and black Americans are part of the lower socioeconomic groups. The following statement helps explain the effect that social class can have on vocational opportunities:

> Occupational choice is much more restricted in the lower classes . . . because of fewer opportunities for education and training, lowered expectations, ignorance of alternatives, need for early income, probably a greater stress on immediate gratification of desires, the lack of informed and sympathetic adult advice, and the greater operation of chance (Berelson & Steiner, 1964).

Even the black American or brown American with high competence has trouble getting a job. "We'd like to hire you as a salesman, but our customers are all white." "I'm sure you're a good engineer, but a lot of our employees might not understand." "Your experience as a nurse is fine, but our patients might not like it." "You can't get a job here without a union card and you can't get a union card without someone sponsoring you, and I don't know anyone in the union who would sponsor you." These are representative of the statements made when a minority group member applies for jobs. Among the questions he must answer are: (1) If he is interested in a career that seems closed to him, should he train for that position or for another position that might be easier to get—or both? (2) If he cannot find a job appropriate for his abilities and training in his own community, should he look elsewhere, take a lesser job, or fight for what he feels he deserves? (3) If he is offered a reasonable position by a company with an apparent policy of never promoting members of his ethnic group, should he accept it with the idea of proving himself or take a lesser job with more future promise? How would you decide such dilemmas?

Recently many employers have gone out of their way to hire people of non-Anglo backgrounds. Initially such hiring took the form of adding one minority group person and placing him conspicuously for visitors to see, then returning to old hiring practices. Often the person hired had high-level training. Slowly, however, some employers became aware that nondiscriminatory hiring had to be accomplished at all ability levels, and a few companies even instituted reverse discrimination, making special efforts to hire and promote minority group members to help equalize the previous imbalance. Federal and state laws have been passed to outlaw discrimination in hiring based upon sex, age, or ethnic background, but the success of these laws is still to be determined.

Other characteristics. Additional individual characteristics that enter into career planning include physical health and stamina, appearance and size, sensory acuity such as good vision and hearing, citizenship, criminal record, having a driver's license, and present marital status. By and large, you can evaluate the relevance of these characteristics to your career choices, and then determine how you qualify for each.

To plan a career, an individual should know about himself and about the variety of career possibilities. He needs to consider his own unique pattern of background, personality, and abilities and to relate these to what various vocational fields offer and require.

Job Characteristics in Career Planning

So far the discussion has emphasized the qualities of the job holder, but careful consideration of the characteristics of the job and the job market is also essential. Do you have a clear picture of the career field you intend to enter? What are its requirements? What does it offer you? Some of the more important considerations in evaluating a career field include the job market, job requirements, job description, working conditions, advancement opportunities, income and other material benefits, the social status of the job, and the opportunity for personal growth and satisfaction. (Figure 20–3 shows how one large group of college students evaluated the important aspects of their future careers.) Keep in mind that you may be well suited for more than one vocational field. How would you prepare under such circumstances?

Getting the Job

Even a good career plan loses some value if a student does not know how to look for a job. Many unnecessary frustrations may be eliminated by a carefully planned and conducted job search.

1. Begin to search for a position at least eight to ten weeks before graduation.
2. Use all available sources: classified advertisements, government job listings, friends and relatives, and college and other placement bureaus.
3. Apply to several organizations.
4. Be prepared to wait—personnel decisions may take several weeks.
5. Have references all lined up.
6. Have a well-executed biographical outline mimeographed; these outlines can be left with references, enclosed in letters to prospective employers, used to supplement application forms, and sent to friends to keep an eye out for you.
7. For job interviews, dress appropriately, be relaxed, and do not try too hard to impress the interviewer; honesty is the best policy.

The Job Market

Our country is a dynamically changing nation. Entire vocational fields are born and disappear each decade. Automation is eliminating certain careers while creating new ones. The funeral director, the kindergarten teacher, the commercial artist, the policeman, and the receptionist are all likely to be around for a while; but miners, railroad firemen, dock workers, and certain types of white-collar workers are going the way of the blacksmith.

Not all job fields are equally crowded. At any given time, certain career areas have an overabundance of qualified people while other fields suffer shortages. Also, the job market in your community may differ from the job market 100 or 1,000 miles away. Because of the changing nature of the job market, training and education beyond high school become important in providing career flexibility, so that you can move easily from one job field to a related one. Without a doubt, your career plan is made more effective by careful consideration of the job market, both present and future, and both local and national.

Job Requirements

Different vocations have different requirements. Experience, education, human-relations skills, and good written and spoken English are merely a few of the many types of demands that must be met to succeed in certain vocational fields.

Job requirements must be known before any career plan can be established. Many students talk casually about becoming dentists or atomic physicists only to learn to their dismay that these careers demand seven, eight, or more years of college. Others decide to become electricians or television stagehands and do not find out soon enough that they must enter a highly selective union.

Standards in many vocational fields are being upgraded. Sixty years ago, teachers and social workers did not even need a high school diploma in many states; but today most such positions demand a minimum of a college degree. The nurse, pharmacist, funeral director, librarian, and military officer have all seen their fields tighten requirements for entrance. Some states now demand that barbers, policemen, and real estate salesmen pass written examinations.

Earlier it was stated that career planning demanded an awareness of personal characteristics. Job requirements are the other side of the coin, and the career plan should attempt to match personal characteristics with job requirements. (You may prefer to consider job requirements as pertaining not only to getting the position, but also to success and satisfaction on the job.)

Job Description

What, precisely, will you be doing on your eventual job? Strangely enough, many students do not bother to investigate carefully. It sounds romantic to be an FBI agent, but what does he do on a typical day? Some girls think nurses spend all their time helping kindly old women and unhappy little children, but what do nurses actually do? The work of an airplane pilot or a reporter may seem exciting, but what do they really do?

Exactly what tasks do the potential jobs in your career field call for? Will you sell to people? Buy from people? Give orders? Take orders? Make decisions? Carry out decisions of others? Use a pencil? A lathe? A typewriter? Be subject to stress? To time pressures? Sit behind a desk? Work outside? Travel around the country? Around the city? The things

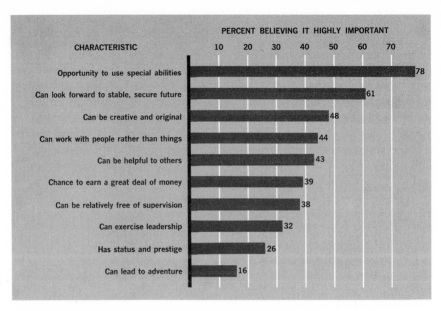

PERCENT BELIEVING IT HIGHLY IMPORTANT

CHARACTERISTIC	Percent
Opportunity to use special abilities	78
Can look forward to stable, secure future	61
Can be creative and original	48
Can work with people rather than things	44
Can be helpful to others	43
Chance to earn a great deal of money	39
Can be relatively free of supervision	38
Can exercise leadership	32
Has status and prestige	26
Can lead to adventure	16

Figure 20–3.

Career characteristics considered important by college students (Goldsen et al., 1960).

you do from day to day will be a controlling element in your enjoyment of your career. Too often people allow the **image** of their job field to blind them to the importance of the daily routines.

Working Conditions

Health, safety, cleanliness, comfort, having a private office and a personal secretary, being indoors or outdoors are working conditions that inevitably require consideration in career planning.

The forest ranger spends much time alone; the skilled automobile mechanic gets greasy; the beautician handles chemicals; the riveter works under noisy conditions (as does the nursery school teacher); the stockbroker wears a business suit and sits all day in an office.

Literally hundreds of potential factors determine working conditions, ranging from the hours, the shift, and the travel requirements to the dirt, the temperature, and the smells.

Advancement Opportunities

Advancement can come within a vocation or by changing to a related vocation, within a company or by changing companies. The plumber opens a plumbing-equipment shop and becomes a businessman; then he sells his business and is appointed vice-president of a company manufacturing plumbing equipment. Another plumber becomes increasingly successful, takes on several helpers, yet remains a plumber himself. Both have advanced.

Certain careers offer only limited advancement. To make matters worse, some positions look good at first and offer a fairly good salary; then, after several years, the employee realizes that he cannot advance and that he would have to take a severe salary cut if he changed jobs. These dead-end jobs are very frustrating, because a look into the future reflects an image of the present. To contemplate many more years of disagreeable work is hardly a pleasant thought, but, fortunately, additional education or training often enables a person to advance within his own company or to move to a better position elsewhere.

Income and Other Benefits

Some people have a great need for money, and others get along well on a moderate amount. One element of career planning is the evaluation of how the individual's needs would be satisfied by his probable income in various fields. Although such information is available, many students overestimate their own future income potential.

Salary is not the only form of payment. Various fringe benefits, including vacations and extra pay for overtime, cost large employers an estimated 27% of their payroll and are increasing twice as rapidly as base salaries (Zollitsch, 1964). The value of fringe benefits varies greatly from field to field and from job to job.

Social Status of the Job

When people are asked to rank jobs according to status, they do so with remarkable consistency (Deeg & Paterson, 1947), and the average rankings today are not much different from those of 30 years ago. One of the main reasons students attend college is to be able to get a "better" job, that is, a job with better social status as well as income.

Gene Machover had been working as a wholesale milk delivery man for 12 years. Unlike the door-to-door delivery man, who usually carries only two or three bottles at a time, Gene had to carry two or three dozen at a time. Considering his lack of job skills, the pay was good; but two things bothered Gene: (1) his income was remaining fairly constant and promotion was unlikely, since administrative positions were usually given to college graduates; and (2) his back was beginning to bother him. He began to look for a new career field and soon found a position representing a canned-goods producer. His job was to visit food markets to see that his company's products were well displayed, to introduce new products, and to take care of complaints. His initial income dropped by 30%, but Gene anticipated he could make that up over the years. In addition, he proudly listed other advantages: he drove a company car; he did not have to wake up at 4:30 in the morning; he could stay clean all day; and he had no heavy lifting. Also, his wife took pride in hanging white shirts on the clothesline instead of his uniform shirts.

Gene improved his working conditions, his advancement opportunities, and his job status, even though his income dropped temporarily. Evidence exists that higher-status positions lead to feelings of greater personal satisfaction (Hoppock, 1935).

Opportunity for Personal Growth

The purpose of career planning is to help the individual be as satisfied as possible with his career. If the career choice is appropriate, the person should find opportunity for personal growth and self-actualization. Work can be very satisfying when the individual is able to use his present talents and develop new ones, when he feels he has done a good job, when he feels his work has benefited others and that they appreciate him, when he can express himself through his work, when a challenge exists, and when the nature of the work is felt to reflect the individual's "real" self.

When a person feels he is no longer improving, no longer learning, no longer finding new ways to do things, he begins to mark time. The working day becomes a time to be gotten through as quickly and easily as possible, and important satisfactions come primarily from sources outside work.

Many of us think that a person must achieve something big in order to feel he is self-actualizing. The following is an example of just the opposite:

Elton Baintree * had a very small role in a Broadway show starring Helen Hayes. Although well into his fifties at the time, Mr. Baintree had never known an actress he had admired more than Miss Hayes. His great joy from merely sharing the stage with such a fine actress undoubtedly outshone the satisfaction some of the more important actors received from what, to them, was just another acting job. On one occasion,

---

* Elton Baintree is not the correct name of the actor. However, the remainder of the anecdote is as accurate as my memory of an incident that occurred over 25 years ago. The meeting with this exciting man made a great impact upon me at the time, and I still carry his enthusiasm with me.

*"It's not so much the money that interests me, as
the chance to do the kind of work I'm fitted for."*

**Figure
20–4.**

Finding personal satisfaction more important than income is common in many jobs.
Courtesy Ed Fisher.

Miss Hayes told him that his two lines (he had only three in the entire
show) brightened up the final moments of the second act. These words
were a great treasure for Mr. Baintree.

Mr. Baintree worked with his three lines and few minutes of action
to give more meaning to his role. Few people recalled him after leaving
the theater, but Elton Baintree gained a great amount of satisfaction and
personal growth from his work in the play. Not many people have Mr.
Baintree's gift for seeing a small part as having meaning in terms of a
larger production; neither do many have the ability to strive constantly
for growth and improvement.

Self-actualization is possible in any career. Like Elton Baintree, each
individual has the option of turning a small role into something meaning-

ful, or else he can just go through the motions and do an adequate job. One person can achieve great personal growth through being an artist or a writer; another will find maximum self-actualization by being a landscape gardener, a government official, a housewife, or an insurance salesman.

Each person is unique, with a unique set of abilities, interests, and other characteristics. Thus each person must find self-actualization through work in his own way. Planning for the career that seems to offer the greatest possibilities for self-actualization is a difficult but fruitful task.

Job Satisfaction

So far the discussion has focused on the broader outlines of careers, but within each career field are innumerable jobs. The person planning his career will eventually have to think in terms of specific jobs and the potential satisfaction each one offers.

Speaking primarily to those with some training after high school, the well-known management consultant Peter Drucker stated that job satisfaction depends less upon specific aptitudes than upon having a job for which the person is temperamentally suited (Drucker, 1968). Drucker suggests that the job seeker answer four questions:

1. Do I want security and a work routine I can depend upon, or do I want challenge and creative opportunity but with a high chance of failure?

2. Do I want a large organization, or do I prefer a smaller organization?

3. Do I wish to start at the bottom and work my way up slowly but upon a firm base, or do I want to begin much higher up and risk falling off?

4. Do I want to specialize, to become an expert in a small area, or do I want to be a generalist, to have breadth rather than depth (Drucker, 1968)?

These questions become particularly important in light of the fact that recent graduates often find their first postgraduate jobs a great disappointment. At least half leave their first jobs within a brief period of time (Schein, 1968). The frustrations met by the men investigated in this study were numerous. One of the biggest shocks was finding out that their ideas were usually rejected or ignored, even when they were specifically asked to come up with an idea and regardless of the value of the idea. They had just not learned enough about the human side of business and industry, and they expected their supervisors to respond in terms of business logic, rather than in terms of their own personal needs and biases. These new graduates also underestimated the resentment they aroused in management, who saw them as overly ambitious, impatient, immature, and inexperienced. The fact that they were often better educated than their supervisors merely added fuel to the fire (Schein, 1968).

To be a satisfying *first* job, the position should offer the employee the opportunity to test himself to see how good he is; the chance to learn and to grow and to make use of his abilities and education; the right to retain his integrity and individuality and avoid forced conformity; and the chance to work for an organization that is dynamic and receptive to new ideas (Schein, 1968).

Note the factors in Figure 20–5 that were considered most important in determining job satisfaction and those that led to dissatisfaction. The former related to what the person does, and the latter referred to the job environment (Herzberg, 1968). This result implies that the opportunity for self-actualization makes a job worthwhile, whereas a restriction of the work environment makes a job unpleasant. In an article that carefully reviewed existing research on job satisfaction, two psychologists (Zander & Quinn, 1962) found that job satisfaction was based upon the opportunity for self-actualization and decision making, satisfying relationships with co-workers and supervisors, and perception of self-adequacy through pay, status, and recognition.

Job satisfaction is important not only to the worker, but also to his

Factors Leading to Job Satisfaction	*Factors Leading to Job Dissatisfaction*
1. Achievement	1. Company policy and administration
2. Recognition for achievement	2. Supervision
3. Nature of work	3. Salary
4. Opportunity to take responsibility	4. Interpersonal relations
5. Opportunity for advancement	5. Working conditions

Figure 20–5.

Determinants of job satisfaction and dissatisfaction of engineers and accountants (Herzberg, 1968).

employer, since employees expressing high job satisfaction tend to do better work (Herzberg, Mausner, Peterson, & Capwell, 1957). Although exceptions occur, research shows that accidents are fewer, absenteeism is lower, and performance is better when employee attitudes toward work are good (Brayfield & Crockett, 1955).

Management personnel have become very much aware of the importance of job satisfaction. At one time, the emphasis in business and industry was to simplify jobs as much as possible, so that they could be done quickly and easily, without much thought. However, this simplification made the jobs dull and without challenge for many workers, and both production and turnover changed for the worse. As a consequence, **job enlargement** has begun. Job enlargement gives workers considerably more responsibility, a wider range of tasks, and more opportunity to make decisions regarding the method used or the best work pace; and in general, it produces jobs with higher skill-level demands (Hulin & Blood, 1968).

Job Success

What does it mean to be successful on the job? Some desire the satisfaction of feeling that a job has been well done and that the results have some meaning. Others feel success comes from money or fame or prestige. Still others consider themselves successful if they can be creative or test out new ideas or be equal to some challenge. Success means different things to different people, depending upon their personal needs.

What makes a person successful on a job? Some of the factors leading to success are fairly obvious: intelligence, education and train-

Characteristic	Percentage of Students Believing It Important
Hard work	62%
Personality	57%
Know "right people"	32%
Brains	31%
Luck	5%

Figure 20–6.

Qualities needed for advancement, according to college students (Goldsen et al., 1960).

437

Career Planning and the World of Work

ing, human-relations skills, appropriate personality, proper abilities, and effective career planning (recall the beginning of this chapter). Figure 20–6 indicates the characteristics that college students believe will lead to advancement, which is certainly one type of success.

Personal and emotional stability are also related to job success. The work adjustment of a group of young employed people was found to be higher when their personality adjustment, tested some years earlier, was better (Havighurst, Bowman, Liddle, Matthews, & Pierce, 1962); and anxiety seems to reduce work output (Hanes & Flippo, 1963). Various personality problems will affect job performance. The rigid person, although he might do well enough under normal conditions, may be unable to function in an unusual situation; an anxious person might communicate his worrying to others; and a fearful person might be afraid to make a decision.

Whatever qualities a person has, there is rarely a substitute for hard work in achieving job success. Hard work does not necessarily mean physical labor, nor does it mean that every minute must be spent poring over the drawing board, recording numbers, reading books, or oiling machines. Hard work means doing the job completely, on schedule, as well as possible, and every time.

It is true that some of our work customs, such as the reluctance to fire a man who is supporting a family, protect certain incompetent and lazy workers. It is also true that occasionally the fellow who plays the angles seems to succeed. In the long run, however, diligent workers receive the rewards. Ironically enough, when they are rewarded for hard work by being promoted to a managerial position, they find themselves working still harder. Professional and managerial personnel have much less free time than plant workers and office clerks (Lehner & Kube, 1964). However, the professional and managerial people enjoy their work more (Hoppock, 1935) and feel they accomplish more and self-actualize more, which may explain their willingness to work longer hours.

Success in Supervision

The role of the supervisor is more complex than many people realize. First of all, the supervisor must be able to perform many of the functions he supervises. A sales manager should be a reasonably good salesman; a charge nurse should have been a competent floor nurse. The supervisor must also make decisions and accept the blame when he is wrong. He must be able to get along with those whom he supervises and with those who supervise him. In addition, it is his task to communicate the messages of each group in the language of the other. For example, the superintendent of maintanance of a chain of banks may supervise 50 or 60 people, and he must communicate their feelings about their work and explain highly technical maintenance matters to a vice-president, who may know little about maintenance and may have had limited contact with the maintenance crew.

According to one expert, supervisors should base their actions on five principles:

1. *Fair evaluation of work.* Supervisors should give appropriate praise and criticism, taking care not to embarrass workers.

2. *Effective delegation of authority.* Supervisors must be able to know what tasks their subordinates can perform satisfactorily. Too many supervisors try to do too much themselves and do not know how to distribute work satisfactorily.

3. *Fair treatment for all.* All employees deserve equal treatment and need to be considered as worthy human beings.

4. *Availability to employees.* Supervisors should be available for employees to call upon them and discuss appropriate matters with them.

5. *Employee participation in decision making.* Employees often respond better when allowed to participate in decision making, even if they are used in a strictly advisory capacity. If the decision affects the employees, their reactions to the decision are important and their help may be valuable (Blum, 1956).

The same author also suggests that the supervisor avoid the following: (1) taking advantage of his superior position; (2) pretending he knows things when he does not, especially regarding the tasks at hand; (3) interfering with an employee's work or looking over his shoulder too much; (4) showing favoritism or discrimination; (5) criticizing employees in public; (6) spending too much time and effort on minor details; (7) giving orders that conflict with previous orders or with orders of other supervisors; and (8) giving unnecessary orders (Blum, 1956).

Government and business organizations have learned that employees wish to feel like a part of the company and to feel respected, unique, and important. A series of studies conducted 40 years ago showed that industrial production increased when employees felt they were meaningful to the success of the company. Later studies showed that feeling a part of the company did even more to improve production than did financial rewards (Roethlisberger & Dickson, 1939).

These realizations created a new problem, as well as increased success, for supervisors. They needed to recognize that financial rewards and various threats are not necessarily effective in improving production or reducing absenteeism. Supervisors today are encouraged to be sensitive to the feelings, the frustrations, and the needs of those they supervise. Although maintaining such sensitivity is not an easy task, it can pay rich rewards.

Being a supervisor carries prestige, opportunity for further advancement, and increased income, as well as more problems and more opportunities for satisfaction and self-actualization. Unfortunately, as many learn to their dismay, the qualifications for being a good supervisor differ from the qualifications for being a good worker.

Sources of Career-planning Information

For effective career planning, the student must have information both about himself and about the various vocational fields. Information sources for the latter are readily available, but learning about yourself is much more difficult and gives rise to some interesting problems.

Information About Vocational Fields

Many publications describe jobs and career fields. The college counselor or public library may have files of occupational information, including books, pamphlets, and even films discussing various careers. These sources give the income potential, educational requirements, advancement opportunities, work description, and other information relevant to specific careers. Much occupational information, however, paints an unduly attractive picture of the specified career and underestimates its disadvantages.

Good sources of occupational information include people currently in the field, people who have recently left that field, and college counselors, who usually have a large fund of information through their personal experience.

Information about the Job Seeker

Learning about yourself is difficult for several reasons: (1) Psychologists can measure some human characteristics with reasonable accuracy, but they have not been so successful in measuring personality attributes such as motivation to succeed on the job or ability to make sound decisions. (2) People often resist accepting their limitations or admitting their inadequacies. (3) People tend to interpret information about themselves so that they are placed in a favorable light. (4) Even when much information is available, it is not always known how this information about the individual relates to vocational fields.

Sources of Information Concerning Job Availability

Newspaper classified ads. Most newspapers have extensive listings of available jobs. By reading these listings for several months before the time for applying, a person can gain insight into the type of position he might wish. One warning is necessary: certain help-wanted ads, especially those recruiting commission salesmen, may exaggerate the earning potential or misrepresent the actual work to be done; following these up may be a waste of time. *Employment agencies.* The United States Employment Service has branches in all major cities in the country. The USES makes job arrangements without cost, and frequently maintains extensive job listings. Private agencies, however, will charge a fee either to the employer or the employee. Reputable agencies make this charge only if the person takes the job. Since the better private agencies often get job listings not available to the USES, their services are useful. It is better to pay an agency 10% of the first year's salary than to remain unemployed four weeks longer than necessary or to accept an inferior position.

Government Civil Service listings. The proportion of city, county, state, and federal government jobs has been increasing steadily over the years. Some of these positions require competitive written examinations, but others do not. Lists of available jobs, job requirements, and examination dates are easily obtained through the proper authorities.

Personal contacts. An amazingly high proportion of jobs are obtained through personal contacts. You hear of a friend who has been promoted, and the company needs to fill his position; your father's old Army friend is assistant manager of a furniture store, and you are interested in retailing and fulfill the job requirements.

Personal initiative. Sending a direct letter to the personnel director of an organization or making a personal call are very appropriate methods of job hunting.

Many colleges provide counseling facilities, where trained personnel can aid you in understanding yourself. In addition, the instructor of this course can probably give you help or can refer you to someone who can. Whether self-evaluation is done through a counseling center or in class, the individual will have to take into account his interests, his aptitudes and previous achievements, and his needs and personality.

Preparing for a future career is certainly one of the major purposes of college education in America today. Colleges provide training in skills necessary for jobs, and increase understanding and appreciation of others, of ourselves, and of the world around us, all of which may indirectly affect future job performance. Careers can be planned haphazardly, they can be virtually the result of a string of accidents, or they can be planned in a thoughtful, organized way. The characteristics both of

441

Career Planning and the World of Work

the individual and of the career field must be considered in such planning.

Summary of Important Ideas

1. Except for housewives, the disabled, and the retired, almost all adults work for financial return.

2. Choice of career and the subsequent success and satisfaction are highly significant in many ways.

3. Job success and job satisfaction are important to the adequacy of the self-concept and the enjoyment of life.

4. Students and others often lack the necessary information and understanding for career planning.

5. For an effective career plan, the individual should be able to evaluate his interests, needs, values, personality, and ability. He should also be aware of how his educational level, age, health, and other characteristics affect his career potential.

6. The individual planning his career also needs to be informed about the characteristics of the job and of the job market.

7. Different job fields offer differing opportunities and have differing requirements.

8. Vocational selection necessitates an awareness of the day-to-day demands of the job, that is, the job characteristics, as well as such factors as income and fringe benefits, working conditions, advancement opportunities, and the opportunity for satisfaction and personal growth.

9. Career plans should carefully consider the individual's temperament and personality needs. Finding a job with challenge and the opportunity for self-expression and personal responsibility is often important.

10. Job success is defined differently by different people. For some, supervisory responsibility is a sign of success, but supervision requires capabilities often not demanded for the job being supervised.

11. Numerous sources of information are available regarding jobs: for example, booklets, people in the field, college instructors, occupational-information files, and films. The student seeking a job who wishes to know more about himself can receive testing, counseling, and help with self-evaluation through the college counseling office or a comparable facility elsewhere.

Appendix I

*College Orientation**

College success depends upon more than attending classes and studying for examinations. It requires that you integrate your learning into something meaningful to you and related to your personal and vocational life. College administrators and faculty members provide many resources to help students achieve these goals. These resources include the setting up of a major, so that your courses can be taken in proper sequence and made personally and vocationally meaningful; a variety of campus activities to enrich student life in ways that the classroom cannot do; and many sources of information and counseling to help you make your own decisions concerning your future. As a result, it is hoped, each student will become aware of his own capabilities and of the skills and understanding necessary to develop these capabilities.

Planning Your College Program

Did you know what your major would be before you entered college? Have you changed your mind? Regardless of how you answered these questions, you will find many other college students like yourself. College not only provides courses for growth in understanding, information, and skills, but it also encourages personal growth and maturity through self-evaluation and sometimes painful reappraisals. The important thing to remember in planning your college program is to choose courses that make sense to you and lead to the goals that allow you the greatest use of your capacities. Thus, both vocational and personal considerations must be taken into account.

[handwritten note: Points to remember]

In deciding on a major, you might ask yourself the following questions:

---

* The markings in this appendix show how one person used emphasis marks while reading. See page 469 for further explanation.

1. Will this field help me become the sort of person I wish to become?

2. Will it provide the satisfactions I especially desire?

3. Will it be sufficiently challenging to provide the stimulation for self-actualization?

4. Will it provide a sense of accomplishment?

5. Will it help me reach my vocational goals?

6. Will it enable me to develop the talents I think I possess?

7. Will I be able to learn what I want to learn?

8. Will I enjoy the courses I must take and be able to take the courses I want to take?

9. Will I be able to take courses with the faculty members I want to get to know?

Are there any questions you would wish to add?

Selecting Your Courses

You have only limited freedom in deciding which courses to take. You must, for example, satisfy any general requirements set by the ① college for all students; second, you must satisfy all field requirements established by the professors in the department of your major; and third, ② you may need to satisfy certain options allowed for your major, which ③ give you some leeway. Then you may select from a great variety of courses to complete your graduation credits.

You will be further limited if you wish to transfer to a similar program at a similar college or to a much different program at a much different kind of college. In either case, you will need to consider the demands of the college you wish to enter and the demands of the college you are now attending.

Since the courses required by your major, your minor (if you have one), and your general program account for most of the units needed for graduation, you will have only a limited number of free-elective courses. What criteria can you set up to determine which free electives to take? One guideline, which some students follow carefully, is the "will-it-help-me-make-a-buck" criterion. Each possible elective is evaluated by its potential contribution to future income, and the student registers for the courses that pay off the most financially. *one possibility*

The author does not favor this approach. The time you spend in college may be your best opportunity to sample the great store of knowledge and understanding available through higher education. Your free electives offer you the chance to investigate topics about which you have always been curious, or to take a course with a highly regarded *Author's Bias* professor, or to fill what you consider to be a gap in your educational background.

Did you enjoy art classes in high school? Try a course in figure drawing. Do you find pleasure in reading poetry to a friend? Register for a literature course. Do you feel you need to know more about fixing automobiles? Sign up for an introduction to auto mechanics. Do you hope to travel? Take a cultural and political geography course. Do you think you might run for political office some day? Try a course or two in political science. Have you thought about increasing your enjoyment of leisure? Try photography or cooking or creative writing or stage design. Do you want a real intellectual challenge? Consider advanced courses in philosophy or math or history or science. The possibilities are limited only by your time and your energy.

A great deal of discussion is heard about whether a student should take more courses in his specialty or whether he should experiment more. A survey of college graduates showed that about one-third wished they had specialized more and one-fifth felt they had specialized too much (Havemann & West, 1952). Thus, the degree of specialization desired seems to be a matter of individual taste.

Survey results for exam

Selecting Your Instructors

You may have trouble evaluating professors, since the most common source of information is other students, who have well-known biases. Sometimes one professor will strongly recommend another, but faculty members are reluctant to show partiality. If you use student evaluations, learn why your informant feels as he does: the business-law instructor is liked by Jack Gerson because he knows his field, but disliked by Ed Meadows because he is frequently sarcastic. The sophisticated student will check on faculty members through several different sources, learning not only whether they are liked, but—more important—*why* they are liked and *for what classes* they are liked.

important to author

The College Catalogue

Although most students probably read their college catalogue before entering college, they too often ignore it once they begin to take classes. This neglect is unfortunate, since the catalogue contains not only descriptions of courses and requirements for majors, but also such information as the history of the school, available scholarships and loans, the academic background of the faculty members, graduation requirements, and a host of rules and regulations. Consider a few of the questions answered in the catalogue:

1. What courses are required to graduate in your major? How many units are required in the major? In a minor? In general education courses?

2. Which set of rules do you operate under if a new catalogue appears during your second year on campus and changes the requirements?

3. If a college regulation creates a particular hardship for you, what can you do about it? For example, if your college requires three credits of speech, but you completed a similar two-credit course at another college, can you arrange to meet the present obligation? What system of petitions does your college have?

4. What is the meaning of "probation" at your school? How long can you remain on probation? How do you get off probation?

5. What does the grade *Incomplete* signify? How long do you have in which to make it up? What happens if you do not make it up? It is amazing how often students wait until the last minute to make up an Incomplete, only to find out the professor is on leave, or that he is no longer willing to administer an examination that should have been taken ten months earlier, or that he has taken a job elsewhere.

6. Your campus has an outstanding professor who is an excellent lecturer, but you do not wish to take his course for credit. Can you arrange to listen to his lectures?

7. How do you compute your grade-point ratio? What would the grade-point ratio be for the following, assuming A equaled 4 points: English, A (3 credits); Psychology, B (3 credits); Physical Education, B (1 credit); Shop, C (3 credits); Government, C (3 credits); Chorus, C (1 credit)? *be Able to figure GPR*

8. Can you get credit for any course by taking an examination instead of the course itself?

9. How much time do you have to drop a course without risking a failing grade? What is the deadline for dropping courses that you are passing?

10. If you fail a course, then take it over and get a C, how do you compute your grade-point ratio?

11. How can you arrange to take a course at another college during the summer and transfer the credits back to your own college?

12. What courses require prerequisites, and how important is it to have had the prerequisites before registering for a course?

Appendix I

Campus Activities

Keep
in
mind

The academic program is assumed to be the most important part of college life. However, American colleges usually provide extensive activity programs, some with little or no relationship to specific course work. Since your future growth and satisfactions will certainly not come completely through your vocation, your on-campus growth and satisfaction need not come solely through classroom experience.

Colleges provide a wide assortment of social, athletic, creative, and political activities that contribute to the learning process. Faculty and administrators essentially accept the value of these activities, although they show concern when students begin to ignore their classwork because they become so involved with activities.

In the 20 years between 1930 and 1950, several studies indicated that students who participated in activities also received better grades (for example, Gustad, 1952), earned more money after graduation (Jepsen, 1951), and were better adjusted (Stone, 1951). However, more recent research suggests that this situation might have changed (Kalish & Bartos, 1960; C. Watson, 1965). Since *Sputnik* startled American educators into placing greater emphasis on academic work, many of the better students no longer have the interest or the time to participate in school activities. The effects of this recent trend, which has been observed both in high schools and in colleges, are still unknown.

Social Organizations and Social Activities

Although many campus organizations include a social program along with their other activities, most campuses have social clubs that promote social affairs for their own members and, on occasion, for the entire student body.

Pros
&
Cons
of
Social
Clubs

These clubs, especially if they have the status of fraternities and sororities, are simultaneously much admired and much disliked. The negative responses are based upon the clubs' selection practices, which emphasize racial, religious, and social-class factors; snobbery in restricting dating and other social relationships; numerous instances of organized cheating and violation of college regulations; and demands for conformity. Those favoring the clubs cite their efforts in building school spirit and school loyalty, their participation in student government, their promotion of sincere friendships among members, and their value in providing contacts and experiences that will be useful after graduation.

College Orientation

Social activities, however, are not limited to members of organized groups. Colleges provide a variety of social programs, ranging from Saturday-evening formals to coffee-shop bull sessions. Social life has a definite place on campus. It breaks the routine of study, provides relaxation and enjoyment, and has educational value, since students are responsible for much of the planning and organizing of social activities.

Dangers in an exaggerated social life occur both for club members and for nonmembers. Social life can become too time-consuming and energy-consuming for anyone who lets it. Even the seemingly harmless coffee break may stretch into a two-hour session.

Athletics

Is the college athlete *the* "Big Man on Campus"? Or is he "just a slob who gets paid to play football"? Both interpretations are heard on our college campuses. One psychologist did learn that athletes (in high school, however) tended to become leaders during flight training with the United States Air Force (Krumboltz, Christal, & Ward, 1959). We can all point to certain well-known figures, such as Supreme Court Justice Byron White, who were once athletes. Some psychologists do believe that team sports "build character" and are "a great leveler in a democracy" (McKinney, 1960).

In spite of this and additional evidence, we do not actually know whether intercollegiate competitive sports have a beneficial effect upon the participants. Certainly the pressures to win are sufficiently great at some colleges that all else becomes secondary, including studies. The author was told by one of his students that he had seen a nationally famous football player rifling the drawer of a professor's desk to look at the next day's examination—the player had bribed the janitor to let him into the office. (The student, by the way, was also on the football team and was amused rather than disturbed by the incident, which had occurred several years earlier.) This is, of course, an isolated incident, but it does show the pressures under which college athletes are placed by their extremely demanding schedule.

In addition to having a handful of athletes who participate in intercollegiate competition, many colleges encourage all students to join in intramurals and informal athletic activities as much as possible. The opportunity for exercise is good for students who spend most of their day sitting in the classroom, the library, and the snack bar. Also, since exercise is recommended for the postcollege years, college is an excellent time to develop your capability to play whatever sports you enjoy and can easily continue after you leave college. Some examples that fit these criteria include tennis, volleyball, handball, golf, archery, swimming, and bowling. (After all, how many of you will have access to the people and the facilities necessary for football, baseball, or basketball after you leave college?)

At the very least, athletics provide a source of achievement, an opportunity to let off steam, good exercise, an expression of teamwork and cooperation, and a competitive challenge. Both the participant and the observer can profit, although the former receives much more than the latter. When athletics are at their finest, they approach the heroic. When they are corrupt, they corrupt the entire campus.

learn
this—Exam
quest.

The Arts

Many schools offer their students the opportunity to participate in dramatics, music, art, dance, photography, debate, and both creative and journalistic writing. As with athletics, the training is available to those few with professional hopes and to the many who wish to express themselves and gain satisfaction through a leisure activity.

The United States is at present going through what some have termed a "culture boom." Hundreds of communities have established amateur theater groups; dozens of big and small cities have their own orchestras; art exhibits are seen everywhere; and hundreds of magazines offer authors of fiction, nonfiction, and poetry the chance to be published. College is an excellent place to begin to develop your own talents in one or more of these activities, which can lead to much leisure-time satisfaction and pleasure in the years following college.

Student Politics

Student politics fall into two distinct and almost unrelated categories: student government and off-campus politics. Each offers excitement and experience—and hazards.

Student government provides a training for future community leaders. Students receive valuable experience in administration, making decisions, influencing others, learning their own capacities and limitations, and—to some extent—learning the complexities of political action. Some campuses have dozens, perhaps hundreds, of opportunities to participate in student-government committee work each year.

Unfortunately, most students ignore their governing body except for a flurry of excitement around election time. The similarity to the national lack of interest in government is obvious and distressing. Although some student apathy undoubtedly results from the student government's power being so limited, the greater part probably stems from plain indifference.

Renewed interest in campus politics occurred when students began to feel that they wished to participate in the decision-making processes

*Figure
Ap I–1.*

Both athletics and the creative arts have a place on college campuses. *Top:* Courtesy UCLA. *Bottom:* Courtesy California State College at Los Angeles.

in their colleges and universities. Student concern—and, frequently, protest—touched upon such issues as the role of the ROTC on college campuses, university support for war-directed research, ethnic discrimination in admissions policies and practices, initiation of black-studies centers, and campus disciplinary practices. These issues were quite different from the matters that occupied student officers in the past (for example, dorm hours or disbursing funds for dances), and it is entirely possible that campus politics of the future will be involved with overall college policy.

Off-campus politics is another matter entirely. From the end of

Figure
Ap I–2.
       "Remember the good old days—when it was just panty raids?"

Student activities have changed since 1950. Courtesy Ed Fisher.

World War II until the early 1960s, students were frequently criticized for not paying sufficient attention to the nation and the world. Then students became involved in national politics, initially with the civil rights movement and later with the peace movement. The candidacies of Barry Goldwater in 1964 and Eugene McCarthy in 1968 also aroused considerable enthusiasm among the 18- to 22-year-olds.

Although only a minority of students ever participated in off-campus politics, those who were involved received attention far out of proportion to their numbers. This interest occurred partly because the news media gave them extensive coverage; but the student activists apparently had the sympathies of many people both on and off campus, and they were ② addressing themselves to important issues. Many community leaders ③ preferred that students get excited over football games and dormitory hours, to keep them away from involvement with the major policy issues of the day. Beginning in 1965, the more active students had divorced themselves from student government and were demanding participation */new trend/* in making significant decisions previously reserved for faculty and administration and for local leaders (see Chapter 19).

Nonetheless, most college students, like most of their parents, continued to avoid any political involvement other than voting and criticizing. Why do you suppose this lack of interest occurs? Are the students afraid to be associated with certain movements? Are they too involved in their own small world of classes, dates, and part-time jobs? Do they feel so set apart from the world or so powerless that activity seems a meaningless gesture? Are they "playing it cool," remaining emotionally uninvolved? Do they prefer to let others do the work for them? These are *think about this* some of the explanations offered. How would you explain it?

A variety of campus activities, in addition to those mentioned, are conducted at many schools. Some examples are a social and educational club in which foreign and American students can meet; an organization to help tutor children from culturally deprived areas; preprofessional clubs for students with interest in nursing, teaching, psychology, or business management; clubs affiliated with different religious groups; and national and international groups like Phi Beta Kappa, National Student Association, and World University Service.

Campus activities allow a change in routine, lead to personal growth through social opportunities, give some students the chance to excel, and encourage artistic and creative endeavor. Also, some learning is directly related to later job demands, especially in human relations and leadership.

Special Groups with Special Adjustments

Compared to the college of 50 years ago, the college of today has *try to learn* more older students, more working students, more married students, and more foreign students. Each of these groups has its own special challenges to success.

Appendix I

Older Students

Most tax-supported colleges and junior colleges have a substantial number of students in their thirties and older. At some colleges, one-fourth or more of the students are 30 years old or older. The needs motivating these students to return to school include such practical desires as more rapid promotions, higher income, and more flexibility in shifting to a new job field. Other motives include the desire to understand more of the world, to receive better insight into oneself, and to experiment with new areas of knowledge. If this author's observations are accurate, older students are more aware of the significance of self-actualization. Many of them have left well-paying jobs to return to college; others add college courses to their normal workload at the sacrifice of leisure. These students have come to college precisely because their present situation does not allow them the opportunity to use their capacities, and, often in spite of good incomes, they are frustrated by the lack of creative, challenging opportunities.

Working Students

I disagree, look for more info.

The combination of work and study can actually improve study effectiveness, *if* the combination does not demand too much time and too much energy. Full-time students can work up to about 12 hours a week without harming their studies, but beyond that their grades go down (McKinney, 1960). The work-plus-study load a person can successfully carry varies greatly from individual to individual.

get general idea

A study conducted just after World War II showed that nearly one-fourth of all male college graduates and about one-tenth of female graduates had put themselves through college solely with their own earnings; only one in six men and less than half the women were financed fully by their parents. However, working during college showed little relationship either to grades or to participation in college activities (Havemann & West, 1952). Today, an even higher proportion of students earn part or all of their college expenses.

Married Students

fact to remember

Between 25% and 30% of all college students currently enrolled are married, many of them also being older and working (see above sections). Regardless of age or work status, they all share the problem of having important family responsibilities in addition to their study demands. Their academic success depends upon the cooperation of their spouse and, sometimes, of their children. Financial problems are often pressing. Nonetheless, research shows that the grades of male students are higher after marriage than before (Wilder, 1967).

One particular danger of student marriages, especially if both husband and wife are young, is that the husband, who usually continues in college, may become more intellectually aware and demanding, while his wife is too busy with her work and her household to have time for reading or studying. Many wives of students make a special effort to find

Figure Ap I–3.

Married students are a common sight on college campuses. Photograph by John G. Warford.

time for keeping up with their husbands, but others are in possible danger of realizing too late that their spouse has drifted away.

International Students

An estimated 74,000 international students were studying in the United States in 1965 (estimate of International Institute of Education). Some foreign students are supported by their governments or the United States government; others are financed by their parents, the college they are attending, or themselves. They come from the familiar countries such as Germany, France, Japan, and Italy, as well as from little-known lands like Nepal, Sudan, Gabon, Kuwait, and Surinam.

Foreign students, fearful of how they will be treated by American students, often spend a great deal of time with each other and do not get to know the country in which they are studying. Foreign students are frequently a much better source of information on some subjects than are textbooks or professors. At the same time, they need the opportunity to learn about the United States, so that they may take back to their own countries a friendly and realistic interpretation.

Foreign students have major adjustment problems when they begin their studies in the United States, and they again must make an adjustment when they return to their own countries. One typical pattern is to feel excited and elated upon arriving in the United States; to become increasingly frustrated and unhappy after the initial enthusiasm wears off and the problems of adjusting to an alien culture make themselves felt; to learn to deal with these frustrations and enjoy the educational experience; to return to the home country and find changes in themselves that make them less fit to live in their home country; and to learn to deal with this second set of frustrations and readjust to their own country (Gullahorn & Gullahorn, 1963).

Confusing—
look
over
Carefully

Sources of Help

Extensive facilities are available on some college campuses to help students cope with their problems and make the most of their capabilities, although other schools have almost nothing. College students state time and time again that they are interested in discussing their problems with someone, but those same students often neglect the opportunities when offered. Over 40% of the residents of a women's dormitory at one university expressed a desire to meet with a counselor of some sort (Will, 1957); at another large state college, over 80% of the entering freshmen signed up for noncredit, voluntary freshman-orientation discussion groups that met weekly.

which Came
first —
Chicken
or Egg?

Those students who do seek help seem to benefit from it. Counseled students get better grades, participate more in activities, and appear better adjusted than a group similar except for counseling (Gustad, 1951). One study showed that before counseling began, counseled students received lower grades than noncounseled students of equal ability; after counseling, both groups were getting the same grades, suggesting that the counseling definitely helped (Ivey, 1962).

good
Study

Two cautions need to be sounded: first, counseling is not magic, and some students profit little or not at all from counseling; and second, students should consider other help provided by the college besides direct counseling.

Occasionally, someone expresses the view that getting help is for weak people, and that strong people go it alone. Such an attitude wins neither wars nor college degrees. Actually, the strong person is willing to accept help when it is needed, since the help is aimed at getting him to help himself use his capacities better. *[handwritten: Sounds like me 2 yrs. ago.]*

The reason for seeking counsel may range from wanting the answer to a simple question about course requirements to wishing help in dealing with a highly disturbing emotional problem. Although colleges do not provide all the facilities an individual might need, someone will at least be able to refer him to the proper facility.

Faculty Adviser

At most colleges, each student is either assigned to a faculty adviser or encouraged to request such an assignment, usually with someone in his major field of concentration. The primary task of the faculty adviser is to counsel the student concerning the academic program, the selection of courses, the interpretation of rules and regulations, and vocational and personal goals.

The faculty adviser—and most other faculty members as well—are willing to listen to a student's problems, either personal or academic, and to try to be of help. However, the mere fact that someone is a professor (or doctor or lawyer or teacher) does not automatically make him competent to deal with such problems. Aware of this limitation, many faculty members will refer students to other campus facilities or, occasionally, to off-campus agencies.

Counseling Centers

Most colleges have some sort of counseling center where students can discuss virtually any kind of problem with someone trained in counseling. The counselor may be a clinical psychologist or psychiatrist who is especially qualified to discuss more disturbing personal and emotional problems; or he may be a specialist in student personnel work and more interested in study problems, vocational problems, or academic planning. Counselors will combine discussion, supplying of information, and psychological tests in their sessions.

College counseling centers perform two major functions. (First,) *[circled: 1]* counseling may give necessary information: Can I shift majors without losing credit? Can I get credit for military service? Are jobs available for people like me after I get my degree here? What courses outside my major would help me become a good short-story writer? (Second) counsel- *[circled: 2]* ing helps the student understand himself better. He learns about his abilities and interests through tests, about his qualifications for certain job fields through occupational information, and about his own personality and motivation through discussion with the counselor. Sometimes counseling requires consideration of personality problems more properly in the province of a clinical psychologist or psychiatrist. Under such circumstances, the counselor may continue to see the student regularly over a period of time, or he may refer the student to another individual or to an agency in the community.

This very brief description of counseling may make it appear simple; it is not. Learning about ourselves is much more difficult than it might seem. Everyone has weaknesses he does not wish to expose to others. Sometimes, you are not even able to see past these "blind spots" yourself:

> Don Griggs had decided, during a stint in the Army Medical Corps, that he wanted to be a surgeon. He knew that high school science courses had given him trouble, but he felt he could make it up in college. By the end of his first year in college, he had a C average in his nonscience courses and a D average in his science courses. The low grades put him on probation. When he went for counseling, he learned that his aptitude tests showed him to be very weak in science. He even admitted to the counselor that he did not like science courses, but he insisted that he wanted to go to medical school. After two difficult years in college, Don re-enlisted in the Medical Corps.

College Medical Facilities

Most campus medical facilities offer a variety of services, ranging from dispensing nosedrops to emergency service for broken legs. Some colleges, especially those with dormitories, usually include extensive medical care and even hospitalization on campus. The dispensary may also give immunization injections, provide consultation for weight problems, and offer many sorts of medical advice.

Library

One of the best sources of counsel and information is the college library. Here you can find the wisdom of the centuries (admittedly, along with a great deal of ignorance). A staff of trained professionals, often specialists, is available to help you locate what you wish. Do you have a religious conflict? What did St. Augustine say? What would Albert Schweitzer or Paul Tillich say about your conflict? Are you confused about your major? The library has biographies of famous men and women in your future vocation; it also has a collection of information about job opportunities. Are you having trouble filling out your income tax? The library has books on how to do it.

Other Sources

A variety of individuals affiliated with colleges can supply advice or other forms of help. These sources include the college pastor or other religious advisers, residence-hall advisers, the veterans' adviser, the foreign-student adviser, and the job-placement counselor. At the same time, individual faculty members have information and contacts; after all, business and government leaders frequently come to professors for advice.

Sometimes, when the need for help results from a severe emotional problem and when campus facilities are inadequate, the student may wish to look for help in the local community, although these resources often require a lengthy waiting period. Someone on the college faculty or in the administration can usually help a student locate an appropriate community facility or provide the name of a competent psychotherapist. If help is not available at his own school, a student can contact another college or university in the area to get such information or ask a local physician or minister for a referral. The Yellow Pages of the telephone book usually carry a list of psychologists and psychiatrists, but not all of them are necessarily qualified. Since many "psychoquacks" masquerade as qualified psychotherapists, a person seeking help should make certain he is using the proper channels.

— Not in Dictionary

Sometimes an attempt to obtain help meets with frustration. You get yourself all ready to talk with someone and then find that all appointments are booked for ten days. Or you finally decide to get low-cost psychotherapy and learn that your community has no facilities. It is best to be persistent. Once you have taken the first step, make certain you get the help you desire.

In general, college campuses provide innumerable resources for those needing help, but, unlike in high school, help rarely comes looking for the student. In college, the student must take the initiative.

A Final Word

This appendix has covered some of the topics discussed in a college orientation course, but others have been ignored on the assumption that they are already well known to you. For example, this discussion has said nothing about the importance of learning where things are located on your campus, about knowing the history and traditions of your college, about the value of school spirit, or about the specific majors available on various campuses.

Perhaps the most important point is one mentioned in Chapter 19: a college is a community of scholars who come together to share their learning and to try to learn more. The more you participate in this community, the more you will gain, the greater maturity you will develop, and the greater feeling of accomplishment and satisfaction you will have.

Summary of Important Ideas

1. Success in college depends upon more than attending classes and studying for examinations; it depends upon integrating learning into something meaningful and relating it to other facets of life.

2. The student must decide what his major field of study will be; sometimes he must select a minor.

3. The student must select his courses and try to choose effective teachers.

4. Campus activities are available at most colleges. They may supplement course work, may relate to future vocational goals, or may seem totally unrelated to either, but lead to personal enjoyment, personal growth, or pure relaxation.

5. Campus activities include social life and social clubs, spectator and participant athletics, the arts, and both on-campus and off-campus politics.

6. Older students, married and working students, and international students have their own special problem areas.

7. Most campuses supply numerous sources of help for students, including faculty advisers and counseling centers.

Appendix II

Study Methods*

At various points in the book, suggestions have been made for improving study methods, for instance, applying learning principles to study, using the SQ3R method to study textbooks, and establishing goals to improve study effectiveness. In this appendix, some additional methods for improving study effectiveness are outlined. For those who have taken study-methods courses, the following pages will serve as a review; for those who have not had such a course, these pages will provide some concrete suggestions. However, since your present course is not in study methods but in human behavior, the author does not feel it appropriate to present a full treatment of the topic here.

This appendix will cover time schedules, note-taking, notebooks, textbook reading, examinations, and term papers.

Time Schedules

Several things must be kept in mind when making out a time schedule, in addition to the caution "Be realistic":

1. Balance. A balance of academic work, social life, campus and off-campus activities, and outside work if appropriate is desirable.

2. Flexibility. A time schedule is to serve you, not to run your life for you. Therefore, a good schedule will permit a certain amount of easy substitution, so that last-minute opportunities and unexpected demands can be handled.

3. Own time. College is not preparation for life. College *is* life. The years of college should not be seen as mortgaged against a day when "real life" will begin, but should be viewed as a part of real life. Therefore, you deserve a certain amount of time that is completely your

---

* Appendix II has been adapted from *Making the Most of College* (2nd ed.), by Richard A. Kalish, © 1969 by Brooks/Cole Publishing Company.

own and that can be spent in any way you wish, regardless of what is "good for you."

4. Health.   Without physical health, a student cannot achieve any goals. Consideration, then, must be given to adequate time for meals, rest and sleep, and some exercise.

5. Time intervals.   The length of time a student can study will depend upon many factors, including the type of work the course demands, the student's level of ability in that course, and the time of day and fatigue level when the study occurs. Some students study more effectively in the morning or afternoon, and others are night owls.

Figure Ap II–1.

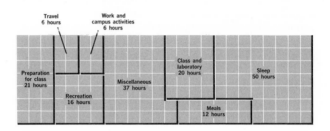

This chart shows how a sample of University of Hawaii students used their time during a seven-day period (Dole, 1959).

6. Breaks.   Each student must determine his own ability to work without becoming fatigued, and he must learn to schedule his breaks accordingly. Short breaks, five to ten minutes per hour, are long enough to have the desired effect of reducing the feeling of monotony, without letting the student get too involved with other matters and without wasting time.

Some students carry such a heavy load that for them the above comments are irrelevant. One student in this category was a 30-year-old man who had a wife and two children and who held down a full-time job while carrying almost a full-time course load. Thanks to a cooperative family and an excellent ability to organize his time, he was able to continue like this for five years until getting his degree. Many who have attempted such a schedule have found it impossible.

Constructing a Study Schedule

First, using a schedule like that shown on page 462, fill in all hours that cannot be changed, such as class and laboratory hours, transportation to and from campus, and eating and sleeping times. You might wish to make a preliminary schedule for one week as you observe how you can actually spend your time.

Second, using a different-colored pencil, schedule your flexible commitments during the remaining hours. Estimate the number of study hours each course is likely to demand, and schedule them accordingly. Also schedule time spent on campus activities, social life, and work. In doing this, consider the following suggestions:

Specify the particular course you will study, rather than merely marking "Study" on the schedule.

Allow from 50 to 90 minutes for studying each course at any one time interval. Less than 50 minutes is usually inefficient; more than 90 minutes can be boring or fatiguing.

Make effective use of in-between hours, such as the hour from the end of your 9:00 A.M. class to the beginning of your 11:00 A.M. class.

Try to schedule study time for a class just after it has ended or just before it begins.

Allow three to five minutes before and after each class to review lecture notes and textbook notes relevant to that class.

Allow about 20 minutes between the end of studying in the evening and going to bed; this is to help you unwind.

Leave a couple of free hours on Sunday to review all the work from the past week.

Make use of free minutes. Waiting for the bus, sitting in the barbershop, or waiting for a late appointment all provide a few minutes during which certain types of study are possible. These moments are useful for memorizing foreign language vocabulary, silently rehearsing a speech, or proofreading a composition.

Give yourself the luxury of *at least* one full evening a week as your own time.

Third, once the schedule is made up, carry it with you for a week and look at it from time to time to see how well you are following it. If it is impractical to follow, make changes, but allow sufficient time to accomplish the required study for each course. Flexibility is necessary, since unexpected personal and academic events constantly occur. In such cases, make certain that for each hour that is changed from "Study" to "Meet airplane" or "Type term paper," you change another hour back to "Study," at least for that week.

Fourth, keep one copy of the final schedule near your study desk and carry another copy with you for immediate reference. Remember that the schedule belongs to you; you do not belong to it.

The importance of a study schedule cannot be exaggerated. There

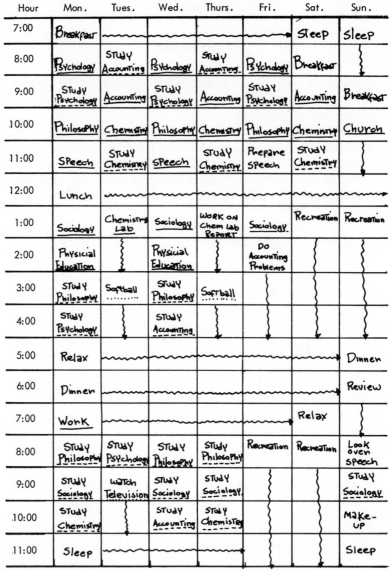

Hour	Mon.	Tues.	Wed.	Thurs.	Fri.	Sat.	Sun.
7:00	Breakfast					Sleep	Sleep
8:00	Psychology	Study Accounting	Psychology	Study Accounting	Psychology	Breakfast	
9:00	Study Psychology	Accounting	Study Psychology	Accounting	Study Psychology	Accounting	Breakfast
10:00	Philosophy	Chemistry	Philosophy	Chemistry	Philosophy	Chemistry	Church
11:00	Speech	Study Chemistry	Speech	Study Chemistry	Prepare Speech	Study Chemistry	
12:00	Lunch						
1:00	Sociology	Chemistry Lab	Sociology	Work on Chem Lab Report	Sociology	Recreation	Recreation
2:00	Physical Education		Physical Education		Do Accounting Problems		
3:00	Study Philosophy	Softball	Study Philosophy	Softball			
4:00	Study Psychology		Study Accounting				
5:00	Relax						Dinner
6:00	Dinner						Review
7:00	Work					Relax	
8:00	Study Philosophy	Study Psychology	Study Philosophy	Study Philosophy	Recreation	Recreation	Look over speech
9:00	Study Sociology	Watch Television	Study Sociology	Study Sociology			Study Sociology
10:00	Study Chemistry		Study Accounting	Study Chemistry			Make-up
11:00	Sleep						Sleep

Figure Ap II–2A.

Name _____Tom Frosh_____

Tom Frosh's schedule for one week.

is little difficulty in constructing one, but there may be considerable difficulty in adhering to it.

Tom Frosh's Study Schedule (See Figure Ap II–2A.)

Tom's college is on the semester system, and Tom is majoring in business administration. He is taking three-credit courses in psychology, accounting, English, and speech, plus a two-credit data-processing course

Study Methods

and a one-credit physical education class. Accounting takes a long time, particularly with having to work out the problems; English and psychology take a little less than the expected amount of time; data processing comes easily; and speech makes no demands except immediately before the six talks Tom has to give. Physical education is strictly an activity class at Tom's college.

In addition to the specifically assigned study hours, Tom has allocated several hours a week as *flexible time,* some during the day and

Week beginning	Mon.	Tues.	Wed.	Thurs.	Fri.	Sat.	Sun.
Jan 6	Registration for self	Registration for new students	First day of class		Date-Ted	Date- George	
Jan 13					ℓ Begin work English theme Date-George?	Date-Ted ? Prepare speech	
Jan 20		Brief Speech	Is theme almost done?		English theme	Last day drop class	Study for English quiz
Jan 27			English quiz				
Feb 3	Prepare Speech	Basketball Is theme almost done?	Brief Speech		English theme	No date History midterm	STUDY HISTORY
Feb 10	History midterm	Study Broadcasting	Lincoln's Birthday →	Broadcasting Midterm Basketball			Prepare Speech Study English
Feb 17		Brief speech	English quiz Theme?		English Theme	Major Dance George	
Feb 24	Finish first draft English theme					Leap Year Dance George	Father's birthday
Mar 2	Finish final draft English theme	Basketball Long Speech			Basketball History paper	Begin Intensive study History	Type English theme
Mar 9	Begin intensive study English	English major theme			Begin intensive study BDcasting	No dates!! Finals!!	Brush up Public spking
Mar 16	S	Final Exam History T	Final Exam Broadcasting U	D	Final Exam English Y		

Name ▶ *Jean Coed*

Figure Ap II–2B.

Jean Coed's schedule for the coming quarter.

some during the evening. These flexible hours are to allow for the extra time demands of studying for exams, working on term papers, or compensating for time lost through illness. Later in the semester, he might use some of these hours for playing volleyball or for participating in a social club. Notice that Tom has kept four evenings a week for himself.

Not only does each week need scheduling, but a schedule for the entire semester or quarter is also useful. Note how Jean Coed uses this device.

Lecture Notes

Both the form and the content of lecture notes are important, although the content is the more vital. In order to increase the value of the content, it is necessary to listen and evaluate critically, rather than to attempt to scribble down every word of the lecture. It is usually best to determine the important elements of the lecture and to try to grasp its organization (true—some professors seem to have no organization to their lectures, but most do), and then to include the important facts and the lecture organization in your notes. The form in which notes are taken is also important. The form a student uses provides organization to his notes.

*The Paragraph Form**

Form influences organization—must have some method, show major points, secondary, relationship between these, details. Paragraph Form —easiest, poorest, write until idea changes, begin new para. Sentence Form—more difficult, but better; numbered statements, minimal organization. Standard Outline Form—best organization, most *difficult;* uses Rom. numerals, letters, numbers, indentation to show org. Dash Outline Form—adaptation of SOF, but uses dashes not symbols; good organization, simple. Preference: SOF and DOF, perhaps combine.

As you can readily observe, this form shows organization through the use of punctuation. However, good organization is difficult to de-

---

* The decision to use short phrases for certain samples of note-taking and sentences for others was made arbitrarily.

velop. Also, reading over notes written in solid paragraphs may become tiring.

The Sentence Form

1. The form of taking notes is important.
2. It provides organization by showing major points, minor points, their relationship to each other, and details.
3. The paragraph form is the easiest to use and the poorest.
4. For the paragraph form you write a paragraph until the idea changes.
5. The sentence form, a little more difficult and a little better, is a series of numbered statements.
6. The standard outline form is the best for organization, but the most difficult to use.
7. It uses roman numerals, letters, numbers, and various types of indentation.
8. The dash outline form is a variation of the standard outline form, but uses dashes instead of symbols.
9. It has organization, and avoids the complexity of the standard outline system.
10. The standard outline form and the dash system are best, although you may prefer to combine forms.

The sentence form uses no organization to speak of, but it is a little easier to read than the paragraph form.

The Standard Outline Form

I. Form of taking notes
  A. Form is important
  B. Form provides organization
    1. Major pts
    2. Minor pts
    3. Relationships between them
    4. Details

II. Comparison of forms
  A. Paragraph form
    1. Easiest
    2. Poorest
  B. Sentence form
    1. More difficult
    2. Better

   C. Standard outline form
     1. Best for organization
     2. Most difficult
     3. Indenting
     4. Symbols
   D. Dash outline form
     1. Like standard
     2. With dashes instead of complex symbols
     3. Fairly simple
     4. Good organization
III. Preferable: standard or dash or a combination

This form shows good organization. Major points fit under minor points, and the method of indenting emphasizes the organization.

The Dash Outline Form

—Form of taking notes
  —important because provides organization
    —major points, minor points, relationships between them, details
  —Paragraph form
    —easiest, but poorest
    —write until idea changes; begin new paragraph
  —Sentence form
    —more difficult, but better
    —series of numbered statements
  —Standard outline form
    —best for organization, but most difficult
    —uses roman numerals, letters, numbers, indentation
  —Dash outline form
    —like standard, but uses dashes
    —has good organization
  —best: standard or dash
    —may combine forms

This form is similar to the standard outline form, but omits the complex system of symbols. Although it gains in simplicity, it does lose a little in organization by depending solely on indentation for form.

Sample Lecture Notes

Figures Ap II-3A and Ap II-3B are based on the following excerpt from a classroom lecture:

It really does make a difference how far a student sits from the professor in a class. There are students who always come in late and sit far away from the professor. These tend to be the students who do not do very well. Of course, because they come in late, the professor feels that they probably aren't interested. Yet I had one student, a girl—she was editor of the campus newspaper and very active on campus. She came in late to one of my classes and would sit far in the back; sometimes, although not often, she would cut class. She received excellent grades in my class and in every other class. I wondered about this until I learned that she studied diligently and compensated for coming late. And in spite of sitting far in the back, she paid close attention to what was going on in class. As a matter of fact, she sat in the back just to prove it could be done, because she didn't believe what I said about sitting in front.

As I recall, it was largely because of her that I ran a little experiment in class. Of course, it wasn't a real experiment in technical terms, but I did it just for fun and to see what would happen. The day after an examination, I passed a piece of paper around the class—I didn't have required seating in the class and there was plenty of room for students to spread out in the classroom—and asked the students to write their names according to where they were sitting. Then I divided the class into three groups: the first group consisted of the 40 students sitting in the first four rows; Group *B* consisted of the 20 students sitting in the next three rows; Group *C* was made up of the remaining 20 students—they spread out for at least eight to ten rows.

Sure enough, just as I figured—the first group averaged the grade of low B—; the last group, those in the back, averaged a low C—; the middle group averaged a little above a straight C. I think that proved my point.

I'd say several factors influenced this result: (1) better students tend to seek out positions in the front of the class; (2) students sitting farther back have more distractions, more moving heads in front of them, more opportunity to look outside the window or through open doors. I remember one student who became fascinated by a couple holding hands outside of the classroom. He couldn't keep his eyes off them—kept looking through the window and paid no attention to class. Later I found out it was his best friend and a former girl friend—oh, well. Another reason is that students who sit in the back are often under the misapprehension that they can write letters, sleep, or daydream without being noticed. At any rate, you should try to avoid sitting in the back of a classroom, especially if the room is large. I'd say any seat in the front half is all right.

Notebooks

Good notebooks, like many other study aids, show much individual variation. Approaches successful for some people may be unsuccessful

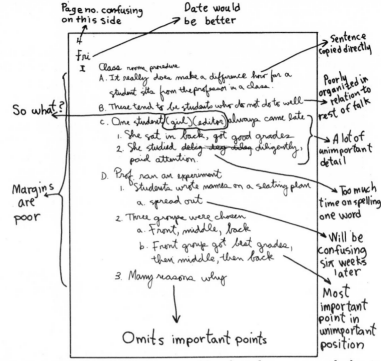

Page no. confusing on this side →
Date would be better →

→ Sentence copied directly

Poorly organized in relation to rest of talk

So what? →

→ A lot of unimportant detail

Margins are poor →

→ Too much time on spelling one word

→ Will be confusing six weeks later

Most important point in unimportant position

Omits important points

Figure Ap II–3A.

This outline shows many obvious errors, although it does cover much that is important. Organization is poor, and important points are missed. It would be difficult to read and understand this material eight or ten weeks later.

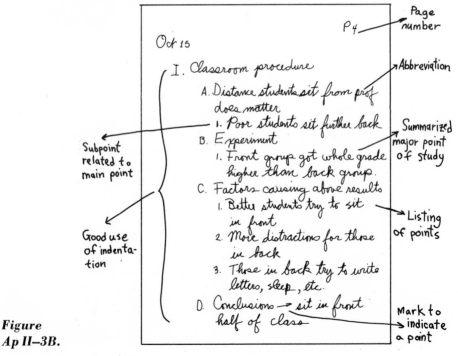

Page number →

Abbreviation →

Summarized major point of study →

Subpoint related to main point →

Listing of points →

Good use of indentation →

Mark to indicate a point →

Figure Ap II–3B.

A good set of lecture notes.

for others. The suggestions listed below have been found useful by many students. Before evaluating their effectiveness, use them for six to eight weeks so they can become part of your pattern of study habits.

—Use a standard 8½″ × 11″ notebook. Large notebooks are often awkward to carry and worse than awkward to spread out on the arms of chairs; small notebooks lead to cramped writing.
—Use a notebook or spiral book, rather than a clipboard, loose sheets, or tear-off pads.
—Write your name, address, and telephone number inside each notebook.
—Enter the date each time class begins.
—Number each page.
—Separate reading and lecture notes.
—Keep each course separate from other courses.
—Try to use a fountain pen or ballpoint.
—Use only one side of the page for taking notes. The other side is then available for comments, questions, doodling, assignments, and a summary paragraph of each day's notes.
—Use an appropriate outline form.
—Indicate your own ideas to differentiate your thoughts and interpretations from the lecturer's comments.
—Use your own words whenever possible.
—Use emphasis marks.
—Be brief, but be explicit.

Studying Textbooks

An excellent approach to studying textbooks, the SQ3R method, was described on page 74. This section will merely add a few suggestions on how to take SQ3R notes and how to mark textbooks. Look back at Appendix I to see the way one person applied emphasis marks while reading it. The SQ3R notes taken by this person are shown below.

How do you plan a college program?
you figure out what you need
for your major and minor
and other required courses,
then try to get good instructors.

What is the purpose of the College Catologue?
  To provide information

What kinds of Campus activities are there?
  Social activities, athletics, creative art, and student politics

What are the special student groups?
  Older, working, and married students -- much overlap -- and foreign.

What are the sources of help?

  Faculty advisors, community agencies, and counseling center.

Examinations

Most examination questions can be categorized as either objective items or essay questions. Objective-test questions can be answered by one or two words or by indicating which of several alternatives is correct; essay questions requiring writing from as little as a couple of sentences to as much as several pages. Sometimes an examination will involve showing your skill in doing something, such as typing, performing a mechanical operation, or demonstrating proper nursing procedures upon a dummy; such examinations demand a different type of study from that described below. However, the common belief that essay and objective exams require different types of study is highly dubious.

A number of suggestions can be made about how students can prepare for and take examinations.

Study Methods

Preparing for Examinations

—Try to predict what questions will be asked. The Q step of SQ3R should be helpful in this effort, and your professor has undoubtedly given hints. Perhaps you will be allowed to look at back exams your professor has given.

—Keep up to date in your study. This is probably the most important requirement for effective preparation, since last-minute cramming has numerous hazards.

—Get a good night's sleep before the examination.

—Schedule extra time for study before the exam, but remember that time allocated to study is worthless if not combined with concentration.

—Don't overlook cramming *in addition to* distributed learning.

—Try studying with others taking the course, but make certain that you spend the time studying and asking each other questions, not having a bull session and debate over the merits of the instructor and the course.

—If it is to be an essay exam, practice writing answers to questions you predict.

Taking the Examination

—Read *all* directions carefully.

—Try to figure out how long the exam will take. Space your efforts to complete the exam and to give some answer to every item.

—Read each question all the way through, including multiple-choice questions, even though you think you know the answer after reading the first few words.

—Unless there is a penalty for guessing, put down some answer for every question, and guess on multiple-choice items.

—Don't spend too much time on any one item, but be sure to mark an omitted item so that you remember to return to it.

—If you are using an IBM answering sheet, follow directions carefully.

—Be careful to observe such words as *explain, describe, evaluate,* and *list,* or *probably, tendency,* and *always.* Answer accordingly.

—To review (if you have time), cover the answers to your questions; then try to answer the question in your mind, and compare your new answer with your previous answer.

—If the test consists of a few long essay questions, spend a couple of minutes outlining each answer before writing it; also use a brief introduction and a summary or concluding statement.

—Longer answers are better than shorter answers, unless you have to "pad" or bring in irrelevant information.

—Be as careful as possible with grammar and spelling and try to write legibly.

The multiple-choice and true-false forms of examination are frequently used at the college level. Photograph by John G. Warford.

—Be careful to answer the question that is asked, not some related question.
—Proofread essay tests. Double-check objective tests to make sure you have answered every item.
—When you get the examination back, check over not only your errors but also your correct responses. This is an excellent method for *overlearning*.

**Figure
Ap II–5A.**

Examples of good and poor essay answers.

---

1. Evaluate the French Impressionist movement in modern art:

STUDENT A:

The French Impressionist movement included men like Van Gogh, Gauguin, Renoir, and Matisse. These men used to meet frequently in Paris cafes and discuss their progress. They didn't paint exactly what the thing they were painting looked like, but they brought in shadow effects and painted impressions, such as the name of their movement indicated. They were not very popular at that time, but have subsequently become popular, although I still think they are silly.

STUDENT B:

The French Impressionist movement signaled the breaking from traditional, photograph-like art. Its followers made use of shadow effects and impressions rather than exact likenesses. The movement enabled painting to free itself of having to stick by so-called reality and to make greater use of imagination. The artists became less restricted, experimented in color and form, and created many new schools of art. At the same time, freedom seemed to be licence for some artists, and they moved to painting abstractions, which - in my opinion - retarded the field of painting.

Both of these students knew the material quite well, although the latter expressed himself much better. The major difference, however, is that the first answer does not evaluate, but rather describes, the movement—until the final clause in which the writer "evaluates" by saying he doesn't like it. The second answer shows greater depth of understanding, as well as a grasp of the meaning of the question.

Figure Ap II–5B.

2. List the four presidents preceding Eisenhower and state one accomplishment of each:

STUDENT A:

Truman – War in Korea
Roosevelt – Depression, War with Europe
Hoover – helped Belgians
Coolidge – Prosperity.

STUDENT B:

Harry Truman – prosecuted Korean War almost to its conclusion
F. D. Roosevelt – led the country through depression and through the Second World War
Herbert Hoover – developed programs to try to offset the depression
Calvin Coolidge – led the country during great prosperity

Appendix II

The first answer is satisfactory, but minimally so. Hoover's work with the Belgians took place before he was President and was not so important in its impact on the United States as his attempts to curb the depression. The second answer, although also very brief, expresses the ideas much more clearly.

Figure Ap II–5C.

3. What is SQ3R and how does it work?

STUDENT A:

SQ3R is a method for reading textbooks with greater efficiency. It works by making the student pay greater attention to what he reads. This is achieved through the five steps: (1) Survey – skim the chapter and read the summary. (2) Question – turn headings into questions. (3) Read – read the section under the heading. (4) Recite – answer the questions of the Q-step. (5) Review – review notes and perhaps skim again and read summary.

STUDENT B:

SQ3R is when you read Textbooks by using five things – you survey, question, read, recite, review. You survey when you look over the chapter; you question when you makeup questions; you read when you read; you recite when you answer questions; Then you review

The first answer gives a fairly good, brief response, covering both parts of the question. The second makes several errors: (1) it never states what SQ3R is; (2) it uses very poor grammar and rhetoric; (3) it answers superficially and vaguely.

Figure Ap II–5D.

4. Compare the problems of the student sitting at the back of a classroom with one sitting at the front. (This question is based on the notes taken earlier.)

STUDENT A:

At the back, the student has lots of distractions and he thinks he can dream, while he really can't because Professors know what They are doing. Students in front dont have these Problems.

STUDENT B:

Students sitting in the back of a classroom find more distractions. the heads of the students in front of them, the opportunity of looking out the window – I guess if its a fellow, good-looking girls – all these are distractions. In back he is more likely to be with other students who are not good students, but who may be writing letters or daydreaming or goofing off. The students in front, on the other hand, may feel that other students think they're polishing the apple.

STUDENT C:

Sitting in back of a classroom brings about trouble to a lot of students. They sit back there and they find that they don't do as well as students who sit up front. Those up front, according to one experiment, get better grades. They are also better students, while the ones in the back of the class are not so good. I think sitting in the middle is about best.

The first answer is minimal. Student A remembered two facts from the lecture and put them down with no imagination and with poor organization. He also said nothing about the problems of students up front. The lecture had made no mention of such problems, so the students answering the question were called upon to think on their own. Student B gave a very informal answer, but he covered the ground quite well. Student C used a lot of words; however, he said almost nothing, and, as he continued to write, he lost sight of the original question and began to answer a different question.

Writing Papers

Term papers have several purposes. They enable you to pursue a topic in greater depth than the classroom situation permits; they acquaint you with the wide variety of available source materials; they permit you to work independently; and they require that you integrate the thinking of several other people and evaluate their work.

Steps in Writing a Term Paper

1. *Selecting the topic* is usually the first and, often, the most important decision that must be made. Choose a topic that interests you and one that can be adequately covered within the limits of your projected paper.

2. *Scheduling the work* is necessary, since term papers are assigned in addition to other studying, and they are too often postponed until the last minute. Somehow, they always take more time than you originally anticipated.

3. *Collecting sources* can begin as soon as you know your topic.

4. *Collecting ideas* can begin at the same time.

5. *Reading and taking notes* starts as soon as you have collected sources. As you read, you will undoubtedly supplement your original collection of sources.

6. *Outlining the paper* before beginning to write is essential for any paper over a page or two. You can use one of the outlining methods described in the section on note-taking.

7. *Writing the first draft* can be done quickly if the outline is well-constructed and complete. Introductory and concluding paragraphs are usually important.

8. *Revising the paper* depends upon how much effort was put in on the outline and the first draft. Different people have different styles; some prefer a painstaking first draft with little revision; others set down a quick first draft, then revise it carefully.

9. *Prepare the final copy* carefully. You may want to show it to someone else or read it to yourself right before this final step.

10. *Proofread* the paper before handing it in.

Miscellaneous Study Problems

Some study problems may arise from home or dormitory conditions. For example, you must learn to contend with distractions. You may need to ask other students to quiet down or—more probably—find another

Study Methods

"I don't care whether I really understand Pragmatism or not—
as long as I can pass the exam about it."

Figure
Ap II–6.

Have you ever heard yourself making this comment? Courtesy Ed Fisher.

study area. Even parents may need to be asked to cooperate—four out of five college freshmen in one survey complained that parents hindered their study in one way or another, most commonly by family conversations, walking through the study room, parental attitudes, and television and household noise (Feinberg, 1963). Although students do become accustomed to noise—sometimes even to chaos—relative quiet and privacy are normally best for study.

You may have noticed advertisements in newspapers offering you easy ways to study or to learn. One of these methods is a device that supposedly enables you to learn while you sleep; another is a speed-reading program that makes fantastic promises; a third promises you unlimited ability to concentrate; a fourth guarantees you an amazing memory. The sleep-learning device, according to research (Simon & Emmons, 1955), is next to worthless and may even rob you of sleep. Some of the other programs have merit, but they should be evaluated carefully.

Appendix II

Before buying an expensive package with extravagant claims, see what your campus has to offer. The valid aspects of these programs are often incorporated into programs on your campus. However, if after checking into a commercial program, you feel it is worth your while, give it a try, but make certain that you follow the instructions carefully and complete all the requirements.

Appendix II has attempted to outline some of the more important elements of effective study, supplementing what has been written elsewhere. For more thorough discussions of study methods, see the following books:

Kalish, Richard A. *Making the most of college.* (2nd ed.) Belmont, Calif.: Brooks/Cole, 1969.

Libaw, Frieda B., & Martinson, William D. *Success in college.* (2nd ed.) Glenview, Ill.: Scott, Foresman, 1967.

Morgan, Clifford T., & Deese, James. *How to study.* (2nd ed.) New York: McGraw-Hill, 1966.

Pauk, Walter. *How to study in college.* Boston: Houghton Mifflin, 1962.

Robinson, Francis P. *Effective study.* (Rev. ed.) New York: Harper, 1961.

Voeks, Virginia. *On becoming an educated person.* (2nd ed.) Philadelphia: Saunders, 1964.

Your instructor or your college counselor can suggest other books and sources of study-methods materials, some of them specifically related to the problems that concern you. The ability to study effectively is too important to leave to chance or casual learning. It requires an ability to be self-critical, a willingness to try new approaches, and a desire to continue to seek methods of self-improvement.

*Glossary**

Ability: The actual power to perform an act.

Achievement: The present level of competence in performing a particular task.

Adaptation: A change in the organism permitting it to cope with the demands of the environment; for example, sensory adaptation is a change in the sensory apparatus that permits it to cope with changes in the environment.

Affective disorders: A group of psychotic reactions characterized by inappropriate emotional response and mood.

Agitated depression: A type of affective disorder in which depression is marked by considerable, often rapid, movement.

Alcoholic: A compulsive drinker; an individual who cannot control his drinking. An alcoholic is *not* the same thing as a heavy drinker.

Alienation: The feeling of being isolated from the general community and from reference groups.

Amnesia: Lack of memory under circumstances in which normal forgetting is unlikely.

Anxiety: An unpleasant emotion, similar to fear, marked by a vague feeling that something unpleasant is going to occur in the future. Because of the vagueness of the cause, it is very difficult to overcome anxiety.

Anxiety reaction: A form of neurosis in which the person is in a constant state of anxiety (*see* Anxiety).

Apathy: In the sense used in Chapter 14: a withdrawal from emotional threat by retreating into a position of not caring, although the unconscious feeling may be that of caring very much. Sometimes used as a defense mechanism.

Approach-approach conflict: A conflict in which two positive goals are available, but the selection of one goal eliminates the possibility of selecting the other.

---

* In devising these definitions, the author has leaned heavily upon *A Comprehensive Dictionary of Psychological and Psychoanalytical Terms,* by Horace B. and Ava C. English, published by Longmans, Green, 1958.

Approach-avoidance conflict: A conflict in which the same goal has both positive and negative features, so that it attracts and repels simultaneously.

Aptitude: The potential to gain competence, assuming that training and experience are available (*see* Achievement).

Attention: The active selection of and emphasis upon one aspect of the environment at a time; the relative limiting of what is responded to.

Attitude: A continuing, learned tendency to behave in a consistent way toward an object or class of objects.

Auditory: Pertaining to hearing.

Authoritarian: A method of control or leadership in which the individual establishes procedures and judges results without others sharing in the decision-making process.

Autonomy: The ability to control the environment or be self-regulating. Closely related to independence.

Avoidance-avoidance conflict: A conflict in which both alternative goals are repelling, and the individual has to select one or the other.

Behavior: The acts an organism performs; anything an organism does.

Behavior therapy: A form of psychotherapy that makes substantial use of operant learning and reinforcement.

Belief: An emotional acceptance of an idea or statement upon what the individual considers adequate grounds; the individual has not necessarily examined the bases for his beliefs, but may have accepted them without evaluation.

Biochemistry: The chemical basis for and functioning of plant and animal, including human, life.

Body-image: The image or picture an individual has of his physical appearance and physical body; may include clothing, hair style, deformities, and hidden scars.

Brainwashing: The process of causing an individual to alter his attitudes, values, or behavior in the direction of those guiding the process; a number of specific techniques are involved. Brainwashing is one form of persuasion.

Case-history method: An intensive study of a single individual, utilizing a great variety of sources of information, such as school records, vocational evaluations, interviews, medical records, tests, and family history.

Glossary

Catatonic schizophrenia: A form of schizophrenia marked by frequent apparent stupor; extreme excitement and activity are occasionally exhibited.

Chronic anxiety: An emotional state in which feelings of anxiety are continually present.

Chronic brain syndrome: A condition, frequently psychotic, that results from relatively permanent, largely irreversible damage to brain tissue.

Classical conditioning: A form of learning in which two stimuli are presented close together in time on numerous occasions until the response caused by one stimulus is also elicited by the second stimulus, although the latter originally did not produce this response.

Clinical psychologist: A psychologist who is involved with studying or treating individuals with mental illness or personal-adjustment problems.

Compulsion: That which forces a person to do something or feel or think something against his "will"; may contribute (as a ritual form used to ward off an obsessive thought) to the form of neurosis termed obsessive-compulsive reaction.

Concept formation: The abstraction of a common quality from several stimuli, or the generalization to a common quality from several stimuli; for example, the sky, your friend's eyes, the ink in your fountain pen, and your new sweater all share the common quality of *blue*.

Conflict: A type of stress produced when a person is motivated by two or more needs, in such a fashion that the satisfaction of one need is believed to mean the nonsatisfaction of another need, or that the satisfaction of one need is believed to involve unpleasant consequences.

Conformity: Behavior, including attitudes and judgments, that complies with the demands and expectations of a particular group; the behavior may or may not be consistent with the values of the person conforming.

Conscious: Referring to the state of being aware of what is occurring.

Control group: A group of subjects, similar in every way possible to another group of subjects *except* that the latter group is treated in some predetermined fashion, so that any differences between the two groups after the experimental treatment can be tentatively assumed to result from the treatment conditions.

Conversion reaction: A form of neurosis in which the person displays such bodily symptoms as paralysis or sensory loss (blindness, deafness) without corresponding biochemical changes.

Counseling psychologist: A psychologist whose primary interests are in research and treatment involving people with vocational and academic problems or those needing information and rehabilitation. His work overlaps with that of the clinical psychologist.

Cross-sectional: In research design, refers to the study of variables at one point in time (*see* Longitudinal).

Culture: The pattern of all behavior and of all material things that members of a society have adopted, shared, and communicated to future generations.

Defense mechanism: An attitude or other form of behavior which is used by the individual—without his awareness—to maintain the adequacy of his self-concept.

Deficiency-motivation: The process of satisfying needs for things the organism lacks. Hunger is a deficiency motive, but the desire (or need) to enjoy food is a growth motive (*see* Growth-motivation).

Delusion: A false belief. A person may have the delusion that he is president of the world, that he is a great baseball player, or that his family is stealing all his money. Although these delusions indicate severe personality disturbance, less serious delusions can also occur.

Demographic: Referring to the study of human population, including changes and distributions.

Depressive reaction: A form of neurosis in which depression is the major symptom.

Derived status: The position one has in the community as reflected from the status or accomplishments of a parent or other relative (*see* Primary status).

Developmental psychologist: A psychologist whose primary interests are in the development of human behavior, with special emphasis on a particular age group (for example, children, the aged) or on principles of development throughout the life cycle.

Discrimination: (1) In learning, the act of learning to recognize the difference between two stimuli and to respond accordingly; (2) in social psychology, the act of showing preference to one individual or group as opposed to another.

Displaced aggression: Redirected aggression, or hostile action directed away from the real cause of the aggressive or hostile feeling and onto another victim (*see* Scapegoat).

Displacement: The redirection of feelings, often anger or dislike, from the original cause usually to a less harmful person, object, or idea. The implication is that the person is prevented from directing his feelings toward the appropriate object. Occurs without awareness, and is often a defense mechanism.

Dissociative reaction: A form of neurosis in which the primary symptom is dissociation, that is, the separation of mental processes so that they cease to have the normal association between idea and emotion.

Distributed practice: Learning spaced out over a period of time, with intervening rest periods or periods of other activities; studying one hour each day for an examination would be an example.

Drug addict: An individual who takes drugs compulsively; he has developed a strong need for a particular drug and may display bodily changes if deprived of it.

Dynamic: A condition implying change, in which a change affecting one aspect of the organism instigates other changes that may affect the initial change; for example, a gradual self-concept change, from submissive to moderately aggressive, will lead to new experiences that, in turn, may affect the direction of change in the self-concept.

Educational psychologist: The psychologist whose primary interests are in educational testing and measurement, curriculum planning, evaluation of teacher and pupil effectiveness, and other educational problems.

Effector organs: The cells and structures with which the organism responds: muscles and glands.

Emotion: A feeling or state of arousal of the organism which stirs it to observable action or to internal change.

Engineering psychologist: The psychologist whose primary interests are in studying and improving the effectiveness of man's use of machines of all sorts.

Enuresis: Bed-wetting that occurs well beyond the age at which the child can be expected to maintain control; the term can be applied to any uncontrolled act of urinating.

Esteem needs: Needs, as adapted from Abraham Maslow, for an individual to be respected by others and to respect himself.

Ethnic group: A group of individuals sharing a common language, religion, national origin, race, or cultural heritage.

Ethnic-group identification: The feeling of having membership in a particular ethnic group; association and affiliation with an ethnic group.

Experimental method: A research method in psychology and other fields. Implies a systematic approach in which one group of subjects is given one set of conditions and another group of subjects, another set; or in which the conditions are systematically varied to determine the effect of the change.

Experimental and physiological psychologist: A psychologist whose primary interests are in studying the biological bases for human behavior, animal behavior, learning and emotion, sensation and perception, and related matters.

Exploratory need: The need of an individual, especially an infant or child, to examine his environment.

Extinction: In learning theory, the diminishing and eventual cessation of a response to its stimulus.

Fantasy: (1) An image that occurs as part of the thought process and that is fairly coherent; the image of a dream or daydream; (2) a type of withdrawal through daydreaming; sometimes a defense mechanism. The term may also be applied to a situation in which an individual purposely relives a previous action, rehearses a future action, or attempts some creative activity.

Feedback: A direct report regarding the effect of one's behavior upon others.

Forgetting: The inability to recall because of attention lack, disuse, or inability to make associations.

Fraternal twins: Twins, not necessarily similar in appearance and not necessarily of the same sex, resulting from two separately fertilized eggs.

Frustration: The unpleasant emotional state that results when a person's desired goal is blocked.

Fugue or fugue state: A lengthy period of amnesia or lack of recall for past events while previous learning of skills and other aspects of life are remembered. The person may wander from his home and live under another identity.

Functional psychosis: Mental illness caused by stress that exceeds the individual's stress tolerance; caused by environmental stress, as opposed to direct biochemical changes.

General-adaptation syndrome: A theory that physiological changes in the human body in response to stress occur in three stages: alarm reaction, resistance, and exhaustion.

Genetic: Pertaining to, or occurring as the result of, genes. Genes are elements that control many characteristics of the child and are transmitted from parents to child at the time of conception.

Group: A number of individuals having some characteristic in common.

Group decision: A decision made with the participation of the entire group and achieved with the active or tacit consent of each member of the group; a decision arrived at not by vote but by general acceptance.

Growth-motivation: The process of activating behavior as the result of satisfying the need to make use of one's capacities and talents (*see* Deficiency-motivation).

Growth spurt: The relatively sudden increase in growth that occurs shortly before puberty.

Guilt: The feeling, giving rise to discomfort or anxiety, that one has violated moral principles.

Guilt society: A culture in which internalized values and conscience provide the major form of social control.

Halfway house: A facility for alcoholics, addicts, delinquents, mental patients, and others after their release from a hospital or other institution, to enable them to maintain some professional support while readjusting to the community; may be substituted for hospitalization.

Hallucination: A perception that occurs without relevant stimuli but that is accepted as real.

Healthy personality: A person who not only shows a relative absence of emotional disturbance, but also is able to satisfy his needs adequately, including the need for self-actualization; implies a positive, growth-motivated life.

Hebephrenic schizophrenia: A form of schizophrenia marked by silliness, giggling, and a general return to an earlier and immature condition.

Hereditary: Pertaining to the characteristics or influences that parents transmit biologically to their children at the time of conception.

Hierarchy of needs: As adapted from Abraham Maslow, a ranking of needs in terms of those that demand most immediate satisfaction; that is, the more basic needs are ranked lowest and are placed at the base of the hierarchy. They must be reasonably well satisfied before the individual can turn his attention to the next most basic set of needs.

Homosexuality: A form of sexual deviation in which an individual prefers sex relationships with members of his own sex rather than with the opposite sex.

Hostile-aggressive: Pertaining to an act of aggression that also involves hostility.

Hypothesis: A tentative explanation for an event, relationship, or other form of occurrence. Psychologists will frequently test hypotheses by collecting and analyzing relevant data.

Hysterical: Referring to the result of conversion reaction (*see* Conversion reaction)—hysterical blindness, hysterical paralysis. Other meanings of this term are not relevant to this book.

Ideal self: The individual as he would like to be; the self the individual sees as the best "me" possible.

Identical twins: Twins, very similar in appearance and of the same sex, resulting from one fertilized egg.

Identification: Association or affiliation with a group or another person; acceptance as your own of the values and purposes of another person or group. Frequently used, without awareness, as a defense mechanism to improve the self-concept.

Identity: Although there are innumerable meanings for this word, only one is primarily relevant here: the awareness an individual has of himself as a unique individual; of how he relates to the rest of society; and of his place in society and in the world.

Identity, search for: The attempt of an individual to understand his relationship to the rest of society, his place in the world, and himself as a unique individual.

Illusion: A mistaken perception (*see* Delusion *and* Hallucination).

Image: The "picture in the mind's eye" an individual has of a typical representative of a group of people or things; for example, many adults have an unfair image of a typical adolescent. This is only one use of this term.

Industrial psychologist: The psychologist whose primary interests are in the behavior of people at work. This field includes selection and placement of personnel, personnel testing, labor-management relations, human relations in industry, and evaluation of advertising and marketing practices.

In-group: A group whose members have a strong need for association with each other and a strong need to exclude those not of the group.

Inherited predispositions: Tendencies—to behave in particular ways or contract particular illnesses—that parents transmit genetically to their children at conception.

Insight: (1) The understanding of your own motives and other mental processes; (2) the understanding of some meaning, process, pattern, or use.

Insight learning: The process through which the meaning, significance, pattern, or use of an object or situation becomes clear.

Intellectualization: An attempt to withdraw from the emotional impact of a conflict by approaching a problem in purely intellectual terms; usually a defense mechanism.

Intelligence: The ability to grasp abstract concepts and symbols, to learn and to solve problems, and to cope with new situations.

Internalization: The taking on of the values, attitudes, beliefs, ideas, wishes, and goals of another person as your own; the general cultural values are transmitted from parent to child in this fashion.

Internal senses: The senses *within* the body, for example, the senses of hunger and thirst.

Intolerance of ambiguity: A type of rigidity; an inability to deal with uncertainty; a need for clear-cut explanations.

Intrauterine environment: The environment of the individual within the mother's womb between conception and birth. The degree to which experiences and events in this environment affect later development is not well understood.

Involutional psychosis: A form of affective disorder involving depression that occurs most commonly to people in their fifties.

Job enlargement: An increase in the variety of demands, tasks, and responsibilities of a job.

Job satisfaction: The degree to which an individual is pleased with his job; the amount of positive regard he has for his position.

Kinesthetic sense: The sense that enables an individual to be aware of his movement through space.

Glossary

Laissez faire: In social psychology, a type of leadership in which the leader exerts a minimum amount of control and makes minimum demands.

Latent dream content: The "real" meaning of a dream; the meaning that underlies what the individual "sees" and recognizes (*see* Manifest dream content).

Leader: A person who modifies, directs, or controls the attitudes or actions of one or more others; especially, the individual in the group who exhibits the most of such influence.

Learning: A process that occurs whenever a relatively permanent change in behavior results from experience.

Level of aspiration: The degree of competence, learning, achievement, and so on, the individual anticipates gaining.

Longitudinal: In research design, refers to the study of variables as they change over a period of time (*see* Cross-sectional).

Long-range goal: An end result toward which a person is working and which takes a long time to achieve.

Love needs: Needs, as adapted from Abraham Maslow, to feel the love, the warmth, and the affection of physical and emotional contact with others.

Lying-in: An arrangement in a hospital whereby a new baby can be placed in the same room with the mother, who can then care for the infant within a few hours of its birth; also called *rooming-in*.

Manic: Pertaining to a condition, often found in the mentally ill, of great excitability and elation.

Manic-depressive psychosis, circular type: A form of affective disorder in which the person is highly excited and elated for a period, then highly depressed for a period; there may be a period of relative normality in between.

Manifest dream content: That aspect of the dream that the individual "sees" (*see* Latent dream content).

Massed practice: Learning that takes place continuously without rest or other occurrences interrupting. Frequently applied to study; cramming for an examination would be an example.

Maturation: Development; particularly those developmental changes that occur relatively inevitably in all normal members of the species provided with a relatively suitable environment. No special learning is required for maturation.

Glossary

Menopause: The period during which a woman's menstrual cycle becomes irregular and eventually ceases, ending her ability to conceive. It usually occurs during the late forties or early fifties.

Mental age: The level of intellectual development, determined by comparing the person's performance on an intelligence test to the average performance of others at various chronological age levels.

Mental illness: Behavior disorder or behavior maladjustment; a breakdown in adjustment that necessitates some form of professional help or hospitalization.

Motivation: The process of setting behavior into action because of a need.

Motor abilities: Abilities related to movements, such as running, walking, or hammering.

Multiple personality: A form of dissociative reaction (neurosis) in which the individual maintains two or more distinct personalities, each of which appears separately at various times; an extremely rare condition.

Natural childbirth: A process through which a pregnant woman prepares herself, both physically and emotionally, for the birth of her child with minimum dependence upon anesthetics.

Need: A lack of something in the organism which, if present, would increase the satisfaction of the organism. There are numerous ways of classifying needs, including systems by Abraham Maslow and Henry Murray. Satisfying the need may be necessary to maintain existence, to provide stimulation, or to increase satisfactions.

Neonate: The infant between birth and about two or three weeks of age; a newly born infant.

Nervous system: The brain, the spinal cord, and the nerves.

Neurosis: A relatively mild personality disturbance that does not incapacitate the individual or necessitate his hospitalization; the neurotic person remains in contact with reality.

Nonverbal communication: The transmission of a message without written or oral words, as through gestures or body movements.

Norm: A standard with which the performance of an individual can be compared. If, on a test of verbal ability, your score is compared to scores obtained by 1,000 entering freshmen, the 1,000 freshmen constitute the norm group.

Glossary

Nurture: (1) The totality of environmental factors that influence an individual at any point in the life-span; (2) the providing of food, love, and care that permits an individual to develop.

Observational method: A research method for studying behavior; it consists of watching relevant occurrences either in person or with some mechanical aid such as a tape recorder. Controlled observations are carefully recorded in some objective fashion.

Obsession: An idea that seems to haunt a person, usually associated with dread or anxiety; may contribute to the form of neurosis termed obsessive-compulsive reaction.

Obsessive-compulsive reaction: The behavior pattern in which *obsessive* feelings elicit *compulsive* behavior.

Operant learning: The form of learning in which the correct response to a stimulus is gradually selected out from among all potential responses.

Organic: Referring to the body and its anatomical and biochemical makeup, rather than to the surrounding environment, the self-concept, or the personality.

Organic psychosis: Mental illness caused by structural damage to the brain.

Other-directed: Pertaining to the internalization of only one important value—that the approval and acceptance of the group is of primary importance.

Overindulgence: A giving in to the demands and whims of another more often than is appropriate; usually used in reference to child rearing.

Overlearning: Learning in which practice goes beyond the point where the act can be performed with only the required degree of excellence; learning beyond the minimal level of adequacy, but without the implication that unnecessary learning has taken place.

Overprotective: Providing greater care than necessary, usually in reference to an infant or child; implies an unnecessary reduction in the opportunity of the individual to satisfy certain stimulation needs.

Parallel play: The play of very young children; each plays by himself in the presence of the other with only occasional interaction.

Paranoid: Marked by systematic, apparently logical, delusions. The person is often mentally ill, but able to remain out of the hospital.

Paranoid schizophrenia: A form of schizophrenia characterized by unrealistic thinking, hallucinations, and delusions (especially of grandeur or persecution).

Peer group: A group consisting of one's equals. The term is usually used to refer to others of similar age, although it could also refer to equality of intelligence, competence, or social class.

Percentile: One of 99 scores that divide a group of scores into 100 equal parts. Thus, the student whose score is at the 53%ile (percentile) has received a higher score than 53% of those with whom he is being compared. (It does not mean he answered 53% of the questions correctly.)

Perception: The process through which the various sensations are interpreted and organized into meaningful patterns.

Personality: The dynamic organization of characteristic attributes leading to behavior and distinguishing one individual from other individuals. It refers to the total individual and includes needs, motives, methods of adjusting, temperament qualities, self-concept, role behaviors, attitudes and values, and abilities.

Personality psychologist: A psychologist whose primary interests are in the study of personality (*see* Personality).

Phobia, phobic reaction: A form of neurosis in which the person develops a dread, morbid, and exaggerated fear of something.

Physiological needs: Needs that result from lack of satisfaction of tissue requirements such as hunger, thirst, oxygen, rest, and sex. Physiological needs may demand satisfaction for survival or for stimulation.

Physiological psychologist: *See* Experimental and physiological psychologist.

Population explosion: A term applied to the rapid increase in population throughout the world, resulting primarily from the reduction in the death rate in general and infant mortality in particular.

Prejudice: An evaluation or belief, either positive or negative, developed without sufficient information or understanding and resistant to change. Prejudices often form about an individual as the result of the ethnic, religious, sex, age, or vocational group to which he belongs.

Preliterate: Being without a written language; usually applied by anthropologists to groups of people living under primitive conditions.

Prenatal: Pertaining to the period between conception and birth.

Primary status: The position one has in the community resulting from one's own worth and accomplishments, rather than the worth and accomplishments of a parent or other relative (*see* Derived status).

Probability: The likelihood that an event will occur.

Problem solving: The process of determining a proper solution for accomplishing a task; implies that some thinking is involved rather than only trial and error.

Projection: The process of attributing your own feelings, motives, or shortcomings to others. Occurs without conscious awareness, and is usually a defense mechanism.

Projective test: A psychological test, most frequently using ambiguous stimuli, that requires the subject to interpret the stimuli in light of his own feelings, experiences, and needs.

Propaganda: Actions or expressions of opinion deliberately designed to influence beliefs, values, attitudes, opinions, or behavior of others. Propaganda *may* have educational value, and education *may* have propaganda value.

Psychiatrist: A medical doctor whose primary concern is with mental illness and problems of personal adjustment.

Psychoanalyst: An individual, usually a medical doctor, who studies and treats mental illness and personal-adjustment problems on the basis of Sigmund Freud's principles or some modification of these principles. A person must complete a carefully specified course of study to become a psychoanalyst.

Psychologist: An individual who studies behavior in order to understand, describe, predict, and influence this behavior; he uses research to lead both to theories of behavior and to effective practical applications directed at immediate and long-range problems. There are many types of psychologists.

Psychology: The discipline, field, or science that deals with behavior and the behaver (*see* Psychologist).

Psychosis: A relatively severe personality disturbance that often incapacitates the individual and may necessitate his hospitalization. The psychotic may lose contact with reality.

Psychosomatic: Pertaining to physical symptoms produced by biochemical changes initiated by emotional stress. Psychosomatic problems can do tissue damage, are often treatable through a combination of medical and psychiatric methods, and are not in the least imaginary.

Glossary

Psychotherapy: The use of any psychological technique in helping an individual deal more effectively with personal or social problems; often restricted to trained psychotherapists operating in a situation in which they confront the person or persons receiving the help.

Psychotic depression: A form of affective disorder marked by extreme depression and frequently precipitated by the immediate environment rather than by experiences in the early years of the victim's life.

Puberty: The period of human development during which the individual becomes sexually mature; usually between ages 12 and 14, but with wide variations.

Puberty rites: A ceremony, taking place around the time of puberty, that intiates the individual as a regular member of the community.

Questionnaire: A set of questions on a given topic or several topics to investigate beliefs, attitudes, preferences, actual or potential behavior, or other individual characteristics; it is usually readily scorable.

Rationalization: An attitude or other behavior that presents a plausible reason for something that would otherwise disrupt the self-concept. The individual is unaware of his purpose in using it; usually a defense mechanism.

Reaction formation: The establishment of a personality trait or behavior directly opposed to certain unconscious motives or feelings; usually a defense mechanism.

Receptor: A specialized part of the human or lower-animal organism sensitive to such forms of energy as light (for vision) or sound (for hearing); it changes this energy into a form that enables its impact to be transmitted to the brain.

Reference group: The people with whom an individual compares and judges himself.

Reflex: A simple action that occurs automatically and without the control of the individual, for example, the knee jerk in response to a tap or sneezing in response to having the nose tickled.

Regression: The return to an earlier form of behavior; sometimes a defense mechanism.

Reinforcement: The increasing of the probability that an indicated response will follow a given stimulus; the strengthening of the bond between stimulus and response through rewarding the correct response.

Relative deprivation, law of: The theory that a person's satisfaction or dissatisfaction will result from how much he has compared to how much he feels he should have (reflected by what he sees around him); thus, a poor Asian farmer feels less deprived than an American farmer because the latter is surrounded by wealth, but the former is surrounded by poverty.

Reliability: The consistency of a rating, test, or other psychological measurement. If you receive the exact same grade relative to others on every quiz or examination you take in your psychology course, your scores would be considered highly reliable (or dependable or consistent).

Repression: The process leading to being unaware of or being unable to recall something, as a defense against the anxiety or guilt that the awareness or recollection would produce; having such a strong need to be unaware or unable to recall that lack of awareness or recollection results. A defense mechanism.

Response: An instance of behavior that is stirred up or stimulated by an event, a situation, or other behavior.

Retarded depression: A type of affective disorder in which depression is marked by apathy, reduced movement, and lack of overt activity.

Reward: The satisfaction of a need in such a way as to increase the chance that the reward-eliciting behavior will occur the next time the need becomes motivating.

Role: The behavior expected of an individual who occupies a particular position in the social scheme; positions include age position, leadership position, vocational position, and innumerable others.

Safety needs: Needs, as adapted from Abraham Maslow, to feel safe and secure and not to fear physical violence or loss of property.

Scapegoat: The victim of displaced aggression; the person or thing that receives the displaced-aggressive or hostile actions of another.

Schizophrenia: A group of psychotic reactions characterized by basic confusion regarding reality, by inappropriate emotional response, and by other forms of disturbed behavior.

School psychologist: A psychologist who functions inside a school setting and is usually concerned with testing, curriculum, counseling, and related matters; tends to be concerned with day-to-day problems, rather than with the theoretical and research issues that occupy the educational psychologist.

Segregation: Forced separation of an individual from a group or of one group of individuals from another group. Often used in relationship to ethnic groups.

Self: All that constitutes an individual; the "real me" (*see* Self-concept). Some authors define this term in other ways.

Self-actualization: The process of making the most of your capabilities, developing your talents, and acting naturally or being yourself.

Self-concept: The idea an individual has of himself; what a person sees himself as. The similarity between self and self-concept varies from person to person.

Self-fulfilling prophecy: A statement about what will happen in the future that helps cause the predicted circumstance to occur; a student who predicts he might fail in a course may behave in such a fashion, because of his prophecy, that he does fail.

Senile psychosis: Mental illness affecting the aged, usually assumed to have at least some organic basis.

Sensation: That which occurs when some stimulus excites a receptor. Sensation has no meaning, except as it is interpreted by the organism.

Separation anxiety: The concern felt by a young child because of being apart from his parents; this concern is reflected in later life when people become unhappy at temporary or permanent separations from others.

Set: A readiness to act or react; it may be a readiness to move, a readiness to perceive, or a readiness to accept a thought or idea.

Sex role: The behavior expected of an individual because of his sex.

Shame: An unplesant emotion produced by the feeling that others disapprove of your behavior or some other characteristic; there is some implication that the individual himself also disapproves of the behavior or other characteristic.

Shame society: A culture in which disapproval, ridicule, or criticism by others provides the major form of social control.

Sibling: The term used to refer to brother or sister, without regard to sex; your sibling may be either a sister or a brother.

Sibling rivalry: The competition between two or more children in the same family for the attention and approval of the parents or other significant figures; it occurs at all ages.

Glossary

Significant others: Individuals who have an extremely important and continuing impact upon the development and behavior of an individual, especially of a child; the mother is most commonly a significant other, as is the father to a slightly lesser degree.

Simple schizophrenia: A form of schizophrenia marked by limited involvement with the external world and limited adequacy in interpersonal relationships.

Social class: A grouping of individuals sharing certain social characteristics that enable them to interact with each other as approximate equals. Your social class affects your social environment, which affects values and many types of behavior.

Social-class mobility: The ability to move from one social class to another; the ability to be accepted as a member of a social-class group other than that of birth.

Social psychologist: A psychologist whose primary interests are in the study of groups, of attitudes and beliefs, and of communication, and in general, of the effects upon behavior of the social environment and social interactions.

SQ3R: A method for improving learning and reducing forgetting in reading, especially in studying textbooks.

Statistical psychologist: A psychologist whose primary interests are in evolving and utilizing quantitative approaches in research.

Status: The position or standing a person is given by his group.

Stereotype: A rigid and oversimplified or biased perception or conception of an aspect of reality, especially of persons or social groups.

Stimulation needs: Those unlearned (although not uninfluenced by learning) needs that cause the individual to explore and manipulate his environment.

Stimulus: An object or event that stirs up or arouses behavior.

Stimulus generalization: The process through which the individual learns to respond to stimuli that resemble the stimulus originally eliciting the response.

Stress: A strong emotional force producing tension or discomfort.

Stress tolerance: The amount of stress an individual can withstand without exhibiting adjustment problems.

Suppression: A purposeful attempt to forget or ignore something; not a defense mechanism.

Survival needs: Those unlearned needs necessary to the maintenance of the life of the organism, for example, hunger, thirst, and sleep needs.

Tension: The feeling of emotional strain that results from stress, most often discomforting and motivating the organism toward its elimination.

Thinking: Judging, abstracting, reasoning, evaluating, recalling, imagining, anticipating, or performing a comparable intellectual task; does not include perceiving.

Threshold: The point at which a stimulus is just strong enough to cause a response.

Toilet training: The method through which the child learns to control his elimination processes until he can find a socially acceptable location for eliminating.

Trait (personality):   A characteristic behavior pattern that differentiates people from each other.

Tranquilizer: A type of drug that reduces unpleasant emotional states such as anxiety and guilt and induces a feeling of calmness.

Trial: A single performance; a single attempt to respond properly to a stimulus.

Unconscious: Referring to the state of being unaware of what is occurring.

Unconscious motivation: The process of setting behavior into action because of a need or lack of something in the organism of which the person himself has no awareness.

Validity: The capacity of a test, rating, or other psychological measurement to measure what it is intended to measure. Your grade in psychology is valid to the extent that it measures how much you know about the material of the psychology course.

Value: A belief about what is good or bad. Each individual internalizes many values, which then may serve to motivate behavior. Values are often held without the individual's full awareness.

Value system: Several values related to each other and interdependent to some extent, so that a change in one value would probably produce at least a slight change in the others.

Variable: Anything that can change. In psychology, any attribute or property that changes as the result of another attribute, property, process, or event; for example, the variable *obedience* changes as the result of the event *spanking*.

Glossary

Vestibular sense: The sense that enables an individual to maintain balance and to be aware of his position.

Visual: Pertaining to seeing.

Warm-up: A brief period of getting ready to do something during which the individual gains the proper set or readiness; derived from baseball.

Weaning: The process by which a child (or young lower animal) is taught to become accustomed to being without his mother's milk; the process by which any individual reduces his dependency upon a person or thing.

Withdrawal: An action or pattern of behavior in which an individual removes himself from a stressful situation in an attempt to reduce the feelings of tension or maintain a satisfactory self-concept.

Zygote: The cell, formed by the union of the male sperm and the female ovum, from which a new individual matures.

References

Abelson, Philip H. LSD and marihuana. *Science,* 1968, **159,** 1189.

Adams, James F. An introduction to understanding adolescence. In James F. Adams (Ed.), *Understanding adolescence: Current developments in adolescent psychology.* Boston: Allyn & Bacon, 1968. Pp. 1–12.

Adorno, Theodore W., Frenkel-Brunswik, Else, Levinson, Daniel J., & Sanford, R. Nevitt. *The authoritarian personality: Studies in prejudice.* New York: Harper, 1950.

Albee, George W. Conceptual models and manpower requirements in psychology. *American Psychologist,* 1968, **23,** 317–320.

Allport, Gordon W. *The nature of prejudice.* Reading, Mass.: Addison-Wesley, 1954.

Allport, Gordon W., & Kramer, B. M. Some roots of prejudice. *Journal of Psychology,* 1946, **22,** 9–39.

Allport, Gordon W., & Ross, J. Michael. Personal religious orientation and prejudice. *Journal of Personality and Social Psychology,* 1967, **5,** 432–443.

Allport, Gordon W., Vernon, Philip E., & Lindzey, Gardner. *Study of values.* (3rd ed.) Boston: Houghton Mifflin, 1960.

Alper, T. G., & Boring, E. G. Intelligence test scores of northern and southern white and Negro recruits in 1918. *Journal of Abnormal and Social Psychology,* 1944, **39,** 471–474.

Anastasi, Anne. *Differential psychology.* (3rd ed.) New York: Macmillan, 1958.

Anderson, Richard C. Educational psychology. *Annual Review of Psychology,* 1967, **18,** 129–164.

Argyle, Michael. *The scientific study of social behaviour.* London: Methuen, 1957.

Argyle, Michael. *Religious behavior.* New York: Free Press, 1959.

Arkoff, Abe. *Adjustment and mental health.* New York: McGraw-Hill, 1968.

Asch, Solomon E. Effects of group pressure upon the modification and distortion of judgment. In Harold S. Guetzkow (Ed.), *Groups, leadership, and men.* Pittsburgh: Carnegie Press, 1951. Pp. 177–190.

Astin, Alexander W., & Nichols, Robert C. Life goals and vocational choice. *Journal of Applied Psychology,* 1964, **48,** 50–58.

Ausubel, David P. *Theory and problems of adolescent development.* New York: Grune & Stratton, 1954.

Ax, Albert F. The physiological differentiation between fear and anger in humans. *Psychosomatic Medicine,* 1953, **15,** 433–442.

References

Bacon, Margaret K., Child, Irvin L., & Barry, Herbert. A cross-cultural study of correlates of crime. *Journal of Abnormal and Social Psychology,* 1963, **66**, 291–300.

Bandura, Albert. Behavioral psychotherapy. *Scientific American,* 1967, **216**(3), 78–86.

Banta, Thomas J., & Hetherington, Mavis. Relations between needs of friends and fiancés. *Journal of Abnormal and Social Psychology,* 1963, **66**, 401–404.

Barrett, William. *Irrational man.* Garden City, N. Y.: Doubleday, 1958.

Barry, Herbert, & Lindemann, Erich. Critical ages for maternal bereavement in psychoneurosis. *Psychosomatic Medicine,* 1960, **22**, 166–181.

Bayley, Nancy. On the growth of intelligence. *American Psychologist,* 1955, **10**, 805–818.

Bayley, Nancy, & Oden, Melita H. The maintenance of intellectual ability in gifted adults. *Journal of Gerontology,* 1955, **10**, 91–107.

Beloff, Halla. Two forms of social conformity: Acquiescence and conventionality. *Journal of Abnormal and Social Psychology,* 1958, **56**, 99–103.

Benedict, Ruth F. *The chrysanthemum and the sword.* Boston: Houghton Mifflin, 1946.

Bennett, Margaret E., & Lewin, Molly. *Getting the most out of college.* New York: McGraw-Hill, 1957.

Berelson, Bernard, & Steiner, Gary A. *Human behavior: An inventory of scientific findings.* New York: Harcourt, Brace & World, 1964.

Berkowitz, Leonard. Impulse, aggression, and the gun. *Psychology Today,* Sept. 1968, **2**, 19–23.

Berne, Eric. *Games people play: The psychology of human relationships.* New York: Grove, 1964.

Biderman, Albert D. The image of "brain-washing." *Public Opinion Quarterly,* 1962, **26**, 547–563.

Bieber, Irving. *Homosexuality: A psychoanalytical study.* New York: Vintage, 1965.

Birns, Beverly, Blank, Marion, & Bridger, Wagner H. The effectiveness of various soothing techniques on human neonates. *Psychosomatic Medicine,* 1966, **28**, 316–322.

Birren, James E. *The psychology of aging.* Englewood Cliffs, N. J.: Prentice-Hall, 1964.

Block, Jack, & Thomas, Hobart. Is satisfaction with self a measure of adjustment? *Journal of Abnormal and Social Psychology,* 1955, **51**, 254–259.

Block, Jeanne H., Haan, Norma, & Smith, M. Brewster. Activism and apathy in contemporary adolescents. In James F. Adams (Ed.), *Understanding adolescence: Current developments in adolescent psychology.* Boston: Allyn & Bacon, 1968. Pp. 198–231.

References

Blood, Robert O., Jr. *Anticipating your marriage.* New York: Free Press, 1955.

Blood, Robert O., Jr. "Uniformities and diversities in campus dating preferences. *Marriage and Family Living,* 1956, **18**, 37–45.

Blood, Robert O., Jr., & Wolfe, Donald M. *Husbands and wives.* New York: Free Press, 1960.

Blum, Milton L. *Industrial psychology and its social foundations.* (Rev. ed.) New York: Harper, 1956.

Bogart, Leo. American television: A brief survey of research findings. *Journal of Social Issues* 1962, **18**(2), 36–42.

Bogdonoff, M. D., Klein, R. F., Estes, E. H., Jr., Shaw, D. M., & Back, K. W. The modifying effect of conforming behavior upon lipid responses accompanying CNS arousal. *Clinical Research,* 1961, **9**, 135. Cited in David Krech, Richard S. Crutchfield, & Egerton L. Ballachey, *Individual in society.* New York: McGraw-Hill, 1962. P. 521.

Boneau, Alan. Psychology's manpower: Report on the 1966 National Register of Scientific and Technical Personnel. *American Psychologist,* 1968, **23**, 325–334.

Bowlby, John. Separation anxiety. *International Journal of Psychoanalysis,* 1960, **41**, 89–113.

Boys' Clubs of America. *Needs and interests of adolescent Boys' Club members.* Boys' Clubs of America, 1960.

Bradway, Katherine P., & Thompson, Clare W. Intelligence at adulthood: A twenty-five year follow-up. *Journal of Educational Psychology,* 1962, **53**, 1–14.

Brayfield, Arthur H., & Crockett, Walter H. Employee attitudes and employee performance. *Psychological Bulletin,* 1955, **52**, 396–424.

Bridges, Katherine M. B. Emotional development in early infancy. *Child Development,* 1932, **3**, 324–341.

Bronson, Gordon W. The fear of novelty. *Psychological Bulletin,* 1968, **69**, 350–358.

Brown, Daniel G. Masculinity-femininity development in children. *Journal of Consulting Psychology,* 1957, **21**, 197–202.

Brown, William F., & Holtzman, Wayne H. A study-attitudes questionnaire for predicting academic success. *Journal of Educational Psychology,* 1955, **46**, 75–84.

Bruner, Jerome S., & Goodman, C. C. Value and need as organizing factors in perception. *Journal of Abnormal and Social Psychology,* 1947, **13**, 33–44.

Bugental, Daphne E., & Lehner, George F. J. Accuracy of self-perception and group-perception as related to two leadership roles. *Journal of Abnormal and Social Psychology,* 1958, **56**, 396–398.

Burgess, Ernest W., & Cottrell, Leonard S., Jr. *Predicting success or failure in marriage.* Englewood Cliffs, N. J.: Prentice-Hall, 1939.

References

Burgess, Ernest W., & Wallin, Paul. *Engagement and marriage.* Philadelphia: Lippincott, 1953.

Buxbaum, Robert E. Homosexuality and love. *Journal of Religion and Health,* 1967, **6**, 17–32.

Byrne, Donn, & Blaylock, Barbara. Similarity and assumed similarity of attitudes between husbands and wives. *Journal of Abnormal and Social Psychology,* 1963, **67**, 636–640.

Caldwell, Bettye M., & Hersher, Leonard. Mother-infant interaction during the first year of life. *Merrill-Palmer Quarterly,* 1964, **10**, 119–128.

Calvin, A.D., & Holtzman, Wayne H. Adjustment to the discrepancy between self-concept and the inferred self. *Journal of Consulting Psychology,* 1953, **17**, 39–44.

Capel, W. C. Continuities and discontinuities in attitudes of the same persons measured through time. *Journal of Social Psychology,* 1967, **73**, 125–136.

Caplan, Nathan. Treatment intervention and reciprocal interaction effects. *Journal of Social Issues,* 1968, **24**(1), 63–88.

Cattell, Raymond B. Are I.Q. tests intelligent? *Psychology Today,* 1968, **1**(10), 56–62.

Chatterjee, M. N. *Society in the making.* Ann Arbor, Mich.: Edwards Brothers, 1942.

Clark, Kenneth B., & Clark, Mamie P. Racial identification and preference in Negro children. In Eleanor E. Maccoby, Theodore M. Newcomb, & Eugene L. Hartley (Eds.), *Readings in social psychology.* (3rd ed.) New York: Holt, 1958. Pp. 602–611.

Cohen, E. L. The incidence and localization of acne. *British Journal of Dermatology,* 1945, **57**, 10–14.

Cohen, Nathan. The Negro and the American dream. *UCLA Alumni Magazine,* 1968, **42**(4), 5–9.

Cole, Luella, & Hall, Irma N. *Psychology of adolescence.* (6th ed.) New York: Holt, 1964.

Coleman, James C. *Personality dynamics and effective behavior.* Glenview, Ill.: Scott, Foresman, 1960.

Coleman, James C. *Abnormal psychology and modern life.* (3rd ed.) Glenview, Ill.: Scott, Foresman, 1964.

Coleman, James S., Mood, A. M., Campbell, E. Q., et al. *Equality of educational opportunity.* Washington, D. C.: U.S. Office of Education, 1966.

Conrad, H. S., & Jones, H. E. A second study of familial resemblance in intelligence: Environmental and genetic implications of parent-child and sibling correlations in the total sample. *39th Yearbook National Society for the Study of Education,* 1940, Part II, 97–141.

Cooley, Charles H. *The nature of human nature.* New York: Scribner's, 1902.

References

Coughlan, R. Control of the brain. *Life*, Mar. 8, 1963, **54**, 90–106; and Mar. 15, 1963, **54**, 81–94.

Cumming, Elaine, & Henry, William E. *Growing old*. New York: Basic Books, 1961.

Datta, Lois, & Parloff, Morris B. On the relevance of autonomy: Parent-child relationships and early scientific creativity. *Proceedings of 75th Annual Convention of the American Psychological Association*, 1967, **2**, 149–150.

Deeg, Maethel E., & Paterson, Donald G. Changes in social status of occupations. *Occupations*, 1947, **25**, 205–208.

Dement, William. The effect of dream deprivation. *Science*, 1960, **131**, 1705–1707.

Diamond, Solomon. *Personality and temperament*. New York: Harper, 1957.

Dick-Read, Grantly. *Childbirth without fear: The principles and practice of natural childbirth*. (4th ed.) New York: Heinemann, 1960.

Dole, Arthur A. College students report on their use of time. *Personnel and Guidance Journal*, 1959, **37**, 633–637.

Dollard, John, Doob, Leonard W., Miller, Neal E., Mowrer, O. H., & Sears, Robert R. *Frustration and aggression*. New Haven, Conn.: Yale University Press, 1939.

Domhoff, G. William. *Who rules America?* Englewood Cliffs, N. J.: Prentice-Hall, 1967.

Douvan, Elizabeth, & Adelson, Joseph. The psychodynamics of social mobility in adolescent boys. *Journal of Abnormal and Social Psychology*, 1958, **56**, 31–44.

Drucker, Peter F. How to be an employee. *Psychology Today*, 1968, **1**(10), 63–65, 74.

Dublin, Louis I. Suicide: A public health problem. In E. Shneidman (Ed.), *Essays in self-destruction*. New York: Science House, 1967. Pp. 251–257.

Durham, Philip, & Jones, Everett L. *The Negro cowboys*. New York: Dodd, Mead, 1965.

Ebbs, J. H., Tisdall, F. F., & Scott, W. A. The influence of prenatal diet on the mother and child. *The Milbank Memorial Fund Quarterly*, 1942, **20**, 35–36.

Edwards, Allan L. *Edwards personal preference schedule*. New York: Psychological Corporation, 1954.

Elkind, David, & Elkind, Sally. Varieties of religious experience in young adolescents. *Journal for the Scientific Study of Religion*, 1962, **2**, 102–112.

English, Horace B., & English, Ava C. *A comprehensive dictionary of psychological and psychoanalytical terms: A guide to usage*. New York: Longmans, Green, 1958.

English, O. Spurgeon, & Pearson, Gerald H. J. *Emotional problems of living*. (3rd ed.) New York: Norton, 1963.

References

Engström, L., Geijerstam, G. af, Holmberg, N. G., & Uhrus, K. A prospective study of the relationship between psycho-social factors and course of pregnancy and delivery. *Journal of Psychosomatic Research,* 1964, **8,** 151–155.

Erikson, Erik H. The problem of ego identity. *Journal of the American Psychoanalytic Association,* 1956, **4,** 56–121.

Escalona, Sibylle K. Some determinants of individual differences. *Transactions of New York Academy of Sciences,* 1965, **27,** 802–816.

Eysenck, Hans J. New ways in psychotherapy. *Psychology Today,* 1967, **1**(2), 39–47.

Farberow, Norman L., & Shneidman, Edwin S. (Eds.) *The cry for help.* New York: McGraw-Hill, 1961.

Feifel, Herman. Attitudes toward death in some normal and mentally ill populations. In Herman Feifel (Ed.), *The meaning of death.* New York: McGraw-Hill, 1959. Pp. 114–130.

Feinberg, Mortimer R. College student in residence. *New York Times Sunday Magazine,* Oct. 13, 1963. P. 93.

Festinger, Leon. Motivations leading to social behavior. In Marshall Jones (Ed.), *Nebraska symposium,* 1954. Pp. 191–219.

Festinger, Leon. *A theory of cognitive dissonance.* Evanston, Ill.: Row, Peterson, 1957.

Fey, William F. Correlates of certain subjective attitudes toward self and others. *Journal of Clinical Psychology,* 1957, **13,** 44–49.

Fisher, Sarah C. Relationships in attitudes, opinions, and values among family members. *University of California Publications in Culture and Society,* 1948, **2,** 29–100. Cited in Henry C. Smith, *Personality adjustment.* New York: McGraw-Hill, 1961. P. 223.

Flacks, Richard. The liberated generation: An exploration of the roots of student protest. *Journal of Social Issues,* 1967, **23**(3), 52–75.

Ford, Clellan S., & Beach, Frank A. *Patterns of sexual behavior.* New York: Harper, 1951.

Frankel, Edward, Characteristics of working and non-working mothers among intellectually gifted high and low achievers. *Personnel and Guidance Journal,* 1964, **42,** 776–780.

Freedman, Marvin B. The sexual behavior of American college women: An empirical study and an historical survey. *Merrill-Palmer Quarterly,* 1965, **11,** 38–48.

Frenkel-Brunswik, Else. Intolerance of ambiguity as an emotional and perceptual personality variable. *Journal of Personality,* 1949, **18,** 108–143.

Friedan, Betty. *The feminine mystique.* New York: Norton, 1963.

Fromm, Erich. *Escape from freedom.* New York: Holt, 1941.

Fromm, Erich. *The art of loving.* New York: Harper, 1956.

References

Gallup, George, & Hill, Evan. Youth: The cool generation. *Saturday Evening Post,* Dec. 23, 1961. Pp. 63–80.

Garrison, Karl C. Physiological changes in adolescence. In James F. Adams (Ed.), *Understanding adolescence: Current developments in adolescent psychology.* Boston: Allyn & Bacon, 1968. Pp. 43–69.

Getzels, Jacob W., & Jackson, Philip W. *Creativity and intelligence: Explorations with gifted students.* New York: Wiley, 1962.

Gibb, Cecil A. *Leadership.* In Gardner Lindzey (Ed.), *Handbook of social psychology,* Vol. 2. Reading, Mass.: Addison-Wesley, 1954. Pp. 877–920.

Gibson, Eleanor J., & Walk, Richard D. The "visual cliff." *Scientific American,* 1960, **202,** 64–71.

Goldsen, Rose K., Rosenberg, Morris, Williams, Robin M., Jr., & Suchman, Edward A. *What college students think.* Princeton, N. J.: Van Nostrand, 1960.

Goodenough, Florence L. *Measurement of intelligence by drawings.* Chicago: World Book, 1926.

Gordon, Albert I. *Intermarriage: Interfaith, interracial, interethnic.* Boston: Beacon Press, 1964.

Gorer, Geoffrey. *Himalayan village.* London: M. Joseph, 1938.

Gowan, John C. Relationship between leadership and personality measures. *Journal of Educational Research,* 1955, **48,** 623–627.

Gregory, I. Anterospective data following childhood loss of parent. *Archives of General Psychiatry,* 1965, **13,** 99–109.

Gross, Edward. *Work and society.* New York: Crowell, 1958.

Group for the Advancement of Psychiatry, Committee on Adolescence. *Normal adolescence.* New York: Scribner's, 1968.

Gullahorn, John T., & Gullahorn, Jeanne E. An extension of the U-curve hypothesis. *Journal of Social Issues,* 1963, **19**(3), 33–47.

Gustad, John W. Changes in social attitudes and behavior: A review of the literature. *Educational and Psychological Measurements,* 1951, **11,** 87–102.

Gustad, John W. Factors associated with social behavior and adjustment: A review of the literature. *Educational and Psychological Measurements,* 1952, **12,** 3–19.

Haire, Mason. Projective techniques in marketing research. *Journal of Marketing,* 1950, **14,** 649–656.

Hanes, Bernard, & Flippo, Edwin B. Anxiety and work output. *Journal of Industrial Engineering,* 1963, **14,** 244–248.

Harlow, Harry F. The nature of love. *American Psychologist,* 1958, **13,** 673–685.

Harlow, Harry F., & Harlow, Margaret K. The effect of rearing conditions on behavior. *Bulletin of the Menninger Clinic,* 1962, **26,** 213–224. (a)

References

Harlow, Harry F., & Harlow, Margaret K. Social deprivation in monkeys. *Scientific American*, 1962, **207**, 136–146. (b)

Harlow, Harry F., & Harlow, Margaret K. The young monkeys. *Psychology Today*, 1967, **1**(5), 40–47.

Harlow, Harry F., Harlow, Margaret K., & Meyer, Donald R. Learning motivated by a manipulation drive. *Journal of Experimental Psychology*, 1950, **40**, 228–234.

Harrell, Ruth F. Further effects of added thiamin on learning and other processes. *Contributions to Education*, 1947, No. 928. Teachers College, Columbia University.

Harris, Dale B. Work and the adolescent transition to maturity. *Teachers College Record*, 1961, **63**, 146–153.

Harris, Florence R., Wolf, Montrose M., & Baer, Donald M. Effects of adult social reinforcement on child behavior. *Young Children*, 1964, **20**(1), 8–17.

Harris, Louis. The Harris poll. In the *Los Angeles Times*, Mar. 18, 1965. P. 12.

Havemann, Ernest, & West, Patricia S. *They went to college.* New York: Harcourt, Brace, & World, 1952.

Havighurst, Robert J., Bowman, Paul H., Liddle, Gordon P., Matthews, Charles V., & Pierce, James V. *Growing up in River City.* New York: Wiley, 1962.

Havighurst, Robert J., Robinson, Myra Z., & Dorr, Mildred. The development of the ideal self in childhood and adolescence. *Journal of Educational Research*, 1946, **40**, 241–257.

Heron, Woodburn. The pathology of boredom. *Scientific American*, 1957, **196**, 52–56.

Herzberg, Frederick. Motivation, morale, and money. *Psychology Today*, 1968, **1**(10), 42–45, 66–67.

Herzberg, Frederick, Mausner, Bernard, Peterson, Richard O., & Capwell, Dora F. *Job attitudes: Review of research and opinion.* Psychological Service of Pittsburgh, 1957. Cited in Bernard Berelson & Gary A. Steiner, *Human behavior: An inventory of scientific findings.* New York: Harcourt, Brace & World, 1964. Pp. 410–411.

Hess, Robert D., & Goldblatt, Irene. The status of adolescents in American society: A problem in social identity. *Child Development*, 1957, **28**, 459–468.

Hetherington, E. Mavis. Effects of paternal absence on sex-typed behaviors in Negro and white pre-adolescent males. *Journal of Personality and Social Psychology*, 1966, **4**, 87–91.

Hilgard, Ernest R., & Atkinson, Richard C. *Introduction to psychology.* (4th ed.) New York: Harcourt, Brace & World, 1967.

Himmelweit, Hilde T. A theoretical framework for the consideration of the effects of television: A British report. *Journal of Social Issues*, 1962, **18**(2), 16–28.

References

Hoefer, C., & Hardy, M. C. Later development of breast fed and artifically fed infants. *Journal of the American Medical Association*, 1929, **92**, 615–619.

Holland, James C. Teaching psychology by a teaching machine program. Unpublished mimeographed report, 1960. Cited in Bernard Berelson & Gary A. Steiner, *Human behavior: An inventory of scientific findings.* New York: Harcourt, Brace & World, 1964. P. 150.

Hollingshead, August B. *Elmtown's youth.* New York: Wiley, 1949.

Honzik, Marjorie P. Developmental studies of parent-child resemblance in intelligence. *Child Development*, 1957, **28**, 215–228.

Hoppock, Robert. *Job satisfaction.* New York: Harper, 1935.

Hovland, Carl I. Human learning and retention. In S. S. Stevens (Ed.), *Handbook of Experimental Psychology.* New York: Wiley, 1951.

Hovland, Carl I., Campbell, Enid H., & Brock, T. The effects of "commitment" on opinion change following communication. In Carl I. Hovland et al., *The order of presentation in persuasion.* New Haven, Conn.: Yale University Press, 1957. Pp. 23–32.

Hughes, Helen MacG., & Watts, Lewis G. Portrait of the self-integrator. *Journal of Social Issues*, 1964, **20**(2), 103–115.

Hulin, Charles L., & Blood, Milton R. Job enlargement, individual differences, and worker responses. *Psychological Bulletin*, 1968, **69**, 41–45.

Hurlock, Elizabeth B. *Developmental psychology.* (2nd ed.) New York: McGraw-Hill, 1959.

Hyman, Herbert H. The value system of different classes: A social psychological contribution to the analysis of stratification. In Reinhard Bendix & Seymour M. Lipset (Eds.), *Class, status, and power.* New York: Free Press, 1953. Pp. 426–442.

Hyman, Herbert H. *Political socialization: A study in the psychology of political behavior.* New York: Free Press, 1959.

Inselberg, Rachel M. Social and psychological factors associated with high school marriages. *Journal of Home Economics*, 1961, **53**, 766–772.

Ivey, Allen E. The academic performance of students counseled at a university counseling service. *Journal of Counseling Psychology*, 1962, **9**, 347–352.

Izard, Carroll E. Personality similarity and friendship: A follow-up study. *Journal of Abnormal and Social Psychology*, 1963, **66**, 598–600.

Izard, Carroll E., & Manhold, John H. Correlates of peer leadership ratings: I. Medical complaints. *Medical Research Reports*, United States Naval School of Aviation, 1954.

Jacob, Philip E. *Changing values in college: An exploratory study of the impact of college teaching.* New York: Harper, 1957.

Janis, Irving. When fear is healthy. *Psychology Today*, 1968, **1**(11), 46–49, 60–61.

References

Jeans, Philip C., Wright, F. Howell, & Blake, Florence G. *Essentials of pediatrics.* (5th ed.) Philadelphia: Lippincott, 1954.

Jeffers, Frances C., Nichols, Claude R., & Eisdorfer, Carl. Attitudes of older persons toward death: A preliminary study. *Journal of Gerontology,* 1961, **16,** 53–56.

Jepsen, Victor L. College activities and vocational success. *Occupations,* 1951, **29,** 345–347.

Johnstone, John W. C., & Rosenberg, Larry. Sociological observations on the privileged adolescent. In James F. Adams (Ed.), *Understanding adolescence: Current developments in adolescent psychology.* Boston: Allyn & Bacon, 1968. Pp. 318–336.

Jourard, Sidney M. *Personal adjustment: An approach through the study of healthy personality.* (2nd ed.) New York: Macmillan, 1963.

Kagan, Jerome. The many faces of response. *Psychology Today,* 1968, **1**(8), 22–27, 60.

Kagan, Jerome, & Moss, Howard A. *Birth to maturity: A study in psychological development.* New York: Wiley, 1962.

Kalish, Richard A. An approach to death attitudes. *American Behavioral Scientist,* 1963, **6,** 68–70.

Kalish, Richard A. Of children and grandfathers: A speculative essay on dependency. *The Gerontologist,* 1967, **7,** 65–70.

Kalish, Richard A. Suicide: An ethnic comparison in Hawaii. *Bulletin of Suicidology,* December 1968, pp. 37–43.

Kalish, Richard A. *Making the most of college.* (2nd ed.) Belmont, Calif.: Brooks/Cole, 1969.

Kalish, Richard A. The old and the young: Generation gap allies. *The Gerontologist,* 1969, **9,** 83–89.

Kalish, Richard A., & Bartos, Otomar. Survey of student attitudes toward campus activities. *Personnel and Guidance Journal,* 1960, **39,** 292–299.

Kalish, Richard A., Maloney, Michael, & Arkoff, Abe. Cross-cultural comparisons of college student marital-role preferences. *Journal of Social Psychology,* 1966, **68,** 41–47.

Kallmann, Franz J. *Heredity in health and mental disorder.* New York: Norton, 1953.

Kaplan, Max. *Leisure in America, a social inquiry.* New York: Wiley, 1960.

Katz, Joseph. Quoted in the *Los Angeles Times,* Nov. 19, 1968, Section H. P. 6.

Keith-Spiegel, P., & Spiegel, D. Perceived helpfulness of others as a function of compatible intelligence levels. *Journal of Counseling Psychology,* 1967, **14,** 61–62.

Kelley, Harold H., & Volkart, Edmund H. The resistance to change of group-anchored attitudes. *American Sociological Review,* 1952, **17,** 453–465.

References

Kelly, E. Lowell. Consistency of the adult personality. *American Psychologist,* 1955, **10**, 659–681.

Keniston, Kenneth. The sources of student dissent. *Journal of Social Issues,* 1967, **23**(3), 108–137.

Keys, Ancel B., Brožek, Josef, Henschel, Austin, Michelsen, Olaf, & Taylor, Henry L. *The biology of human starvation,* Vol. 2, Minneapolis: University of Minnesota Press, 1950.

Kidd, Aline H., & Rivoire, Jeanne L. (Eds.) *Perceptual development in children.* New York: International Universities Press, 1966.

Killian, Lewis M. The significance of multiple-group membership in disaster. *American Journal of Sociology,* 1952, **57**, 309–314.

Kinsey, Alfred C., Pomeroy, Wardell B., & Martin, Clyde E. *Sexual behavior in the human male.* Philadelphia: Saunders, 1948.

Kinsey, Alfred C., Pomeroy, Wardell B., Martin, Clyde E., & Gebhard, Paul H. *Sexual behavior in the human female.* Philadelphia: Saunders, 1953.

Kirkpatrick, Clifford. Religion and humanitarianism: A study of institutional implications. *Psychological Monographs,* 1949, **63**.

Kobler, Arthur L., & Stotland, Ezra. *The end of hope: A social-clinical study of suicide.* New York: Free Press, 1964.

Kohn, Melvin L. Social class and parental values. *American Journal of Sociology,* 1959, **64**, 337–351.

Kollar, Edward J., Slater, Grant R., Palmer, James O., Docter, Richard F., & Mandell, Arnold J. Stress in subjects undergoing sleep deprivation. *Psychosomatic Medicine,* 1966, **28**, 101–113.

Krech, David. The chemistry of learning. *Saturday Review,* Jan. 20, 1968, **51**, 48–50, 68.

Krech, David, Crutchfield, Richard S., & Ballachey, Egerton L. *Individual in society.* New York: McGraw-Hill, 1962.

Krumboltz, John D., Christal, Raymond E., & Ward, Joe H., Jr. Predicting leadership ratings from high school activities. *Journal of Educational Psychology,* 1959, **50**, 105–110.

Kuhlen, Raymond G. Motivational changes during the adult years. In Raymond G. Kuhlen (Ed.), *Psychological backgrounds of adult education.* Center for the Study of Liberal Education for Adults, 1963. Cited in James E. Birren, *The psychology of aging.* Englewood Cliffs, N. J.: Prentice-Hall, 1964.

Kuhlen, Raymond G., & Arnold, Martha. Age differences in religious beliefs and problems during adolescence. *Journal of Genetic Psychology,* 1944, **65**, 291–300.

Kukuk, W. Traits of college drinkers. Unpublished master's thesis, 1960. Cited in Henry C. Smith, *Personality adjustment.* New York: McGraw-Hill, 1961. P. 323.

References

Langhorne, M. C., & Secord, Paul F. Variations in marital needs with age, sex, marital status, and regional location. *Journal of Social Psychology*, 1955, **41**, 19–37.

Lavin, David E. *The prediction of academic performance.* New York: Russell Sage, 1965.

Lehmann, Irvin J. Changes in critical thinking, attitudes, and values from freshman to senior years. *Journal of Educational Psychology*, 1963, **54**, 305–315.

Lehner, George F. J., & Kube, Ella. *The dynamics of personal adjustment.* (2nd ed.) Englewood Cliffs, N. J.: Prentice-Hall, 1964.

Leib, J. W., Cusack, Julia, Huges, Deanna, Pilette, S., Werther, Jacqueline, & Kintz, B. L. Teaching machines and programmed instruction: Areas of application. *Psychological Bulletin*, 1967, **67**, 12–26.

Lenski, Gerhard E. *The religious factor.* Garden City, N. Y.: Doubleday, 1961.

Leuba, Clarence J., & John, William F. *Man: A general psychology.* New York: Holt, 1961.

Levine, R., Chein, Isidore, & Murphy, Gardner. The relation of the intensity of a need to the amount of perceptual distortion: A preliminary report. *Journal of Psychology*, 1942, **13**, 283–293.

Levinger, George, & Breedlove, James. Interpersonal attraction and agreement: A study of marriage partners. *Journal of Personality and Social Psychology*, 1966, **3**, 367–372.

Lewin, Kurt. Group decision and social change. In Eleanor E. Maccoby, Theodore M. Newcomb, & Eugene L. Hartley (Eds.), *Readings in social psychology.* (3rd ed.) New York: Holt, 1958. Pp. 197–211.

Lilly, J. C. Mental effects of reduction of ordinary levels of physical stimuli on intact, healthy persons. Psychiatric Research Reports, 1956 (5) 1–28. Cited in Norman L. Munn, *Psychology: The fundamentals of human adjustment.* (4th ed.) Boston: Houghton Mifflin, 1961. P. 175.

Lindemann, Erich. Symptomatology and management of acute grief. *American Journal of Psychiatry*, 1944, **101**, 141–148.

Lippett, Ronald, & White, Ralph K. An experimental study of leadership and group life. In Eleanor E. Maccoby, Theodore M. Newcomb, & Eugene L. Hartley (Eds.), *Readings in social psychology.* (3rd ed.) New York: Holt, 1958. Pp. 496–511.

Lippman, Hyman S. Emotional factors in family breakdown. *American Journal of Orthopsychiatry*, 1954, **24**, 445–453.

Long, Diane, Elkind, David, & Spilka, Bernard. The child's conception of prayer. *Journal for the Scientific Study of Religion*, 1967, **6**, 101–109.

Lorenz, Thomas H., Graham, David T., & Wolf, Stewart. The relation of life stress and emotions to human sebum secretion and to the mechanism of acne vulgaris. *Journal of Laboratory and Clinical Medicine*, 1953, **41**, 11–28.

References

Lowe, C. R. Effect of mothers' smoking habits on birth weight of their children. *British Medical Journal,* 1959, **2,** 673–676.

Luby, Elliot D., Frohman, Charles E., Grisell, James L., Lenzo, Joseph E., & Gottlieb, Jacques S. Sleep deprivation: Effects on behavior, thinking, motor performance, and biological energy transfer systems. *Psychosomatic Medicine,* 1960, **22,** 182–192.

Luckey, Eleanore B. Marital satisfaction and personality correlates of spouse. *Journal of Marriage and the Family,* 1964, **26,** 217–220. (a)

Luckey, Eleanore B. Marital satisfaction and its concomitant perceptions of self and spouse. *Journal of Counseling Psychology,* 1964, **11,** 136–145. (b)

Lynes, Russell. How good are the junior colleges? *Harper's Magazine,* 1966, **233,** 53–60.

Maccoby, Eleanor E. Developmental psychology. *Annual Review of Psychology,* 1964, **15,** 203–250.

Maccoby, Eleanor E., Gibbs, Patricia K., & the staff of the Laboratory of Human Development, Harvard University. Methods of child-rearing in two social classes. In Arthur P. Coladarci (Ed.), *Educational psychology: A book of readings.* New York: Holt, 1955. Pp. 97–121.

Malnig, Lawrence R. Anxiety and academic prediction. *Journal of Counseling Psychology,* 1964, **11,** 72–75.

Mann, Richard D. A review of the relationships between personality and performance in small groups. *Psychological Bulletin,* 1959, **56,** 241–270.

Maslow, Abraham H. A theory of human motivation. *Psychological Review,* 1943, **50,** 370–396.

Maslow, Abraham H. Deficiency motivation and growth motivation. In Marshall R. Jones (Ed.), *Nebraska Symposium,* 1955. Pp. 1–30.

Maslow, Abraham H. *Toward a psychology of being.* Princeton, N. J.: Van Nostrand, 1962.

Matarazzo, Joseph D., Allen, Bernadene V., Saslow, George, & Wiens, Arthur N. Characteristics of successful policemen and firemen applicants. *Journal of Applied Psychology,* 1964, **48,** 123–133.

McCain, Garvin, & Segal, Erwin M. *The game of science.* Belmont, Calif.: Brooks/Cole, 1969.

McCord, Joan, McCord, William, & Thurber, Emily. Effects of maternal employment on lower-class boys. *Journal of Abnormal and Social Psychology,* 1963, **67,** 177–182.

McCord, William, McCord, Joan, & Verden, P. Familial and behavioral correlates of dependency in male children. *Child Development,* 1962, **33,** 313–326.

McGeoch, John A., & Irion, Arthur L. *The psychology of human learning.* (2nd ed.) New York: Longmans, Green, 1952.

References

McGinnies, Elliot, & Vaughan, Willard. Some biographical determiners of participation in group discussion. *Journal of Applied Psychology,* 1957, **41**, 179–185.

McGlothin, William H., & West, Louis J. The marijuana problem: An overview. *American Journal of Psychiatry,* 1968, **125**, 370–378.

McGlothin, William H., & Arnold, David O. Organicity measures following repeated LSD ingestion. *Archives for General Psychiatry,* in press.

McKinney, Fred. *Psychology of personal adjustment.* (3rd ed.) New York: Wiley, 1960.

Mehrabian, Albert. Communication without words. *Psychology Today,* 1968, **2**(4), 53–55.

Menninger, Roy. What troubles our troubled youth? *Mental Hygiene,* 1968, **52**, 323–329.

Merrill, Francis E. *Courtship and marriage.* New York: Holt, 1959.

Milgram, Stanley. Some conditions of obedience and disobedience to authority. In Ivan D. Steiner & Martin Fishbein (Eds.), *Current studies in social psychology.* New York: Holt, 1965. Pp. 243–262.

Miller, George A. The psycholinguists: On the new scientists of language. *Encounter,* 1964, **23**, 29–37.

Mishima, Yukio. Judging the U. S. giant. *Life,* Sept. 11, 1964, **57**, 81–84.

Moberg, David O. Religiosity in old age. *The Gerontologist,* 1965, **5**, 78–88.

Montagu, M. F. Ashley. Some environmental factors which may influence prenatal development. In Jerome M. Seidman (Ed.), *The child: A book of readings.* New York: Holt, 1958. Pp. 42–50.

Morgan, Clifford T., & King, Richard A. *Introduction to psychology.* (3rd ed.) New York: McGraw-Hill, 1966.

Muhyi, Ibrahim A. Women in the Arab Middle East. *Journal of Social Issues,* 1959, **15**(3), 45–57.

Murdock, George P. *Social structure.* New York: Macmillan, 1949.

Murdock, George P. World ethnographic sample. *American Anthropologist,* 1957, **59**, 664–687.

Murray, Henry A. *Explorations in personality.* New York: Oxford University Press, 1938.

Mussen, Paul H. Some personality and social factors related to changes in children's attitudes toward Negroes. *Journal of Abnormal and Social Psychology,* 1950, **45**, 423–441.

Newcomb, Theodore M., & Svehla, G. Intra-family relationships in attitude. *Sociometry,* 1937, **1**, 180–205.

Newson, J., & Newson, E. *Some social differences in the process of child rearing.* Baltimore: Penguin Books, 1967.

References

Newsweek. Book review of Arthur H. Lewis, *Lament for the Molly Maguires,* New York: Harcourt, Brace & World, 1964. Sept. 7, 1964, **64**, 85.

Newsweek. Campus '65. March 22, 1965, **65**, 43–63.

Newton, Niles R. Breast feeding. *Psychology Today,* 1968, **2**(1), 34–35, 68–70.

Nichols, Robert C. Nature and nurture in adolescence. In James F. Adams (Ed.), *Understanding adolescence: Current developments in adolescent psychology.* Boston: Allyn & Bacon, 1968. Pp. 101–127.

Noel, Donald L. Group identification among Negroes: An empirical analysis. *Journal of Social Issues,* 1964, **20**(2), 71–84.

Ort, Robert S. A study of role-conflicts as related to happiness in marriage. *Journal of Abnormal and Social Psychology,* 1950, **45**, 691–699.

Osborne, R. Travis, & Gregory, A. James. The inheritability of visualization, perceptual speed and spatial orientation. *Perceptual Motor Skills,* 1966, **23**, 379–390.

Osgood, Charles E. *Method and theory in experimental psychology.* New York: Oxford University Press, 1953.

Osler, William. To the editor of the *Spectator* (Nov. 4, 1911). In L. Farmer, *Doctor's legacy.* New York: Harper, 1955.

Parker, Seymour, & Kleiner, Robert. Status position, mobility, and ethnic identification of the Negro. *Journal of Social Issues,* 1964, **20**(2), 85–102.

Parkes, C. Murray. Effects of bereavement on physical and mental health—a study of the medical record of widows. *British Medical Journal,* 1964, **2**, 274–279.

Pavlov, Ivan P. *Conditioned reflexes.* (Translated by G. V. Anrep.) New York: Oxford University Press, 1927.

Peissel, Michel. Mustang, remote realm in Nepal. *National Geographic,* Oct. 1965, **128**, 579–604.

Perloff, Robert. Consumer analysis. *Annual Review of Psychology,* 1968, **19**, 437–466.

Pettigrew, Thomas F. *A profile of the Negro American.* Princeton, N. J.: Van Nostrand, 1964.

Piers, Ellen V. Adolescent creativity. In James F. Adams (Ed.), *Understanding adolescence: Current developments in adolescent psychology.* Boston: Allyn & Bacon, 1968. Pp. 159–182.

Powledge, Fred. *To change a child: A report on the Institute for Developmental Studies.* Chicago: Quadrangle Books, 1967.

Prince, Alfred J., & Baggaley, Andrew R. Personality variables and the ideal mate. *Family Life Coordinator,* 1963, **3**, 93–96.

Rahe, Richard H., & Arthur, Ransom J. Life-change patterns surrounding illness experience. *Journal of Psychosomatic Research,* 1968, **11**, 341–345.

Ramirez, Michael, III. Identification with Mexican family values and authori-

References

tarianism in Mexican Americans. *Journal of Social Psychology,* 1967, **73,** 3–11.

Reichard, Suzanne, & Rapaport, D. The role of testing concept formation in clinical psychological work. *Bulletin of the Menninger Clinic,* 1943, **7,** 99–105.

Reiss, Ira J. How and why America's sex standards are changing. *Trans-action,* 1968, **5**(4), 26–32.

Reiter, Henry H. Prediction of college success from measures of anxiety, achievement motivation, and scholastic aptitude. *Psychological Reports,* 1964, **15,** 23–26.

Renne, Karen S. Correlates of dissatisfaction in marriage. Unpublished manuscript, Human Population Laboratory, California State Department of Public Health, 1968.

Ribble, Margaretha A. *The rights of infants: Early psychological needs and their satisfaction.* New York: Columbia University Press, 1943.

Riesman, David, Denney, Reuel, & Glazer, Nathan. *The lonely crowd: A study of the changing American character.* New Haven, Conn.: Yale University Press, 1950.

Rioch, Margaret J. Changing concepts in the training of psychotherapists. *Journal of Consulting Psychology,* 1966, **30,** 290–292.

Robin, Stanley S., & Story, Fae. Ideological consistency of college students: The Bill of Rights and attitudes towards minority groups. *Sociology and Social Research,* 1964, **48,** 187–196.

Robinson, Francis P. *Effective study.* (Rev. ed.) New York: Harper, 1961.

Roethlisberger, Fritz J., & Dickson, William J. *Management and the worker.* Cambridge, Mass.: Harvard University Press, 1939.

Rogers, Carl R. This is me. In Carl R. Rogers, *On becoming a person.* Boston: Houghton Mifflin, 1961. Pp. 3–27.

Rogerson, B. C. F., & Rogerson, C. H. Feeding in infancy and subsequent psychological difficulties. *Journal of Mental Science,* 1939, **85,** 1163–1182.

Rokeach, Milton. *The open and closed mind.* New York: Basic Books, 1960.

Rokeach, Milton. A theory of organization and change within value-attitude systems. *Journal of Social Issues,* 1968, **24**(1), 13–33.

Rosenberg, Leon A. Idealization of self and social adjustment. *Journal of Consulting Psychology,* 1962, **26,** 487.

Rosenfeld, Albert. The psycho-biology of violence. *Life,* June 21, 1968, **64,** 67–71.

Rosenthal, Robert, & Jacobson, Lenore. *Pygmalion in the classroom: Teacher expectation and pupils' intellectual development.* New York: Holt, 1968.

Rosow, Irving. *Social integration of the aged.* New York: Free Press, 1967.

Ross, Sherman, & Lockman, Robert F. *A career in psychology.* American Psychological Association, 1963.

References

Rosten, R. A. Some personality characteristics of compulsive gamblers. Unpublished master's thesis, 1961. Cited in James C. Coleman, *Abnormal psychology and modern life.* (3rd ed.) Glenview, Ill.: Scott, Foresman, 1964. Pp. 360–361.

Ruch, Floyd L. *Psychology and life.* (7th ed.) Glenview, Ill.: Scott, Foresman, 1967.

Sanford, Fillmore H. *Psychology: A scientific study of man* (2nd ed.) Belmont, Calif.: Wadsworth, 1965.

Saxton, Lloyd. *The individual, marriage, and the family.* Belmont, Calif.: Wadsworth, 1968.

Schachter, Joseph, Bickman, Leonard, Schachter, Judith S., Jameson, Jean, Litachy, Stanley, & Williams, Thomas A. Behavioral and psysiologic reactivity in infants. *Mental Hygiene,* 1966, **50**, 516–521.

Schein, Edgar H. The Chinese indoctrination program for prisoners of war: A study of attempted "brainwashing." In Eleanor E. Maccoby, Theodore M. Newcomb, & Eugene L. Hartley (Eds.), *Readings in social psychology.* New York: Holt, 1958. Pp. 311–334.

Schein, Edgar H. The first job dilemma. *Psychology Today,* 1968, **1**(10), 26–37.

Schneider, Louis, & Lysgaard, Sverre. The deferred gratification pattern: A preliminary study. *American Sociological Review,* 1953, **18**, 142–149.

Sears, Robert R. Experimental studies of projection: I. Attribution of traits. *Journal of Social Psychology,* 1936, **7**, 151–163.

Sears, Robert R., Maccoby, Eleanor E., & Levin, Harry. *Patterns of Child Rearing.* New York: Harper, 1957.

Sells, Saul B. The atmosphere effect: An experimental study of reasoning. *Archives of Psychology,* 1936, No. 200.

Selyé, Hans. *The stress of life.* New York: McGraw-Hill, 1956.

Sewell, William H., & Mussen, Paul H. The effects of feeding, weaning, and scheduling procedures on childhood adjustment and the formation of oral symptoms. *Child Development,* 1952, **23**, 185–191.

Shils, Edward A. Primary groups in the American Army. In Robert K. Merton & Paul Lazarsfeld (Eds.), *Continuities in social research: Studies in the scope and method of "The American Soldier."* New York: Free Press, 1950. Pp. 16–40.

Shils, Edward A., & Janowitz, Morris. Cohesion and disintegration in the Wehrmacht in World War II. *Public Opinion Quarterly,* 1948, **12**, 280–315.

Shirley, M. M. *The first two years: A study of 25 babies,* Vol. 2. *Intellectual development.* Minneapolis: University of Minnesota Press, 1933.

Siipola, Elsa M. A group study of some effects of preparatory sets. *Psychological Monographs,* 1935, **46**(No. 210), 27–38.

Silberman, Charles E. *Crisis in black and white.* New York: Random House, 1964.

References

Simon, Charles W., & Emmons, William H. Learning during sleep? *Psychological Bulletin*, 1955, **52**, 328–342.

Sinnett, E. Robert, & Stone, LeRoy A. The meaning of a college education as revealed by the semantic differential. *Journal of Counseling Psychology*, 1964, **11**, 168–172.

Skinner, B. F. *Science and human behavior*. New York: Macmillan, 1963.

Skipper, James K., Jr., & Nass, Gilbert. Dating behavior: A framework for analysis and an illustration. *Journal of Marriage and the Family*, 1966, **28**, 412–420.

Sklare, Marshall. Intermarriage and the Jewish future. *Commentary*, April 1964, **37**, 46–52.

Skodak, Marie, & Skeels, Harold M. A final follow-up study of one hundred adopted children. *Journal of Genetic Psychology*, 1949, **75**, 85–125.

Smith, M. Brewster. The revolution in mental-health care—a "bold new approach." *Trans-action*, 1968, **5**(5), 19–23.

Soffietti, James P. Bilingualism and biculturalism. *Journal of Educational Psychology*, 1955, **46**, 222–227.

Soskin, W. F., Duhl, L. J., & Leopold, R. L. Socio-cultural dilemmas in the world of adolescence and youth. Cited in Roy Menninger, What troubles our troubled youth? *Mental Hygiene*, 1968, **52**, 323–329.

Spence, Donald P., Gordon, Carol M., & Rabkin, Judith. Effects of rejection on psychogenic hunger. *Psychosomatic Medicine*, 1966, **28**, 27–33.

Spitz, Rene A. The role of ecological factors in emotional development in infancy. *Child Development*, 1949, **20**, 145–156.

Spock, Benjamin. *The common sense book of baby and child care*. (Rev. ed.) New York: Pocket Books, 1957.

Stodgill, Ralph M. Personal factors associated with leadership: A survey of the literature. *Journal of Psychology*, 1948, **25**, 35–71.

Stone, Carol L. Sorority status and personality adjustment. *American Sociological Review*, 1951, **16**, 538–541.

Stone, L. Joseph, & Church, Joseph. *Childhood and adolescence*. (2nd ed.) New York: Random House, 1968.

Strodtbeck, Fred L., Simon, Rita J., & Hawkins, Charles. Social status in jury deliberations. In Ivan D. Steiner & Martin Fishbein (Eds.), *Current studies in social psychology*. New York: Holt, 1965. Pp. 333–342.

Sullivan, Harry Stack. *Conceptions of modern psychiatry*. New York: Norton, 1953.

Sulzberger, Marion B., & Zaidens, Sadie H. Psychogenic factors in dermatologic disorders. *Medical Clinics of North America*, 1948, **32**, 669–685.

Sutton, R. L. Acne vulgaris, a pustular lipoidosis. *Southern Medical Journal*, 1941, **34**, 1071–1082.

References

Tanner, John M. *Education and physical growth.* London: University of London Press, 1961.

Tarnopol, Lester. Personality differences between leaders and non-leaders. *Personnel Journal,* 1958, **37**, 57–60.

Taylor, Ronald A. Personality traits and discrepant achievement: A review. *Journal of Counseling Psychology,* 1964, **11**, 76–82.

Telford, Charles W., & Sawrey, James M. *Psychology: A concise introduction to the fundamentals of behavior.* Belmont, Calif.: Brooks/Cole, 1968.

Terman, Lewis M. *Psychological factors in marital happiness.* New York: McGraw-Hill, 1938.

Terman, Lewis M., & Oden, M. H. *The gifted group at mid-life: Genetic studies of genius.* Vol. 5. Stanford, Calif.: Stanford University Press, 1959.

Tharp, Roland G. Psychological patterning in marriage. *Psychological Bulletin,* 1963, **60**, 97–117.

Thigpen, Corbett H., & Cleckley, Hervey M. *The three faces of Eve.* New York: McGraw-Hill, 1957.

Thompson, Helen. Physical growth. In Leonard Carmichael (Ed.), *Manual of child psychology.* New York: Wiley, 1946. Pp. 255–294.

Thompson, Wayne E. Pre-retirement anticipation and adjustment in retirement. *Journal of Social Issues,* 1958, **14**(2), 35–45.

Thompson, Wayne E., & Streib, Gordon F. Situational determinants: Health and economic deprivation in retirement. *Journal of Social Issues,* 1958, **14**(2), 18–34.

Thorne, Frederick C. The incidence of nocturnal enuresis after age five. *American Journal of Psychiatry,* 1944, **100**, 686–689.

Trent, James W., & Craise, Judith L. Commitment and conformity in the American college. *Journal of Social Issues,* 1967, **23**(3), 34–51.

Trent, James W., & Medsker, Leland L. *Beyond high school.* Berkeley: University of California Press, 1967.

United States Department of Labor, Bureau of Labor Statistics. *Retired couple's budget,* 1966.

Vener, Arthur M., & Snyder, Clinton A. The preschool child's awareness and anticipation of adult sex-roles. *Sociometry,* 1966, **29**, 159–168.

Voeks, Virginia. *On becoming an educated person.* (2nd ed.) Philadelphia: Saunders, 1964.

Vogel, William, Broverman, Donald M., Draguns, Juris G., & Klaiber, Edward L. The role of glutamic acid in cognitive behaviors. *Psychological Bulletin,* 1966, **65**, 367–382.

Wallas, Graham. *The art of thought.* New York: Harcourt, Brace & World, 1926.

Wallin, Paul. Cultural contradictions and sex roles: A repeat study. *American Sociological Review,* 1950, **15**, 288–293.

References

Wallin, Paul, & Riley, Rosemary. Reactions of mothers to pregnancy and adjustment of offspring in infancy. *American Journal of Orthopsychiatry*, 1950, **20**, 616–622.

Walster, Elaine, Aronson, Vera, Abrahams, Darcy, & Rottmann, Leon. Importance of physical attractiveness in dating behavior. *Journal of Personality and Social Psychology*, 1966, **4**, 508–516.

Washington, Bennetta B. Growth and cultural conflict. *Vocational Guidance Quarterly*, 1964, **12**, 153–158.

Watson, Charles G. Cross-validation of certain background variables as predictors of academic achievement. *Journal of Educational Research*, 1965, **59**; 147–148.

Wechsler, Henry. Halfway houses for former mental patients: A survey. *Journal of Social Issues*, 1960, **16**(2), 20–26.

Weil, Andrew T., Zinberg, Norman E., & Nelsen, Judith M. Clinical and psychological effects of marihuana in man. *Science*, Dec. 13, 1968, **162**, 1234–1242.

Wenger, Marion A., Jones, F. N., & Jones, M. H. *Physiological psychology.* New York: Holt, 1956.

White, Robert W. *The abnormal personality.* (3rd ed.) New York: Ronald Press, 1964.

Whiting, John W. M., & Child, Irvin L. *Child training and personality: A cross-cultural study.* New Haven, Conn.: Yale University Press, 1953.

Wilder, May C. Relationship of college achievement to marital status. *Dissertation Abstracts*, 1967, **27**(10A), 3326–3327.

Will, Caroline F. A survey of problems confronting Frear Hall residents. Bureau of Testing and Guidance Research Studies on University of Hawaii Student Behavior, 1957, No. 1.

Williams, Allan F. Social drinking, anxiety, and depression. *Journal of Personality and Social Psychology*, 1966, **3**, 689–693.

Winch, Robert F., Ktsanes, Thomas, & Ktsanes, Virginia. The theory of complementary needs in mate selection: An analytic and descriptive study. *American Sociological Review*, 1954, **19**, 241–249.

Wolfe, J. B. Effectiveness of token-rewards for chimpanzees. *Comparative Psychology Monographs*, 1936, **12**(60).

Wrenn, C. Gilbert. Editor's Introduction. In Norman T. Bell, Richard W. Burkhardt, & Victor B. Lawhead (Eds.), *Introduction to college life.* Boston: Houghton Mifflin, 1962. P. v.

Wrenn, C. Gilbert, & Crandall, Elizabeth B. Behavior ratings and scholarship among college freshmen. *Journal of Educational Research*, 1941, **34**, 259–264.

Yarrow, Marian R., Campbell, John D., & Burton, Roger V. *Child rearing: An inquiry into research and methods.* San Francisco: Jossey-Bass, 1968.

References

Yarrow, Marian R., Scott, P., deLeeuw, L., & Heinig, C. Child-rearing in families of working and nonworking mothers. *Sociometry,* 1962, **25,** 122–140.

Zander, Alvin, & Quinn, Robert. The social environment and mental health: A review of past research at the Institute for Social Research. *Journal of Social Issues,* 1962, **18**(3), 48–66.

Zollitsch, Herbert G. Fringes—benefits or burdens? *Personnel,* July/August 1964, **41,** 54–59.

Index

Index

Index

Index

Index

Index

Index